Revising Pentecostal History

Revising Pentecostal History

Scandinavian-American Contributions to the Development of Pentecostalism

EDITED BY
Rakel Ystebø Alegre,
Torbjörn Aronson, AND
David M. Gustafson

FOREWORD BY
Cecil M. Robeck Jr.

AFTERWORD BY
David Bundy

☙PICKWICK Publications • Eugene, Oregon

REVISING PENTECOSTAL HISTORY
Scandinavian-American Contributions to the Development of Pentecostalism

Copyright © 2024 Wipf and Stock Publishers. All rights reserved. Except for brief quotations in critical publications or reviews, no part of this book may be reproduced in any manner without prior written permission from the publisher. Write: Permissions, Wipf and Stock Publishers, 199 W. 8th Ave., Suite 3, Eugene, OR 97401.

Pickwick Publications
An Imprint of Wipf and Stock Publishers
199 W. 8th Ave., Suite 3
Eugene, OR 97401

www.wipfandstock.com

PAPERBACK ISBN: 979-8-3852-2211-7
HARDCOVER ISBN: 979-8-3852-2212-4
EBOOK ISBN: 979-8-3852-2213-1

Cataloguing-in-Publication data:

Names: Alegre, Rakel Ystebø [editor]. | Aronson, Torbjörn [editor]. | Gustafson, David M. [editor]. | Robeck, Cecil M., Jr. [foreword writer]. | Bundy, David [afterword writer].

Title: Revising Pentecostal history : Scandinavian-American contributions to the development of Pentecostalism / edited by Rakel Ystebø Alegre, Torbjörn Aronson, and David M. Gustafson ; foreword by Cecil M. Robeck, Jr. ; afterword by David Bundy.

Description: Eugene, OR: Pickwick Publications, 2024 | Includes bibliographical references and index.

Identifiers: ISBN 979-8-3852-2211-7 (paperback) | ISBN 979-8-3852-2212-4 (hardcover) | ISBN 979-8-3852-2213-1 (ebook)

Subjects: LCSH: Pentecostal churches—History. | Pentecostalism—United States. | Pentecostalism—Sweden—History. | Pentecostalism—Norway—History. | United States—Church history.

Classification: BR1644.5 A44 2024 (paperback) | BR1644.5 (ebook)

VERSION NUMBER 11/04/24

Dedicated to Dr. Edith Blumhofer (1950–2020)

American Pentecostal Historian

Professor of History, Wheaton College, Illinois

Scholar of the Pentecostal Movement whose writings highlighted the ministries of William H. Durham and F. A. Sandgren among Scandinavian immigrants in Chicago.

Her work has inspired scholars around the globe.

Contents

List of Illustrations | ix

List of Abbreviations | xi

Foreword | xiii
—Cecil M. Robeck Jr.

Acknowledgments | xix

Introduction | xxi
—Rakel Ystebø Alegre, Torbjörn Aronson, and David M. Gustafson

Convergence of Streams

1. Before Azusa Street: Scandinavian Pentecosts in America, 1886–1906 | 1
   —Kristina Undheim

2. Scandinavian-American Pentecostal Revival of Chicago, 1906–1912 | 27
   —David M. Gustafson

3. Movement of Scandinavian-American Pentecostals, 1906–1918 | 55
   —Jan-Åke Alvarsson and David M. Gustafson

4. Trans-Atlantic Influence from Norway on Scandinavian-American Pentecostalism, 1906–1930 | 87
   —Rakel Ystebø Alegre

Emergence of Identities

5. Scandinavian-Americans and the General Council of the Assemblies of God (AG), 1906–1952 | 118
  —Darrin J. Rodgers

6. Scandinavian-American Independent Assemblies of God (IAG), 1918–1952 | 147
  —Jan-Åke Alvarsson and David M. Gustafson

7. Between Multiple Worlds: Emerging Scandinavian-American Pentecostal Theology, 1907–1919 | 179
  —Tommy Davidsson

Influence Within Cultures

8. Scandinavian-American Pentecostal Mission to Brazil: Gunnar Vingren and Daniel Berg, 1910–1962 | 208
  —Isael de Araujo and Joel Wright

9. Missionary Tongues of Sophie Hansen: Testimonies of Xenolalia in Shanghai, 1908–1923 | 238
  —Ruth Ma

10. Formation and Transformation of a Scandinavian-American Pentecostal Congregation in South Bend, Indiana, 1907–1967 | 266
  —Beverly C. Johnson-Miller

11. From Scandinavian-American to Trans-Atlantic Relations of Neo-Pentecostals in Sweden and the United States, 1965–2014 | 295
  —Torbjörn Aronson

Afterword | 319
—David Bundy

Appendix: Successor Associations in America Today | 327
List of Contributors | 331
Name Index | 333

List of Illustrations

Image 1   August Davis. First Evangelical Free Church, Minneapolis. Used by permission. | 12

Image 2   Ida Anderson and Mary Johnson, *Räddningslinan*, 1909, Minnesota Historical Society, St. Paul. Photo by David M. Gustafson. | 16

Image 3   J. W. Hjertstrom, *History of the Swedes of Illinois*, Engberg-Holmberg, 1908. Public domain. | 31

Image 4   Second Swedish Baptist Church, 3020 Fifth Avenue (Wells), Chicago. Used by permission from Archives of Bethel University and Converge, St. Paul. | 40

Image 5   Cenna Osterberg. Courtesy of the Osterberg Family. | 60

Image 6   Maren Iversen, *Räddningslinan*, 1909. Courtesy of the Minnesota Historical Society, St. Paul. | 67

Image 7   F. A. Sandgren, Courtesy of the Sandgren Family. | 77

Image 8   Lewi Pethrus, Laura Barratt, T. B. Barratt et al. Courtesy of Norwegian Pentecostal Historical Archive, Oslo, Norway. | 105

Image 9   Salem Gospel Assembly, New York City, 1936. Courtesy of the Ring Family. | 109

Image 10 C. M. Hanson and daughter Anna Hanson Berg. Used by permission of Flower Pentecostal Heritage Center, Springfield, Missouri. | 128

Image 11 Frank J. Lindquist. Used by permission of the Flower Pentecostal Heritage Center, Springfield, Missouri. | 133

LIST OF ILLUSTRATIONS

Image 12   Scandinavian Pentecostal meeting, 1915. Courtesy of Gunnar Vingren Memorial Archives, CPAD, Rio de Janeiro, Brazil. | 149

Image 13   National Convention of Independent Assemblies of God at Philadelphia Church, Chicago, Oct. 5–10, 1943. Philadelphia Church, Chicago. Photo by David M. Gustafson. | 154

Image 14   Full Gospel Assembly (Barry Avenue Church), Chicago, Courtesy Nybakken-Anderson Family. | 156

Image 15   E. C. Erickson and Harry Ring. Courtesy of the Ring Family. | 167

Image 16   Andrew August Holmgren at the Office of *Sanningens Vittne*. Courtesy of the Holmgren Family. | 184

Image 17   Daniel Berg and Gunnar Vingren before traveling to Brazil, 1910. Courtesy of the Gunnar Vingren Memorial Archives, CPAD, Rio de Janeiro, Brazil. | 210

Image 18   Meeting of the Scandinavian Assemblies of God, 1922. Courtesy of Gunnar Vingren Memorial Archives, CPAD, Rio de Janeiro, Brazil. | 228

Image 19   Assemblies of God Conference in Brazil, *Sanningens Vittne*, 1936. Used by permission of the Flower Pentecostal Heritage Center, Springfield, Missouri. | 233

Image 20   Sophie Hansen, Courtesy of the Hansen Family. | 239

Image 21   Missionaries of the Apostolic Faith Mission of China, 1908. Courtesy of the Hansen Family. | 249

Image 22   Samuel Hansen with ministerial students in Shanghai, ca. 1941. Courtesy of the Hansen family. | 261

Image 23   Olof A. and Esther Uldin, 1944. Courtesy of the Uldin Family. | 274

Image 24   South Bend Gospel Tabernacle, 1949, Collection of Beverly Johnson-Miller. | 283

List of Abbreviations

AF	*The Apostolic Faith*
AG	Assemblies of God, Springfield, Missouri
BM	*The Bridegroom's Messenger*
BP	*Byposten*
BR	*Brudgummens Röst*
BD	*Bref-Dufvan*
CB	*Chicago-Bladet*
EH	*Evangelii Härold*
FV	*Folke-Vennen*
HF	*Herald of Faith*
HFCA	*The History of the Fellowship of Christian Assemblies*
IAG	Independent Assemblies of God
KS	*Korsets Seier/ Seir*
LRE	*Latter Rain Evangel*
LRM	Latter Rain Movement
MT	*The Minneapolis Tribune*
NWP	*Nya Wecko-Posten*
PE	*The Pentecostal Evangel*
PT	*Pentecostal Testimony*
SA	*Svenska Amerikanaren*
SAG	Scandinavian Assemblies of God
SBT	*The South Bend Tribune*
SS	*Sanningens Segrar*

LIST OF ABBREVIATIONS

SV   *Sanningens Vittne*
TP   *The Pentecost*
VI   *Världen idag*

Foreword

Cecil M. Robeck Jr.

My paternal grandfather, Axel Edwin Robeck, was born into a Norwegian family in 1889, one of many Scandinavian families that immigrated to the United States during the latter half of the nineteenth century. His father, a layman named Magnus Robeck, and his wife, Julia Ellise (Tollefson) Robeck donated part of their farm, where he planted, built, and pastored a small Lutheran church in Porterfield, Wisconsin, until they could get an ordained pastor. During Axel's late teens and early twenties, companies from Texas advertised in a Norwegian newspaper in Minnesota and Wisconsin, offering jobs to able-bodied men who would come to work in Texas. Since his alternative was to stay and work the eighty-acre family farm, he moved to Kingsville, Texas, about 30 miles southwest of Corpus Christi. He also married my grandmother, Laura Elizabeth Arneson, a member of a Norwegian Free-Free Church. There, he came across a Pentecostal tent meeting, where he was baptized in the Spirit and spoke in other tongues.

My grandparents were not alone. Many Scandinavians on both sides of the Atlantic soon made similar discoveries. Of my grandfather's ten sisters and brothers, however, none of them remained Lutheran; most of them joined Scandinavian free churches or free-free churches, although by 1916, my grandfather, Axel, followed by three of his younger brothers, Andrew Edward, Eddie Olaf, and Elmer Theo, became Assemblies of God ministers who planted many churches from California to Washington.

This book is the first major academic study in English to document some of the stories regarding Scandinavians and Pentecostalism. At the center of much of this story lies the famous Azusa Street Mission, whose revival from April 1906 until 1909, was the subject of ridicule, news stories, and from the 1920s, academic study. Readers may be surprised to find that there are such a large number of primary sources available for such a volume to be written. Interaction between the Scandinavians in Los Angeles, with those along the northern borders of the United States, particularly in the upper plains, or with those in their northern European homelands, was significant from the beginning. Missionaries from Sweden soon met up with Scandinavian missionaries from Los Angeles to take Azusa Street's message across the Pacific. In China, they became part of the vanguard of Scandinavian Pentecostal missionaries throughout the world.

Arguably, the Azusa Street Mission had the most significant impact on Scandinavian Pentecostalism when one considers other impulses of the movement. It would be wrong to claim that Azusa Street was the first place where Scandinavians came into contact with Pentecostal-like activities, or with the message of Pentecost. The emphases of Pietism, Holiness, and even individualism appeared regularly among Scandinavian Lutherans in Europe. Many had participated in prayer meetings and revivals, but subsequently left the State church to focus their attention on specific aspects of spirituality. They formed denominations such as the Evangelical Covenant Church, Evangelical Free Church, and Swedish Baptist Church in their spiritual quest for a closer walk with Jesus Christ. Some of them experienced visions, prophecies, and other manifestations such as speaking in tongues, at the end of the nineteenth century. In a sense, the revival at Azusa Street did not come as a surprise.

In 1905, a group of "patriotic and public spirited men" in Los Angeles formed the Liberal Alliance, "an organization devoted to the interests and welfare of those foreign born residents who desire[d] to become good American citizens."[1] Two years later, this organization published the *International Directory of Los Angeles, 1906–1907*, the only such volume to appear. It listed fifteen groups of Los Angeles residents according to the European nations from which they had come. It included 334 Danish households, 379 Norwegian households, and 1,003 Swedish households. Apparently, however, there was not a sufficient number of

1. *International Directory of Los Angeles, 1906–1907* (Los Angeles: International Publishing Company, 1907).

Finnish households to include them as a separate category. The directory also included nine Scandinavian language churches.[2]

With so many Scandinavians in Los Angeles, it should come as no surprise that the names of several Scandinavians stand out when we think of Azusa Street. The first are Cenna and Louis Osterberg and their son, Arthur, part of a Swedish-American family that played a significant role in making the revival known, in participating in the refurbishing of the Azusa Street Mission, in serving on the board, and remaining loyal friends of Pastor William Seymour for many years. The second was Thomas Ball Barratt, pastor of a Methodist Episcopal Church in Christiana [Oslo] Norway. Although he did not visit Azusa Street during the years 1906 to 1909, it can be said that Azusa Street visited him! While Barratt was on a fund-raising visit to the United States in 1906, he received a copy of Azusa's paper, *The Apostolic Faith,* read it, and then engaged in an exchange of letters with leaders at the Mission. Moreover, through Lucy Leatherman and a group of newly-minted Azusa Street missionaries passing through New York City on their way to serve as missionaries in Liberia and Angola, Barratt experienced his baptism in the Spirit. Once back in Norway, he held a series of meetings, which quickly raised interest in the Azusa Street revival and began the spread of the Pentecostal revival in Europe.

There were other Scandinavians at the Azusa Street Mission, of course, people like Carl Bjorkman, Jennie and Annie Jacobson, Eric and Ida Hollingsworth, and Sigrid [Bengtson] McLean, daughter of a former member of the Swedish Parliament. Aage L. Sulger, son of a Lutheran pastor in Bornholm, Denmark, received his baptism in the Spirit and spoke in tongues at Azusa Street, before repudiating, and strongly opposing Pentecostals after moving to Denver and joining Alma White's Pillar of Fire

---

2. The directory lists: Free Norwegian Lutheran Church, Norwegian-Danish Evangelical Lutheran Church, Norwegian and Danish Methodist Episcopal Church, Swedish Baptist Church, Swedish Christian Church, Swedish Congregational Church, Swedish Evangelical Church, Swedish Evangelical-Lutheran Angelica Church, and Swedish Methodist Episcopal Church. *International Directory*, 1,000.

holiness church.[3] While Frank Bartleman was a German-American, he preached repeatedly throughout Norway, Sweden, and Finland.[4]

A third person who stood out was a young Swede who went by the name of Andrew Johnson when he lived in Los Angeles. By late summer 1906, he had determined to become an Apostolic Faith missionary in the Middle East. Running out of funds by the time he reached Italy, he decided to return to Sweden where he became an early Pentecostal pastor. In Sweden, they knew him as A.G. Jansson, as Andrew Ek, or as Andrew Jonson-Ek. The Swedish and Norwegian press quickly picked up his story, and the revival spread.

Few Americans know that Scandinavian scholars took Azusa Street and the Pentecostal Movement far more seriously than their English-speaking counterparts, and wrote extensively on the revival between 1919 and 1956. They included works by A. A. Holmgren, Emanuel Linderholm, Efraim Briem, G. E. Söderholm, and Nils Bloch-Hoell.[5] Their level of scholarship in English, would not be equaled until the 1970s or later.

In this volume, Rakel Ystebø Alegre, Torbjörn Aronson, and David M. Gustafson and their colleagues have provided a real service to those interested in the Azusa Street revival and Pentecostal movement upon and through Scandinavians. This story has not been widely studied previously, nor has the breadth of its impact been widely explored. This book provides us with a well-conceived perspective on the breadth and the depth of Azusa Street-Scandinavian linked involvement throughout much of the world. This volume covers not only Los Angeles but also Chicago, Scandinavia, Brazil, China, and back to the United States. It

---

3. *The Apostolic Faith*, Dec. 1906, 1; A. Sulger, "Delivered from the 'Tongue' Heresy," *Rocky Mountain Pillar of Fire* (March 27, 1907). Gastón Espinosa, *William J. Seymour and the Origins of Global Pentecostalism: A Biography and Documentary History* (Durham, NC: Duke University Press, 2014), 116, 372, 374–76. Sulger, a native of Bornholm, returned to the U.S. in 1910, listed as a missionary.

4. Frank Bartleman, *Two Years Mission Work in Europe Just before the World War 1912–1914* (Los Angeles: F. Bartleman, 2nd ed., no date).

5. A. A. Holmgren, *Pingströrelsen och dess förkunnelse* (Minneapolis: S.V. Publ. House, 1919); Emanuel Linderholm, *Pingströrelsen: Dess förutsättningar och uppkomst: Ekstas, under och apokalyptik i bibel och nytida Folkreligiositet* (Stockholm: Bonnier, 1924); Efraim Briem, *Den moderna pingströrelsen* (Uppsala: Svenska Kyrkans Diakonistyrelses Bokförlag, 1924); G. E. Söderholm, *Den svenska pingstväckelsens historia 1907–1927* (Stockholm: Förlaget Filadelfia, 1933); and Nils Bloch-Hoell, *Pinsebevegelsen: En Undersøkelse av Pinsebevegelsens Tilblivelse, Utvikling of Særpreg med Særlig Henblikk på Bevegelsens Utformning i Norge* (Oslo: Universitetsforlaget, 1956).

covers classical Pentecostal groups such as the Assemblies of God (AG), groups such as the Scandinavian Filadelfia churches, especially Stockholm's flagship congregation, the Independent Assemblies of God (IAG) with its reception of the Latter Rain Movement, and more recent Neo-Pentecostal churches. Thus, this volume is a welcome addition to Scandinavian historical studies, and to the growing body of literature that documents regional participation in the Pentecostal movement featuring Scandinavia, and the Azusa Street Mission, from which many Scandinavian pastors, congregation, and missionaries received much of their impetus to spread their message around the world.

Cecil M. Robeck, Jr.

Acknowledgments

Revising Pentecostal History is the product of dozens of people. The multiple authors contributed the chapters to fit within a coordinated outline in order to produce a coherent volume. What no single scholar could accomplish, this team of scholars did, proving the value of a multi-author volume.

The authors were dependent upon primary sources that were digitized recently and made available online. Thus, several archivists and librarians are acknowledged here for their work, including Rebekah Bain of the History Center and Archives of Bethel University and Converge in St. Paul; Thomas Cairns of the Archives of the Evangelical Free Church of America in Minneapolis; Emilio Núñez of the David Allan Hubbard Library at Fuller Theological Seminary in Pasadena, California; Lynnette Westerlund of the Minnesota Historical Society in St. Paul; Nathan Thebarge of the Rolfing Library at Trinity Evangelical Divinity School in Deerfield, Illinois, Geir Lie at the Norwegian Pentecostal Historical Archive in Oslo, Norway, Magnus Wahlström of the Pentecostal Archives in Bromma, Sweden, and Glenn Gohr and Darrin Rodgers of the Flower Pentecostal Heritage Center in Springfield, Missouri.

In addition, the authors are indebted to the families and friends who provided non-published source materials and photographs. Descendants of Louis and Cenna Osterberg, F. A. Sandgren, A. A. Holmgren, George and Sophie Hansen, Olof Uldin, and Hanna Holmsten have been exceedingly cooperative and generous with their time and information. In addition, Warren Heckman has been supportive of the project that built upon his research and writing. We acknowledge the encouragement of John Picket at the Philadelphia Church in Chicago, Wayne Wachsmuth of Christian Life College in Mount Prospect, Illinois, and Steve Ekeroth with E4 Ministry Network. Arlene Nybakken Chase donated her collection of newspaper clippings and songbooks. Finally, we thank Donn Ring for sharing his treasure of knowledge, resources, photos, and insights about his father's ministry among Scandinavian-American Pentecostals.

Introduction

RAKEL YSTEBØ ALEGRE, TORBJÖRN ARONSON, AND DAVID M. GUSTAFSON

AMERICAN PENTECOSTAL HISTORY HAS often been an English-language project. This is understandable. Modern Pentecostalism in America began around the turn of the 20th century and most historians of this history have drawn from the available English-language sources. Very few historians of American Pentecostalism knew of source materials in the Scandinavian languages of Norwegian and Swedish, and if they did, fewer numbers possessed the language skills necessary to access them. This brings us to the present volume which argues that American Pentecostal history cannot be understood apart from both the texts and the people who participated in and contributed to the Pentecostal movement in America, including first-generation immigrants from Scandinavia and second-generation Scandinavian-Americans. They were active in American Pentecostalism from the start.

Revising Pentecostal History describes ways in which Scandinavian-Americans have contributed to and played a role in the development of the Pentecostal movement. The volume presents crucial findings from rarely, if ever, used sources which inform how American Pentecostalism is understood. For over a century, periodicals in the Norwegian and Swedish languages have sat dormant in university and historical society archives, unavailable to the vast majority of American researchers. This has left a gap in the body of literature on American Pentecostalism.

The gap is due not entirely from the lack of access to Scandinavian-language sources, however. The ahistorical character of many early

Scandinavian-American Pentecostals contributed to this as well. They were more concerned with soul-saving and missionary-sending than writing and preserving their history. This was especially true of the Independent Assemblies of God (IAG). Their ahistorical character and disinterest in preserving primary sources can be illustrated from recent research indicating that two entire runs of Scandinavian-language Pentecostal periodicals have been lost (or hopefully tucked away in some great grandson's attic still to be discovered!).[1] Thankfully other Scandinavian-language Pentecostal periodicals survived, mostly from the efforts of other bodies or institutions in the United States, Norway, and Sweden.

The chapters of *Revising Pentecostal History* have made extensive use of these periodicals which have been digitized recently.[2] Drawing from these rich sources, the authors of this volume have made precious discoveries that contribute to the understanding not merely of Scandinavian-American Pentecostals but of American Pentecostals in general. These source materials have prompted new questions, affirmed and challenged previously held assumptions, and contributed to fuller and more accurate narratives of American Pentecostalism.

This volume, for example, informs the discussion on the origin(s) of American Pentecostalism, examines Chicago and Los Angeles as original Pentecostal centers, and describes initiatives of Scandinavian-Americans to form Pentecostal churches in the Upper Midwest, Pacific Northwest, and Northeast. It examines the trans-Atlantic nature of Scandinavian-American Pentecostals that set them apart from their English-language counterparts and guided them through theological controversies. In addition to church planting, Scandinavian-Americans launched three schools that continue today as universities. Moreover, this volume describes two Swedish immigrant missionaries from Chicago who began a work in Brazil which today numbers over 22 million members.

---

1. The periodicals are *Pingst-Rösten* (*The Pentecostal Voice*) published in Chicago, and *Sandhedens Tolk* (Interpreter of Truth) published in the Seattle-Tacoma area.

2. This research project included digitizing periodicals that were published in the U.S., namely, *Brev-Duvan* (Swedish), *Sanningens Vittne* (Swedish), *Folke-Vennen* (Norwegian), and *Herald of Faith* (English). The recent digitization of *Byposten/ Korsets Seir* (Norwegian) in Norway was also important to the project. The American periodicals *Chicago-Bladet* (Swedish), *Evangelisten* (Norwegian), and *Evangelii Härold* (Swedish) in Sweden were digitized earlier.

Context of American Culture

Scandinavian-American Pentecostalism emerged from among immigrants to the United States who came from the Scandinavian countries of Norway, Sweden, and Denmark, and to some extent also from the Nordic country Finland. The migration of Scandinavians and their participation in the nascent American Pentecostal movement was significantly shaped by developments in American culture, at the intersection of the Gilded Age (1870–1900) and the Progressive Era (1890–1929).

The Gilded Age witnessed a significant influx of immigrants to America aided by steamships and railroads. City newspapers in Chicago and Minneapolis, for example, including those published in the Swedish- and Norwegian-languages, promoted immigration and reported on the immigrant experience. While the Gilded Age offered the opportunity of the American dream to many and prosperity to a few, the large majority of immigrants endured economic struggles and social hardships. Thus, progressives who inaugurated the Progressive Era, sought to address social injustices of the Gilded Age, taking active roles in matters, for example, of public health and safety, and reform of slum housing.

The context of American culture was also religious. At the juncture of the Gilded Age and Progressive Era, networks of English-language revivalists were active in the United States and Great Britain. In addition to their preaching of personal salvation, they supported temperance as a means to reduce domestic violence and strengthen the nuclear family. These revivalists advocated spiritual renewal, personal and social holiness, and taught the necessity for the Holy Spirit to accomplish such reforms individually, and then as a result, societally. Moreover, these revivalists were often characterized by an ecumenical spirit, cooperating with other Christians across denominational lines. Their influence spanned from the United States and United Kingdom to Scandinavia.

Numbers of Scandinavian immigrants in the United States resonated with these revivalists. In fact, many were prompted to emigrate from their homelands to America not simply to pursue the American dream but because they had embraced the teachings, values, and practices of such revivalists. The *push* of religious discrimination from state churches and the *pull* of freedom to live according to their religious convictions motivated many to migrate to America. Emigration from Scandinavia by Lutheran pietists, Methodists, Baptists, and Free-Mission revivalists was especially pronounced from the 1880s to the

1920s. These Scandinavians were familiar not only with the writings of the well-known Swedish pietist C. O. Rosenius (1816–1868), for example, but also with the writings of the English Baptist C. H. Spurgeon (1834–1892), the American revivalist D. L. Moody (1837–1899), and the American Baptist A. J. Gordon (1836–1895).[3] Familiarity with these English-language revivalists came mostly through periodicals, pamphlets, and books that contained their sermons, having been translated into the Scandinavian languages. In addition, many Scandinavians were acquainted with the writings of R. A. Torrey (1856–1928) whose theology emphasized "the baptism with the Holy Spirit,"[4] and A. B. Simpson (1843–1919) who taught the "four-fold gospel" that included Christ as Savior, Sanctifier, Healer, and Coming Lord.[5]

Socio-Religious Proximity to Pentecostalism

Scandinavians in America who participated in the early Pentecostal movement drew from the pietist, holiness, and revivalist traditions that preceded and prepared them. They were receptive to Pentecostal phenomena and many accepted Pentecostal teachings, contributing to the expansion of the early Pentecostal movement from Los Angeles and Chicago to the Upper Midwest, Pacific Northwest, and Northeast. The "Free-Free" of Minnesota and the Dakotas who were "free in the Spirit" and part of the Swedish Evangelical Free Mission, as well as "Pentecostalized" Swedish Baptists of Illinois, Michigan, and Indiana who belonged to the Swedish Baptist Conference, along with numbers of Norwegian Methodists, were especially receptive to Pentecostalism.[6]

3. David M. Gustafson, *D. L. Moody and Swedes: Shaping Evangelical Identity among Swedish Mission Friends, 1867–1899* (Linköping, Sweden: Linköpings universitet, 2008). Cf. Henry H. Ness, *Demonstration of the Holy Spirit: As Revealed by the Scriptures and Confirmed in Great Revivals of Wesley, Finney, Cartwright, Whitfield, Moody, etc.* (Seattle: Hollywood Temple, n.d.). Also, A. A. Holmgren, *Pingströrelsen och dess Förkunnelse*. Minneapolis: S. V. Publishing House, 1919), (Simpson) 63; (Finney) 130–31; 209; 212–14; (Moody), 211–12; (Wesley), 127–28, 24. Also see Donald W. Dayton, *Theological Roots of Pentecostalism* (Grand Rapids: Baker Academic, 1987, 2011).

4. R. A. Torrey, *The Baptism with the Holy Spirit* (Chicago: Revell, 1895).

5. A. B. Simpson, *The Four-fold Gospel* (New York: Alliance Press, ca. 1890).

6. The word "Pentecostalized" [*pentekostaliserade*] was used by Jan-Åke Alvarsson in reference to a Baptist church in Chicago. Jan-Ake Alvarsson, ed., *Varför reste Lewi Pethrus just till Chicago?: Relationer mellan Sverige och USA inom ramen för pentekostalismen* (Skellefteå, Sweden: Artos, 2019), 36.

With the same socio-religious proximity, many joined the burgeoning Pentecostal movement that emphasized the baptism of the Holy Spirit witnessed by the physical sign of speaking in tongues (glossolalia) along with the expectation of miraculous signs and wonders.[7]

However, differences over Pentecostal teachings and practices between those who became Pentecostals and their former religious bodies created tensions, sparking theological debates and congregational splits beginning around 1910. Some of those who experienced Pentecostal-baptism were soon excluded from or given the cold shoulder by their respective Scandinavian Free Mission, Norwegian-Danish Methodist, and Swedish Baptist churches.[8] These tensions prompted the formation of Scandinavian-American Pentecostal congregations and informal and formal networks of Pentecostal churches.

Chicago was at the center of Scandinavian-American Pentecostal activity beginning in February 1906. Within two decades, the Windy City boasted of having the most Norwegian- and Swedish-language Pentecostal congregations in the United States, well ahead of Los Angeles, Seattle, Minneapolis, St. Paul, and New York City. The Pentecostal revival of Chicago was led by J. W. Hjertstrom (1854–1919) of the Second Swedish Baptist Church. Like other Swedish Baptist ministers who participated in the movement, he led a "Pentecostalized" Baptist congregation. Months after the Chicago revival began, missionaries from the Azusa Street Mission in Los Angeles arrived at William H. Durham's North Avenue Mission in Chicago. Soon dual streams of Pentecostalism functioned in the Windy City with considerable interplay between them. By 1909, Chicago had become the center of *American* Pentecostalism as it had been the center of *Scandinavian-American* Pentecostalism.[9]

---

7. See David D. Bundy, Geordan Hammond, and David Sang-Ehil Han, eds., *Holiness and Pentecostal Movements: Intertwined Pasts, Presents, and Futures* (University Park, PA: Pennsylvania State University Press, 2022).

8. "The proximity of pentecostalism to the holiness movement in the religious environment caused great friction between them." Gerald W. King, *Disfellowshiped: Pentecostal Responses to Fundamentalism in the United States, 1906–1943* (Eugene, OR: Pickwick, 2011), 33.

9. In May 1908, A. H. Argue visited Chicago and reported that "thirteen or fourteen missions" had experienced Pentecostal phenomena. *The Apostolic Faith*, May 1908, 4.

Trans-Atlantic Context

In addition to the trans-Atlantic network of revivalists, the burgeoning Scandinavian-American Pentecostal movement was trans-Atlantic, having exchanges between Scandinavian-American Pentecostals in the United States, and Pentecostals in Norway and Sweden, in particular.[10] With the trans-Atlantic movement of peoples, ideas, and periodicals, Scandinavian-American Pentecostalism developed not simply under the tutelage of American Pentecostal leaders like J. W. Hjertstrom and William H. Durham (1873–1912) of Chicago, but also under T. B. Barratt (1862–1940) of Norway and Lewi Pethrus (1884–1974) of Sweden. Both Barratt and Pethrus visited America to conduct preaching tours among Scandinavian-American Pentecostal congregations. Numbers of immigrants subscribed to their periodicals and looked to them as theological authorities, especially when theological controversies arose.

Moreover, evangelists and pastors moved back-and-forth across the Atlantic to hold evangelistic meetings or to accept pastorates in one context or the other. Of course, from the beginning, the trans-Atlantic nature of the movement had carried American Pentecostalism by Scandinavians to Scandinavia. The pattern of reverse migration seen with Andrew G. Johnson-Ek (1878–1965) and Oscar Halvorsen (1876–1947), along with female missionaries Agnes Jacobson (1880–1955) and Maren Iversen (1876–1970) was not new either. The same pattern of reverse migration occurred decades earlier with Scandinavian revivalist and holiness leaders such as the Swedish Baptist John Ongman (1844–1931), the Swedish revivalist Fredrik Franson (1852–1908), and the Norwegian Methodist Sivert V. Ulness (1865–1937).[11] Needless to say, trans-Atlantic impulses shaped Scandinavian-American Pentecostals, defined their theological and cultural identities, and formed their corporate practices. This set them

---

10. Important studies related to trans-Atlantic migration are: Walter Nugent, *Crossings: The Great Transatlantic Migrations, 1870–1914* (Bloomington: Indiana University Press, 1992), and Annette G. Aubert and Zachary Purvis, eds., *Transatlantic Religion: Europe, America, and the Making of Modern Christianity* (Leiden: Brill, 2021). For Scandinavian-specific volumes, see Hans Norman and Harald Runblom, *Transatlantic Connections: Nordic Migration to the New World after 1800* (Oslo: Norwegian University Press, 1988), and Frederick Hale, *Trans-Atlantic Conservative Protestantism in the Evangelical Free and Mission Covenant Traditions* (New York: Arno, 1979).

11. David Bundy, *Visions of Apostolic Mission: Scandinavian Pentecostal Mission to 1935* (Uppsala: Uppsala Universitet, 2009), 90–94; Gustafson, *D. L. Moody and Swedes*, 118–25, 305, 314.

apart from their English-language counterparts in America and provided a means to contribute to American Pentecostalism.

Thematic Limitations

It is acknowledged that some themes raised in this volume are not fully developed. As mentioned above, the authors drew from Swedish-, Norwegian-, and English-language periodicals that recently have become available through digitization. While technology to digitize these periodicals has contributed to the writing of this highly original volume, the sheer amount of new data placed necessary restrictions on the number of important themes that could be developed, including the subjects of gender and race.[12] In one instance, for example, a Norwegian-language journal identified a young African-American woman in a photo with several Scandinavian-American Pentecostal missionaries in China in 1907.[13] The young woman was identified merely as a member of the Azusa Street Mission. Her name is neither listed with the photo nor was there any mention of her in period sources with the missionaries. Notwithstanding limitations like these, this volume is a step forward in the direction of adding to the body of literature on American Pentecostalism.

Methodologies of the Volume

The authors of this volume are mostly church historians. Others are trained in cultural anthropology, theology, missiology, and higher education. Each contributor brought a set of skills and expertise to the task of writing this volume, whether training in historiographical or qualitative research. Some applied mixed methodologies. In addition to the historical method which draws upon primary and secondary sources, one researcher used qualitative research by conducting personal interviews and gathering data from a focus group. Network mapping was used as well,

---

12. For example, additional research may examine themes of race and gender as described in: Anita Olson Gustafson, *Swedish Chicago: The Shaping of an Immigrant Community, 1880–1920* (Ithaca, NY: Cornell University Press, NY, 2020), and Dag Blanck and Adam Hjorthén, *Swedish-American Borderlands: New Histories of Transatlantic Relations* (Minneapolis: University of Minnesota Press, 2021).

13. Tønnes H. Gundersen, "Øybuen som ville frelse kineserne," *Dalane Folkmuseum Årbok* (2011–2012) 131.

identifying people in relationships with others and tracking how ideas were transmitted from one city or region to another.

An issue in writing historical accounts, especially when describing religious traditions, is bias. Authors do not write in a vacuum but bring their interests and personal perspectives to the task. The goal of this volume has been to pursue scholarly objectivity without abandoning interest in and involvement with the Pentecostal movement. Primary source materials for this volume describe events that may be considered highly supernaturalistic with descriptions of Pentecostal phenomena such as healings, tongue-speaking (glossolalia and xenolalia), prophesying, and other signs and wonders. Generally, the authors of this volume present such accounts from the primary sources at face value and often use direct quotations. The authors have sought to represent fairly the views of both proponents and detractors of the Pentecostal movement.

Arrangement of the Volume

The chapters of this volume are arranged in three sections under rubrics which demonstrate the participation and development of Scandinavian-American Pentecostals. The sections are: (1) "Convergence of Streams" which focuses on antecedent impulses of Scandinavian pietism, American revivalism, and the Holiness movement that led to the early formation of Swedish-American and Norwegian-American Pentecostal congregations; (2) "Emergence of Identities" which traces ecclesial and ethno-linguistic preferences that defined Scandinavian-American Pentecostals along lines of affiliation; and (3) "Influence within Cultures" which demonstrates contributions of Scandinavian-American Pentecostals within the American context and cross-culturally in overseas mission fields.

Convergence of Streams

In chapter 1, "Before Azusa Street: Scandinavian Pentecosts in America, 1886–1906," Kristina Undheim provides a fascinating survey of backgrounds for Scandinavian-American Pentecostalism. The chapter argues that revivals with Pentecostal phenomena occurred in the old countries, as well as in the Upper Midwest of the United States prior to April 1906, the beginning of the Azusa Street revival in Los Angeles. During the 18th and 19th centuries, the pietist movement in Sweden displayed Pentecostal phenomena such as prophesying and speaking in tongues. The chapter then provides multiple examples of Scandinavian-Americans who similarly experienced pre-Azusa revivals in the Upper Midwest, often within pietist, revivalist, and holiness traditions, illustrating that these movements shaped early Pentecostalism.

In chapter 2, "Scandinavian-American Pentecostal Revival of Chicago, 1906–1912," David M. Gustafson examines the people and movements that contributed to the early Pentecostal movement in Chicago. Similar to Undheim's chapter, Gustafson carefully describes the "pre-Azusa Pentecost" of Chicago which began in February of 1906, months before the Azusa Street revival. The Chicago revival was led by J. W. Hjertstrom of the Second Swedish Baptist Church. A few months later, missionaries from Azusa Street arrived to William H. Durham's North Avenue Mission in Chicago. As mentioned above, in Chicago, dual streams of Pentecostalism functioned concurrently with considerable interplay and interchange between them. Gustafson argues that while Scandinavian-American *Pentecostals* began to emerge, they did so in contrast to a number of "Spirit-filled Swedish Baptists" who were content to remain *Baptists*. Chicago was the center of Scandinavian-American Pentecostalism as a result of the concurrent streams.

In chapter 3, "Scandinavian-American Pentecostals: From Los Angeles and Chicago to Nordic America, 1906 to 1918," Jan-Åke Alvarsson and David M. Gustafson examine the spread of Scandinavian-American Pentecostalism. The authors show that with a large number of Scandinavian-Americans receptive or predisposed to the movement, the "Pentecostal fire" spread rapidly. Dozens of Scandinavian-Americans were active in the revival of the Azusa Street Mission in Los Angeles and its daughter Scandinavian Mission. The movement spread not simply north from Chicago to the Upper Midwest, but also from Los Angeles to Seattle by Josef N. Strand (1842–1923). Los Angeles and Chicago, as original centers of the movement had centripetal and centrifugal forces (moving inward and outward) with people visiting and then returning home to establish new Pentecostal missions and churches.

In chapter 4, "Trans-Atlantic Influence from Norway on Nordic-American Pentecostalism, 1906–1930," Rakel Ystebø Alegre examines the trans-Atlantic movement of Norwegians, as well as news in Norwegian-language publications. She argues that at the center of the exchange, the prominent leader, T. B. Barratt, provided theological and ecclesial leadership to Norwegian-American Pentecostals, mostly through his writings but also from his extended tour to the United States. Although the transatlantic influence went both ways, the chapter focuses on the influence from Norway to North America. The chapter draws heavily on periodicals in Scandinavian languages published in Norway and the United States, but particularly upon Barratt's periodical *Byposten*, later named *Korsets Seir*.

Emergence of Identities

In chapter 5, "Scandinavian-Americans and the General Council of the Assemblies of God (AG), 1906–1952," Darrin J. Rodgers presents the history of Scandinavian-Americans in the early Pentecostal movement and their participation in the Assemblies of God (AG) of Springfield, Missouri. While the AG did not form a language branch for Scandinavians in the United States, Scandinavian ministers and Scandinavian-majority churches were located primarily in the Midwest and Northwest. Based on comparative research of ministers and missionaries with the same Scandinavian surnames, this chapter argues that in the years 1935 and 1952, the AG had four to five times the number of ministers and missionaries than those of the Independent Assemblies of God (IAG) that was composed mainly of Scandinavians. Moreover, while certain Scandinavian AG leaders and churches have received attention in historical and scholarly literature, little has been written about Scandinavians in general in AG history and their contributions to American Pentecostalism.

In chapter 6, "Scandinavian-American Independent Assemblies of God (IAG), 1918–1952," Jan-Åke Alvarsson and David M. Gustafson sketch developments of the independent Pentecostals whose preference was not to affiliate with the English-language, American denomination (AG) because of ecclesiological (and ethno-linguistic) reasons. This body of Scandinavian-American Pentecostals of the IAG was shaped initially by William H. Durham and later by Lewi Pethrus of Sweden. Despite a merger of two independent bodies, the IAG later split over the controversy of the Latter Rain Movement.

In chapter 7, "Between Multiple Worlds: Emerging Scandinavian-American Pentecostal Theology, 1907–1919," Tommy Davidsson explores the emerging theology of Scandinavian-American Pentecostals. This chapter examines four theological themes that were especially prevalent, namely, (1) the full gospel and the "finished work of Calvary,"

(2) radical congregationalism, (3) the intermediate state and eternal punishment, and (4) the Oneness debate. Davidsson analyzes these themes based on early Scandinavian-American Pentecostal literature and corresponding literature in Scandinavia. The chapter argues that the development of Scandinavian-American Pentecostal theology was shaped by the intersection of their different "worlds" such as historic Evangelicalism with its streams in pietism, revivalism, and the holiness movement, American Pentecostalism, Scandinavian Pentecostalism, and theological discussions in the wider world. The chapter further proposes that the emergence of a Scandinavian-American Pentecostal theology in 1919, was built on a tense and decade-long process of what doctrines should, or should not, belong to the "Apostolic Faith."

Influence within Cultures

In chapter 8, "Scandinavian-American Pentecostal Mission to Brazil: Gunnar Vingren and Daniel Berg, 1910–1962" the authors, Isael de Araujo and Joel Wright, examine the work of these two Swedish-American missionaries from Chicago who arrived in Brazil in 1910, and established a Pentecostal mission that expanded exponentially to become the Assemblies of God of Brazil. The chapter argues that Vingren's and Berg's mission practice in Brazil not only introduced a full gospel message with a Pentecostal spirituality, but with time recognized the role of indigenous agency to empower Brazilian converts to become leaders of Brazil's Pentecostal movement. This chapter draws from Portuguese, English, and Swedish sources, and is arguably the most developed treatment of these two missionaries in the English language to date.

In chapter 9, "Missionary Tongues of Sophie Hansen: Testimonies of Xenolalia in Shanghai: 1904–1923," Ruth Ma presents her research on the Norwegian-American Sophie Hansen (1864–1925), who along with her husband and children, traveled as missionaries to China in 1907, with the Apostolic Faith Mission, founded by Bernt Berntsen (1863–1933). Ma argues from period sources that a breakthrough in the Hansens' work in Shanghai came in July 1908, when Sophie Hansen spoke Mandarin with natal proficiency, a practice known as xenolalia. In addition to her family, missionaries testified to her claim to have this spiritual gift, along with several Chinese people. While most cases of xenolalia were shown to be suspect and discredited, Ma's research provides what is arguably among the strongest cases of xenolalia in Pentecostal history, providing a window into Pentecostal spirituality.

In chapter 10, "Formation and Transformation of a Scandinavian-American Pentecostal Congregation in South Bend, Indiana, 1907–1967," Beverly Johnson-Miller presents a case study of South Bend Gospel Tabernacle (SBGT) of South Bend, Indiana, highlighting the church's theological vision and spiritual practices that shaped a Pentecostal faith-formation. Johnson-Miller posits that while this South Bend church had roots as a "Pentecostalized" Swedish Baptist Church in the 1910s, it emerged in the 1920s as a flourishing and impactful Pentecostal congregation. In her study, Johnson-Miller shows that the church exacted a high cost on the members in terms of time devoted to the church's ministries and often with a heavy sense of obligation. Despite the downsides, the church environment was spiritually formative and prepared the congregants to engage rather than withdraw from the local culture, as well as to participate cross-culturally in short-term and career missions.

In chapter 11, "From Scandinavian-American to Trans-Atlantic Relations of Neo-Pentecostals in Sweden and the United States, 1965–2014," Torbjörn Aronson discusses and analyzes three major Neo-Pentecostal developments in Sweden. He argues that the late 1960s and early 1970s was a time of transition from an earlier pattern when second-generation Scandinavian-Americans had a mutual exchange with Pentecostals in Sweden to a new development, namely, a trans-Atlantic, "Neo-Pentecostal" exchange. This development occurred with both the Charismatic renewal beginning in the 1960s, and the Jesus People movement of the 1970s.

Pentecostal Origins Theory

This volume does not attempt specifically to address the theory of the origin(s) of 20th century Pentecostalism. As mentioned above, there were pre-Azusa revivals that shaped the Scandinavian-American Pentecostal movement. Many of those who experienced these revivals with demonstrations of Pentecostal phenomena later joined the Pentecostal movement, and related their earlier experiences to it. Certainly, the Azusa Street revival played an important role in rallying people around the Pentecostal understanding that in the last days God would "pour out his Spirit on all flesh" (Acts 2:17). It is clear that the Azusa Street

Mission brought an evangelistic and missionary impulse to the early Pentecostal movement.

To understand the revival of the Azusa Street Mission from 1906 to 1909 as a rallying point of the Pentecostal movement, it is important to recognize that some prominent figures of Scandinavian-American Pentecostalism experienced Pentecostal-baptism at the Azusa Street Mission, and their ministries were profoundly affected. Although William H. Durham was not of Scandinavian descent, he experienced Pentecostal baptism at the Azusa Street Mission, and returned to Chicago where he ministered to hundreds of Norwegian, Danish, and Swedish immigrants, who joined the Pentecostal movement.

In addition, several Scandinavian immigrants participated in the Azusa Street revival. Among them were: Cenna Osterberg, Andrew G. Johnson-Ek, Agnes Jacobson, Gustav S. Lundgren, Ellen Carlson (Lundgren), Adolph Johnson, and Hanna Holmsten.[14] In addition, there were Finnish-born immigrants, namely, Mary Bjorkman and Linda Erickson (Johnson), as well as Norwegian-born immigrants, Josef N. Strand, Maren Iversen, and Bernt Berntsen. A Dane by the name of Auge Sulger also participated for a time. All of these Scandinavian-Americans were active in the Azusa Street revival, and launched ministries as Pentecostal evangelists or missionaries from America's West Coast to the mission fields of Norway, Sweden, Denmark, China, Fiji, and India.

While the revival in Los Angeles was not the only source of the Pentecostal movement, it must be recognized that Azusa Street, as mentioned above, was a rallying point that set into motion Scandinavian-American ministers, laypeople, and missionaries in the United States and overseas.[15] In turn, thousands were influenced by them as they told stories of their experiences at the Azusa Street Mission.

Another case for the Azusa Street revival as a rallying point of the burgeoning movement comes from the prominent figure of Scandinavian-American Pentecostalism, A. A. Holmgren (1866–1949) of Minneapolis, who served for decades as editor of *Sanningens Vittne* (Witness of Truth), a Swedish-language Pentecostal periodical. Holmgren was

---

14. David M. Gustafson, "The Scandinavian Mission of the Azusa Street Revival of Los Angeles, 1907–1913," *Swedish-American Historical Quarterly* 72 (July 2021) 167.

15. Gastón Espinosa, *William J. Seymour and the Origins of Global Pentecostalism* (Durham, NC: Duke University Press, 2014), 30. For more on multiple sources of Pentecostalism, see Jay Riley Case, *An Unpredictable Gospel: American Evangelicals and World Christianity, 1812–1920* (New York: Oxford University Press, 2012), 231–54.

among the most knowledgeable of the movement, especially among the Independent Assemblies of God (IAG). Although he was closely tied to Chicago as the center of Scandinavian-American Pentecostalism, he referred to Los Angeles and 312 Azusa Street, in particular, as "the center of the outpouring of the Spirit (*medelpunkten för andeutgjutelsen*) in 1906 and 1907."[16] The Azusa Street revival certainly rallied a critical mass that set the Pentecostal movement and missionary activity in motion. However, as will be shown, Chicago played a similar role, and the interplay between Chicago and Los Angeles as two centers of Pentecostalism cannot be underestimated, especially as Chicago emerged by 1908 as the new center of American Pentecostalism with Scandinavians playing an important part.

Process of Producing the Volume

The research project involved scholars from the United States, Sweden, Norway, Brazil, and China in dialogue with each other. Earlier, most contributors had produced journal articles, dissertations, or books on Scandinavian-American Pentecostals, writing in English, Swedish, Portuguese, or Norwegian. The scholars who contributed chapters were invited by the volume editors to participate in hopes of producing a book that would broaden the previous understanding of the nature and sources of American Pentecostalism.

Concurrently, initiatives were carried out to digitize source materials that allowed the authors to access sources on the internet. Several institutions contributed to the digitization process including Flower Pentecostal Heritage Center in Springfield, Missouri; Minnesota Historical Society in St. Paul; Archives of the Evangelical Free Church of America in Minneapolis; Archives of Bethel University and Converge in St. Paul; Fuller Theological Seminary in Pasadena, California; and Trinity Evangelical Divinity School in Deerfield, Illinois.

The Symposium on Scandinavian-American Pentecostalism was part of this research project. This meeting, hosted by Trinity Evangelical Divinity School on April 21–22, 2023, provided the opportunity for the authors, whether in-person or participating via Zoom, to present their findings and receive peer feedback. Before and after the Symposium,

---

16. *Sanningens Vittne*, January 1934, 5. Cf. Holmgren, *Pingströrelsen och dess Förkunnelse*, 24–25.

the team of scholars generated strings of email correspondence by which they carried out collaborative research, discussed source materials, forwarded information relevant to other chapters, and offered constructive criticism.

This book represents the significant and fruitful collaboration between these scholars in order to produce a coordinated and coherent work on Scandinavian-American Pentecostalism. Through this process, findings from the research highlight the important contributions of Scandinavian immigrants and their children to the development of American Pentecostalism. These findings have prompted a revising of Pentecostal history.

Chapter One

Before Azusa Street

Scandinavian Pentecosts in America,
1885–1906

Kristina Undheim

WHEN NEWS OF THE Azusa Street revival reached Scandinavian-Americans, the nature of the revival was familiar to them as they were reminded of previous experiences and stories heard from earlier generations, both in Scandinavia and America. Anders O. Morken, a Norwegian immigrant from Audubon, Minnesota, reported in December 1906 that, "A copy of the *Apostolic Faith* has been sent to us [from Los Angeles], and we were much blessed when we read and saw that God baptized His children with the Holy Ghost exactly the same way as He has done here. It is two years ago since God began to baptize His children in this place and some are talking with tongues, some have the gift of prophecy."[1]

Furthermore, a number of preachers from the Swedish Evangelical Free Churches were receptive to the Pentecostal movement in its earliest years. In his seminal book, *Northern Harvest*, published in 2003, Darrin J. Rodgers gives an account of pre-Pentecostal impulses among Scandinavians in the Upper Midwest.[2] Three years later, Rodgers published an

---

1. A. O. Morken, *Apostolic Faith* (*AF*), December 1906, 3.
2. Rodgers, *Northern Harvest*, 4–20.

article titled "Rediscovering Pentecostalism's Diverse Roots" in which he illustrates how more than twenty pre-Azusa Scandinavian-American congregations practiced glossolalia and healing. These churches served to shape the burgeoning Pentecostal movement in America alongside the revival at the Azusa Street Mission.[3]

Accounts of pre-Azusa, Pentecostal phenomena were known in Scandinavia too. In 1907, an article in the Chicago-based newspaper *Svenska Amerikanaren* (The Swedish American) attested to a revival in Sweden 70 years earlier when participants spoke in tongues and prophesied.[4] Even William J. Seymour in his book titled *Doctrines and Disciplines of the Azusa Street Apostolic Faith Mission*, mentioned such phenomena happening in Sweden between 1841 and 1843.[5]

The purpose of this chapter is to examine pre-Azusa Pentecostal experiences among Scandinavian-Americans, or what may be described as "Scandinavian Pentecosts in America." This chapter argues that *pre-Azusa* Pentecosts with Pentecostal phenomena occurred in the old countries, particularly in Sweden and Norway as well as in the Upper Midwest of the U.S., prior to April 1906, the start of the Azusa Street revival. In the 18th and 19th centuries, Scandinavian Pietist movements witnessed revivals that displayed Pentecostal phenomena such as prophesying and speaking in tongues. Similarly, Scandinavian immigrants experienced pre-Azusa Pentecosts in America. While these Scandinavian-Americans were rooted in Pietism in the old countries, they drew from other sources in the new country including American Revivalist and Holiness movements. In part, this chapter demonstrates why a number of Scandinavian immigrants were so sympathetic with and receptive to the Pentecostal revival of Azusa Street in 1906.

Previous Research

In 1946, author Stanley H. Frodsham listed eleven claims of glossolalia (speaking in tongues) in the U.S. between 1850 and 1900.[6] According

---

3. Rodgers, "Rediscovering Pentecostalism's Diverse Roots," 50.

4. "Talande med tungor för 70 år sedan." *Svenska Amerikanaren* (*SA*), March 5, 1907, 5. Trans. by David M. Gustafson.

5. Seymour, *Doctrines and Disciplines*, 46. Cf. V. P. Simmons, "History of Tongues," *The Bridegroom's Messenger* (*BM*) February 1, 1908, 4.

6. Frodsham, *With Signs Following*, 9–17, cited in Rodgers, "Rediscovering Pentecostalism's Diverse Roots," 51.

to Frodsham, these occurred in New England, Ohio, Minnesota, South Dakota, North Carolina, Tennessee, and Arkansas. Unfortunately, he did not cite his sources. Similarly, historians Carl Brumback and William Menzies repeated Frodsham's list. Menzies noted that these were isolated revivals of merely local importance, which is reason for later historians omitting them altogether.[7] For instance, historian Edith W. Blumhofer did not include these accounts in her 1989 history of the Assemblies of God.[8] Such accounts were likely dismissed as hear-say, unverified by historical evidence.

As already mentioned above, in 2003, Darrin Rodgers published his groundbreaking book *Northern Harvest: Pentecostalism in North Dakota*, which was followed by several articles and book contributions. In these publications, Rodgers provides detailed evidence and cites multiple sources from newspapers, books, and transcripts that attest to pre-1900 revivals accompanied by signs of divine healing and glossolalia. In his article from 2006, for instance, he lists twenty places in the Dakotas and Minnesota where these people met in organized churches or home meetings.[9] According to Rodgers, such revivals among Scandinavian settlers in the northern Great Plains "provided precedents and leaders for the emerging movement."[10]

In response to Rodgers, Edith W. Blumhofer questioned whether the existence of glossolalia among Scandinavian-Americans could be characterized as Pentecostal "because the participants viewed tongues as a gift [of God], but not necessarily as uniform evidence of Spirit Baptism."[11] In contrast, Gary B. McGee, in his book *People of the Spirit*, published in 2004, drew upon Rodgers's research and characterized the experience of these Scandinavian immigrants as Pentecostal.[12]

---

7. Brumback, *Suddenly from Heaven*, 12–17.

8. Rodgers, "Pentecostal Origins in Scandinavian Pietism on the Great Plains," 302.

9. Rodgers, "Rediscovering Pentecostalism's Diverse Roots," 52–53. Rodgers notes that the congregations in central Minnesota were in: Alexandria, Audubon, Detroit Lakes, Evansville, Fergus Falls, Lake Eunice, Moorhead, and Tordenskjold. In northwest Minnesota: Argyle, Fosston, Hallock, Holt, Karlstad, Lake Bronson, Stephen, Thief River Falls, and Warren. In eastern North Dakota: Grafton and Hillsboro. In southeast South Dakota: Greenfield.

10. Rodgers, "Rediscovering Pentecostalism's Diverse Roots," 50.

11. Blumhofer, "Response to: 'Rediscovering our Diverse Roots' by Darrin Rodgers" cited in Rodgers, "Pentecostal Origins in Scandinavian Pietism on the Great Plains," 302–3.

12. McGee, *People of the Spirit*, 25, 69, 88.

In the book *Miracles, Mission and American Pentecostalism*, McGee concludes: "Since they [Scandinavian-Americans] apparently had no contact with Charles F. Parham's Apostolic Faith movement, to label them 'Pentecostal' becomes problematic since they did not espouse his doctrine of evidential tongues for the Pentecostal baptism. While not 'Classical Pentecostal' as the term would later be understood—wrapped with distinct theological, denominational, and cultural connotations—a 'Pentecostal' spirituality thrived."[13]

Hence, for the purpose of this chapter, the designation "Pentecostal" will address those Scandinavians who practiced glossolalia and healing even though they had no direct connection to Parham, to Azusa Street, or to a doctrine of speaking in tongues as the evidence of Spirit baptism.[14]

Additional authors have built upon the work laid by Rodgers. In 2012, Roger E. Olson in his article "Pietism and Pentecostalism: Spiritual Cousins or Competitors?" demonstrated that Pentecostalism is a descendant of Pietism.[15] In 2015, David M. Gustafson wrote an article titled: "August Davis and the Free-Free: Pentecostal Phenomena among the Swedish Evangelical Free," in which he traced Pentecostal activity back to 1885 among the Free-Free (*de fri fria*) of the Swedish Free Mission.[16] Gustafson published a second article in 2017, titled "Mary Johnson and Ida Anderson: 'Free-Free' Missionaries of the Scandinavian Mission Society USA," and posited that these two women are identified in Pentecostal historiography as the first Pentecostal missionaries.[17] In 2019, Jan-Åke Alvarsson edited a volume that examines the transAtlantic exchanges between Pentecostals in Sweden and the U.S. In this volume, Alvarsson introduces the topic by drawing upon Rodgers's research and highlighting the importance of the Norwegian-American C. M. Hanson and the "Free-Free" of the Scandinavian Mission Society USA.[18] In addition to Rodgers, these authors provide a picture of Scandinavian *Pentecosts* in America between 1885 and 1905.

---

13. McGee, *Miracles, Missions, and American Pentecostalism*, 91.
14. Rodgers, "Pentecostal Origins in Scandinavian Pietism on the Great Plains," 303.
15. Olson, "Pietism and Pentecostalism?," 319–44.
16. Gustafson, "August Davis and the Free-Free," 201–23.
17. Gustafson, "Mary Johnson and Ida Anderson," 55–77.
18. Alvarsson, *Varför reste Lewi Pethrus just till Chicago?*, 18–20.

Pre-Azusa Pentecostal Experiences in Scandinavia

Several historical precedents prepared Scandinavians for the Pentecostal movement. According to Roger E. Olson, "Pietism is an important ingredient in that network of movements that prepared the way for the emergence of Pentecostalism."[19] Clearly, Pietism's emphases on the subjective experience of living faith and the Great Commission of proclaiming the gospel to all nations, ranks among the top impulses that Scandinavians brought with them to America.

Scholars trace the origin of Pietism to Philip Jakob Spener, a German Lutheran, who in 1675, wrote *Pia Desideria* (Pious Desires). Spener said: "It is not enough that we hear the Word with our outward ear, but we must let it penetrate to our heart, so that we may hear the Holy Spirit speak there, that is, with vibrant emotion and comfort feel the sealing of the Spirit and the power of the Word. Nor is it enough that we are baptized, but the inner man, where we have put on Christ . . . must also keep Christ on and bear witness to him in our outward life."[20]

Olson claims that the historical movement of Pietism spanned from 1675 to about 1750. After this, Pietism's *ethos* entered mainstream Christianity, which included Lutheranism, Methodism, and Congregationalism. The effects of Pietism were felt also among Scandinavian-American bodies such as the Augustana Lutheran, Swedish Baptist, Norwegian-Danish Methodist, Mission Covenant, Evangelical Free, and Pentecostal.[21] Pietism promoted the need for personal repentance and acknowledgement of one's need of divine grace, in light of one's unworthiness before God.

Furthermore, repentance and faith led to a sanctified or pious life. Though, according to the Norwegian scholar Kari Guttormsen Hempel, not as pious as the Puritans.[22] Due to the Pietistic focus on emotion and personal conviction, the first Norwegian immigrants were not as prone to impose religious rules and regulations on their followers as their Puritan English neighbors. In her doctoral thesis, titled, "Is Not a Sin in One Place Not a Sin in Another?," Hempel notes how Lee Hansen, a priest of a Norwegian immigrant church in 1857, asked the Norwegians to stop having fun after the Sunday services due to the bad reputation

---

19. Olson, "Pietism and Pentecostalism," 321.
20. Olson, "Pietism and Pentecostalism," 325.
21. Olson, "Pietism and Pentecostalism," 324.
22. Guttormsen Hempel, "Is Not a Sin in One Place a Sin in Another?," 98.

they had obtained among the English Americans. This brought a debate about sin and morality to Norway.[23]

Furthermore, Pietism prompted an interest in mission activity, in God's kingdom on earth through revivals, and in Christ's imminent return—all features of early twentieth-century Pentecostalism.[24] It must be noted, however, that all Pietists were not Pentecostal as such, even though Pietists propagated a heart-felt Christianity emphasizing the personal experience of Christ and an emotional display, even when restricted to crying quietly.[25] On the other hand, early Scandinavian-American Pentecostals viewed themselves as heirs of Pietism. For instance, in 1928, Arthur F. Johnson, a Swedish-American leader of the Independent (Scandinavian) Assemblies of God, questioned the drift of other Scandinavian denominations away from the Pietist origins and mentioned the Swedish Pietists Carl O. Rosenius, P. P. Waldenström, Karl Palmberg, Svenning Johansson, C. A. Björk, August Pohl, J. G. Princell, and Fredrik Franson.[26]

One of the more influential Pietistic revivals in Norway was propagated through the lay preacher Hans Nielsen Hauge (1771–1824) who prompted what became known as the Haugean movement. Some of the first Norwegian settlers in the U.S. were deeply affected by the movement. Darrin Rodgers notes, "While some members of these early Pentecostal churches [in North Dakota] were Swedes, most were Norwegians, many of whom had Haugean Lutheran backgrounds."[27]

During his ministry, Hauge was repeatedly convicted of breaking Norway's Conventicle Law. This law prohibited people from assembling without the presence or consent of a priest. All the Scandinavian countries had their version of this law. It was seldom observed after Hauge's lifetime, and as the first country in Scandinavia, Norway repealed its Conventicle Law in 1842.[28]

---

23. Guttormsen Hempel, "Is Not a Sin in One Place a Sin in Another?," 98.

24. Olson, "Pietism and Pentecostalism," 326. Olson does not mention mission in the article "Pietism and Pentecostalism" however, in his book he notes that the Moravians sent missionaries to many parts of the world that had not been touched by Christianity. Olson, *Story of Christian Theology*, 484.

25. Olson, *Story of Christian Theology*, 485.

26. *Sanningens Vittne (SV)*, December 1928, 3.

27. Rodgers, "Pentecostal Origins in Scandinavian Pietism on the Great Plains," 312.

28. Guttormsen Hempel, "Is Not a Sin in One Place a Sin in Another?," 81.

The repeal of this law caused a substantial increase in the lay Christian movement, the founding of several Christian societies, and with them the establishment of thousands of prayer houses or meeting houses (*Bedehus*). The numbers of people attending these pietistic revivals led to the growth of home devotions. The prayer houses facilitated the growth of the low-church tradition that included lay-led prayer meetings and sermons, as well as a commitment to home and foreign missions.[29]

In some places, the prayer houses functioned as the local church. Weather and geographical conditions often made these houses the nearest and only option for Christian assemblies during the week, as well as on Sundays.[30] Increasingly throughout the 1800s, volunteer work became the backbone of Norwegian Christians due to the establishment of these Christian societies. The immigrants brought this with them, and by 1916, they founded about 6,700 churches in the U.S.[31] In the book titled, *People of the Spirit*, McGee points to the Scandinavian familiarity with home prayer assemblies as an important premise for the immigrants who started new churches. They knew how to bring the fervency of the prayer meetings into regular Sunday services.[32]

As for early Pietism in Sweden, Moravian missionaries from Germany introduced house meetings with particular Pietist songs and literature.[33] An early meeting was held in Lillhärdal, in Härjedalen towards the end of the eighteenth century and spread across the middle part of Sweden towards the eastern coast. A female farmer named Karin Olofsdotter, who was given the nick-name "Bång-Karin," along with the Lutheran priest, Mårten Larsson Thunborg (1719–1775), led the Pietist revival. Bång-Karin claimed she had received divine revelations and preached a message of repentance. At first, Thunborg was skeptical towards her charismatic sermons and expressions, though he had no objection to female preachers. He soon endorsed her, believing she had spiritual gifts from the Holy Spirit including the gift of prophecy. Not long after he joined the revival, Mårten Thunborg was released from the priesthood and exiled from Lillhärdal. Followers of this revival were said to have bodily convulsions, fall into a sleep-like state of mind, and speak in tongues.[34] In the

29. Weihe, "Bedehus."
30. Weihe, "Bedehus."
31. Guttormsen Hempel, "Is Not a Sin in One Place a Sin in Another?," 92.
32. McGee, *People of the Spirit*, 68–69.
33. Berntson, Nilsson, and Wejryd, *Kyrka i Sverige*, 230.
34. Bygdén, *Hernösands Stifts Herdaminne*, 84.

early 1920s in Norway, the Lillhärdal revival was used as an example to warn people about dangers of the Pentecostal movement.³⁵

Another predecessor of the Pentecostal movement is mentioned in the writings of Philip Schaff, as well as William J. Seymour and Henry H. Ness, as mentioned above.³⁶ The revival in Sweden from 1841 to 1843 was referred to commonly as the "preaching sickness."³⁷ This spiritual awakening in the southern part of Sweden—particularly in Götaland—spread quickly with different expressions but soon ended. It was known for its passion, ecstasy, fire-and-brimstone preaching, and shouting inspired by the Holy Spirit.³⁸ Lutheran bishop J. A. Butsch (1800–1875) reported in *Aftonbladet* that "the sermons consisted of simple admonitions to repentance and the renunciation of sins such as card-playing, dancing, drunkenness and pride."³⁹ The "shouters" who cried out during the revival, were said to have no control over how or when they would shout.⁴⁰

Though there are few records of those who participated, the participants were deemed to be "sick" due to their convulsions and ecstatic outbursts. Spasms were said to accompany the "sickness." Hospital records show that 45 young participants were hospitalized with "religious ecstasy."⁴¹ According to historian Peter Aronsson, it is estimated that between 2,000 to 3,000 people were touched by the "shouters."⁴² In 1860, W. M. Wilkinson claimed that 3,000 people in the Skaraborg alone were affected by the "preaching sickness."⁴³

Referring to an account by Butsch, Wilkinson describe those "afflicted with the sickness." They would shake, then speak with a clear and

---

35. "Pinsebevægelsen," *Trondhjems Adresseavis*, March 14, 1922, 4.

36. Ness writes, "In the *History of the Christian Church*, by Philip Schaff, volume I, page 237, of the edition of 1882, he shows that the phenomenon of speaking in tongues among the early Quakers and Methodists, the Readers (followers of Lasare) in Sweden in 1841–1843." Ness, *Demonstration of the Holy Spirit*, 9–10.

37. Stephenson, *Religious Aspects of Swedish Immigration*, 31.

38. Aronsson, "Pigornas Rop Och Överhetens Diskurs," 246–47.

39. *Aftonbladet*, September 6, 7, 1842, cited in Stephenson, *Religious Aspects of Swedish Immigration*, 31.

40. Aronsson, "Pigornas Rop," 254.

41. Aronsson, "Pigornas Rop," 248–49. The average age was 20 to 21. Most were single young people from the lower level of society, from small farms, for example, domestic servants. The youngest being a 12-year-old boy and an 8-year-old girl. Aronsson, "Pigornas Rop," 248–49.

42. Aronsson, "Pigornas Rop," 266.

43. Wilkinson, *Revival*, 185. Similar phenomena was experienced in Finland by the Laestadian movement. Mantsinen, "Finnish Pentecostal Movement," 114.

eloquent but unusual language "by a certain immediate and miraculous influence of God."[44] Then, they would be calm, exceedingly well and happy. Some observed or testified that there was a "frequent heaviness in the head, heat at the pit of the stomach, prickling sensation in the extremities, convulsions and quaking; finally the falling, frequently with a deep groan, into a profound fainting fit or trance . . . They seemed disposed for visions and predictions. They declared that the words they spoke were given to them by someone else, who spoke by them."[45] The sickness produced "a religious state of mind, which was strengthened by the apparently miraculous operations within."[46] This was a revival marked by Christian language, and what Butsch described as true Christian thoughts and feelings. In his concluding remarks about the sickness, Wilkinson noted that "the good effect it produced on the mind of many a hardened sinner remains to testify of its truth and reality."[47]

While period sources did not specifically mention glossolalia, in 1907, the article published in Chicago's *Svenska Amerikanaren*, mentioned above, claimed that people spoke in tongues during the 1841–1843 revival,

> Hearing about the recent phenomena from several places, that people in a spiritual state of ecstasy (*hänförelse*) have the ability to "speak with tongues" in the biblical sense like that of the first disciples at Pentecost, reminds us of a spiritual movement which about 70 years ago took place in southern Västergötland—and perhaps in other places in Sweden also, although we only know about it happening there. Even then, it came across as "language-speaking" (*tungomålstalande*), although in a few rare cases, it might be considered to be "incomprehensible speech" (*obegripligt språk*). Nevertheless, the spiritual revival messages given in a state of physical and mental excitement by completely untrained and often "non-expressive people," was much more common.[48]

The meetings from 1841 to 1843 in Sweden were held at secretly agreed-upon places in the woods due to Sweden's Conventicle Law that

---

44. Wilkinson, *Revival*, 180.
45. Wilkinson, *Revival*, 178–79.
46. Wilkinson, *Revival*, 179.
47. Wilkinson, *Revival*, 185.
48. "Talande med Tungor för 70 År Sedan," *SA*, March 5, 1907, 5.

banned all religious gatherings not sponsored by the state church. *Svenska Amerikanaren* continued,

> Occasionally, as the leaders spoke, before or after speaking, they were affected and began to experience such things as violent twitching of the muscles or the shaking of their whole body, and sometimes fell into a state like unconsciousness. Then, all of a sudden, their message might switch to an entirely new topic. However, at times, they had such severe seizures that their speech became simply a string of obscure sounds tied together, or they became silent altogether. Soon, such verbal utterances became equally common among those who were listening.... When listeners at the meeting were given the gift of speaking with tongues, they sat down, huddled on the ground, rocked their bodies and sat silently until all of a sudden one or the other—or often all at once—fell completely over on the ground, or they stood on their feet, yet, in a crooked position, and they began talking again.... This [revival] movement, which dissolved and died out unnoticed, lasted about three years.[49]

From this account, it is evident that some Scandinavians either remembered or recognized similarities between the "preaching sickness" in their homeland and what was described in news reports of the Azusa Street revival. Yet, while Pentecostal-like phenomena were familiar to both, as Roger Olson underscores, there were significant theological differences between them.[50]

Pre-Azusa Pentecostal Experiences among Scandinavians in the USA

After the end of the American Civil War in 1865, waves of emigrants from the Scandinavian countries, mainly Swedes and Norwegians, washed upon the eastern shore of America and flowed into the upper Midwest, particularly to regions surrounding Chicago and Minneapolis. As many as 840,000 Norwegians emigrated to the U.S. between 1865 and 1938,[51] with 1.5 million Swedes emigrating from Sweden between 1865 and 1914.[52]

49. "Talande med tungor för 70 år sedan," *SA*, March 5, 1907, 5.
50. Olson, "Pietism and Pentecostalism," 341–44.
51. Hegdal and Bauge, "Nordmennenes møte med Amerika," 49.
52. Alvarsson, *Varför Reste Lewi Pethrus Just till Chicago?*, 10.

In addition to Chicago, Scandinavians in Minnesota and on the plains of the Dakotas began to report glossolalia, as well as cases of divine healing.[53] Evangelists, itinerant preachers, and missionaries soon formed regional networks such as the Scandinavian Mission Society USA, known commonly as Sällskapet (the Society)—the first district of the Swedish Evangelical Free Mission.

The Scandinavian Mission Society was organized by August Davis (originally August Davidsson, 1852–1936) and John Thompson (originally Jan Tomasson, 1854–1940).[54] The wider body of the Swedish Evangelical Free Mission, known simply as the "Free" (*fria*), drew inspiration from Swedish Pietists such as Carl O. Rosenius and P. P. Waldenström, as well as from the American revivalist D. L. Moody, and his Swedish disciple, Fredrik Franson.[55] In contrast to other Swedish Free Mission Friends, August Davis and the Scandinavian Mission Society, known commonly as the "Free-Free" (*fri fria*), promoted Pentecostal phenomena, commissioned female evangelists, and preferred itinerant preachers over resident pastors. At first this was a district society in Minnesota but expanded to Wisconsin and the Dakotas.[56]

---

53. Rodgers, "Rediscovering Pentecostalism's Diverse Roots," 50.

54. August Davis was born as August Davidsson on July 13, 1852, in Enslöv, Sweden. John Thompson was born as Jan Tomassson on August 10, 1854, in Södra Finnskoga, Sweden.

55. Gustafson, "August Davis and the Free-Free," 202.

56. Gustafson, "Mary Johnson and Ida Anderson," 58.

August Davis. Courtesy of First Evangelical Free Church of Minneapolis.

In addition to an emphasis on holiness, members sought divine healing and spoke in tongues. August Davis gained a reputation for emotional preaching and "strange demonstrations."[57] From his earlier years in Pennsylvania, he adopted free Methodist elements that he incorporated into his ministry.[58] In 1890, Axel Mellander of the Swedish Mission Covenant, writing to P. P. Waldenström of Sweden, described the Davis movement, saying, "A certain August Davis who is now pastor of the Free church in Minneapolis is the leader of a special faction among the Free whom we call the 'Free-Free.' He pushes the doctrine of perfection to an extreme and communicates the Holy Spirit though the imposition of hands. The procedure is as follows: The assembled carry on for hours with loud outcries and strenuous gestures. The preacher lays his hands on them and breathes on them. Then [the assembled] fall on the floor, are seized by convulsions, weep, laugh, thrash around, kick, etc."[59]

Earlier, Davis testified to his own experience of the Holy Spirit. While serving as an itinerant preacher he came to the conviction that

57. Gustafson, "August Davis and the Free-Free," 202.
58. Brolund, *Missions-vännerna*, 18; Olsson, *By One Spirit*, 329.
59. Waldenström, "Handlinger," 60–61, cited in Olsson, *By One Spirit*, 331.

it was possible to have greater spiritual power in his ministry and so "he sought after and was baptized with the Holy Spirit," and preached what he had experienced.[60] In 1885, the Swedish-language periodical *Chicago-Bladet* published his account.

> [Davis] prayed to God that he might experience such blissful experiences himself. And it happened one morning in Galesburg [Illinois] during prayer to God. [Davis] claimed that at that moment he experienced heavenly bliss and could do nothing other than utter unintelligible sounds (*utstöta orediga ljud*) which frightened all those who were in the house. Then another time during an evening meeting in Missouri, he said that he experienced such power that it was as if it would carry his prayer straight up to heaven. Later he often had such blissful experiences; at times it had felt as though his chest would burst. Sometimes the mouth was drawn closed, and it was as if his face shone brightly. Such experiences could not be of the devil.[61]

Davis continued to discuss Spirit-baptism, and at the turn of the century, the periodical *Chicago-Bladet* reported about a meeting of Free Mission Friends in Boone, Iowa. The question was raised: "What does it mean to be baptized with the Holy Spirit and with fire," (Matt. 3:11)? Are Spirit-baptism and fire-baptism the same? If not, what is the difference?"[62] A. L. Stone who submitted the question said that he did so for his own benefit but also believed that it would be of benefit to others. He said: "One often hears, for example, the prayers of some people who pray to be baptized with the Holy Spirit and with fire." He explained that "there were some African-Americans in Chicago who asked that God would baptize them with a baptism of fire."[63] The first to respond to the question was August Davis who said:

> I would like to read Matt. 3:10–11 "The axe is already at the root of the trees, and every tree that does not produce good fruit will be cut down and thrown into the fire. I baptize you with water for repentance. But after me will come one who is more powerful than I, whose sandals I am not fit to carry. He will baptize you with the Holy Spirit and with fire." John [the Baptist] speaks about a people for whom he came to prepare

---

60. Lindberg, *Looking Back Fifty Years*, 12.
61. *Chicago-Bladet* (*CB*), October 20, 1885.
62. *CB*, July 16, 1901. Cf. Synan, *Holiness-Pentecostal Tradition*, 52–58.
63. *CB*, July 16, 1901.

the way for the coming of the Messiah. He did this by preaching about repentance and baptism. The same people who were baptized with water would then be baptized with the Holy Spirit and with fire. I know well enough that some people try to distinguish between these two and hold that baptism of fire deals with the wicked. But I believe that Spirit-baptism and fire-baptism are the same because on the day of Pentecost there came *tongues of fire* [emphasis his], as we read, when the Spirit was poured out upon them.[64]

Hence, Davis maintained his distinct view of the Holy Spirit. For several years, he and John Thompson worked as board members of the Scandinavian Mission Society, an organization that they founded. John Thompson served as pastor of the Swedish Free Mission in Moorhead, Minnesota, for twenty-three years.[65] This church experienced several prolonged revivals in the late 1890s and early 1900s. During the revivals, God's Spirit would come upon members and they would experience Pentecostal baptism and speak in tongues.[66] Henry H. Ness (1894–1970) wrote:

> My first personal witness to the demonstrations of the Spirit was in Oslo, Norway, in 1906. God gave Norway a most remarkable revival through that well known, godly man, Pastor T. B. Barratt, who at that time was one of the leaders of Methodism in Norway. . . . Another account of early Pentecostal outpourings of the Holy Spirit in America took place in the Swedish Mission Church, Fourth Ave. and Tenth St. N., Moorhead, Minn., where the Rev. John Thompson was pastor: This spiritual revival began in 1892 and continued many years. There were many remarkable healings, and very often as Pastor Thompson was preaching, the power of God would fall, people dropping to the floor and speaking in other tongues as the Spirit gave them utterance.[67]

In addition to pastoring the congregation in Moorhead, John Thompson served as the pastor of the Free Mission of Enderlin, North Dakota, and the Free Mission Church in Detroit Lakes, Minnesota. In 1912, N. A. Martinson wrote to *Sanningens Vittne*, a Swedish-language

64. *CB*, July 16, 1901. Cf. August Davis, "Faderns löfte om den Helige Ande," *Sanning och Ljus*, August 1931, 62.

65. Gustafson, "August Davis and the Free-Free," 219.

66. Rodgers, *Northern Harvest*, 2.

67. Ness, *Demonstration*, 11.

Pentecostal periodical in Minneapolis, saying: "This Pentecostal movement was new in Moorhead 15 to 20 years ago [1892–1897], and some of the older believers who have read your newspapers have said, 'This is just how it was here then.'"⁶⁸

Regarding the revivals in the early 1900s, Peter B. Thompson, son of John Thompson and later a minister of the Assemblies of God, wrote in *Pentecostal Evangel* describing the revival of 1903, saying, "God graciously poured out His Spirit with signs following. Many received the glorious Baptism in the Holy Ghost speaking in other tongues as the Spirit of God gave utterance. At that time we had not heard of any other places having received a like experience, but later we heard of people in California and Winnipeg, Canada, having received a like precious outpouring of the Holy Spirit."⁶⁹

Later, when the Swedish Evangelical Free Church took a position that did not embrace particular Pentecostal doctrines, John Thompson began to attend the Fargo Gospel Tabernacle, later called First Assembly of God, that had been started by Ness.⁷⁰

While still in Moorhead, John Thompson welcomed to his congregation Carrie Johnson and her four daughters. The youngest daughter was Mary Johnson (1884–1968).⁷¹ In 1904, Mary was sent by the Moorhead Evangelical Free Mission as a missionary of the Scandinavian Mission Society to South Africa. She traveled with her co-worker, Ida Anderson (1871–1964). The two women had ministered together earlier, working to establish Swedish Free churches in Minnesota. In 1902, Ida joined the Scandinavian Evangelical Free church in Minneapolis where August

---

68. *SV*, April 1912, 3. Cf. N. A. Martinson, "Huru står det skrifvit?" *Sanning och ljus*, December 1913, 4. In this Swedish Evangelical Free Church periodical edited by August Davis, N. A. Martinson of Moorhead, Minnesota, provides a theological treatment of Spirit-baptism and speaking in tongues.

69. Thompson, "Pentecostal Outpouring of Thirty-four Years Ago," 8, cited in Rodgers, *Northern Harvest*, 12–13, 216. Carl E. Martin suggested the revival happened in 1893. *SV*, May 1933, 5. Peter Thompson of Detroit Lakes, Minnesota, was a member of the Scandinavian Mission Society. *CB*, June 29, 1906, 3.

70. While the Swedish Evangelical Free Church, especially "the Free-Free," accepted Pentecostal phenomena such as healing and speaking in tongues, the Free Church as a body of independent congregations did not adopt Pentecostal theology of speaking in tongues as the initial evidence of Spirit-baptism. The The Davis movement was part of the Free Church but not entirely the Free Church. Oskarson, "History of the Doctrinal Emphasis of the Evangelical Free Church from 1930 to 1950," 34. See also *CB*, May 13, 1930; *SV*, June 1930, 3–4; *CB*, August 3, 1937, 2.

71. Rodgers, *Northern Harvest*, 11.

Davis served as pastor. For nearly two years, Mary Johnson accompanied Ida Anderson, leading singing and playing music during evangelistic meetings which they held.[72]

Ida Anderson and Mary Johnson, *Räddningslinan*, September 1909, Minnesota History Center, St. Paul. Photo by David M. Gustafson

In 1904, Mary and Ida attended the conference of the Scandinavian Mission Society held at Lake Eunice, Minnesota. During the conference, the two women experienced a profound calling to go as missionaries to South-Africa.[73] An account in *Trons Segrar* reflected on Mary's experience at the meeting, saying, "There, God met Mary with the baptism of the Spirit. She also received the gift to speak in tongues. Ida had this experience several years earlier."[74]

When Mary and Ida told others of their missionary calling to Africa, members of the Society agreed to support them. William Melin, secretary of the Society gave an account in *Bref-Dufvan*, saying, "It was in the autumn of 1904, and strictly speaking October 29, when sister Mary Johnson was called, not by any human being or through

72. Reinholdz, *Trons Segrar*, August 23, 1968, 10.
73. Gustafson, "Mary Johnson and Ida Anderson," 62–63.
74. Reinholdz, *Trons Segrar*, August 23, 1968, 10.

any human instrument but by God, to go out as a missionary to Africa. God's Spirit came in such power upon sister J[ohnson] that she was beside herself for a long time. But God's power not only came upon her greatly—when the Spirit of God came over her—but upon the whole meeting."[75] An account of the meeting reported,

> Those present were: John Thompson, Louis Olson, George Anderson, John Moline, Wm. Melin, H. M. Brandt, Alf Bakke, Wm. Bergström, O. A. Löfgren, Gottfrid Svenson and Albert A. Nelson. In addition to these were some prophesying daughters, Ida Anderson, Mary Johnson, Sabina Johnson, Thea Johnson, Ida C. Moen, Christina Sjölander, and Augusta Johnson, and many guests from various locations in Minnesota and neighboring states. We were together in sweet fellowship, to consider the importance of the mission, when the Spirit of God rested so powerfully upon the meeting that it was almost impossible to hold our business meeting. It was at this meeting that the Africa Mission as this little story is about, was born. A young sister, short in stature, modest and shy, attended the meeting. God's Spirit came upon her so mightily that she could not sit still, but got up, and ran with all her might back and forth in the meeting room, praising God, and in the Spirit she began to speak of Africa and the people and the country there, and right then she was called by the Lord, together with sister Ida Anderson, to go to this continent to proclaim the gospel of salvation, to those in the darkness and distress of paganism. The sister's name is Mary Johnson.[76]

In January 1905, Ida and Mary arrived by ship to Durban, South Africa. They spent their lives in South Africa as missionaries, establishing a mission station at Filipi near Port Shepstone. In addition to sharing the gospel, they witnessed Spirit-baptism among the Zulu converts.[77] Ida and Mary received financial support from churches of the Scandinavian Mission Society, and when some became Pentecostal congregations, like Fargo Gospel Tabernacle (later First Assembly of God) and Kulm Gospel Tabernacle (later Kulm Assembly of God), they continued

---

75. *Bref-Dufvan (BD)*, April, 1918, 4. William Melin was born December 14, 1866, in Dalarne, Sweden, came to America at sixteen, and lived in Minneapolis where he studied under August Skogsbergh and August Davis. Halleen et al., *Golden Jubilee*, 148; *Wright County Journal Press*, May 19, 1960, 1.

76. *BD*, March 1928, 3.

77. Gustafson, "August Davis and the Free-Free," 221. Gustafson cites *Bref-Dufvan*, April 1918. Gustafson, "Mary Johnson and Ida Anderson," 62.

to support the two missionaries. After the Swedish-language Pentecostal periodical *Sanningens Vittne* began in 1910, Ida Anderson regularly sent news of their ministry in South Africa.[78]

Henry H. Ness gathered additional accounts of Pentecostal activities in Minnesota and the Dakotas beyond Moorhead and Lake Eunice. He reported, "Another remarkable outpouring of the Spirit took place at Greenfield, S.[outh] D.[akota], in the First Methodist Church where the Rev. Rasmus Kristensen [Christiansen] was pastor. This was in 1896. As Brother Kristensen was preaching the power would fall, the people being filled with the Holy Ghost and speaking in other tongues and many other wonderful manifestations of God being witnessed."[79] In addition to revival in Greenfield, the Swedish Evangelical Free Mission of Brooklyn Township near Beresford experienced revival in 1897, when numbers of people were converted to faith.[80] During this period, the congregation was served by itinerant preachers of the Scandinavian Missionary Society including August Davis.[81]

Rasmus Christiansen (1848–1922) of Greenfield was a native of Rudkøbing, Denmark, and immigrated to America in 1865, arriving to South Dakota in 1869. In addition to farming, he took up preaching in Greenfield, south of Beresford. In 1904, Christiansen published an article in *Folke-Vennen*, a Norwegian-language periodical in Chicago, that spoke of his own baptism in the Holy Spirit and experience of speaking in tongues. He wrote: "God has gifted me to speak in foreign languages, so I neither subtract from it nor add to it. I speak whatever the Spirit gives."[82] In March 1906, *Folke-Vennen* published another article in which Christiansen described the gifts of the Holy Spirit and the necessity of living a life of obedience and faith according to the Word.[83] As a farmer-preacher, his Pentecostal ministry touched several families in the Beresford area.

In 1904, several of these Scandinavian families sensed God's call to go as missionaries to South Africa.[84] Whether by coincidence or

---

78. *SV*, May 1928, 8; December 1933, 7; October 1934, 7; December 1934, 7; September 1, 1935, 6; October 1, 1936, 7; May 1, 1938, 7; May 1, 1939, 6.

79. Ness, *Demonstration*, 10–11.

80. Halleen, *Golden Jubilee*, 68.

81. August Davis, "Besök i Beresford, So. Dak." *Sanning och frihet*, December 1897, 134; March 1898, 26.

82. Rasmus Christiansen, "De Aandelige Gaver," *Folke-Vennen* (*FV*), May 12, 1904, 1.

83. Rasmus Christiansen, "Greenfield, So. Dak.," *FV*, March 8, 1906, 5.

84. "Fra Syd Dakota til Sydafrika," *St.Paul Tidene*, December 2, 1904. In 1916, B. F.

planned, they joined Ida Anderson and Mary Johnson in Minneapolis on their way to South Africa. The group comprised a total of twenty-six people.[85] Twenty-four were from Beresford and were led by Henry C. Henricksen (1870–1953), a native of Tanstrup, Denmark. Henricksen was considered the group's "prophet." In addition to Henricksen's wife and three children, the "South Africa missionary band" included Folker Hansen, his wife and ten children; Nels Knudsen, his wife and daughter; and four single adults, namely Rasmus Robertson, Emelia Hansen (Robertson), Anne M. Larsen (Flyger), and Christine Villadsen. Before their departure for South Africa, a farewell was held at the Free Methodist Church in Beresford. Some members of the missionary band had ties to the Brooklyn Township Swedish Free Mission.[86]

Soon after the missionary band departed Beresford, Rasmus Christiansen remained with his family in Greenville. He received some word of divine warning that he would die on a certain day, apparently due to the fact that he "did not accompany his brethren" across the Atlantic Ocean.[87] Fortunately for him, the day passed without incident, and he remained in the land of the living.

Twenty-two members of the Beresford missionary band returned within two years.[88] In addition to their difficulty in finding land for farming and suitable work, some adults including Henricksen, found learning the native Zulu language difficult.[89] In contrast, Emelia Hansen, one of the single adults, acquired the language very quickly and

---

Lawrence reported that between 1900 and 1903, God's Spirit fell in South Dakota upon a band of people (presumably Norwegians) who then traveled to Africa. The group was accompanied to Chicago by a preacher named Bakke. Lawrence, *Apostolic Faith Restored*, 46–47, cited in Rodgers, "Rediscovering Pentecostalism's Diverse Roots," 61.

85. "Quit the Dakotas for South Africa: Scandinavian Families Desert the Wheat States and Go to Cape Town," *Minneapolis Daily Times*, November 26, 1904.

86. Karen M. Hansen, and Rev. J. H. Mars, pastor of the Swedish Free Mission, in "Many from Here Attend Services for Former African Missionary," *Beresford Republic* 43 (August 18, 1938) 1.

87. "For No Man Knoweth: South Dakota Farmer Didn't Die on Self-Appointed Day," *Sioux City Journal* December 17, 1904, 3; *Union County Courier*, December 1, 1904.

88. "Back from South Africa," *Turner County Herald*, July 13, 1905, Prophet Returns: Founder of New Sect Forsakes the Promised Land in Africa, *The Mitchell Capital*, April 20, 1906, 1; *The Black Hills Weekly Journal* May 4, 1906.

89. The South African Travelers, *Turner County Herald*, June 8, 1905; *The Black Hills Weekly Journal*, September 8, 1905.

began teaching a class of Zulu boys.[90] When the members of the South Africa missionary band arrived back in South Dakota, they returned to various churches in the area including Methodist, Evangelical Free, Nazarene, and Seventh-Day Adventist, evidence of their pietist, revivalist, and holiness impulses.

In addition to the Greenfield and Beresford area, Pentecostal activity was observed 320 miles north in Audubon, Minnesota, as mentioned above. Henry H. Ness wrote, "at Audubon, Minn., God wonderfully poured out His Spirit in 1897."[91] The most influential leader in this revival in Audubon was Jakob O. Bakken (later changed to Balken). Jakob Bakken and his brother, Ole, sister Anna, and mother Mary, were all involved during the early days of the Pentecostal movement. They were members of the Scandinavian Mission Society along with August Davis and John Thompson.[92] Although located 320 miles north of Greenfield, South Dakota, the Bakkens of Audubon and Christiansens moved in the same circles.[93]

Jacob O. Bakken (1870–1961) was born in Søre Storrustbakken, near Dovre, Norway. He, along with Anders O. Morken (1856–1931) who was born in Kvam of Nord-Fron, Norway, visited several communities in east central Minnesota, holding house meetings, proclaiming the gospel, and witnessing people convert to Christ.[94] In 1904, A. O. Morken reported in *Folke-Vennen* about Pentecostal phenomena happening in the area, saying:

> Some of the gifts of the Spirit from apostolic times have appeared among us, as some have received the grace to speak with tongues in diverse languages. It does not seem to be any known language but that of angels, because under the influence of the Spirit they are gripped by a power that completely

---

90. Emelia Hansen and Rasmus Robertson were the only missionaries from Beresford that decided to stay in Africa. In 1906, after they became husband and wife, they joined the Scandinavian Alliance Mission, organized years earlier by Fredrik Franson. The couple later relocated to Swaziland, but sadly, Emelia died in 1908 and Rasmus in 1912. *Union County Courier*, September 19, 1912, 8; Grauer, *Fifty Wonderful Years*, 191.

91. Ness, *Demonstration*, 12.

92. *BD*, December 1909, 8, in Gustafson, "August Davis and the Free-Free," 221. Bakken attended meetings with August Davis and John Thompson. *CB*, July 31, 1906, 8.

93. This is demonstrated by the fact that Rasmus Christiansen's daughter married Ole Bakken, Jakob O. Bakken's brother.

94. Rodgers, *Northern Harvest*, 5.

possesses them. What they speak is incomprehensible to themselves and others, the Spirit Himself has given interpretation [*tydning paa*] of some of it, which seems to be an encouragement and admonition for the children of God to be alert and praying, because Jesus is returning soon. I have often wondered where the power and the spiritual gifts are that should be present in a church (1 Cor. 12–14).[95]

In this account, Morken acknowledged that God's power was not only visible to them, but had become visible in other places of Minnesota too. Moreover, Morken viewed the outpouring of the Holy Spirit and the bestowal of spiritual gifts as a prelude to Christ's Second Coming, noting that when God plans to bring great changes in the world, he communicates these plans in advance to his children.

To the east of St. Paul, Minnesota, in the town of Dallas, Wisconsin, a Pentecostal assembly began in 1900.[96] Meetings were held in the farm homes of Nels Kringle, Gilbert Wahl, and John Wahl. Nels Kringle, an immigrant from Sør-Aurdal, Norway presided over the work from 1900 to 1914. Among those saved and baptized in the Spirit were Julia Wahl and Nora Severude.

Another important figure was Carl M. Hanson (1865–1954) who originally worked with the Free Mission Friends (*frimissionsvännerna*).[97] Hanson had a profound spiritual influence in the late 1890s and early 1900s among Scandinavian-Americans, with manifestations of glossolalia and healings. Hanson traveled across Minnesota and the eastern Dakotas, Wisconsin, and Iowa, promulgating Pentecostal experiences. Later, he became a recognized leader among Scandinavian-American Pentecostals in the Assemblies of God (AG), earning him the nickname, "Daddy" Hanson.[98]

C. M. Hanson was born in Lemond, Minnesota, to parents who had immigrated from Norway. He came to Christ as a student in the preparatory program at Augsburg Seminary, a Lutheran School in Minneapolis. After being healed of severe blood poisoning in 1895, he

---

95. A. O. Marken, "Fra Vor Egen Læsekreds: Audobon, Minnesota: Til Folkevennens Udgiver!," *Folke-Vennen*, February 29, 1904. Translation by Kristina Undheim. This article is signed A. O. Marken but most records are A. O. Morken.

96. G. Raymond Carlson, "Pentecostal Outpouring Dates Back to 1900: The Story of the Pentecostal Revival in Wisconsin," *Assemblies of God Heritage*, 5 (Fall 1985) 3.

97. *Svenska Folkets Tidning*, March 15, 1905, 5.

98. Rodgers, "Rediscovering Pentecostalism's Diverse Roots," 53.

traveled as a Free Mission evangelist. During a meeting at the farm of Hendriek N. Russum, near Grafton, North Dakota, a young girl spoke in tongues.[99] In the following year, Hanson experienced Pentecostal-baptism himself while at home in Minneapolis.

C. M. Hanson preached in homes, small churches, and in the open-air, similar to the format of the Salvation Army.[100] Manifestations of the Holy Spirit including tongues-speaking, prophesying, floor-rolling, and divine healing occurred in his meetings. Henry H. Ness described an occasion when Hanson experienced divine power in a strange manner, writing, "Then, while he [Hanson] was conducting services at Lake Eunice, Minn., he was on his knees praying on the platform during one meeting. Suddenly he was picked up by the power of God and carried through the air to the rear of the church where he found himself speaking in other tongues to a group of persons who were standing looking on. One man reached out his arm to grab Pastor Hanson but his arm became stiff and he could do no harm."[101]

Some manifestations were reminiscent of the "preaching sickness" of Sweden mentioned earlier, prompting strong reactions against him and his fellow evangelists. In some cases, objections to his methods of evangelism ended in threats of violence. For instance, in 1903, on a "dark night when Hanson and two of his disciples were returning home from a meeting in the country near Fergus Falls ... unsuspectingly, the three were startled by a shot and a bullet which kicked up the dust a few feet in front of them. A few minutes later a second bullet struck behind them."[102] In 1905, a witness in Fergus Falls, Minnesota, described what happened during a meeting there, saying,

> [Hanson] began praying in a moderate tone of voice which he gradually raised to a very high pitch, keeping his eyes fastened steadily on Miss [Olga] Nelson and a young girl who was sitting beside her. As the prayer ceased both young girls fell to the

---

99. Hanson, "My Experiences of the Graces of Salvation," *Tract*, 1906. Rodgers, "Rediscovering Pentecostalism's Diverse Roots," 53; and Rodgers, "Pentecostal Origins in Scandinavian Pietism on the Great Plains," 306. According to Rodgers, historians provided differing dates for these events. Frodsham and Brumback repeated Hanson's claim that the Grafton revival occurred in 1895, while Menzies dated the revival 1896, and Ness placed it at 1898.

100. *The Minneapolis Journal*, March 13, 1905, 9.

101. Ness, *Demonstration*, 12.

102. "Missionary Is Driven from City: Hanson Saved," *The Minneapolis Tribune* (*MT*), March 13, 1905, 9.

floor and began rolling and tossing and throwing themselves wildly about, at the same time quivering in every muscle and talking in what, appeared to be some strange language . . . Mr. Hanson himself cheerfully admits that his converts frequently roll about upon the floor but says this is due to the good and evil spirits combatting for mastery. He also claims that he is frequently given the gift of tongues, and that his converts often have a like experience.[103]

In this case, Hans Nelson, the father of Olga Nelson who appeared to have lost her reason, brought charges against Hanson who was arrested and fined $39.[104] It was rumored that the fine of $39 saved him from receiving "a coat of tar and feathers." The fine came with the understanding that Hanson would leave town immediately.

Following this event, he traveled widely, even to Chicago, where he became active with the North Avenue Mission. In February 1905, he published an article about Spirit-baptism in *Folke-Vennen*, and in 1909, he was ordained by Chicago Pentecostal leader William H. Durham of Chicago, and eight years later, transferred his ministerial credentials to the Assemblies of God.[105]

Conclusion

This chapter has examined pre-Azusa revivals among Scandinavian-Americans and their leaders, many of whom later either joined or identified closely with the Pentecostal movement. Rooted in Pietism with impulses from Anglo-American Wesleyan Holiness movement and Premillennialism, Scandinavian-Americans who were mostly associated with the Free-Free (*fri fria*) of the Swedish Evangelical Free Mission were known for their Pentecostal phenomena.

These Scandinavian immigrants were literate and well-versed in theological subjects. They emphasized home devotions and religious meetings that included singing, testimonies, prayer, and Scripture reading. They focused on mission and evangelism that prompted their

---

103. "Missionary Is Driven from City: Hanson Saved," *TMT*, 9. Hanson also claimed that an older lady had been gifted the German language without prior knowledge of it. *Fergus Falls Daily Journal*, March 10, 1905, 3.

104. "Missionary Is Driven from City: Hanson Saved," *TMT*, 9.

105. Rodgers, "Pentecostal Origins in Scandinavian Pietism on the Great Plains," 310.

travel to other towns and regions to proclaim the gospel. With an emphasis on revival, they witnessed manifestations of the Holy Spirit that included glossolalia, divine healing, and prophesying. The pre-Azusa *Pentecosts* among Scandinavian-Americans were mostly among evangelists and itinerant preachers of the Scandinavian Mission Society in Minnesota, Wisconsin, and the Dakotas. This society propagated activities and phenomena that later would be identified as *Pentecostal*. Among the pre-Azusa Pentecostals were: August Davis, John Thompson, Ida Anderson, Mary Johnson, Rasmus Christiansen, Henry C. Henricksen, Jakob O. Bakken, A. O. Morken, and C. M. Hanson. Most of them observed a continuity between their earlier experiences and the Pentecostal revival of Azusa Street.

Moreover, people like Henry H. Ness, author of *Demonstration of the Holy Spirit*, included accounts of many of these people in his book, being familiar with them and their stories. He was equally familiar with Pentecostal phenomena, testifying that his "first personal witness to the demonstrations of the Spirit was in Oslo, Norway, in 1906 . . . through that well known, godly man, Pastor T. B. Barratt."[106] Ness viewed the accounts that he described in Minnesota and the Dakotas as equally valid as his experiences within the wider Pentecostal movement.

Bibliography

Primary Sources

NEWSPAPERS USED

The Apostolic Faith (*AF*), Los Angeles, 1906–1908
Beresford Republic, Beresford, SD, 1893–
Black Hills Weekly Journal, Rapids City, SD, 1885–1930
Bref-Dufvan (*BD*), Buffalo, MN, 1909–1933
Bridegroom's Messenger, Atlanta, GA, 1907–1970
Chicago-Bladet (*CB*), Chicago, IL, 1877–1952
Fergus Falls Daily Journal, Fergus Falls, MN, 1883–1972
Folke-Vennen (*FV*), Chicago, IL, 1879–1933
Minneapolis Journal, Minneapolis, MN, 1888–1939
Minneapolis Daily Times, Minneapolis, MN, 1901–1905
The Minneapolis Tribune (*MT*), Minneapolis, MN, 1867–
Sanning och frihet, Minneapolis, MN, 1896–1913
Sanning och ljus, Minneapolis, MN, 1913–1936

---

106. Ness, *Demonstration of the Holy Spirit*, 11.

Sanningens Vittne (SV), Minneapolis, 1911–1939
Sioux City Journal, Sioux City, SD, 1864–
Svenska Amerikanaren (SA), Chicago, 1877–1914
Svenska Folkets Tidning, Minneapolis, 1881–1927
Trons Segrar, Askersund, Sweden,1890–1993.
Turner County Herald, Hurley, Dakota, SD, 1883–1918
Union County Courier, Elk Point, South Dakota, 1871–1913

Other Primary Sources

Hanson, Carl M. "My Experiences of the Graces of Salvation, Healing and Baptism in the Holy Spirit." Tract. 1906.
Lawrence, B. F. *Apostolic Faith Restored*. St. Louis: Gospel Publishing House, 1916.

Secondary Sources

Alvarsson, Jan-Åke Alvarsson, ed. *Varför reste Lewi Pethrus just till Chicago?: Relationer mellan Sverige och USA inom Ramen för Pentekostalismen*. Skellefteå, Sweden: Artos, 2019.
Andersen, Arlow W. *The Salt of the Earth: A History of Norwegian-Danish Methodism in America*. Nashville: Norwegian-Danish Methodist Historical Society, 1962.
Aronson, Peter, "Pigornas Rop Och Överhetens Diskurs. Ett Tolkningsförsök Av En Väckelse På 1840-Talet." *Scandia: Tidskrift För Historisk Forskning* 55 (2008) 245–89.
Blumhofer, Edith. "Response to: 'Rediscovering our Diverse Roots' by Darrin Rodgers." Annual meeting of the Society for Pentecostal Studies, Milwaukee, Wisconsin, March 2004, Flower Pentecostal Heritage Center.
Brumback, Carl. *Suddenly from Heaven: A History of the Assemblies of God*. Springfield, MO: Gospel Publishing House, 1961.
Bygdén, Leonard. *Hernösands Stifts Herdaminne: Bidrag till Kännedomen Om Prästerskap Och Kyrkliga Förhållanden till Tiden Omkirng Luleå Stifts Utbryning*. Stockholm: Almquist & Wiksell, 1926.
Carlson, G. Raymond. "Pentecostal Outpouring Dates Back to 1900: The Story of the Pentecostal Revival in Wisconsin." *Assemblies of God Heritage* 5 (1985) 3–13.
Frodsham, Stanley H. *With Signs Following*. Springfield, MO: Gospel Publishing House, 1946.
Grauer, O. C. *Fifty Wonderful Years: Missionary Service in Foreign Lands*. Chicago: Scandinavian Alliance Mission, 1940.
Gustafson, David M. "August Davis and the Free-Free: Pentecostal Phenomena among the Swedish Evangelical Free." *Pneuma* 37 (2015) 201–23.
———. "Mary Johnson and Ida Anderson." *Pneuma* 39 (2017) 55–77.
Guttormsen Hempel, Kari. "'Is Not a Sin in One Place a Sin in Another?' Menighetsliv i Norskamerikanske Immigrantmiljø i 1870–1917, kontinuitet og endring." PhD Thesis, Universitetet i Tromsø, 2011.

Halleen, E. A., et al. *Golden Jubilee: Reminiscences of Our Work under God, Swedish Evangelical Free Church of the U.S.A., 1884–1934*. Minneapolis: Swedish Evangelical Free Church, 1934.

Lindberg, Frank T. *Looking Back Fifty Years: Over the Rise and Progress of the Swedish Evangelical Free Church of America*. Minneapolis: Lindberg, 1935.

Mantsinen, T. T. "The Finnish Pentecostal Movement." In *Charismatic Christianity in Finland, Norway, and Sweden: Case Studies in Historical and Contemporary Developments*, edited by Jessica Moberg and Jane Skjoldli, 109–135. London: Palmgrave-Macmillan, 2018.

McGee, Gary B. *People of the Spirit: The Assemblies of God*. Springfield, MO: Gospel Publishing House, 2004.

———. *Miracles, Missions, and American Pentecostalism*. Maryknoll, NY: Orbis, 2010.

Ness, Henry H. *Demonstration of the Holy Spirit: As Revealed by the Scriptures and Confirmed in Great Revivals of Wesley, Finney, Cartwright, Whitfield, Moody, etc.* Seattle: Hollywood Temple, n.d.

Olson, Roger E. "Pietism and Pentecostalism: Spiritual Cousins or Competitors?" *Pneuma* 34 (2012) 319–44.

———. *The Story of Christian Theology: Twenty Centuries of Tradition & Reform*. Downers Grove, IL: InterVarsity, 1999.

Olsson, Karl A. *By One Spirit*. Chicago: Covenant, 1962.

Oskarson, Paul J. "A History of the Doctrinal Emphasis of the Evangelical Free Church from 1930 to 1950." Thesis, Trinity Seminary and Bible College, Chicago, 1956.

Rodgers, Darrin J. *Northern Harvest: Pentecostalism in North Dakota*. Bismarck, ND: North Dakota District Council of the Assemblies of God, 2003.

———. "Rediscovering Pentecostalism's Diverse Roots: Origins in Scandinavian Pietism in Minnesota and the Dakotas." *Refleks* 5 (2006) 50–64.

———. "Pentecostal Origins in Scandinavian Pietism on the Great Plains." In *A Light to the Nations: Explorations in Ecumenism, Missions, and Pentecostalism*, edited by S. M. Burgess and P. W. Lewis, 301–28. Eugene, OR: Wipf & Stock, 2017.

Stephenson, George M. *The Religious Aspects of Swedish Immigration: A Study of Immigrant Churches*. Minneapolis: University of Minnesota Press, 1932.

Thompson, Peter B. "Pentecostal Outpouring of Thirty-four Years Ago." *Pentecostal Evangel* n.d. (November 27, 1937) n.d.

Wilkinson, W. M. *The Revival in Its Physical, Psychical, and Religious Aspects*. London: Chapman & Hall, 1860.

Chapter Two

Scandinavian-American Pentecostal Revival of Chicago, 1906–1912

David M. Gustafson

WHEN THE PENTECOSTAL AWAKENING began in Los Angeles in April 1906, similar phenomena were happening in Chicago. Reports of spiritual awakenings in 1905 in Wales were published earlier in Chicago's Swedish- and Norwegian-language newspapers, sparking interest in revival among a number of Chicago's Scandinavian immigrants.[1]

At this time, Chicago was home to 50,000 immigrants from Sweden, 22,000 immigrants from Norway, 10,000 from Denmark, and 400 from Finland, comprising 14 percent of all foreign-born residents in the Windy City.[2] Many of these immigrants had joined Chicago's Lutheran, Baptist, Methodist, and Evangelical Free churches.

Swedish Baptist pastors and their congregations were at the front of Chicago's Scandinavian Pentecostal movement that began in 1906. This movement brought renewed spiritual life to many churches and conflict

---

1. *Folke-Vennen* (*FV*), June 1, 1905, 2; *Nya Wecko-Posten* (*NWP*), February 27, 1906, 5.

2. "What Chicago's Immigrant Population Looked Like in 1900," *Stackers*, June 27, 2022.

to others.[3] The "new movement" as it was called, prompted numbers of "Pentecostalized" Swedish Baptists to leave their congregations in order to form new congregations of Spirit-baptized, tongues-speaking Christians.[4] In others cases, members of the newly "Pentecostalized" Baptist churches left their congregations to join less-animated Swedish Baptists.

This chapter examines the Pentecostal movement among Scandinavian-Americans in Chicago between 1906 and 1912, introducing several people central to the early development of the movement. Many highlighted in this chapter are described more fully in subsequent chapters.

Chicago—situated geographically between Los Angeles, New York, Houston, and Minneapolis—soon became the center of Pentecostal activity and exchange. Just as America's railroads crisscrossed Chicago, the Windy City linked Pentecostals in the west, east, north, and south. Although the Azusa Street Mission of Los Angeles played an important role as a rallying point for the nascent Pentecostal movement, especially from 1906 to 1909, this chapter argues that the Pentecostal movement began two months earlier in Chicago, and by 1909, became the center of the Pentecostal movement in America, with Scandinavian-Americans playing a vital role in its growth and development.[5]

Pentecostal Stirrings in Chicago

An important personality among Scandinavian immigrants in the Upper Midwest was Carl M. Hanson (1865–1954), mentioned in the previous chapter. Hanson had ties early in his ministry with the Free Mission Friends of Minnesota. In February 1905, he published an article on Pentecostal baptism[6] in the Chicago-based, Norwegian-language newspaper *Folke-Vennen*.[7] Moreover, Hanson had ties with the American F. A. Graves (1856–1927) who was associated initially with the Christian

---

3. Ericson, *Harvest on the Prairies*, 49–50.

4. *Sanningens Vittne* (SV), May 1934, 5.

5. Synan, *Holiness Pentecostal Tradition*, 132–33. Cf. Espinosa, *William J. Seymour*, 30.

6. In this chapter, the expressions "Pentecostal baptism," "Spirit-baptism," and "baptism of the Holy Spirit," are used synonymously according to a classical Pentecostal understanding, and refer to the spiritual experience that may happen at the same time or subsequent to initial salvation (regeneration) and is evidenced by speaking in tongues (glossolalia).

7. *Folke-Vennen* (FV), February 2, 1905, 5.

utopian community founded by John Alexander Dowie (1847–1907) in Zion City, Illinois, forty miles north of Chicago.[8] Graves later joined the Pentecostal movement as did Hanson.

This chapter describes how the Pentecostal movement began in Chicago in February 1906, two months before the Pentecostal awakening in Los Angeles. The movement in Chicago was led by the Swedish Baptist pastor J. W. Hjertstrom (1854–1919) who was soon joined by other Swedish Baptist pastors, many who founded Scandinavian Pentecostal churches or led Pentecostalized Baptist Churches.

While Swedish Baptists such as J. W. Hjertstrom held to the historic Christian faith, their expectations of the Holy Spirit's presence and power to bring revival was rooted in the teachings of such people as the Swedish pietist C. O. Rosenius (1816–1868), the English Baptist C. H. Spurgeon (1834–1892), the American revivalist D. L. Moody (1837–1899), and the American Baptist A. J. Gordon (1836–1895).[9] Their pietist, holiness, and millennarian influences prepared and shaped the burgeoning Scandinavian-American Pentecostal movement.

J. W. Hjertstrom and "Pentecostalized" Swedish Baptists

J. W. Hjertstrom served as pastor of the Second Swedish Baptist Church of Chicago. Historian C. George Ericson of the (Swedish) Baptist General Conference, known today as Converge, remarked that after Hjertstrom experienced Pentecostal-baptism, he "threw himself with all the force of a strong personality into this movement."[10] In addition to Hjertstrom, Petrus Swartz, pastor of the Lake View Swedish Baptist Church of Chicago became involved with the movement, as did B. M. Johnson of Salem Swedish Baptist Church. In addition, F. A. Sandgren, assistant editor of *Folke-Vennen*, Carl Vingren, a Swedish Baptist missionary to China, and

---

8. Rodgers, "Carl M. Hanson," 10. It should also be noted that Zion City and Chicago were visited briefly prior to 1906 by Charles F. Parham (1873–1929), the initial leader of the Pentecostal movement from Topeka, Kansas. "En Ny Profet i Zion," *Vårt Land*, October 11, 1906, 7. Moreover, William J. Seymour (1870–1922), the leader of the Azusa Street Mission in Los Angeles visited Chicago briefly before locating to Houston and then Los Angeles. Robeck, *Azusa Street Mission*, 35.

9. Olson, *Centenary History*, 4, 13–17, 240, 590–59.

10. Olson, *Centenary History*, 588.

Olof Hedeen, professor of the Swedish Baptist Theological Seminary in Chicago, joined the Pentecostal movement in Chicago.[11]

The revival began on February 5, 1906, at the Second Swedish Baptist Church, located at 3020 Fifth Avenue (later Wells), near Wentworth and 30th streets. Since 1902, however, Hjertstrom and members of his congregation met to study the Bible's teaching about the Holy Spirit.[12] In January 1906, they gathered to "examine the Bible's teaching on the Spirit as the gift of faith."[13] In an interview published on February 6, 1906, in the Swedish-Baptist periodical *Nya Wecko-Posten*, Hjertstrom described this study, saying, "In the spring four years ago [1902], we began to gather on Monday evenings to pray for the Spirit and to read God's Word to learn about the person and work of the Spirit."[14]

Hjertstrom explained that when members, with tears in their eyes, asked him, "Pastor, do you know if I possess the Holy Spirit?," he said that he did not know how to answer them. As a result of their Bible study, however, some members of the congregation experienced the baptism of the Holy Spirit, spoke in tongues, and began to testify about the Spirit's work to bring spiritual renewal.[15]

---

11. In 1906, when Sandgren was an editor, *Folke-Vennen* published excerpts of J. W. Hjertstrom, showing a relationship between them. *FV*, July 19, 1906, 5.
12. Olson, "Brief History of Theological Struggles," 6.
13. *NWP*, January 30, 1906, 4.
14. *NWP*, February 6, 1906, 4.
15. Olson, *Centenary History*, 589; Granquist, "Smaller Religious Groups," 224–25.

J. W. Hjertstrom, *History of the Swedes of Illinois*, Engberg-Holmberg, 1908. Public domain.

John Wilhelm Hjertström was born in Stockholm, Sweden.[16] He converted to faith and at twenty-two years of age was water-baptized by Pastor Theodor Truvé in Gothenburg's archipelago.[17] Two years later, Hjertstrom enrolled in Bethel Seminary in Stockholm, graduating in 1881. He then entered the pastorate at Västervik, and later held pastorates in Nyköping and Falun. In 1891, he immigrated to America and came to Worcester, Massachusetts, where he served as pastor for six years. Then he accepted a call to the Fourth Swedish Baptist Church in Chicago; a role he held from 1897 to 1899. He then moved to Jamestown, New York, where he served as pastor of the Swedish Baptist congregation until 1901, when he returned to Chicago, receiving a call from Second Swedish Baptist Church. His study of the Scriptures led him in 1906 to publish a book titled *Delight in the Holy Spirit*.[18]

With heightened interest in the Holy Spirit, Hjertstrom and other Swedish Baptist pastors in Chicago planned to hold an edification

16. Olson et al., *History of the Swedes of Illinois*, 103.
17. *Vestkusten*, April 10, 1919, 3.
18. Hjertström, *Fröjd i den Helige Ande*.

conference with times of prayer, March 8-11, 1906. During this conference, all who attended would pray for "the outpouring of the Spirit" and expected to "experience greater joy in the Holy Spirit than ever before."[19] Following this conference, *Nya Wecko-Posten* reported: "Quite a few were present at the meetings, not only from the congregations within the city along with their pastors, but also from congregations in other parts of the country. A sister came all the way from Worcester, Mass., to attend the meeting."[20] Hjertstrom described one session, saying,

> Around 9:30 in the evening, the power of God's Spirit was felt so powerfully present that one clearly sensed something special was about to happen. A brother was just about to testify when his expression of words suddenly changed and it became clear to the leader of the meeting that this was now a holy moment . . . People were urged then to say calmly and quietly if they wanted more of God. Many of the believers present gestured that they wanted the Spirit's infilling. They needed not to make any gesture unless they had a sincere desire of heart, and this point was made clear. This was not a matter of emotions but dealt with the real nature of salvation, which gives to believers ongoing and lasting power for life. Then, just as everyone bowed down to their knees, the whole assembly was seized (*greps*) by such a wonderful power from God that young and old began to cry out, some cried for mercy and compassion, others cried out of blessed rapture (*salig hänförelse*). Some rushed out in terror and waited in the vestibule for what would happen next. For a while, this experience was both delightful and terrifying.[21]

After this took place, someone began to lead the group in prayer but the murmurs of the crowd made it nearly impossible for others to hear. When it seemed that the time was right, Hjertstrom read selected Bible verses. The reading of Scripture continued even though some needed to leave. Those who remained continued in a spirit of prayer. Some embraced each other and praised God while others prayed or sang. Professor Olof Hedeen, and pastors Henry Nelson and Petrus Swartz concluded, "This is a work of God."[22] During the following day,

19. *NWP*, February 6, 1906, 4.
20. *NWP*, March 13, 1906, 4.
21. *NWP*, March 20, 1906, 4. Cf. *NWP*, March 20, 1906, 4; *SV*, Jun 1, 1939, 4-5.
22. *NWP*, March 20, 1906, 4. Cf. "the outpouring of the Spirit (*Andeutgjutelse*) in *NWP*, March 20, 1906, 4. Henry Nilson or Nelson (1861-1930), born in Färlöf, Sweden, served Baptist congregations in La Porte and South Bend, Indiana, and worked in Chicago in 1906. For Swartz see *SV*, June 1, 1939, 4-5.

when another session was held, some people shared testimonies of being "taken by God's Spirit" (*fattats af Guds Ande*), saying that they had "either experienced the Spirit's infilling or had the conviction (albeit once disputed) that they received a particular gift of God."[23]

Following the conference, interest piqued in other Swedish Baptists. Professor Olof Hedeen of the Swedish Baptist Theological Seminary in Morgan Park—a department of the Divinity School of the University of Chicago—began a series of meetings to examine the New Testament's teaching on the Holy Spirit.[24] Olof Hedeen (1860–1936), a native of Undersåker, Sweden, and a former student of the Fjellsted School and Uppsala University in Sweden, as well as Augustana Seminary in Illinois, had served years earlier in Lutheran and Baptist churches before teaching Greek and New Testament at the Chicago Baptist seminary.[25] Hedeen was well-connected not merely with students in Chicago and Swedish Baptist pastors in the United States, but also with Baptists in Sweden such as his younger brother, Carl Hedeen, who played a role in the Pentecostal movement on both sides of the Atlantic.

In March 1906, J. W. Hjertstrom called for others to join him for a night of prayer. A hundred people attended the gathering including Olof Hedeen, Petrus Swartz, Henry Nelson, and B. M. Johnson. Hjertstrom reported that "all differences of social rank between believers and social classes were forgotten."[26] In the following month, Salem Swedish Baptist Church, led by B. M. Johnson, began a series of prayer meetings. Johnson said, "We all sit down as disciples, without rank and titles, and let the Holy Spirit be the teacher. Praise be to God that we sit down in peace and observe the person and work of the Holy Spirit in all his fullness, and in all things the Spirit is not ashamed to be the teacher . . . Oh, beloved children of God, may we experience a greater and fuller measure of God himself. . . . 'Do not be drunk with wine, which is debauchery, but be filled with the Spirit.' Eph. 5 18."[27]

23. *NWP*, March 20, 1906, 4. The disputed gift may refer to speaking in tongues.
24. *NWP*, February 20, 1906, 4; *NWP*, Mar 6, 1906, 5.
25. Olson, *Centenary History*, 487–88.
26. *NWP*, March 27, 1906, 4–5.
27. *NWP*, April 17, 1906, 4.

Pentecostals from Los Angeles Arrive in Chicago

While the Pentecostal revival in Chicago began two months before the Pentecostal revival in Los Angeles, the Scandinavian-American Pentecostal movement gained momentum when evangelists and missionaries from the Azusa Street Mission arrived in Chicago. The first missionaries bound for Palestine had left Los Angeles in July 1906. They traveled by train to Oakland, California, where they held meetings for several days, and then boarded a train to Denver, and then to Chicago. They stayed several days in the Windy City, visiting the North Avenue Mission led by the English-speaking William H. Durham (1873-1912).[28]

One of the missionaries bound for Palestine was Andrew G. Johnson-Ek (1878-1965), originally of Skövde, Sweden. Johnson-Ek had attended meetings of the Azusa Street Mission where he experienced Pentecostal baptism and spoke in tongues, which he suspected were Middle Eastern languages, prompting his sense of a divine call to missionary work in Palestine.[29] After this experience, Johnson-Ek, along with two American women, Louisa M. Condit and Lucy Leatherman, who had similar experiences, joined him on the journey to Palestine.[30] They were commissioned by William J. Seymour as the first missionaries sent out from the Azusa Street Mission.

When the "Palestine Missionary Band" arrived in Chicago, they met Durham and piqued his interest in the revival in Los Angeles.[31] Durham's North Avenue Mission was a natural stopping point for Johnson-Ek, Condit, and Leatherman, likely because of Johnson-Ek's connections with Cenna and Louis Osterberg in Los Angeles.[32] The Osterbergs had known Durham personally for years and corresponded with him at the beginning of the Azusa Street revival.[33] Durham later wrote: "About the month of April, 1906, I heard of the mighty outpouring of the Holy Ghost in the City of Los Angeles, accompanied by the speaking in other tongues, and my heart rejoiced over what God was

---

28. Alvarsson, "När Örebro Blev Sveriges Los Angeles," 30.
29. [Johnson] Ek, *Då Elden Föll*.
30. *FV*, Jan 10, 1907, 4; Newberg, "Palestine Missionary Band," 83.
31. Alvarsson, "När Örebro blev Sveriges Los Angeles," 30.
32. Gustafson, "Scandinavian Mission of the Azusa Street Revival," 173.
33. Blumhofer, "William H. Durham," 129.

doing, for I had no doubt that it was a mighty work of God and told my little congregation so."[34]

Moreover, F. A. Sandgren (1863–1933), an editor of *Folke-Vennen*, was a natural point of contact at the North Avenue Mission. This newspaper published accounts of the Scandinavian Pentecostal revivals in the Upper Midwest as early as February 1904, as well as C. M. Hanson's article in 1905, mentioned above.[35] Although Sandgren was a Swede, born in Lidköping, Sweden, he was fluent in English, Swedish, and Norwegian, and in January 1906, he became Durham's assistant pastor, focusing on ministry to Scandinavian immigrants.[36]

In addition to the visit by the Palestine Missionary Band in August 1906, Durham welcomed Mable and Jessie Smith, who also arrived from the Azusa Street Mission. Durham invited them to testify about the phenomena of healings and speaking in tongues that they had witnessed in Los Angeles.[37] Mable Smith (1868–1913), originally from Texas, spoke nightly to overflowing crowds at Durham's storefront mission.[38]

At the end of 1906, a few people from Durham's congregation, along with its sister mission at 328 West 63rd Street led by John C. Sinclair, had experienced Pentecostal-baptism and spoke in tongues.[39] Then, on January 14, 1907, several members of the North Avenue Mission experienced the Pentecostal baptism which drew others to come to the mission in order to observe this phenomenon.[40] Despite this outpouring of the Spirit at Durham's mission, apparently the "Pentecostal fire" had not yet fallen on Durham.

William H. Durham was born in Kentucky to a Baptist family of English descent. He came to Chicago when he was seventeen years old

---

34. *Pentecostal Testimony* (*PT*), March 1909, 6. Interestingly, when Johnson-Ek described meeting Durham at the North Avenue Mission, he recalled, "He told his friends that he did not doubt that we had sincere hearts but that we must be crazy." [Johnson] Ek, *Då elden föll*, 10.

35. *FV* February 2, 1905, 5; February 25, 1904, 4.

36. Sandgren came to the United States at a young age, and was fluent in English, Swedish, and Norwegian. *La Grange Citizen*, January 19, 1933.

37. *The Weekly Evangel*, March 4, 1916, 4.

38. Alexander, "The Role of Women in the Azusa Street Revival," 65–66. Also, *Bridegroom's Messenger*, April 15, 1911, 3. Mable Smith had worked earlier with Parham in Texas.

39. *PT*, March 1909, 6; Cf. *PT*, August 1912, 3. After 1909, the address of Durham's second mission was 228 West 63rd Street.

40. *Pentecostal Evangel*, June 23, 1923, 10.

and soon afterwards moved to Tracy, Minnesota. He came into contact with evangelists of the World's Faith Missionary Association (WFMA), and was ordained as an evangelist with this nondenominational fellowship in 1902.[41] His preaching activities in 1904 included meetings at Skandia Evangelical Free Mission in Slayton, Minnesota, a congregation closely tied with August Davis and John Thompson of the "Free-Free."[42] Although Durham was active preaching in the Upper Midwest, he began to focus on Chicago, working especially in the Humboldt Park neighborhood with its population of Scandinavian immigrants.[43] The North Avenue Mission was located at 943 West North Avenue, but in 1909, the street address was renumbered 2836 West North Avenue.[44]

William H. Durham's Visit to Los Angeles

After Durham's visit by the Azusa Street missionaries, and after he saw those in his congregation experience Pentecostal baptism and speak in tongues, he responded to the invitation from his "old friends, the Osterbergs" to come to Los Angeles and experience the revival for himself.[45] When he arrived to 312 Azusa Street in early February 1907, he was deeply affected by what he saw and heard, and on March 2, he experienced the Pentecostal baptism himself.[46] After this experience, he remained several days with the Osterbergs. During this time, William Seymour prophesied over Durham that wherever he would preach, the Holy Spirit would come upon the listeners.

---

41. Blumhofer, "Urban Pentecostalism: Chicago, 1906–1912," 158, 165.

42. Blumhofer, "William H. Durham," 127. John Thompson ordained Andrew Carlson and August Olson of Slayton. *Chicago-Bladet (CB)* December 4, 1900.

43. Blumhofer, "William H. Durham," 127.

44. North Avenue Mission was later called the Full Gospel Mission, *PT*, March 1909, 8–9; July 1910, 16. *Plan of Re-Numbering City of Chicago* (Chicago: Chicago Directory Co., 1909), 107.

45. Blumhofer, "William H. Durham," 127.

46. *The Apostolic Faith (AF)*, February-March, 1907, 4. *FV*, March 26, 1908, 4; *PT*, July 1912, 3.

Scandinavian Immigrants at the North Avenue Mission

When Durham arrived back in Chicago, he turned the North Avenue Mission into a center for the Pentecostal movement.[47] He taught many of Seymour's theological and social views, and patterned the meetings after those of the Azusa Street Mission.[48] Durham's already diverse congregation became increasingly multiethnic, as well as mission-minded. At a congregational meeting in September 1907, the mission elected three trustees of Scandinavian descent—brothers Jensen, Peterson, and Olsen.[49] Durham also launched a monthly periodical called *Pentecostal Testimony* that promoted the new movement in Chicago and across the country.

Others at Durham's mission also experienced Pentecostal baptism. On March 16, 1907, Sophie P. Hansen (1864–1925), originally of Skinnarbøl, Norway, received the baptism of the Spirit and spoke in the Chinese language which was understood by a former missionary living in Chicago.[50] Having earlier sensed God's call to China, Sophie and her husband, George (Jørgen) Hansen (1868–1928), along with their children, were commissioned by the North Avenue Mission, described further in chapter eight. The Hansens traveled to Seattle where they joined other Scandinavian-American Pentecostal missionaries, including six with ties to the Azusa Street Mission in Los Angeles, on their way to China.[51]

Durham's Pentecostal experience in Los Angeles and his partnership with Sandgren in Chicago to reach Scandinavians with the "full gospel" soon reached a new level. As early as 1910, Durham was recognized as "the informal leader of the Pentecostal movement," especially among those in the Midwest.[52] People thronged to his meetings, often staying into the early morning hours. Thousands of listeners—American and Scandinavian—heard him preach and became convinced of their need for salvation and Spirit-baptism.

Generally, 25 to 30 pastors attended his meetings. The North Avenue Mission with a seating capacity of 200 often overflowed into the

---

47. Blumhofer, "William H. Durham," 141. The name of his mission was later named the North Avenue Full Gospel Assembly.

48. Espinosa, *William J. Seymour*, 20.

49. Blumhofer, "William H. Durham," 132.

50. *Latter Rain Evangel*, August 1911, 13; *SV*, November 1, 1921, 6; *Pentecostal Evangel*, April 1, 1922, 4.

51. Gustafson, "Scandinavian Mission," 183–84.

52. Faupel, *Everlasting Gospel*, 237.

street.⁵³ Notable people such as William H. Piper, A. H. Argue, Luigi Francescon, E. N. Bell, Andrew D. Urshan, and Aimee Semple-McPherson—who visited Durham's mission—became Pentecostal leaders.⁵⁴ In addition, numbers of Scandinavians attended Durham's meetings, many with ties to the "Pentecostalized" Swedish Baptists of Chicago such as B. M. Johnson, to the Free Mission Friends or "Free-Free" of the Upper Midwest such as C. M. Hanson, and to the Azusa Street Mission such as F. A. Sandgren (via Durham).⁵⁵ This prompted the interplay of various Pentecostal impulses that shaped the burgeoning Scandinavian-American Pentecostal movement in Chicago.

Swedish Baptist Pentecostals

Second Swedish Baptist Church of Chicago hosted a second major edification conference February 11–14, 1909, that drew hundreds of people.⁵⁶ The number of Swedish Baptist pastors who joined Hjertstom expanded. Following this conference, he wrote:

> During this meeting there were many items of prayer, particularly for those who as believers, wished to be filled with God's Holy Spirit . . . Professors Arvid Gordh and O. Hedeen and pastors P. Swartz, B. M. Johnson, Magnus Johnson, Carl Oberg, Carl Vingren, and C. H. Ekblad were willingly used of God as his instruments to highlight the truths of the kingdom of heaven . . . In addition to the above-mentioned brothers, others who participated were: Isak Hedberg and G. A. Johnson—the latter from Menominee, Michigan—A. A. Holmgren, and F.[rank] Tolleen . . . Brothers O. Dahlén, P. A. Hjelm, G. Wallendorf, H.[enry] Nilson [Nelson], and T.[horsten] Clafford, all from Chicago, attended giving talks and testimonies.⁵⁷

---

53. Edith Blumhofer notes, "On December 12, the [North Avenue] congregation purchased the mission property for $5,000 and assumed a $3,000 mortgage. The purchase made renovations possible, and Durham added an extension, nearly doubling the seating capacity. In 1908, the congregation installed a baptistery where, in the next two years, Durham immersed 800 people." Blumhofer, "William H. Durham," 132.

54. Robins, *Pentecostalism in America*, 35–36.

55. Parham formulated the theological tenet that speaking in tongues is the initial evidence of Spirit-baptism. Seymour later taught this and Durham brought the teaching to Chicago. Carlsson, "American Influences on the Swedish Pentecostal Movement Since 1910," 159.

56. *NWP*, February 9, 1909, 4; February 23, 1909, 4.

57. *NWP*, February 23, 1909, 4. For Gordh, see Olson, *Centenary History*, 589–90.

In his report of the conference, Hjertstrom referenced the meeting held earlier, in 1906, but noted that the recent meeting had a much larger attendance. He added: "Meetings were held on Sunday and Tuesday evenings when the spacious 'basement' was filled, not only with people but with the God of grace who powerfully occupied the people, in a way that was truly a foretaste of heaven."[58] Henry Nelson of Chicago provided a detailed description, saying:

> The meeting was attended by hungry souls, many who had come several hundred miles to receive a divine awakening (*gudomlig vederkvickelse*) over these days . . . A brother said, "I feel like I am standing on holy ground. I met God's Spirit in the stairway; suddenly I felt like I was in a holy room." It could not be otherwise, for one even felt the power when hearing all the cries of prayer from the side rooms and in the church pews. . . . Yes, I would just listen; I cannot describe it with my pen; I will not try either. The examples were far too holy to be interpreted in human speech. Only the heart which has full spiritual fellowship has any idea of this in reality . . . An old and famous brother among us, who has been in the ranks of the Lord's army for many years, but has always been more or less opposed to such meetings and utterances (*yttringar*) of the Spirit, stood up in the large gathering during the meeting and confessed, "Brothers, this work is of God. I throw myself on God's mercy. I want to receive the good things that God's Spirit communicates. I have been wrong and blind. Pray for me, I need power from on high. Oh God, I have been opposed to shaking, but now shake me, if you will.[59]

Among the manifestations of the Holy Spirit at this conference was divine healing and several testified of this publicly.

Therefore, it came as no surprise that the conference was met with ridicule. There were times "when the Spirit of the Lord filled [people] with the joy and peace of Jesus in overwhelming measure," and some moments were described as "intense spiritual rapture."[60] For this reason, Petrus Swartz responded to one critic, saying: "This movement is not a work of man so that it would depend and rest on any man. It is a work of God and continues toward victory despite ridicule and resistance."[61]

58. *NWP*, February 23, 1909, 4.
59. *NWP*, February 23, 1909, 4.
60. *NWP*, February 16, 1909, 4; March 2, 1909, 4; March 9, 1909, 5.
61. *NWP*, March 16, 1909, 5.

Second Swedish Baptist Church, 3020 Fifth Avenue (Wells), Chicago, Swedish Baptists gathered in 1902 for a Conference event. Used by permission from Archives of Bethel University and Converge.

As American Pentecostals such as Durham promoted the "initial evidence theory" that speaking in tongues is the initial evidence of Spirit-baptism,[62] the majority of Swedish Baptists held that speaking in tongues was not essentially tied to Spirit-baptism.[63] Soon tensions rose over the importance of speaking in tongues and whether this was the initial evidence of Spirit-baptism or not. Some Baptists rejected the Pentecostal phenomena altogether.[64] Others were sympathetic to it. Some Baptists became Pentecostals but were content to remain in Baptist churches. Some who had experienced Pentecostal-baptism accused those who did not as "carnal, not yielded to the Spirit."[65]

With rising tensions, some Pentecostalized Baptists left their congregations to join Pentecostal friends in establishing new Pentecostal assemblies.[66] Generally, these congregations were shaped more by the theology

62. Carlsson, "American Influences," 159.
63. *NWP*, May 11, 1909, 1, 4.
64. Olson, *Centenary History*, 590.
65. Olson, "Brief History of Theological Struggles," 6.
66. Olson, *Centenary History*, 590. The initial evidence theory remained a matter of debate not only among the Swedish Baptists and Scandinavian Pentecostals in

of Durham than the theology of Hjertstrom, but not always. The tensions between 1906 and 1912 over Pentecostal phenomena and theology prompted the publishing of articles and news stories in Swedish Baptist periodicals. Some articles were written to clarify Baptist teachings on the subject, with some in favor and others against the new movement.[67]

Scandinavian Pentecostal Church on Barry Avenue

An example of Scandinavians planting a new Pentecostal congregation in Chicago is the Scandinavian Pentecostal Church (*Skandinaviska Pingst Församlingen*) on Barry Avenue.[68] In 1908, when the North Avenue Mission lacked space, this Swedish-language Pentecostal mission began. Durham wrote, "God led a number of Swedish brethren who had come in and received the Holy Ghost, to go and open a mission in their own language, and for nearly two years that work has gone on, with the blessing of God upon it."[69] By the spring of 1910, B. M. Johnson became the congregation's pastor, joining Oscar Frizen, John Frizen, P. A. Dahlman, Nels Anderson, and Josephine C. Anderson who had organized the work.[70] Each of these lay leaders had "received the infilling of the Holy Spirit according to Acts 2:4" at the North Avenue Mission under Durham.[71] In 1909, the address of the church became 944 W. Barry Avenue, and the small mission was popularly known as the "Barry Avenue Church."[72]

The pastor, B. M. (Bengt Magnus) Johnson (1865–1940), was born in Virestad, Sweden. He had immigrated to America in 1883, and

---

America but also within the Swedish Pentecostal Movement of Sweden. Lewi Pethrus was initially "uncertain about the sign" but later adopted the view that "when the Spirit falls, we speak in tongues." Sahlberg, *Pingströrelsen och tidningen Dagen*, 31, cited in Carlsson, "American Influences," 159. Carlsson adds that by 1939, Pethrus took a stand against an extreme position, believing that a person could be baptized in the Holy Spirit without speaking in tongues.

67. Olson, "Brief History of Theological Struggles," 6.

68. *Word and Work*, May 1910, 155; *SV*, July 1911, 4. The church was also called The Apostolic Faith Assembly. *SV*, September 1929, 8; *Herald of Faith* (*HF*), October 1944, 28.

69. *Word and Work*, May 1910, 155.

70. *PT*, July 1910, 15. Per Axel Dahlman (1863–1931) became a Pentecostal pastor in Norway, Michigan, and Chicago. *SV*, June 1931, 6.

71. Heckman, *History of the Fellowship of Christian Assemblies* (*HFCA*), 123.

72. *SV*, July 1911, 4. Heckman, *HFCA*, 123. *Plan of Re-numbering City of Chicago*, 12.

settled with his parents in Duluth, Minnesota, converting to faith soon afterwards.[73] In 1898, Johnson sensed God's call to ministry which led him to Chicago where he enrolled in the Swedish Baptist Theological Seminary in Morgan Park.[74] In 1904, the Salem Swedish Baptist Church of Chicago called him as the pastor. He became active in the Pentecostal revival with Hjertstrom in the spring of 1906, and by November, left to accept a new pastorate in Norway, Michigan.

In addition to the Pentecostal revival with Hjertstrom and the Swedish Baptists, B. M. Johnson was inspired by Durham, even consulting with him regarding his assurance of Spirit-baptism.[75] Similar to the North Avenue Mission, Johnson's assembly on Barry Avenue grew as "souls were converted and baptized in the Holy Spirit."[76] In 1911, he launched his own periodical titled *Pingst-Rösten* (*The Pentecostal Voice*) that spread the Pentecostal message from Chicago to Scandinavian-Americans across the country.[77]

Humboldt Park Swedish Baptist Church at Fairfield and Cortland

In contrast to the Scandinavian Pentecostal Church led by B. M. Johnson, the Humboldt Park Swedish Baptist Church was "Pentecostalized" but remained a Swedish Baptist congregation. The church was led by Martin Carlson (1864–1953), a native of Aryd, Sweden. Carlson immigrated to America in 1882, locating in Manistique, Michigan.[78] Like others, he came to Chicago to attend the Swedish Baptist Theological Seminary. He graduated from the seminary in 1895, and became pastor of Humboldt Park Swedish Baptist Church, serving the congregation for his first term of five years. He ministered in other churches in the Midwest and worked as an evangelist in Washington state until 1909, when he returned to Humboldt Park for his second term of service to the congregation, and soon found himself in the middle of the Pentecostal revival. In 1910, Durham's *Pentecostal Testimony* reported,

73. *HF*, July 1940, 9.
74. *General Register of the Officers and Alumni, The University of Chicago, 1892–1902*, 173.
75. *SV*, May 1934, 5. Cf. *Brudgummens Röst*, September 1916, 129–30.
76. *HF*, July 1940, 9.
77. Holmgren, *Pingströrelsen och dess Förkunnelse*, 42.
78. Leonard, and Marquis, *Book of Chicagoans*, 118.

... it was stated that the Lord was beginning to work in the Humboldt Park Swedish Baptist Church, and that its three deacons had received the Holy Ghost. A little later the Lord met and baptized the pastor [Martin Carlson], and a few days ago one of the deacons told me that more than one hundred people have received the Holy Ghost up to date, including all the officers (so far as I know) and a large percentage of the members. Best of all, the Lord continues to work, and this church is literally transformed into a Pentecostal Assembly. So far as I know they are taking the same firm stand for the truths of Pentecost that we take. Glory to God for this great work which He has wrought in the power of the Holy Ghost![79]

Despite the report in the *Pentecostal Testimony*, historian Adolf Olson of the (Swedish) Baptist General Conference wrote that with "extreme emotionalism, tongues speaking and other ecstasies, [as well as] bodily exercises such as jerking and jumping," the Humboldt Park church found it "exceedingly difficult . . . to weather the storm."[80] Nevertheless, it remained a Swedish Baptist congregation. In this situation, several of those who were supportive of the Pentecostal movement joined Durham and Sandgren at the North Avenue Mission, or later formed a new Pentecostal church in the Humboldt Park neighborhood.

F. A. Sandgren and William H. Durham

F. A. Sandgren continued his work alongside Durham, and experienced Pentecostal-baptism himself in 1907.[81] For the next two years, these two men "labored together as one man in God's work."[82] After Durham's wife, Bessie Mae, died in August 1909, Sandgren accompanied him to the burial in Tracy, Minnesota. It was on this trip that Sandgren sensed God's call to leave *Folke-Vennen* where he had worked for several years as assistant editor, and "from then on, to preach the gospel."[83]

79. *PT*, July 1, 1910, 15.

80. Olson, *Centenary History*, 278; cf. *SV*, April 1912, 3; Ericson, *Harvest on the Prairies*, 49, 75–76.

81. Rodgers, "Pentecostal Origins in Scandinavian Pietism," 325.

82. *SV*, July-August, 1912, 6. Cf. *Pentecostal Evangel*, April 1, 1922, 10. Sandgren was ordained October 6, 1907, and later received a Certificate of Ordination from the Full Gospel Assembly, 700 Jenks St., St. Paul, September 17, 1922.

83. *SV*, July-August 1912, 6; August 19, 1909, 4; *FV*, January 20, 1910, 8; February 10, 1910, 4. Also, F. A. Sandgren, "Er Bibelen Livets Ord?" *FV*, July 22, 1909, 4.

In 1910, Sandgren served as pastor of the Swedish Baptist Church in South Bend, Indiana.[84] His ministry in this congregation represented a different direction of interplay between Pentecostal impulses in Chicago. Sandgren had felt the influence of the Azusa Street Mission through Durham and yet he served a "Pentecostalized" Swedish Baptist Church in Indiana, described more fully in subsequent chapters. In addition to Sandgren's role in South Bend, he traveled as an evangelist, holding meetings in Swedish, Norwegian, and English in such places as the Apostolic Faith Mission in Brooklyn, New York, the Full Gospel Assembly in St. Paul, Minnesota, and the Scandinavian Pentecostal Camp Meeting in Newington, Connecticut.[85]

When Sandgren left his role at the North Avenue Mission, Durham collaborated with C. M. Hanson. In September 1909, Durham ordained Hanson as a minister of the gospel, and four years later, Hanson served this congregation.[86]

From 1909 to 1912, Durham traveled extensively, holding conventions around the country, in addition to his preaching responsibilities at the North Avenue Mission and editing the *Pentecostal Testimony*. In January 1911, while traveling to the West Coast, he spent ten days in Minneapolis. Arthur Berg who attended Durham's meetings reported: "Every night the altars were filled with men, women, and children seeking God. A great number were saved and about 25 were filled with the Holy Spirit."[87]

Durham continued his journey to Los Angeles with his new associate, Harry Van Loon. Not long after their arrival, it was reported that 200 people were baptized in the Holy Spirit and a congregation of 600 was organized.[88] In addition to his preaching role at the new Pentecostal church, Durham held meetings in Oakland, Portland, Seattle, and

---

84. *PT*, July 1, 1910, 16.

85. *Latter Rain Evangel*, November 1911, 12; *Word and Witness*, November 20, 1913, 3; *Weekly Evangel*, July 24, 1915, 4; *Svenska Amerikanska Posten*, January 25, 1933, 12; *SV*, January 1912, 4. Later Sandgren published *Lifvets Frågor*.

86. Hanson's ordination certificate was signed by Durham, Van Loon, and John Sinclair. Hanson transferred his ordination to the Assemblies of God (AG), September 11, 1917. Rodgers, "Carl M. Hanson," 12; *SV*, May-June 1913, 8. Hanson also worked in Minnesota and the Dakotas. Rodgers, "Carl M. Hanson," 9.

87. Berg, "Early Days of the Pentecostal Renewal in Minnesota," 6.

88. *SV*, July-August 1912, 6.

Winnipeg. Although based in Los Angeles briefly, he returned to Chicago for a large Pentecostal convention in February 1912.[89]

In Chicago, Durham and Sandgren worked together again for three months. Sandgren reported, "Sinners were saved, and children of God who for years prayed and waited for the biblical baptism in the Holy Spirit and fire, had their prayers answered as they were filled and experienced a real Pentecostal awakening.... For the first three weeks or so, 93 received the baptism of the Holy Spirit."[90]

During this time, a Baptist pastor and journalist from Minneapolis named A. A. Holmgren traveled to Chicago to attend Durham's convention. Holmgren met several Scandinavian-American ministers there including Petrus Swartz, Martin Carlson, B. M. Johnson, F. A. Sandgren, Henry Nelson, C. M. Hanson, Eric Hallden, Petrus Hultgren (of Saskatchewan, Canada), and C. Otto Mellquist, a layman from Chicago.[91] Durham's convention was held in the Persian Pentecostal Mission at Sheffield Avenue and Montana Street where Andrew D. Urshan was the pastor.[92] Holmgren noted that among the gospel truths proclaimed by Durham was "Christ's finished work on Calvary."[93] Despite the favorable results of the meetings, Holmgren reported that Durham became increasingly weak during the convention, requiring that Sandgren take over leadership of the sessions.

At the close of the convention, Durham and his new bride, Harriet, along with Durham's children, departed Chicago for Los Angeles. Five days later, after their arrival to LA, news came that Durham had died. He was forty years of age. Durham's impact on the nascent Pentecostal movement was significant, nevertheless. During his final two years, 382,000 copies of his periodical were distributed across the country.[94]

Scandinavian Leaders in the Pentecostal Movement

With Durham's relocation to Los Angeles in 1911, and his premature death in 1912, a leadership vacuum was left within Chicago's

89. *SV*, January 1912, 3; *PT*, May 1912, 13.
90. *SV*, April 1912, 4.
91. *SV*, April 1912, 2–3.
92. *SV*, April 1912, 4.
93. *SV*, April 1912, 4; *PT*, January 1912, 14.
94. *PT*, January 1912, 15; July 1912, 16.

Pentecostal movement. For English-speaking American churches, William H. Piper of Stone Church in Chicago stepped into this role. In 1914, his congregation hosted the second General Council of the Assemblies of God. However, for Scandinavian-American Pentecostals, the leadership vacuum was filled by such people as B. M. Johnson, C. M. Hanson, F. A. Sandgren, and Petrus Swartz.

As mentioned earlier, Petrus Swartz (1860–1939), pastor of Lake View Swedish Baptist Church, joined the Pentecostal friends.[95] Swartz was born in Osby, Sweden, and while in military service he joined the First Baptist Church of Stockholm.[96] When he sensed God's call to become a minister, he enrolled at Bethel Seminary in Stockholm, completing his theological studies in 1885, the same year when he left for America. Arriving in Chicago, he continued his studies at the Swedish Baptist Theological Seminary, graduating in 1889. After serving congregations in Rockford, Illinois, and Omaha, Nebraska, he returned to Chicago in 1898, to serve Lake View Swedish Baptist Church, and took an active role in the Pentecostal revival of 1906. In the following year, he accepted the pastorate of the Swedish Baptist Church in Kansas City, Missouri, but returned to Chicago in 1909, to lead the Edgewater congregation. He served this church for eight years, and in 1917, he left the Baptists to join the Pentecostals as pastor at the West Auburn Park Church which had disaffiliated with the Swedish Baptist Conference to become a Swedish-language Pentecostal Assembly.[97]

Carl Vingren and His Nephew, Gunnar Vingren

Carl A. Vingren (1865–1947) actively supported the Pentecostal revival. He came from Bälinge, Sweden, and converted to faith at seventeen years of age. He attended the Baptist Theological Seminary in Stockholm, graduating in 1890. He was then appointed by the Baptists of Sweden to be their first missionary to China, where he labored for four years.[98] In 1896, he left the mission field, and traveled to Kansas City, Missouri,

95. *Svenska Amerikanska Posten*, May 24, 1939, 6.
96. Olson, *History of the Swedes of Illinois*, 345.
97. Olson, *Centenary History*, 279. In 1924, when Lewi Pethrus visited Chicago, Swartz was serving as pastor of the West Auburn Park Church. *Evangelii Härold*, May 8, 1924; May 29, 1924, referenced in Alvarsson, "Relationer mellan Sverige och USA," 33. Cf. Heckman, *HFCA*, 127.
98. Olson, *Centenary History*, 359.

where he spent time regaining his health. While there, he welcomed his nephew, Gunnar Vingren, from Sweden.

Gunnar Vingren (1879–1933) immigrated to the United States in October 1903, staying briefly with his uncle before moving to St. Louis and then to Chicago for theological studies.[99] He graduated from the Swedish Baptist Theological Seminary in May 1909, and accepted the pastorate of the Swedish Baptist Church in Menominee, Michigan.[100] Nonetheless, he returned to Chicago later that year to attend a large conference held November 17–21, 1909, at the Second Swedish Baptist Church, led by Hjertstrom.[101] At the conference, Gunnar Vingren met Daniel Berg (Höberg, 1884–1963), a native of Västra Tunhem, Sweden. A. A. Holmgren also attended this conference, and later recalled:

> In all the rooms of the church, there were souls longing for the baptism of the Holy Spirit. In a small room to the left of the pulpit, from which steps led to the front platform, Sister [Hannah] Mellquist had crouched down in a corner, and there, God baptized her in the Holy Spirit for which she still praises and glorifies the Lord. On the steps to the platform, Gunnar Vingren was lying on his back under the power of God and pounded his heels on the second and third steps. Oh, what a meeting! . . . How many others besides Sister Mellquist received the baptism of the Spirit at this conference, I do not remember now, but among those who were eagerly longing for it then were brothers B. M. Johnson and Gunnar Vingren.[102]

On Sunday afternoon of the conference, B. M. Johnson stepped up to the platform to give a testimony but did not say much before "he fell under the power of God and remained under this power for the rest of the day."[103]

On Monday, evening Johnson, Holmgren, and Vingren met with friends at the home of Otto and Hannah Mellquist in the Humboldt Park neighborhood for a "prayer-and-waiting meeting" (*bön och väntemöte*).[104]

---

99. Fernandes, *Christianity in Brazil*, 81.

100. Alvarsson, "Relationer mellan Sverige och USA," 30.

101. *NWP*, November 9, 1909, 5; November 23, 1909, 4; *SV*, May 1934, 5.

102. *SV*, May 1934, 5.

103. *SV* May 1934, 5. Johnson was helped to the nearby home of Mark Svedberg. Years later, Svedberg, a layman, led Bethany Pentecostal Assembly (*Betania pingstförsamling*) in Chicago. *SV*, November 1937, 8.

104. In 1909, C. Otto and Hannah Mellquist lived at N. Fairfield Avenue, Chicago.

Just two weeks earlier, Otto Mellquist had experienced Pentecostal baptism. In addition, C. W. Helm attended the Mellquist prayer meeting, along with "some brothers from the Swedish Baptist Church in Humboldt Park... and some sisters from the south side of Chicago."[105] Shortly after midnight some needed to leave because of work responsibilities in the morning but others continued praying and waiting. Holmgren reported, "At about 3:30 in the morning on [Tuesday] November 23, [1909] I saw fire in various forms hover (*sväva*) over Gunnar Vingren's chest, and repeatedly I was compelled to shout out: 'Now he has it; now he has it!' And immediately afterwards, he cried out in a long utterance of speaking in tongues, and with bodily demonstrations like I had never seen before nor have I ever seen since."[106]

Due to tensions between Swedish Baptists over such Pentecostal phenomena, Vingren's experience in Chicago led to his short pastorate in Menominee. For him and other Baptist pastors with Pentecostal experiences, it was difficult to minister in certain Baptist congregations after testifying about the Pentecostal baptism.[107] Thus, Vingren accepted an invitation to work with F. A. Sandgren at the Swedish Baptist Church in South Bend, Indiana, where members had accepted the Pentecostal teaching.

In South Bend, Vingren was joined on a Saturday afternoon by Daniel Berg at the home of Olof A. Uldin, a native of Övre Ullerud, Sweden. As the three met together, Uldin prophesied that Vingren and Berg should go to "Pará."[108] Within months, Vingren and Berg arrived in the city of Belém in the state of Pará, Brazil, as Pentecostal missionaries, described more fully in chapter eight.

Andrew August Holmgren and *Sanningens Vittne*

As the Pentecostal message spread, the movement took root in other cities too, including Minneapolis. A. A. Holmgren who had participated in the two edification conferences with Swedish Baptists in 1909, and in Durham's conference in 1912, became a leading proponent of the Pentecostal

---

105. *SV*, May 1934, 5. For Helm, see *SV*, May 1934, 5.

106. *SV*, May 1934, 5. Cf. *Brudgummens Röst*, September 1916, 129–30.

107. Heckman, *HFCA*, 28. Vingren left Menominee because members forced him to leave. However, 31 members became Pentecostals and formed a local Pentecostal assembly, the Full Gospel Mission on North Broadway. *SV*, July 1911, 4.

108. Chesnut, *Born Again in Brazil*, 26.

movement in the Upper Midwest. When Holmgren was in Chicago in May 1910, he was baptized in the Spirit at the Humboldt Park Swedish Baptist Church.[109] In the following year, he served as pastor of the Scandinavian Christian Assembly, a new Pentecostal congregation located at 2517 Central Ave. N. E., in Minneapolis.[110] Holmgren left his role as editor of the Swedish Baptist periodical *Baneret*, and in 1911 launched his own Swedish-language Pentecostal paper titled *Sanningens Vittne* (Witness of Truth). His new publication, like *Pingst-Rösten* of Chicago, spread news of Scandinavian Pentecostal meetings, conferences, church activities, and missions. For example, in 1911, *Sanningens Vittne* published a report from Anna M. Kjöl of Ingalls, Michigan, saying:

> God put His holy power on a sister, who was wonderfully blessed, and now she expects God soon to complete His work and baptize her in the Holy Spirit ... Half a year ago there was not a single Spirit-baptized person here; now there are 6 of us and 8 more who are earnestly seeking [the gift] ... Those whom God has sent here to give us the whole gospel are B. M. Johnson, Gunnar Vingren (now a missionary in Brazil), K. Knutson [from Menominee], F. A. Sandgren, A. A. Holmgren, C. M. Hanson, and [P. A.] Dahlman from Norway [Michigan].[111]

Within less than a decade, *Sanningens Vittne* had a circulation of 7,000 to 10,000 subscribers. Some issues reached as far as "Mother Svea [Sweden], bringing glad tidings of Pentecost to many hidden places, with some issues going as far as Finland, Denmark, Norway, Russia and Estonia."[112]

---

109. *SV*, May 1934, 5.

110. *SV*, July 1911, 4.

111. *SV*, July 1911, 4.

112. Holmgren, *Pingströrelsen och dess Förkunnelse*, 42. In addition, major Scandinavian-language newspapers reported the Pentecostal movement, mostly what was happening in Norway and Sweden. For instance, in a detailed account from Seattle-Tacoma, *Pacific Tribune* published an article titled, "Man 'Speaks in Tongues' in Sköfde." This article described the ministries of both Barratt in Norway and Johnson-Ek in Sweden, concluding that their activities "seem to be from the same source." From an interview with Johnson-Ek, the article reported that "in a prayer meeting in Los Angeles, California, he had encountered the new movement which in America has ... the gift of speaking in tongues." "Man 'talar med tungor' i Sköfde," *Pacific Tribune*, February 20, 1907, 4–5. Cf. "Humbug vid tungomålstalandet," *Svea*, February 6, 1907, 1; "Märklig andlig rörelsen i Sköfde," *CB*, February 19, 1907, 7.

J. W. Hjertstrom and the West Auburn Park Church

The interplay of Pentecostal impulses in Chicago produced a variety of congregations from Pentecostalized Swedish Baptists to Scandinavian Pentecostals. Interestingly, J. W. Hjertstrom who led Chicago's Pentecostal revival remained a Pentecostalized Baptist. He served the Second Swedish Baptist Church until late 1910, when he accepted the pastorate of a congregation in Cokato, Minnesota. In December 1911, he launched a monthly journal titled *Sanningens Segrar* (Victories of the Truth).

During his time away from Chicago, a new Swedish Baptist Church was organized on December 31, 1910, in the West Auburn Park neighborhood.[113] David Holmberg was called as pastor, and services were held on West 69th Street. After two years, Holmberg left and was succeeded by Hjertstrom who returned to the Windy City.[114]

Hjertstrom began as the pastor in 1912, but two years later, he suffered a stroke that paralyzed his right side.[115] His health condition improved, however. He continued to publish his journal and in 1915, wrote that among the signs of his day that pointed to Christ's imminent return was "the outpouring of the Holy Spirit," quoting Joel 2:28, "I will pour out my Spirit on all flesh."[116]

In 1916, West Auburn Park congregation decided to leave the Swedish Baptist Conference. Historian C. George Ericson wrote, "The work seemed to prosper, but soon the Pentecostal element gained control, and in 1916 it was reported to the [Swedish Baptist] Conference that the West Auburn Park Baptist Church had ceased to be a Baptist church. Members who were still of the Baptist persuasion sought membership in other Baptist churches."[117] The church had become a Pentecostal congregation.[118]

Although Hjertstrom had been at the center of the Scandinavian Pentecostal revival, he remained a Baptist.[119] In 1916, he even wrote an article that was critical of certain Pentecostal extremes, saying,

---

113. Ericson, *Harvest on the Prairies*, 103.
114. *Sanningens Segrar* (SS), January 1914, 21.
115. *Scandinavia*, September 16, 1914, 10.
116. SS, March 1915, 51.
117. Ericson, *Harvest on the Prairies*, 103.
118. Heckman, *HFCA*, 77.
119. For articles in *Sanningens Segrar* (SS) related to the Swedish Pentecostal Baptist perspective, for example see Petrus Swartz, "Ära nyfödelse och Andedop identiska begrepp?" SS, March 1912, 63–65; April 1912, 85–88; "Andeuppfyllelse," SS, September-October, 1912, 212; J. W. Hjertstrom, "Skall jag lämna församlingen?," SS, November

> I have met numerous people who have spoken in tongues, who possess the fruit which we have just mentioned which are characteristic of the life of the Spirit. But nothing in our religious activity has caused more trouble in recent years than the activity connected with the so-called speaking in tongues. The harsh judgments on those who do not speak in tongues have been dreadful. We have heard that their lot will be death and the abyss, that they will not be part of the first resurrection, etc. Well, for my own part, with great care I have judged these friends and their works and have no need to change tactics. But it would probably be desirable if Christian wisdom and calm find a place in several quarters. It is certain, however, that the tongue-speakers' movement is an expression of seeking after God, and God who understands the needs of sinful human beings better than we do, will sufficiently guide everything in the right direction.[120]

In the following year, Hjertstrom left the West Auburn Park assembly to become pastor of the Swedish Baptist Church in San Jose, California.[121] When his health declined, he returned to Chicago where he died in 1919.[122]

Conclusion

After J. W. Hjertstrom left Chicago for Cokato, Minnesota, and after William H. Durham died rather unexpectantly, people such as F. A. Sandberg, C. M. Hanson, Petrus Swartz, and B. M. Johnson stepped into leadership roles in the Pentecostal movement. As early as August 1912, B. M. Johnson led a Scandinavian Pentecostal Conference in Chicago held at the Persian Pentecostal Mission where Durham had held his conference a few months earlier. In anticipation of the conference, Johnson announced, "We pray that God, through these meetings, will unite his

---

1912), 226–34; "Hafven i fått den Helige Ande sedan i Mottagen edert Andedop?," SS, October 1913: 185–86; Magnus Johnson, "Andens Gåfvor—särskildt tungotalandet—i ljuset af Pauli lära," June 1914), 108–10. Magnus Johnson (1867–1958), originally from Gräsmark, Sweden, was a Pentecostal Baptist who served Baptist churches in Providence, Rhode Island, and San Francisco.

120. J. W. Hjertstrom, "Gammaldags kristendom och s.k. 'nya rörelse,'" SS, March-April 1914, 56. Cf. "Andedop"—kifämne, SS, April 1916, 305.

121. Vestkusten, April 10, 1919, 3.

122. His periodical, Sanningens Segrar, ceased publication at this time. CB, April 1, 1919, 5; Brev-Dufvan, April 1919, 8.

people, as never before, and that he will pour out his Spirit, [and] that signs and wonders may take place in the name of Jesus Christ."[123]

The burgeoning Scandinavian-American Pentecostal movement in Chicago brought renewed spiritual life to thousands but sparked tensions, even divisions among Swedish Baptist pastors and congregations. While some churches became Pentecostalized Baptist congregations, others left the Swedish Baptist Conference altogether in order to form independent Scandinavian Pentecostal congregations. Despite conflicts and criticisms, the movement spread from the Windy City—the Pentecostal movement's new center—to Scandinavian enclaves in other cities, regions, and nations of the world.

Bibliography

Primary Sources

NEWSPAPERS USED

The Apostolic Faith (*AF*), Los Angeles, 1906–1908
Bref-Dufvan (*BD*), Buffalo, MN, 1909–1933
Bridegroom's Messenger, Atlanta, GA, 1907–1970
Brudgummens Röst, Stockholm, Sweden, 1911–1922
Chicago-Bladet (*CB*), Chicago, IL, 1877–1952
Folke-Vennen (*FV*), Chicago, IL, 1879–1933
Herald of Faith (*HF*), Duluth, MN, Chicago, 1936–1950
Latter Rain Evangel, Chicago, 1908–1939
Nya Wecko-Posten (*NWP*), Chicago, 1884–1918
Pentecostal Evangel, Plainfield, IN, Springfield, MO, 1913–2014
Pentecostal Testimony (*PT*), Chicago, 1909–1912
Sanningens Segrar (*SS*), Cokato, MN, 1911–1919
Sanningens Vittne (*SV*), Minneapolis, 1911–1939
Scandinavia, Worcester, MA, 1887–1918
Svenska Amerikanska Posten, Minneapolis, 1885–1940
Vestkusten, San Francisco, 1887–2007
Vårt Land, Jamestown, NY, 1890–1920
The Weekly Evangel, St. Louis, MO, 1915–1918
Word and Witness, Malvern, AR, 1912–1915
Word and Work, Framingham, MA, 1919–1940

---

123. *SV*, July–August 1912, 3. Cf. *SV*, June 1912, 4.

Other Primary Sources

General Register of the Officers and Alumni, The University of Chicago, 1892–1902. Chicago: University of Chicago Press, 1903.
Hjertstrom, J. W. *Fröjd i den Helige Ande*. Chicago: J. W. Hjertström, 1906.
Holmgren, A. A. *Pingströrelsen och dess Förkunnelse*. Minneapolis: S.V. Publ. House, 1919.
[Johnson-] Ek, Andrew. *Da°Elden Föll: Av ett Ögonvittne*. Mariestad, Sweden: Ek, 1933.

Secondary Sources

Alexander, Estrelda. "The Role of Women in the Azusa Street Revival." In *The Azusa Street Revival and Its Legacy*, edited by Harold D. Hunter and Cecil M. Robeck Jr., 61–77. Eugene, OR: Wipf & Stock, 2006.
Alvarsson, Jan-Åke. "När Örebro Blev Sveriges Los Angeles." In *"Azusa Street i Örebro": Pingstväckelsens intåg i Sverige. Rapport från ett symposium på Örebro Teologiska Högskola, den 23 november, 2006*, edited by Nils-Eije Stävare and Tommy Wasserman, 22–50. Örebro: Örebro Missionsskola, 2008.
Berg, Anna. "Early Days of the Pentecostal Renewal in Minnesota." *Assemblies of God Heritage* 16 (1996–1997) 5–7, 27.
Blumhofer, Edith L. "William H. Durham: Years of Creativity, Years of Dissent." In *Portraits of a Generation: Early Pentecostal Leaders*, edited by James R. Goff Jr. and Grant Wacker, 123–42. Fayetteville: University of Arkansas Press, 2002.
———. "Urban Pentecostalism: Chicago, 1906–1912." In *Turning Points in the History of American Evangelicalism*, edited by Heath W. Carter and Laura Rominger Porter, 154–79. Grand Rapids: Eerdmans, 2017.
Chesnut, R. Andrew. *Born Again in Brazil: The Pentecostal Boom and the Pathogens of Poverty*. New Brunswick, NJ: Rutgers University Press, 1997.
Erickson, C. George. *Harvest on the Prairies: Centennial History of the Baptist Conference of Illinois, 1856–1956*. Chicago: Baptist Conference Press, 1956.
Espinosa, Gastón. *William J. Seymour and the Origins of Global Pentecostalism*. Durham, NC: Duke University Press, 2014.
Faupel, David W. *The Everlasting Gospel: The Significance of Eschatology in the Development of Pentecostal Thought*. Blandford: UK: Deo, 2009.
Fernandes, Sílvia. *Christianity in Brazil: An Introduction from a Global Perspective*. London: Bloomsbury, 2022.
Granquist, Mark A. "Smaller Religious Groups in the Swedish-American Community." *Swedish-American Historical Quarterly* 44 (October 1992) 217–30.
Gustafson, David M. "The Scandinavian Mission of the Azusa Street Revival of Los Angeles, 1907–1913." *Swedish-American Historical Quarterly* 72 (2021) 165–208.
Heckman, Warren. *History of the Fellowship of Christian Assemblies (HFCA)*. Beaverton, OR: Good Book, 2011.
Leonard, J. W., and A. N. Marquis. *The Book of Chicagoans*. Chicago: A. N. Marquis, 1911.
Newberg, Eric N. "The Palestine Missionary Band and the Azusa-Jerusalem Connection." *Journal of the European Theological Association* 1 (2011) 81–92.

Olson, Adolf. *A Centenary History as Related to the Baptist General Conference of America*. Chicago: Baptist Conference Press, 1952.

Olson, Ernst W., et al. *History of the Swedes of Illinois*. Chicago: Engberg-Holmberg, 1908.

Olson, Virgil. "A Brief History of Theological Struggles within the Baptist General Conference." *The Baptist Pietist Clarion* 8 (2009) 1, 4–9, 14.

Robeck, Cecil M., Jr. *The Azusa Street Mission and Revival: The Birth of the Global Pentecostal Movement*. Nashville: Nelson, 2018.

Rodgers, Darrin J. "Carl M. Hanson: Scandinavian Harbinger of Pentecost." *Assemblies of God Heritage* 26 (2006) 8–15.

———. "Pentecostal Origins in Scandinavian Pietism." In *A Light to the Nations: Explorations in Ecumenism, Missions, and Pentecostalism*, edited by Stanley M. Burgess and Paul W. Lewis, 301–28. Eugene, OR: Wipf & Stock, 2017.

Sahlberg, Carl-Erik. *Pingströrelsen och tidningen Dagen*. Uppsala: 1976.

Synan, Vinson. *The Holiness Pentecostal Tradition*. Grand Rapids: Eerdmans, 2000.

"What Chicago's Immigrant Population Looked Like in 1900." *Stackers*, June 27, 2022. https://stacker.com/illinois/chicago/what-chicagos-immigrant-population-looked-1900.

Chapter Three

Movement of Scandinavian-American Pentecostals, 1906–1918

Jan-Åke Alvarsson and David M. Gustafson

Pentecostals began as a loosely-organized social network of people who came together because of shared spiritual interests and experiences, as well as pursuit of corporate practices reminiscent of the primitive church in the Book of Acts. With heightened interest from word-of-mouth and published testimonies of Spirit-baptisms, healings, prophesying, and glossolalia, people visited Chicago's Full Gospel Assembly on North Avenue, and Los Angeles's Apostolic Faith Mission on Azusa Street. After one's "own Pentecost" of being Spirit-filled and speaking with other tongues as the Spirit gave utterance (Acts 2:4), a person could return home and hold similar meetings, or open a Pentecostal mission on the same pattern, with expectations of the Pentecostal phenomena to manifest.

An example is E. N. Bell who traveled to Chicago's North Avenue Mission in 1907. Later, Bell became the first chairman of the Assemblies of God (AG). F. A. Sandgren described Bells's experience, saying, "After the first visit of Brother Bell, Brother Durham turned to me at the close of the service and said: who do you think that big fellow is, sitting way back in the mission . . . [;] he looks pretty sharp? The next night Brother Bell sat in the front and we got to know that he was a Baptist minister from Ft. Worth, Texas, and that the Lord had talked to him in these words, 'Abide in the city until you are endued with power from on high.' He tarried in the city, and after about eleven months was baptized in the Holy Spirit."[1] In the year after Bell's Pentecostal-baptism, in 1909, he became pastor of a Pentecostal congregation in Malvern, Arkansas, and launched his own monthly publication, *Word and Witness.*

This chapter argues that with numbers of Scandinavian-Americans already shaped by pietist, revivalist, and holiness traditions, many were predisposed, or at least receptive, to the Pentecostal movement. Thus, the "Pentecostal fire" spread rapidly, moving from Chicago and Los Angeles to other regions of North America. The movement spread generally along previously-formed lines of cultural-linguistic, relational, and ecclesial networks.

The period from 1906 to 1918 was characterized by spontaneity and unity. Evangelists, itinerate preachers, and resident pastors cooperated with one another to hold evangelistic meetings and large conferences that rallied Pentecostals together and expanded the reach of the movement. Along the way, independent congregations of Spirit-baptized, tongues-speaking Christians who identified as "Pentecostals" were planted in Scandinavian enclaves, from Seattle to New York City.

To show the receptivity of Scandinavians, especially those from pietist, revivalist, and holiness traditions, this chapter first examines the spread of the Pentecostal movement from the Azusa Street Mission in Los Angeles to the Pacific Northwest. Second, the chapter traces the movements from Chicago to the Upper Midwest and Canada. Third, the chapter describes developments among Scandinavian-American Pentecostals in the Northeast.

Azusa Street and the Pacific Northwest

Three important figures of the Azusa Street revival belonged to the same Swedish-American family. They were Cenna Osterberg and her husband, Louis Osterberg, and their oldest son, Arthur G. Osterberg. Their ties to the Full-Gospel Churches that emphasized holiness and

1. *Pentecostal Evangel*, July 21, 1923, 8. Later, Sandgren and Durham accompanied E. N. Bell to Louisville, Kentucky, to meet with A. S. Worrell who had written a new English translation of the Greek New Testament. *Folke-Vennen* (*FV*), August 20, 1908, 4.

divine healing soon merged with the burgeoning Pentecostal movement in Los Angeles.[2]

Cenna and Louis Osterberg

Cenna was born as Cenna Samuelsson in Billinge, Sweden.[3] In 1873, she immigrated with her father and siblings to the U.S., arriving in Chicago where she met and married Louis Osterberg. The couple, along with their children, attended First Swedish Baptist Church of Chicago. When Cenna became deathly ill and lay unconscious for several days at their home in Chicago, Louis called for John Levi, a deacon of the church, to come and anoint her with oil and pray for her according to James 5:16. Although "Brother Levi" had never done this before, the next day Cenna returned to consciousness and said to her husband, "Louie, I want you to get my clothes. The Lord has told me to get up. And the Lord has told me, 'Daughter if you will be my witness I shall raise you up and you shall be a witness to my power.'"[4]

In 1893, Cenna came into contact in Chicago with a Full-Gospel preacher and her interest in divine healing grew, especially after Louis, who worked as a carpenter, cut his hand severely with a chisel. Despite the serious injury he was healed miraculously when Dr. William D. Gentry, a physician-preacher accompanied by an African-American man named Isaac Seymour, or simply, "Chicago Seymour," prayed for him.[5] Following this experience, Louis and Cenna left the Swedish Baptist Church and joined Gentry's Full-Gospel Chapel located in Chicago's Englewood neighborhood.

When the Osterbergs moved to Benton Harbor, Michigan, they and others formed a Full-Gospel Mission, and called Gentry to come and hold revival meetings for them.[6] In addition, they invited William H. Durham of the North Avenue Mission in Chicago to hold meetings two or three times a year.[7] This began their friendship with Durham.

---

2. Sanders, *William Joseph Seymour*, 82.

3. Gustafson, "Pentecostal Evangelist Cenna Osteberg," 16.

4. Arthur G. Osterberg, Oral History Interview Transcript, Reel #3, 2, March 1966, Archives of the Flower Pentecostal Heritage Center, Springfield, Missouri.

5. Osterberg, Transcript, #3, 4–5. For William D. Gentry, see Williams, *Spirit Cure*, 41, 46. 52.

6. Osterberg, Transcript, #3, 12.

7. Osterberg, Transcript, #2, 3.

In 1903, the Osterbergs moved from Benton Harbor to Los Angeles. Gentry suggested that they contact William R. Manley, a Full-Gospel preacher whom he knew personally.[8] They visited Manley's church and were impressed by his teachings. Besides promoting family prayer, he encouraged every family to begin a weekly home prayer meeting and invite their neighbors to attend. As a result of their growing ministry, in 1905, the Osterbergs built a wooden chapel named the Full Gospel Tabernacle, located at Denver Avenue and 68th Street in Los Angeles. Arthur was only nineteen years old at the time when he became the pastor.[9] In addition to his pastoral duties, he worked at the J. B. McNeil Construction Company.

North Bonnie Brae Street Meetings

When Cenna went to the Crocker Street Hospital in Los Angeles to pray for a young man who had broken his leg, an African-American woman walking down the hallway heard Cenna praying, knelt down, and joined her in prayer.[10] Afterwards the woman introduced herself and told Cenna about a prayer meeting on North Bonnie Brae Street and invited her to come.[11] At dinner Cenna told her family that she would like to attend. The meeting, held on March 26, 1906, was led by William J. Seymour at the home of Ruth and Richard Asberry. Cenna witnessed how this group of men and women preached, prayed, and prophesied about a forthcoming outpouring of God's Spirit on Los Angeles. Seymour announced that he and the others would begin a ten-day fast and pray for the baptism of the Holy Spirit.

The next day, Cenna testified at the Full Gospel Tabernacle about the meeting and urged others to attend. Despite Arthur's misgivings, the church's deacons were interested and decided to visit the Asberry home. Arthur reluctantly agreed and attended the next meeting with his mother and others, joining an estimated 75 to 100 people. For Arthur this was his first time to attend a meeting of blacks and whites. All of his earlier

---

8. Osterberg, Transcript, #3, 7, 14.
9. Wacker, *Heaven Below*, 213.
10. Osterberg, Transcript, #1, 5.
11. Gustafson, "Scandinavian Mission of the Azusa Street Revival," 170. In 1913, the Scandinavian Mission of Los Angeles joined the Swedish Evangelical Free Church. Cf. *Sanningens Vittne* (*SV*), May-June 1913, 6.

concerns disappeared as he witnessed people praying "with such earnestness that tears were running down their faces."[12]

Then, on April 9, 1906, after Seymour and Lucy Farrow (an African-American holiness preacher from Houston) laid hands on Edward Lee for healing, he was baptized in the Holy Spirit and began to speak in tongues. Later that evening, Jennie Evans Moore (later Seymour's wife) also experienced Pentecostal-baptism.

Apostolic Faith Mission at 312 Azusa Street

Due to the growing numbers of people who attended, on April 13, the group decided to lease a property at 312 Azusa Street in LA. The building was an old Methodist church but at the time was used by a contractor as a warehouse. Since the old building was in desperate need of cleaning, Cenna asked Arthur if he would organize a work crew. He agreed and gathered people from the Bonnie Brae meetings, friends of the family, and Mexican laborers employed with him at the McNeil Construction Company.

The building was ready for Easter Sunday in 1906, and people flocked to attend. Within months, the Apostolic Faith Mission on Azusa Street was the largest congregation in Los Angeles, with as many as 1,500 people attending weekly.[13] An estimated 750 to 800 people would squeeze inside the old building. Soon, in addition to attending meetings of the newly formed Apostolic Faith Mission, Cenna launched a daughter mission—the Scandinavian Mission—that met at 8th and Wall streets in LA.[14]

---

12. Osterberg, Transcript, #3, 15.
13. Osterberg, Transcript, #1, 13.
14. *The Apostolic Faith* (*AF*), September 1907, 1.

Cenna Osterberg
Courtesy of the Osterberg Family

In addition to the Osterbergs, another Swede involved early in the Azusa Street revival was Andrew G. Johnson-Ek (1878–1965), mentioned in the previous chapter. He came to LA in December 1903, converted to faith the following year, and like the Osterbergs, entered the fellowship of William F. Manley.[15] Johnson-Ek described Manley as "a preacher made alive by the Word and richly equipped by the power of the Spirit."[16] In 1905, Johnson-Ek was water-baptized in the Pacific Ocean by Manley. The following day, Manley set him apart for the work of an evangelist. Johnson-Ek's ministry began in LA and included distributing evangelistic literature, but soon he was traveling up the coast to San

---

15. Alvarsson, "Scandinavian Pentecostalism," 20.
16. Gäreskog, *Andrew Ek*, 32.

Francisco, Oakland, Portland, Tacoma, and Seattle, sharing the gospel "on the streets" and "in the worst neighborhoods."[17]

In the spring of 1906, when back in LA, Johnson-Ek attended meetings of the Azusa Street Mission where he experienced Pentecostal baptism and received the gift of speaking in tongues. When this happened, he thought he had the gift to speak the modern Hebrew language. The thought of speaking an unlearned language prompted interest in foreign missions, hoping to win others to faith by offering the gospel to people in their own tongue.[18]

The first missionaries left LA for Oakland where they had several days of meetings, and then boarded a train to Denver and then to Chicago where they met William H. Durham of the North Avenue Mission, piquing his interest in Pentecostal baptism.[19] After Johnson-Ek and the two women left Chicago, they continued by train to New York City where T. B. Barratt (1862–1940), a British-Norwegian Methodist pastor from the Christiania City Mission (Oslo) was visiting at the time.[20] After his own Pentecostal baptism, Barratt joined the nascent movement.

Scandinavian Mission of Los Angeles

In the meantime, Cenna Osterberg in Los Angeles led the Scandinavian Mission at the corner of 8th and Wall streets. This daughter mission of the Azusa Street Mission drew numbers of Scandinavians who were in their early-to-mid 20s, and had immigrated to America from Sweden, Finland, Denmark, and Norway as young adults. While this fellowship was characterized by Pentecostal phenomena similar to the meetings on Azusa Street, the Scandinavian Mission provided a place for mostly Swedish-language speakers to sing gospel songs, hear the Scriptures read and taught, offer words of praise, give testimonies, and pray. It is important to note that the Finnish immigrants who attended the meetings, in addition to Swedes, also spoke Swedish, and that the Swedish language could be understood by Norwegians and Danes.[21]

---

17. Gäreskog, *Andrew Ek*, 33.
18. Bloch-Hoell, *Pentecostal Movement*, 43, 87.
19. Alvarsson, "När Örebro blev Sveriges Los Angeles," 30; Wacker, *Heaven Below*, 261.
20. *AF*, December 1906, 3.
21. Bloch-Hoell, *Pentecostal Movement*, 43–44.

While commonly known as the "Scandinavian Mission" or "Swedish Mission," it was named "The Scandinavian Apostolic Faith Mission."[22] The mission was important to the young immigrants who sought to reach their fellow Scandinavians with the gospel. In addition to the work in LA, in 1907, the mission sent missionaries to Sweden, namely, Agnes Jacobson, Eric Carlsson Hollingsworth, and Ida Magnusson Hollingsworth. They also sent missionaries to China including Gustav S. Lundgren, Ellen Carlson (Lundgren), Adolph Johnson, Linda Erickson (Johnson), Mary Bjorkman, and Hanna Holmsten. Within a few years, the Scandinavian Mission of LA commissioned three missionaries to the South Sea Islands, namely, Alma Starkenberg, Alma Ronnberg, and Agnes Jacobson, after she returned from Sweden.[23]

The Osterbergs were at the center of the interchange between the Apostolic Faith Mission on Azusa Street and Chicago's North Avenue Mission. Durham came to LA to experience the revival for himself from promptings of the Osterbergs. On one evening Cenna said to Louis, "I feel led to send for Bro. Durham."[24] She had written him earlier about the Azusa Street revival but his letters in reply only asked questions.[25] Therefore, the Osterbergs decided to invite him and offered to pay his train fare.[26] When he returned to Chicago, he turned his mission into a center of the Pentecostal movement.

Jones Avenue Mission of Seattle

The Pentecostal movement spread rapidly from the Azusa Street Mission in Los Angeles to the Pacific Northwest. Already in October 1906, a Norwegian Free Mission of Ballard (Seattle), Washington, received a letter from Josef N. Strand (1842–1923), an evangelist originally from Ørland, Norway, who earlier held revival meetings at the Seattle mission.[27] Strand's letter described the Pentecostal revival in Los Angeles where he attended meetings at the Azusa Street Mission led by William J. Seymour.

---

22. *AF*, September 1907, 1.

23. Historical Study Manual of Swedish Evangelical Free Church of Los Angeles, 1931/1932, 11. EFCA Archives, Minneapolis, Minnesota.

24. Osterberg, Transcript, #2, 4.

25. Osterberg, Transcript, #2, 3.

26. *AF*, February-March 1907, 4.

27. *FV*, January 5, 1905, 4.

Tobias E. Tonnesen (1856–1925) of the Jones Avenue Mission read Strand's letter that explained how there was an outpouring of the Holy Spirit, how souls were saved from sin, and how people were healed from illnesses. For Strand himself, he also sought the filling of the Spirit as described in Acts 2:4. His letter told of his experience of Spirit-baptism at the Azusa Street Mission and how he immediately gained assurance of God's presence, as well as a new power for gospel witness. He wrote that he wished there was some way he could tell "in words of the glory that was his, but all he could do was praise God for giving him that which Jesus Christ referred to as 'the promise of the Father' [John 14:16]."[28] When Tonnesen finished reading Strand's letter during a meeting, the congregation sat in awe and wonder, and began to seek the baptism of the Holy Spirit. All agreed that their mission needed revival, and soon afterwards a Pentecostal revival came.[29]

As others in Seattle heard reports of revival at the Jones Avenue Mission, they began attending the services. Among them was Serena Helland of Eide, Norway, who in the spring of 1907, experienced Pentecostal baptism. In the following year, she and her daughter, Flora, left Seattle for China as missionaries with the Apostolic Faith Mission.[30] They were joined by Martin and Martine Kvamme, Berthine H. Dahl, and Esther Lenander, also from the Seattle-Tacoma area.

Because the numbers swelled, the building was expanded to nearly twice its size.[31] Years later when the building burned to the ground, the congregation rented a vacant Baptist church on West 56th Street and took the name, Voluntary Scandinavian Pentecostal Mission.[32]

Soon to join Josef Strand in the Pentecostal movement was Henrik S. Langeland (1860–1921), a Norwegian Lutheran pastor in Poulsbo, Washington, originally from Drøsdal, Norway.[33] On November 6, 1906, while in the Ballard area of Seattle, Langeland was baptized in the Spirit and spoke in tongues.[34] He and Strand, as well as Tonnesen,

---

28. Heckman, *History of the Fellowship of Christian Assemblies (HFCA)*, 114.

29. *FV*, March 21, 1907, 5. Thomas and Helen Junk, along with LuLu Miller, went from the Azusa Street revival to Seattle, and reported their work as early as November 1906. *AF*, November 1906, 1; December 1906, 1.

30. *Bridegroom's Messenger*, October 1909, 3.

31. Heckman, *HFCA*, 115.

32. *SV*, May 1, 1920, 8; Philadelphia Church, Seattle, "Our Story."

33. *Kitsap Daily News*, 2011.

34. *Byposten*, March 23, 1907. The letter is dated January 31, 1907.

soon became leaders of the Pentecostal revival among Scandinavians in the Seattle-Tacoma area.[35]

Langeland started a small fellowship of 14 people in Poulsbo, across the Puget Sound from Seattle, where he had served as a Lutheran pastor prior to his Pentecostal baptism.[36] He also launched a Norwegian-language Pentecostal periodical called *Sandhedens Tolk* (Interpreter of Truth) that circulated in the Seattle and Tacoma area.[37] In 1908, William Seymour's periodical in Los Angeles, *The Apostolic Faith*, reported: "Two Pentecostal papers in the Norwegian language are being published, the 'Sandhedans Tolk,' published by Brother H. Langeland, Paulsbo, Wash., and 'Byposten,' by Brother T. B. Barratt, Christiania, Norway."[38]

In 1906, Scandinavians in Tacoma, thirty miles south of Seattle, experienced the Pentecostal revival there, having ties with Tonnesen, as well as Strand and Langeland. In the summer of 1907, tent meetings were held at 11th Street and Cushman Avenue in Tacoma, with mostly Norwegian immigrants attending.[39]

Seattle and the Apostolic Faith Mission of China

The Norwegian-American Pentecostals in Seattle provided a base for Bernt Berntsen in 1907, to gather his missionary band before their departure for China. Berntsen, a Norwegian-American missionary who had served earlier in China, visited the revival of the Azusa Street Mission in 1907, when he experienced Pentecostal-baptism. He soon recruited six members from the Scandinavian Mission in Los Angeles, mentioned above, to join him as missionaries in his new mission named, Apostolic Faith Mission of China.[40] In Seattle, Berntsen and the others were joined by George and Sophie Hansen of the North Avenue Mission in Chicago, along with their seven children. One more Scandinavian immigrant to

---

35. In 1910, Jos. N. Strand lived at 3237 West 68th Street, Seattle, and Henry S. Langeland lived at 3237 (rear) West 68th Street. They were both listed as "missionaries."

36. "Beginnings," Historical Draft of Christ Memorial Church in Poulsbo, WA, August 13, 2008, http://christmemorialhistory.blogspot.com.

37. *Byposten*, October 1, 1909, 79.

38. *AF*, May 1908, 2.

39. *FV*, March 21, 1907, 4.

40. *Bridegroom's Messenger*, May 15, 1908, 2.

join the China missionary band was Emma B. Hansen (Burns), a Norwegian-born, sixteen-year-old from Tacoma, Washington.[41]

In the spring of 1907, Emma Hansen's father, Bendix Hansen, took her to a Pentecostal meeting in Tacoma. They found it strange when they heard people speaking unintelligible languages but afterwards they were drawn to return to the meetings. Emma recalled, "I tried to fight against it until on the 6th day of June [1907], when God won the victory and I sought and found salvation. Two weeks later I received my Pentecost with Bible evidence."[42]

In November, when Bernt Berntsen and his missionary band arrived in Seattle, Emma Hansen heard of their plans to go to Chengtingfu (Zhengdingfu) as missionaries. She wondered if she might join them. She spoke with Berntsen about the possibility. He did not encourage her to do so but he did not rule out the possibility either. Then, just a week before the scheduled departure, she appealed to her parents who said, "If money comes in for your ticket you can go."[43] One day before the ship departed, she received $40, which was nearly half the cost. The rest of the money came in November 29, 1907, while she was standing at the dock waiting to go onboard.

Henrik Langeland continued as editor of *Sandhedens Tolk* until 1913, when the periodical ceased publication. In January 1914, A. A. Holmgren, editor of *Sanningens Vittne* wrote: "With this issue we will add items in the Norwegian language. Numbers of our Norwegian Pentecostal friends read S.V. . . . We have also been asked to do so. Brother H. Langeland in Seattle, who for some years published "Sandhedens Tolk" will cease to do so, and intends during the year to make a trip to the 'old country.'"[44]

When Langeland returned from Norway to Poulsbo, he and L. L. Watland secured a property for their Pentecostal meetings. The name of the property was the "Free Mission Hall" which became a Pentecostal fellowship.[45]

---

41. Emma Hansen, "A Sixteen-Year-Old Missionary," *The Pentecost* (*TP*), June 1909, 4.
42. Hansen, "A Sixteen-Year-Old Missionary," *TP*, June 1909, 4.
43. Hansen, "A Sixteen-Year-Old Missionary," *TP*, June 1909, 4.
44. *SV*, January 1, 1914, 4.
45. "Beginnings," Christ Memorial Church in Poulsbo, WA, August 13, 2008.

Upper Midwest and Canada

The Pentecostal movement spread to Minneapolis. As early as April 1907, three sisters from Azusa Street—Helga, Amanda, and Maren Iversen—visited a newly organized English-language Apostolic Faith Mission at 320 S. Cedar Street in Minneapolis led by Joseph R. Conlee and William Pendleton. All five had recently come from Los Angeles where they participated in the revival of the Azusa Street Mission.[46] Pendleton wrote about the meetings held in Minneapolis, saying: 'It was like some scenes in Azusa, all around lay the slain, Methodists, Baptists, and Lutherans."[47] The Iversen sisters, originally from Norway, reported, "Here in Minneapolis we cannot get away; they want us here to tell about [the] Azusa Mission and our experience . . . The people want us to tell more about Jesus and His wondrous love; they are so hungry among the Swedish and other nations."[48] The Iversen sisters planned to travel to Sweden and Norway, departing on May 17, 1907. Maren wrote the following year from Bjerka, Norway, reporting that many souls were "saved, healed, and sanctified, and others were "waiting in unity and one accord for the outpouring of the Spirit."[49]

---

46. The mission in Minneapolis opened April 15, 1907. *AF* (LA), May 1907, 1. Cf. *The Overcomer*, September 1929, 3-4.

47. *AF*, June-September 1907, 1. Conlee reported on April 15, 1907, that the Minneapolis mission at 320 S. Cedar St. welcomed a group of Dowieites, and later noted, "The Swedish sisters are with us. Their ship sails May 17 [1907]." *AF*, May 1907, 1-2. Cf. *Minneapolis Tribune* (*MT*), June 24, 1907, 5; November 4, 1907, 5. Other sources show that the Iversens were from Norway. In May 1907, the Apostolic Faith Mission met at 16th Avenue and 6th Street. *MT*, May 28, 1907, 7. In 1909, Jackson White, originally from Barrow in Furness, England, took over after J. R. Conlee and Will Pendleton returned to LA. *MT*, March 12, 1910, 13; *SV*, July 1911, 3. White who led the Apostolic Faith Mission at 730 Lake Street, and later at 2415 Riverside Avenue in Minneapolis, had visited the Azusa Street Mission in 1906, while living in Los Angeles. Rodgers, *Northern Harvest*, 48. Will C. Trotter and Florence Crawford also ministered in Minneapolis. *AF*, January 1908, 1.

48. *AF*, May 1907, 2. While in the Twin Cities, Maren Iversen stayed with Ellen Modin at the Scandinavian Women's Alliance Mission Home, associated with the Swedish Evangelical Free Mission, where Iversen trained earlier as an evangelist. "Marin Iverson," *Räddningslinan*, August 1909, 1.

49. *The Apostolic Faith* (Portland), September 1908, 2. For Maren Iversen, see Mentzoni, "*Pinse for alle*," 121-22, 128-29.

Maren Iversen, *Räddningslinan*, 1909, Courtesy of the Minnesota Historical Society, St. Paul, Minnesota

Another Pentecostal mission, the Christian Assembly, located at 1817 Minnehaha Avenue South, was led by the Norwegian, Gerhard Olsen-Smidt who conducted services for Scandinavians.[50] When he left Minneapolis for Norway and Finland, he turned the work over to G. F. Fink from Denver who led English-language services.[51] This prompted A. A. Holmgren who knew Olsen-Smidt and attended the Christian Assembly to begin the Scandinavian Christian Assembly at 2517 Central Avenue, holding three to four Swedish services a week.

A. A. Holmgren, mentioned in Chapter 2, participated in conferences of Swedish Baptists in Chicago in 1909, and in Durham's conference in Chicago in 1912. While visiting Chicago in 1910, Holmgren

---

50. In 1907, Christian Assembly met at 15th and Franklin avenues. *MT*, December 4, 1907, 5. In 1908, when Frank Bartleman visited, the congregation met at 1419 Washington Avenue North. *MT*, May 31, 1908, 9. In 1910, when G. F. Fink first conducted a series of meetings, the congregation met at 1817 Minnehaha Avenue South. *Minneapolis Morning Tribune*, February 20, 1910, 30.

51. *SV*, July, 1911, 3; January 1921, 5. For Olsen-Smidt, see Lie and Andelin, "Olsen-Smidt, Gerhard Martin" 126–127.

experienced Pentecostal-baptism at a meeting of the Swedish Baptist Church in Humboldt Park.[52]

Andrew August Holmgren (1866–1949) was born in Bjurholm, Sweden.[53] In 1886, he converted to faith and joined the Baptists. Soon after, he started preaching the gospel and enrolled for two terms of Bible school at Sundsvall, Sweden. In 1893, he traveled to America and took up residence in Minneapolis. During the next years, he engaged in mission work in northern Minnesota, and accepted pastoral positions in Lake Sarah and Burchard. After a season as a pastor in eastern Iowa, he took a role in publishing the monthly Baptist periodicals *Ungdomens Tidning* (Newspaper of Youth) and *Fyrbaken* (The Beacon) that merged to become *Baneret* (The Banner).[54] In 1904, he returned to Minnesota, living in Minneapolis.

In 1910, historian Algot Strand described Holmgren's periodical, saying, "*Baneret* is the only Swedish religious paper in this country which has been broad-minded enough to open its columns for news from different denominations. . . . It stands for true freedom and is looked upon as an organ for the 'New Movement' or the 'Pentecostal Movement,' and certainly has a large field."[55] In 1911, Holmgren left the Baptist publications and launched the Swedish-language Pentecostal periodical, *Sanningens Vittne*, in Minneapolis, and served as a leading proponent of the movement in the Upper Midwest. In the same year, he helped form the Scandinavian Christian Assembly in Minneapolis, at 2517 Central Avenue.[56]

Holmgren also published a songbook titled *Sånger till Herrens lof* (Songs to Praise the Lord).[57] It was first published in Minneapolis in 1911, for Scandinavian Pentecostal assemblies. In compiling this songbook, Holmgren drew from popular songbooks of the Baptist, Methodist, Pietist Lutheran, and Free churches such as from *Nya Psalmisten* (The New Psalmist), *Fridsröster* (Voices of Peace), *Jubel Sånger* (Jubilant Songs), *Herde-rösten* (The Shepherd's Voice), and *Hemlands-Klockan*

---

52. *SV*, May 1934, 5.
53. Strand, *History of the Swedish-Americans of Minnesota*, 640.
54. Strand, *History of the Swedish-Americans of Minnesota*, 640.
55. Strand, *History of the Swedish-Americans of Minnesota*, 314.
56. *SV*, July 1911, 3–4.
57. A. A. Holmgren, *Sånger till Herrens lof* (Minneapolis: A. A. Holmgren, 1911). *Sånger till Herrens lof* (Songs to Praise the Lord) had subsequent editions in 1916 and 1931.

(Homeland's Clock). Several songs emphasized Pentecostal teaching and experience.[58] Lyrics of songs were written in Swedish, Norwegian, and English. Holmgren included songs composed by T. B. Barratt and Lewi Pethrus.[59]

Nearby, in St. Paul, Minnesota, the Full Gospel Assembly (*Full Evangelisk Församling*), under the leadership of E. S. Stone, held services in 1911, in a small chapel at the corner of Greenbrier Avenue and Jenks Street.[60] Erick Severin Stone (1885–1919), originally of Kvistbro, Sweden, had ties earlier with the Swedish Evangelical Free Mission in St. Paul. Like other Scandinavian Pentecostals, E. S. Stone was influenced by the ministries of William Durham of Chicago, but also by Robert E. McAlister of Ottawa, Canada. Like Durham, McAlister had visited the Azusa Street Mission in LA and experienced Pentecostal-baptism that brought a renewal for evangelistic preaching.

After Stone heard Durham and McAlister preach in Canada, he reported: "At Monday night's meeting, God's power manifested in a wonderful way. One brother fell on the floor; others stood up while they sang the heavenly song led by the Holy Spirit. At the beginning of the meeting, the glory of the Lord appeared in a cloud over the congregation. Someone might ask, 'Can anything like this happen?' Let's open our Bible and read 2 Chr. 29:27–28 and 1 Kings. 8:10–11. His Word says he is the same yesterday, today, and forever. Praise be to his name!"[61]

Stone described not only phenomena of God's presence but also the response of listeners, saying:

> About 38 were baptized in the Holy Spirit and spoke in tongues and praised God as on the day of Pentecost. Nineteen were baptized in water. Hallelujah! Many sick people were healed through Jesus' mighty hand. All glory to him! Many sinners came to Jesus and had their sins forgiven and their souls cleansed by the blood of Jesus. Glory to God! One evening during the sermon

---

58. Among the songs are: No. 71 Dop i eld (Baptism in Fire), No. 73 Hafven I fått den Helige Ande? (Did You Get the Holy Spirit?) No. 74 Har du mottagit den Helige Ande? (Have You Received the Holy Spirit?), No. 76 Andedopet (Spirit-baptism), and No. 243 Døb øs med din Aand (Baptize Us with Your Spirit). Holmgren, *Sånger till Herrens lof*, 59–64, 216.

59. No. 285 Nu brinner Guds eld i mitt hjärta (God's Fire Now Burns in My Heart) by T. B. Barratt, and No. 304 Löftena kunna ej svika (Promises that Never Fail) by Lewi Pethrus. Holmgren, *Sånger till Herrens lof*, 242–43, 262.

60. *SV*, July 1911, 4; March-April 1913, 8.

61. *SV*, January 1912, 3.

when the power of God rested heavily upon the congregation, three hungry souls were baptized in the Holy Spirit right where they sat. At the end of the meeting, an ungodly woman came to the platform where God's children had gathered to pray, and after standing and looking at everything for a while, she sat down in a chair. However, she sat just a few minutes when the power of God came over her. She fell to the floor, weeping, and crying out to the God of Heaven for mercy and salvation for her soul. She was wonderfully saved that night and baptized in the Holy Spirit. All glory to God and the Lamb![62]

Stone's observations of Durham's and McAlister's meetings in Canada shaped his own Pentecostal ministry in St. Paul.

In addition to E. S. Stone, other Swedish Evangelical Free Church pastors joined the Pentecostal movement. Among them was Loth Lindquist (1825–1914), originally of Bjurbäck, Sweden. Lindquist had served Swedish Methodist churches in Illinois and Iowa, and later he ministered with the Swedish Evangelical Free Mission.[63] In 1884, he presided as chairman of the inaugural meeting of the Swedish Free Mission held in Boone, Iowa.[64] Lindquist was well-connected to August Davis of the "Free-Free" who was present also at the 1884 Boone meeting. In addition to Lindquist's interests in Bible prophecy and the holiness doctrine of perfectionism, he joined the Pentecostal movement.[65]

In October 1907, Lindquist wrote to T. B. Barratt in Norway, editor of *Byposten* after an exchange of letters with a Swedish Methodist preacher in Chicago. Lindquist explained to Barratt that he had left the Methodists sixteen years earlier in order to lead Free (*fria*) Bible-reading meetings in Minneapolis.[66] In the meantime, he became convinced from the Scriptures and his own experience that the "outpouring of the Spirit is wonderful, and truly a work of God."[67] Lindquist also reported, "Here in Minneapolis we have had, and still have, glorious meetings led by witnesses from Los Angeles—Spirit-filled men who walk in God's light and preach the full gospel, so that sinners are awakened and saved, children of God are sanctified and cleansed from all sin through the

---

62. *SV*, January 1912, 3.
63. Witting, *Minnen från mitt lif*, 428–33, 509.
64. Gustafson, "1884 Boone Conference of the Free Mission Friends," 256–57.
65. Lindberg, *Looking Back Fifty Years*, 49.
66. For example, *Svenska Folkets Tidning*, February 17, 1897, 10.
67. *Byposten*, October 9, 1907, 94.

blood of the Son of God, Jesus Christ." Moreover, Lindquist said, "As far as I have seen, no less than fifty have been baptized with the Holy Spirit, so that sometimes at our meetings we see and hear from 5 to 10 people at the same time speaking in foreign tongues (*fremande tungsmål*) as happened on the day of Pentecost, as well as in the house of Cornelius in Caesarea and in the church in Ephesus."[68]

Other Scandinavian Pentecostals in Northern States

Pentecostalism continued to spread among Scandinavian Americans in the Upper Midwest. For instance, the movement spread north to Milaca, Minnesota, through the work of Jonas Magnus Shulene (1850–1935), formerly a Swedish Baptist missionary in Wisconsin and Minnesota, and originally from Skön, Sweden.[69]

In Duluth, Minnesota, Hattie Jamieson (1854–1926), wife of the Presbyterian minister, Samuel A. Jamieson, received the baptism of the Holy Spirit in 1908, when visiting a Pentecostal church in Atlanta, Georgia.[70] Her ministry in Duluth led to a small mission which began in a business shop in 1913, and eventually led to the founding of the Pentecostal mission in 1916, by Arthur F. Johnson and other "Spirit-baptized friends."[71]

Arthur F. Johnson, a native of Chicago born to Swedish immigrant parents, soon became a prominent leader of the Scandinavian-American Pentecostals.[72] In 1907, at age nineteen, he converted to faith and was water-baptized at the North Avenue Mission by Durham, and within two years was Spirit-baptized.[73] In 1911, Johnson took up evangelistic work alongside C. M. Hanson. When in Menominee, Michigan, ministering in lumber country, the young Johnson met a female evangelist named Beatrice ("Beda") Farnlof of Norway, Michigan, and soon afterwards, they married.[74]

---

68. *Byposten*, October 9, 1907, 94.
69. *SV*, April 1912, 4.
70. *Pentecostal Evangel*, January 31, 1931, 2.
71. *Evangelii Härold*, June 5, 1924; Heckman, *HFCA*, 75, 129.
72. *SV*, January 1914, 8; Heckman, *HFCA*, 51, 79, 128.
73. *Herald of Pentecost*, May 1953, 9.
74. *SV*, June 1912, 3. Beda Farnlof traveled with K. Knutson.

In the following years, Johnson served as an evangelist, mentored pastors, and organized conferences for new Pentecostal assemblies. As an evangelist, he reported his work in *The Pentecostal Herald*, saying:

> We thank God for His blessings upon us in Duluth. The work is progressing and the mission is filled every Sunday. Some wonderful healings have taken place lately. One young girl about 20 years [old] who was a consumptive and had spent some time in a sanitarium came to the mission for the first time. She asked to be prayed for and so we anointed her with oil and prayed, [and] the Lord healed her then and there. Praise his name. She has since been examined by a doctor and he pronounced her lungs healed. It is wonderful to see the change in this young lady . . . Several seeking the baptism with the Holy Spirit are nearly through and we are praying God to open the floodgates of living waters upon their souls.[75]

Among the young pastors and evangelists that Arthur F. Johnson mentored was E. C. Erickson (1896–1980) who succeeded him at the Pentecostal mission in Duluth.[76] When Elmer Claude Erickson came from Sister Bay, Wisconsin, to Duluth as a Spirit-baptized Baptist, he sought out Scandinavian Pentecostals. In 1919, when Johnson left Duluth, he turned the work of the mission over to Erickson.

Arthur F. Johnson's reputation as an evangelist and conference organizer spread. In July 1918, a periodical in Sweden, *Evangelii Härold*, reported that he was secretary of a meeting held in Chicago of "free preachers in the United States."[77] As a second-generation, Swedish-American, he ministered equally to English- and Scandinavian-language groups. As an evangelist, he traveled in Minnesota, Michigan, Wisconsin, and Illinois. In 1914, he wrote from Rockford, Illinois, saying:

> Friends from the various churches, and quite a few outside the churches, have attended the meetings. Some have come hungry and the Lord has satisfied them with good things . . . Even sinners experience the presence of the Spirit of God in the meetings and we have had the pleasure of seeing two or more redeemed from the dominion of Satan and cleansed in the blood of Jesus. Glory to Jesus! . . . God baptized two brothers and a sister in the Holy Spirit, and we have now received the message from them

---

75. "Duluth, Minn." *The Pentecostal Herald*, April 1918, 3.
76. Heckman, *HFCA*, 14.
77. Alvarsson, "Relationer mellan Sverige och USA," 42.

that four more have had the same experience, for they spoke with tongues and praised God. Hallelujah!⁷⁸

After ministering in Rockford, Johnson traveled to Iron River, Michigan, where meetings were held in the home of Ida E. Segersven, originally from Espoo, Finland. Johnson said: "Sister Segersven received her baptism of the Spirit on Saturday evening, after about a year of waiting. Even on Tuesday, God met us in power when an English [speaking] sister praised God with new tongues for the first time. Among other languages spoken by the Spirit through her was the Finnish language, which is Sister Segersven's mother tongue, and which was well understood by her at this time. Yes, God is the same, despite the fact that people in every conceivable way seek to explain away the outpouring of God's Holy Spirit."⁷⁹

Scandinavian Pentecostals in Canada

In 1908, Scandinavians in Canada learned of the Pentecostal movement from Christina Larson who brought the Pentecostal message from Norway to the village of Weldon, Saskatchewan.⁸⁰ She was among the earliest of Norwegian Pentecostals influenced by T. B. Barratt in Oslo. In 1911, Knut Hagen, a Norwegian immigrant in Rainy River, Ontario, testified that he and his wife, Mathilda, received Spirit-baptism, and that others there were waiting for it.⁸¹

As mentioned in chapter two, in 1912, when A. A. Holmgren of Minneapolis traveled to Chicago to attend Durham's convention, he met Petrus Hultgren of Trossachs, Saskatchewan.⁸² Hultgren, a native of Gothenburg, Sweden, arrived in America in 1908, and four years later was leading Pentecostal meetings. It was reported that in Trossachs "God baptized 18 in the Spirit in 10 days" and "many [souls] were saved and healed and the whole community was stirred."⁸³ News of the Pentecostal

78. *SV*, July-August 1914, 4.
79. *SV*, March-April 1913, 7.
80. Heckman, *HFCA*, 18.
81. *SV*, July 1911, 4.
82. *SV*, April 1912, 2–3.
83. *Pentecostal Testimony*, August 1912, 16. In 1914, a brother "E. Erickson" reported from Trossachs, saying, "It is almost a year since I received the baptism of the Spirit, and I praise my Heavenly Father for I have been able to see more than ever that his yoke is easy and his burden is light." *SV*, March-April, 1914, 6.

revival spread widely among Scandinavians in Canada, especially because of the periodical *Sanningens Vittne*, which in 1912, reported: "Br. A. H. Argue of Winnipeg and R. E. McAlister of Ottawa were expected to attend the [Durham] convention in Chicago, but the Lord brought such a revival in these places that they believed it was God's will to remain [in Canada] in order to continue the harvest."[84]

Danish immigrants were among those touched by Canada's Pentecostal revival. Paul Andreasen, who described himself later as a wandering soul in a spiritual desert, moved to Winnipeg as early as 1907, and while there, was caught up in the Pentecostal revival.[85] In 1916, he completed studies at Moody Bible Institute in Chicago and became a missionary to India. Another example is Anna Jensen Sanders (1869–1955), a Danish immigrant who encountered the Pentecostal movement in Winnipeg at the same time as Andreasen. When Sanders experienced healing from kidney failure and cancer, she sensed God's call to serve as a missionary.[86] She was ordained by the Scandinavian Assemblies of God (SAG) in 1919, and became one of the founders of the Assemblies of God in Mexico.[87]

In Amisk, Alberta, Carl O. Nordin (1882–1957) began an itinerant ministry of evangelism and in 1916, he founded the Pentecostal Church in the Crooked Lake District. He also played a key role in establishing the Amisk Assembly. At the same time, Ole M. Forseth, a farmer in the Peace River area, from Bardu, Norway, pioneered the church at Buffalo Lakes, Alberta.[88]

Northeast USA

The Pentecostal movement soon spread among Scandinavians in the Northeast. Oscar Halvorsen (1876–1947), a native of Nøtterøy, Norway, came to America in 1897, and settled in New York City, where two older brothers lived.[89] In the fall of 1906, Halvorsen met T. B. Barratt at several meetings, and even accompanied him to the harbor in December

---

84. *SV*, April 1912, 4.
85. Christensen, *Unorganized Religion*, 33.
86. Christensen, *Unorganized Religion*, 33.
87. See Bustos and Ziefle, "Anna Sanders," 47–55.
88. Heckman, *HFCA*, 15.
89. Skibsted, *Oscar Halvorsen*, 17.

when Barratt boarded his ship to return to Norway. Halvorsen who had connections earlier to the Salvation Army, American Methodists, and Norwegian Evangelical Free Churches, became interested in Pentecostal baptism. In part, he was impacted by Jen Jensen-Maar's translation of the book by R. A. Torrey, titled *How to Pray*.[90] Then, in January 1907, when Halvorsen was handed a periodical and read an account of the Pentecostal revival in Oslo led by Barratt, he experienced Pentecostal baptism and spoke in tongues.[91] *The Apostolic Faith* of Los Angeles reported, "A Norwegian brother in Brooklyn, New York was reading about the Pentecost in Christiana [Oslo] when he was baptized with the Holy Spirit and began to speak in different languages. It was about midnight January 26, [1907]. His name is Oscar Halvorsen, 293 13th Street. Three others in Brooklyn are speaking in tongues."[92]

The following morning—on Sunday, January 27—Halvorsen visited his friend Theodor "Tom" Christensen, the pastor of a Norwegian Free Friends (*Frie Venner*) mission in Brooklyn. As Halvorsen entered the Free Friends meeting, he began to speak in tongues.[93] Others soon arrived to observe the phenomenon. Halvorsen wrote:

> Well before the meeting began on this Sunday morning, word of what happened spread, and people soon gathered around. I was the first in that place to be Spirit-baptized. At the next meeting the room was packed and a crowd gathered outside. When my brothers and sister-in-law arrived to the meeting and heard me speaking in tongues, they were so bewildered by what they heard that they jumped up, grabbed their chairs, and carried them out into the street. When I went to visit my mother, as soon as I entered her place, I burst into tongues, but she responded more sensibly than the others.[94]

Halvorsen later sensed a divine call to become a fulltime evangelist and began holding meetings in Lincoln Hall. Among those who attended were Bernhard Nilsen, later a missionary to China, and Mikael Hansen who became a pastor of a Norwegian Pentecostal church on Staten Island.[95] Norwegian Evangelical Free Church pastor Ludwig Johnsen

90. Skibsted, *Oscar Halvorsen*, 25.
91. Skibsted, *Oscar Halvorsen*, 32.
92. AF, May 1907, 1.
93. Skibsted, *Oscar Halvorsen*, 33.
94. Skibsted, *Oscar Halvorsen*, 33.
95. Skibsted, *Oscar Halvorsen*, 36; SV, June 1931, 5.

of Newhaven, Connecticut, sent a woman from his church to observe Halvorsen's meetings, and when she was overcome by the power of the Spirit, she became convinced this was from God. Moreover, Gabriel Nilsen, pastor of the Danish Evangelical Free Church of Hartford, Connecticut, visited the meetings and reported all that he saw to his congregation, and he became a Pentecostal himself, leading the Scandinavian Pentecostal congregation in Bridgeport, Connecticut.[96] After Halvorsen ministered in New York City, he held evangelistic meetings in Connecticut. Then, in 1909, he returned to Norway with his wife and daughter where he continued his work of evangelism.[97]

Beginning in May 1907, Dagmar Gregersen (Engstrøm, 1881–1993) and Agnes N. Thelle (Beckdahl, 1876–1968) from Olso, Norway, traveled as evangelists in Denmark, and then to Germany where they were the first to bring the Pentecostal message.[98] In June of 1908, they sailed to Boston, Massachusetts, and held meetings in Connecticut and New York State, witnessing more than two thousand souls redeemed by Christ and filled with the Spirit. The two women attended A. B. Simpson's Missionary Training School before serving as missionaries in India.

F. A. Sandgren's Evangelistic Ministry

In 1911, F. A. Sandgren's ministry of preaching the full-gospel, mentioned in Chapter 2, led him east to Brooklyn, New York, where he visited a mission led by a fellow Pentecostal named Emil Lindstrom. After New York City, Sandgren traveled to Philadelphia and held meetings at Columbia Hall where "many souls were searching for Spirit-baptism."[99] He continued to New Haven, Connecticut, where in December 1911, he preached at a small mission in the English language with several Scandinavian immigrants present. He continued his itinerant tour to New Britain, Connecticut; Providence, Rhode Island; and Boston, Massachusetts. On his return trip to New York City, he passed through New Rochelle in New York State where Thomas Thompson, a Norwegian-immigrant, led the Apostolic Faith Mission.[100]

96. Skibsted, *Oscar Halvorsen*, 37; *SV*, June 1931, 5; Odegaard, *With Singleness of Heart*, 263–64, 525, 562.
97. Lie, *Norsk pinsekristendom og karismatisk fornyelse*, 66.
98. Bundy, *Visions of Apostolic Mission*, 205.
99. *SV*, January 1912, 4.
100. *SV*, April 1912, 4.

F. A. Sandgren. Courtesy of the Sandgren Family.

Scandinavian Pentecostals were clearly active in the Northeast. Their ministries were not limited to Scandinavians, however. When Sandgren returned to Brooklyn, he and Emil Lindstrom visited an Italian family. Sandgren wrote,

> The wife was baptized in the Spirit. Yes, God's power was evident. We bowed down to pray, and the husband who was seeking the baptism of the Spirit fell under the power and began to shake. When we stood up, the house was full of people, mostly Italians, despite this happening on a weekday around the noon hour. Now, whenever someone comes to visit the family, they hold a meeting and focus on all that belongs to God and his kingdom. They meet every night in their home, but they hope to open a mission soon in Brooklyn.[101]

101. *SV*, January 1912, 4.

Meanwhile, from New Britain, Connecticut, an itinerant preacher named Peter Malm was carrying out his evangelistic work. Malm traveled to Worcester, Massachusetts, where a Swede named Adolf Ödman led a small mission. After Malm preached in Worcester, he continued to Manchester and then to Concord, New Hampshire, and finally to Providence, Rhode Island. When Malm returned to New Britain, he held prayer meetings for two weeks, after which he sensed the Spirit's power and presence. He explained:

> A young boy had been baptized in the Spirit before I arrived, and then six were baptized and praised God, after which the Spirit gave them utterance. God's Spirit has been present with power at all the meetings which have been well attended, and so we are amazed ... Sunday, December 10 [1911] was a wonderful day, from Sunday school in the morning until the last meeting in the evening. God's power came mightily upon the people ... At one moment, I myself was so under the power of the Spirit that I could not stand up without help. Two were baptized in the Spirit and praised God in tongues.[102]

Peter Malm (1845–1930) of Delsbo, Sweden, had arrived to America in 1881, and settled in New Haven, Connecticut. He then served as a Swedish Baptist missionary in Worcester, Massachusetts, and Providence, Rhode Island, before relocating to Minneapolis. In July 1911, at the Pentecostal Assembly in Minneapolis, "by means of prayer and the laying on of hands, [he was] set apart to preach in congregations of apostolic faith and confession."[103] After traveling though the Midwest, Malm arrived in New Britain where he took up his ministry of itinerant preaching.[104]

In 1912, Malm's initial meetings in New Britain lasted for three weeks but after F. A. Sandgren arrived, the meetings were extended another week. Malm said that God's power was so powerful upon Sandgren that "it was impossible to sit still."[105] Malm hoped that Sandgren would remain in New Britain longer, saying, "Our prayer is that we may keep him here in the East, for it seems that he is needed more here than in the [Mid]west."[106]

102. *SV*, January 1912, 4. Cf. a similar report in *SV*, April 1912, 3.
103. *SV*, July 1911, 3.
104. *SV*, July 1911, 3–4.
105. *SV*, January 1912, 4.
106. *SV*, January 1912, 4.

New Scandinavian Pentecostal Churches in the Northeast

In regards to meetings held in Manchester, New Hampshire, Malm co-labored with Adolf Ödman. In July 1911, a Danish immigrant named Olof H. Koford wrote about the Pentecostal mission, saying, "My heart is truly full of thanks to God who sent us this blessed Pentecostal revival, so that men and women and even preachers and editors around the world have shown their faith in God by denying themselves and demonstrating their willingness to bear the scorn of Jesus. Here also in M.[anchester] is a small group of Spirit-baptized souls who are hungry for God. The Lord is using Brother Adolf Ödman and his sincere love as an instrument of his divine work here."[107]

In addition to Malm and Lindstrom, Ödman traveled in the Northeast. Adolf Ödman (1871–1941) was born in Ödenäs, Sweden, and had immigrated to America as a gospel preacher in 1907. In 1911, he ministered in Concord, New Hampshire. In the following year, he reported from Jamestown, New York, that "Jesus has already baptized many in the Holy Spirit and fire."[108]

Ödman partnered with a preacher named H. A. Newman and together they "witnessed the Lord moving with victorious power."[109] H. A. Newman served earlier as pastor of the Swedish Baptist Church of Waterbury, Connecticut.[110] However, by April 1913, he had left that position at the request of the congregation and the Swedish Baptist Conference because of "his leadership in the new movement."[111] *Sanningens Vittne* reported: "The Spirit fell in the Swedish Baptist Congregation in Waterbury, Conn. Souls were saved, baptized in the Holy Spirit, spoke in tongues, prophesied, saw signs, and the sick were healed."[112]

H. A. Newman (Helmer August Nyman), originally from Lövånger, Sweden, earlier had served Swedish Baptist congregations in Ishpeming, Michigan, and New Britain, Connecticut, before coming to Waterbury. When the Pentecostal revival came there, a member of the congregation

---

107. *SV*, July 1911, 4.

108. *SV*, April 1912, 4.

109. *SV*, January 1914, 4. For an account critical of Ödman and Lindström see "En varning till allmänheten i Gardner," *Scandinavia*, August 20, 1913, 14. Although Ödman began as a Baptist pastor, he became known as "tungomåltalaren (the tongues-speaking) pastor Adolf Ödman." *Scandinavia*, February 4, 1914, 9.

110. *Minnesskrift, Westbury, Connecticut*, 20–21.

111. *Minnesskrift, Westbury, Connecticut*, 21.

112. *SV*, May-June 1913, 8.

said, "Here in Waterbury we are now about ten baptized in the Holy Spirit, and about the same number are earnestly seeking the same, most having been more or less under the power. We have had and still have wonderfully glorious meetings where the Holy Spirit of God demonstrates his divine attributes, and increasingly reveals Jesus to us."[113] After Newman's dismissal from the Baptists, he worked with "the so-called Swedish Pentecostal Missions" (*Svenska pingstmissionerna*) holding revival meetings in various places before settling in Worcester, Massachusetts.[114]

Ödman also traveled west to Lanse, Pennsylvania, with his final destination of Youngstown, Ohio.[115] In 1913, a Scandinavian Pentecostal mission opened there.[116] Despite the apparent progress, as will be shown in Chapter 7, Ödman and Newman soon promoted "New Light" teachings that caused controversy in the new Pentecostal churches in the Northeast.

In New York City, Emil Lindstrom reported that Scandinavians sought the baptism of the Spirit, and did so among the American, English-speaking Pentecostals as well. Thus, in 1912, Lindstrom said that the number of Scandinavians in his mission—the Apostolic Faith Mission (*Den Apostoliska Trons Mission*) at 211 E. 51st Street—was small.[117] Despite this, he traveled to other towns and cities to spread the Pentecostal message, cooperating, as mentioned above, with Ödman, among others. They were known to "possess a God-given boldness to expose sin in various forms and to emphasize the full gospel that is able to save to the utmost."[118]

Emil J. G. Lindstrom (1864–1932) was born in Stockholm, Sweden. After coming to America, he studied at the Swedish Baptist Theological Seminary in Chicago, and graduated in 1889. He served as a home

---

113. *SV*, January 1914, 8. In Woodbury near Waterbury, Joseph Richter reported that "an American brother was saved from sin, healed from a chronic spinal cord injury, and Spirit-baptized." After this happened, "a Danish sister in the same place was baptized in the Spirit and filled with divine rapture (*gudomlig hänförelse*) and fire." *SV*, January 1914, 8.

114. *Svea*, January 14, 1920. Newman (Nyman) later returned to Sweden, serving the pastorate in Norrviken. In September 1936, he returned to America in the company of Lewi Pethrus.

115. *SV*, April 1912, 4.

116. *SV*, May-June, 1913, 8.

117. *SV*, January 1912, 4; July-August, 1912, 8.

118. *SV*, January 1912, 4. Cf. Erick Erickson of Grand Rapids, Michigan, who preached in Jamestown. *SV*, May-June, 1913, 7.

missionary in the Bronx in New York City, and in Portland, Maine, before becoming pastor of Salem Swedish Baptist Church of Chicago in 1909.[119] While in Chicago, at the height of the Pentecostal revival there, he joined the movement.[120]

After working with Ödman, Lindstrom traveled to Hartford and New Britain, Connecticut. While at Hartford, nine souls were "water-baptized in the Connecticut River in the name of the Father, Son, and Holy Spirit."[121] In New Britain, Lindstrom witnessed believers who spoke in tongues with interpretation.

Lindstrom observed not only that Scandinavians attended meetings of the American English-speaking Pentecostals, but he encouraged it, especially when the meetings were held in conjunction with Scandinavian-language meetings. In June 1913, he announced a meeting to be held in Bridgeport, Connecticut, saying, "The evangelists M.[aria] B. Woodworth-Etter and Mrs. Carrie Judd Montgomery from California will come and lead meetings, if God wills. We expect preachers and tongues-speakers of our own people to come for a Scandinavian meeting that will also be held."[122]

Disputes over the Pentecostal Revival

Disputes soon arose over the Pentecostal revival. In the Baptist periodical, *Nya Wecko-Posten*, the pastor of the Swedish Baptist Church in Jamestown, New York, named C. A. Aldeen, described Ödman as a preacher who had been "expelled from the Baptists."[123] In response, Ödman testified in *Sanningens Vittne*: "Jesus sparked the fire of the Holy Spirit that touched souls in the Baptist Church . . . [and] the Baptists . . . do not like that fire. [This can be said] because several extra meetings have been held to discuss extinguishing the fire. Needless to say, it burns and will burn until Jesus comes. Hallelujah! The people take the matter more philosophically and quote 'Gamaliel's counsel' [Acts 5:38–39]. Yes,

---

119. *Baptist Home Mission Monthly* 31 (1909) 433; *Chicago Blue Book*, 72.

120. SV, January 1912, 4. For Emil Lindstrom, along with Andrew G. Johnson-Ek, Frank Bartleman, and Lewi Pethrus see Gäreskog, *Andrew Ek*, 196–200.

121. SV, July-August 1912, 8.

122. SV, May-June, 1913, 8.

123. SV, April 1912, 4.

with joy and gladness we can exclaim: "The Pentecostal movement has come to Jamestown to stay."[124]

From Organic Movement to Organization

During the years 1914 to 1918, Scandinavian-American Pentecostals were moving from an organic, spontaneous movement toward organization. Some would join ranks with the Assemblies of God (AG). In April 1914, over three hundred English-language, American Pentecostals gathered in Hot Springs, Arkansas, to form the General Council of the Assemblies of God (AG; Springfield, Missouri).[125] More than 300 men and women attended the meetings, representing over twenty states. In the same year, the Stone Church in Chicago held an AG convention that included F. F. Bosworth of Dallas, Texas; A. G. Garr of Los Angeles, California; D. W. Kerr of Cleveland, Ohio; and Arthur F. Johnson of Menominee, Michigan, later of Duluth.[126]

At this time, the Assemblies of God was primarily a ministers' fellowship, comprised mostly of American, English-speaking Pentecostals. In addition to Arthur F. Johnson and E. C. Erickson, other Scandinavian-Americans were ordained by the AG, or served within its ranks, including C. M. Hanson, Henry H. Ness, Frank L. Lindquist, Arthur G. Osterberg, Peter B. Thompson, Emil Samuelson, Rangor S. Peterson, Rasmus S. Rasmussen, and James E. Rasmussen. However, other Scandinavian-American Pentecostals resisted joining the AG, preferring to form other associations that emphasized autonomy and preserved Norwegian, Danish, and Swedish language and identity.

Conclusion

The Pentecostal movement among Scandinavian-Americans spread spontaneously from 1906 to 1918 with little formal organization. The movement emphasized the gifts of the Holy Spirit, speaking in tongues, supernatural healing, and other manifestations of the Holy Spirit. During this time, the movement had little organization besides newly

124. *SV*, April 1912, 4. When the Pentecostal mission in Jamestown began, it was named the Apostolic Assembly, and was led by a Swede named Andrew Forscey (Forse).
125. Blumhofer, *Restoring the Faith*, 116.
126. *The Latter Rain Evangel*, April 1914, 10.

established congregations and cooperative evangelistic meetings and conferences. Periodicals such as *Sanningens Vittne* and *Sandhedens Tolk* were organs established by Pentecostal leaders in order to communicate Pentecostal news and evangelist reports, announce future meetings, spread Pentecostal teaching, solicit funds for missionaries, and report on missionary work abroad. News accounts provided reports in a style similar to those published earlier in William Seymour's *The Apostolic Faith* and other Pentecostal periodicals. The reports were often written with glowing praise for God's supernatural activity with little mention of disappointments, except for perhaps, the soon departures of ministers to their next field of service.

While there was minimal organization during this time, the Scandinavian-American Pentecostal movement was characterized by a zeal for the Pentecostal message and experience. From 1914 to 1918, as the movement grew and matured, particular identities and associations began to emerge along ethno-linguistic and regional lines.

The shared experiences of immigrants from Scandinavian countries (or born to Scandinavian immigrants in America), their use of Scandinavian languages, and their Pentecostal experiences of Spirit-baptism, speaking in tongues, and healings drew them together. Speakers of Danish, Norwegian, and Swedish languages understood one another, generally with minimal exposure to one other's languages. When Norwegians, Danes, Swedes, and Finns looked for a spouse outside their nationality, a fellow Scandinavian was often their choice.[127] This was true when joining a local Pentecostal fellowship as well.

Scandinavian-Americans from pietist, revivalist, and holiness traditions appeared receptive to the Pentecostal message and practices. The "Pentecostal fire" spread not only between Chicago and Los Angeles but to other regions of North America with notable interchange between them. New immigrants who were introduced to the Pentecostal movement in Scandinavia also began to arrive in the United States and Canada that promoted eve wider, trans-Atlantic interchanges.

---

127. Blanck, "Friends and Neighbors?," 18–19.

Bibliography

Primary Sources

Newspapers Used

The Apostolic Faith (AF), Los Angeles, 1906–1908
The Apostolic Faith, Portland, 1908–1929
Baptist Home Mission Monthly, New York City, 1878–1909
Bridegroom's Messenger, Atlanta, GA, 1907–1970
Byposten, Kristiania (Oslo), Norway, 1904–1910
Evangelii Härold, Stockholm, Sweden, 1915–1993
Folke-Vennen (FV), Chicago, IL, 1879–1933
Herald of Pentecost, Duluth, MN, 1950–1956
Latter Rain Evangel, Chicago, 1908–1939
Minneapolis Tribune (MT), Minneapolis, 1867–
Minneapolis Morning Tribune, Minneapolis, 1939–1964
The Pentecost (TP), Indianapolis, Kansas City, 1908–1910
Pentecostal Evangel, Plainfield, IN, Springfield, MO, 1913–2014
The Pentecostal Herald, Chicago, 1915–1923
Pentecostal Testimony, Chicago, 1909–1912
Sanningens Vittne (SV), Minneapolis, 1911–1939
Scandinavia, Worcester, MA, 1887–1918
Svea, Worcester, MA, 1897–1966
Svenska Folkets Tidning, Minneapolis, St. Paul, 1881–1927

Other Primary Sources

Hjertström, J. W. *Fröjd i den Helige Ande*. Chicago: J. W. Hjertström, 1906.
Holmgren, A. A. *Sånger till Herrens lof*. Minneapolis: A. A. Holmgren, 1911.
Minnesskrift öfver Första Svenska Baptistförsamlingens i Westbury, Connecticut, uppkomst och verksamhet, 1892–1917. Westbury, CT: First Swedish Baptist Church, 1917.
Osterberg, Arthur G. Oral History Interview Transcript, March 1966, Archives of the Flower Pentecostal Heritage Center, Springfield, Missouri.
Witting, Victor. *Minnen från mitt lif som sjöman, immigrant och predikant*. Worcester, MA: Burbank, 1904.

Secondary Sources

Alvarsson, Jan-Åke, ed. *Varför reste Lewi Pethrus just till Chicago: Relationer mellan Sverige och USA inom ramen för pentekostalismen*. Uppsala: Artos, 2019.
———. "Scandinavian Pentecostalism." In *European Pentecostalism*, edited by William Kay and Anne Dyer, 19–39. Leiden and Boston: Brill, 2011.
———. "När Örebro blev Sveriges Los Angeles." In *"Azusa Street i Örebro": Pingstväckelsens intåg i Sverige. Rapport från ett symposium på Örebro Teologiska*

Högskola, den 23 november, 2006, edited by Nils-Eije Stävare and Tommy Wasserman, 22–50. Örebro: Örebro Missionsskola, 2008.

Blanck, Dag. "Friends and Neighbors? Patterns of Norwegian-Swedish Interactions in the United States." In *Norwegians and Swedes in the United States: Friends and Neighbors*, edited by Philip J. Anderson and Dag Blanck, 5–20. St. Paul: Minnesota Historical Society, 2012.

Bloch-Hoell, Nils. *The Pentecostal Movement: Its Origin, Development, and Distinctive Character*. Oslo and London: Universitetsforlaget, 1964.

Blumhofer, Edith L. *Restoring the Faith: The Assemblies of God, Pentecostalism, and American Culture*. Urbana and Chicago: University of Illinois Press, 1993.

Bundy, David D. *Visions of Apostolic Mission: Scandinavian Pentecostal Mission to 1935*. Uppsala: Uppsala Universitet, 2009.

Bustos, Donna, and Joshua R. Ziefle. "Anna Sanders: An Unlikely Pioneer of the Assemblies of God in Mexico." *Assemblies of God Heritage* 35–36 (2015–2016) 47–55.

Christensen, Nikolaj. *Unorganized Religion: Pentecostalism and Secularization in Denmark, 1907–1924*. Leiden, Boston: Brill, 2022.

Heckman, Warren. *The History of the Fellowship of Christian Assemblies (HFCA)*. Beaverton, OR: Good Book, 2011.

Gustafson, David M. "The 1884 Boone Conference of the Free Mission Friends: Founding of the EFCA or Theological Discussion?" *Trinity Journal* 34 (2013) 253–77.

———. "Pentecostal Evangelist Cenna Osteberg and the Azusa Street Mission," *Pietisten* 35 (2020) 16–18.

———. "The Scandinavian Mission of the Azusa Street Revival of Los Angeles, 1907–1913." *Swedish-American Historical Quarterly* 72 (2021) 165–208.

Gäreskog, Roland. *Andrew Ek: Några skeden i hans liv som missionär, predikant och nödhjälpsarbetare*. Stockholm: Insamlingsstiftelsen för Pingstforskning, 2015.

Kitsap Daily News. "125 years: Milestone for Poulsbo First Lutheran." 2011. https://www.kitsapdailynews.com/news/125-years-milestone-for-poulsbo-first-lutheran/

Lie, Geir, ed. *Norsk pinsekristendom og karismatisk fornyelse: Ettbinds oppslagsverk*. Oslo: Refleks, 2008.

Lie, Geir, and Jan-Erik Andelin. "Olsen-Smidt, Gerhard Martin." In *Norsk pinsekristendom og karismatisk fornyelse*, edited by Geir Lie, 126–27. Oslo: Refleks, 2008.

Lindberg, Frank T. *Looking Back Fifty Years over the Rise and Progress of the Swedish Evangelical Free Church of America*. Minneapolis: Frank Theodor Lindberg, 1935.

Mentzoni, Torsten. *"Pinse for alle": 100-årsjubileumsbok for pinsevekkelsen*. Skjetten, Norway: Hermon, 2007.

Odegaard, R. Arlo. *With Singleness of Heart*. Minneapolis: Free Church Press, 1971.

Philadelphia Church, Seattle, Washington. "Our Story." https://pcseattle.org/.

Rodgers, Darrin J. *Northern Harvest: Pentecostalism in North Dakota*. Bismarck, ND: North Dakota District Council of the Assemblies of God, 2003.

Sanders, Rufus G. W. *William Joseph Seymour: Black Father of the Twentieth Century Pentecostal/Charismatic Movement*. Sandusky, OH: Xulon, 2003.

Skibsted, Werner. *Oscar Halvorsen, liv og virke; skildring fra denne kjente predikants liv og virke, like fra de bevegede vekkelsestider i begynnelsen av dette århundre og til vår tid*. Oslo: Filadelfiaforlaget, 1947.

Strand, A. E., ed. *A History of the Swedish-Americans of Minnesota, Volume 2*. Chicago: Lewis, 1910.

Wacker, Grant. *Heaven Below: Early Pentecostals and American Culture*. Cambridge, MA: Harvard University Press, 2001.

Williams, Joseph W. *Spirit Cure: A History of Pentecostal Healing*. Oxford: Oxford University Press, 2013.

Chapter Four

Trans-Atlantic Influence from Norway on Scandinavian-American Pentecostalism, 1906–1930

RAKEL YSTEBØ ALEGRE

WHEN THE PENTECOSTAL REVIVAL broke out in 1906, many Scandinavians in the United States embraced the revival and soon Scandinavian Pentecostal fellowships emerged in towns and cities across the country. Most of the early Scandinavian Pentecostals were first- or second-generation immigrants and spoke a Scandinavian language. They read Norwegian, Swedish, and/or Danish newspapers and many corresponded extensively across the Atlantic.[1] Christiania (now Oslo) became one of the early global centers of the Pentecostal movement when the revival broke out in 1906/1907 under the leadership of Thomas Ball Barratt. The revival received a lot of attention from the secular and Christian papers in Scandinavia. Thus, Scandinavians in the U.S. were

---

1. Østrem, *Norsk Utvandringshistorie*, 83–84. Between 1847 and 2010 there were more than 280 different Norwegian-language newspapers published in America.

rapidly informed about "the tongues-speakers" in Norway, and their main leader, T. B. Barratt.[2]

This chapter argues that Norwegian Pentecostalism and especially T. B. Barratt and his followers in Norway influenced the early Scandinavian-American Pentecostals. Though the transatlantic influence went both ways, this study focuses on the influence from Norway to North America. Norwegian Pentecostals in the U.S. were influenced by Pentecostal leaders, writers, evangelists, and pastors in their motherland—primarily through Pentecostal publications and the continued high rate of immigration of Norwegians to North America from 1907 to the 1930s.[3] Norwegian-American Pentecostal churches also recruited pastors and evangelists from Norway and supported Norwegian missionaries. Strong connections were maintained between the Pentecostal communities in the U.S. and Norway. Some of the Norwegian influence extended to the Swedish- and Danish-American Pentecostals—especially through the evangelistic, pastoral, and publishing ministry of T. B. Barratt.

Barratt's Tour in the United States and Baptism in the Spirit

Pentecostalism came to Norway through the ministry of the British-Norwegian Methodist pastor Thomas Ball Barratt (1862–1940). He was born in England but moved to Norway at the age of five. Barratt became a prominent Methodist preacher and pastor in Norway and held different ministerial and leadership positions within the Methodist Episcopal Church from the 1880s to 1906.[4] In 1902 he started the Christiania City Mission among the poor and working class, modeled after the Methodist Central Hall in London, and engaged in social work and creative methods of evangelism. In connection to this, he published his own periodical called *Byposten* (The City Post), beginning in 1904. After some years of

---

2. "Barratt Taler i Tunger," *Nordisk Tidende*, January 24, 1907, 1; "Brev Fra Norge: Fra Minneapolis Tidendes Korrespondent," *Minneapolis Tidende*, January 25, 1907, 5; "Utländska Nyheter," *Svenska Amerikanska Posten*, April 2, 1907, 2; *Aftenposten*, January 13, 1907, 1. The letter in *Minneapolis Tidende* was dated January 6th. The subtitle of the article in *Nordisk Tidende* was: "Den gale Prest fik ildkrone på hodet og Ildtunge" ("The crazy pastor got a crown of fire on his head and tongues of fire"). The article said he was leading religious insanity in Oslo.

3. Østrem, *Norsk Utvandringshistorie*, 33–35.

4. Alegre, "Pentecostal Apologetics of T. B. Barratt," 32–45; Bundy, *Visions of Apostolic Mission*, 141–65; Lange, *T. B. Barratt*, 43–151; Barratt, *When the Fire Fell*, 29–94.

renting different venues, he wanted to build a meeting place for the mission, and so he went on a fundraising tour in the U.S. from 1905 to 1906.[5] During his stay there, he established a network among Scandinavian-American Christians, and he was baptized in the Spirit and spoke in tongues. This happened in New York on November 15, 1906.

Establishing a Network among Christians in America, 1905–1906

When Barratt embarked on his fundraising tour in 1905, he belonged to the Methodist Episcopal Church.[6] He was hoping to get access to the English-speaking churches in America, since they were much wealthier than the Norwegian-speaking churches, but this proved quite difficult. Thus, he visited mostly Methodist churches belonging to the Norwegian-Danish Conference in the Northeast and Midwest, as well as some Scandinavian churches from other confessions. This was during the third large wave of Norwegian emigration and nearly 200,000 Norwegians arrived in America between 1900 and 1910.[7] In the U.S., Barratt met relatives, acquaintances, and friends from his life and ministry. Several of them had been members of Methodist churches that he had pastored or had been part of the City Mission. In the Northeast, Barratt spent much time in Brooklyn. He preached in Norwegian-, Danish-, and Swedish-speaking Methodist churches, and met with several Scandinavian ministers from other denominations.[8] He was also able to preach in a few English-speaking Methodist churches. Moreover, one of the largest Methodist periodicals in the U.S., *The Christian Advocate*, published information about him and his City Mission.[9]

After his stay in New York, Barratt traveled to Chicago. In January 1906, he ministered for three weeks in Moreland Danish-Norwegian Methodist Episcopal Church. The pastor there was Gustav Mathisen, from Sarpsborg in Norway, who longed for revival. Barratt accompanied him on visits to the homes of Norwegians in the area.[10] There was a

---

5. Barratt, *When the Fire Fell*, 93–102; Bundy, *Visions of Apostolic Mission*, 164–7.

6. Barratt left Norway (Stavanger) on October 14th, 1905. T. B. Barratt, "Amerikafærden," *Byposten* (*BP*), October 28, 1905, 127.

7. Østrem, *Norsk Utvandringshistorie*, 33–35.

8. T. B. Barratt, "Amerikafærden," *BP*, November 25, 1905, 134.

9. T. B. Barratt, "Amerikafærden," *BP*, January 13, 1906, 1–2.

10. T. B. Barratt, "Amerikafærden," *BP*, January 27, 1906, 5–7.

Norwegian-Danish Methodist Theological Seminary in Evanston, and professor N. E. Simonsen arranged for Barratt to preach at a large meeting that most Norwegian and Danish Methodist preachers in Chicago would attend.[11] Barratt then held revival meetings at the Norwegian Maplewood Ave. M.E. Church, led by pastor Frederick Ring from Hønefoss in Norway.[12] Here he participated in a large Scandinavian meeting and became known to a number of Swedes from Methodist and Baptist churches.[13] In addition, Barratt had the opportunity to preach several times at the Scandinavian YMCA. He was happy with the outcome of his revival meetings in Chicago, writing that many souls were saved or revived.[14] Significantly, Barratt was able to get quite a few subscribers to his periodical, *Byposten*. Reflecting on his experiences in the city, he said that a much stronger bond should be knit between Christians in Norway and America.[15]

Minnesota was the next stop on Barratt's tour. He held revival meetings and lectures at the Norwegian-Danish Methodist churches in Minneapolis and St. Paul.[16] He went on to hold meetings in Superior, Wisconsin; Duluth, Minnesota; and Forest City, Iowa. Here he made new contacts, especially among Norwegian Methodist ministers, and he continued to gather more subscribers for *Byposten*.[17] After this, Barratt traveled to Des Moines where he participated in a Holiness Camp Meeting, and then briefly visited the Norwegian Methodists in Chicago before he returned to New York in June 1906. His fundraising had been unsuccessful. Therefore, he planned to return to Norway shortly, but the Methodist Bishop William Burt convinced him to stay longer and try out some more strategies to raise funds.[18] The new plan was to ask all Methodists in America to give 5 cents to the City Mission on a specific date, and to travel to different Methodist Conferences to speak about the mission.

11. "Fra vor skole i Evanston," *BP*, March 10, 1906, 17.
12. T. B. Barratt, "Amerikafærden," *BP*, February 10, 1906, 11–12; Strand, ed., *History of the Norwegians in Illinois*, 462–3.
13. "Fra møterne i Chicago," *BP*, March 10, 1906, 19.
14. T. B. Barratt, "Amerikafærden," *BP*, March 24, 1906, 22.
15. T. B. Barratt, "Amerikafærden," *BP*, April 14, 1906, 24.
16. T. B. Barratt, "Amerikafærden," *BP*, May 5, 1906, 37–38.
17. T. B. Barratt, "Amerikafærden," *BP*, June 2, 1906, 46–47; T. B. Barratt, "Amerikafærden," *BP*, June 16, 1906, 53–55; T. B. Barratt, "Amerikafærden," *BP*, June 30, 1906, 57–58.
18. T. B. Barratt, "Amerikafærden," *BP*, July 14, 1906, 61–62.

The Azusa Street Revival and Barratt's Baptism in the Spirit

In July 1906, Barratt moved into A. B. Simpson's Missionary Home in New York. He was unable to realize his travel plans for financial reasons and therefore stayed in and around New York until December.[19] There he preached in different churches, some English-speaking Methodist churches, an evangelical Lutheran free church, and several Norwegian-Danish Methodist churches, and continued to meet Norwegian acquaintances and ministers from different denominations.[20] By September, Barratt was feeling homesick, disappointed that many of his plans had been cancelled, and discouraged by the meager results of his fundraising tour. It had been a very difficult year for him. It was also difficult for his family in Norway, especially since he was not able to send enough money home for his wife, Laura, to pay the rent or buy winter clothes for the children.[21] He was questioning what God's purpose for his stay in the U.S. had been. Therefore, he devoted more time to spiritual renewal and holiness, among other things reading Charles G. Finney's autobiography, visiting meetings, and praying.[22]

It was at this time that he obtained a copy of the first issue of *The Apostolic Faith*, and read about the revival of Azusa Street in Los Angeles. Enthusiastically he translated much of what he read into Norwegian and published it in *Byposten* in October 1906, under the title "Pintsefest paa-ny" ("Pentecost again"). In the text he emphasized the healings, speaking in tongues, baptism in the Spirit, and the experience of divine love.[23] This was the first account that many Norwegians read of the Azusa Street revival. Since Barratt had made so many new acquaintances and gained quite a few new subscribers to *Byposten* during his tour in America, his account of the revival also reached a number of Scandinavian-American readers. For example, on November 22, 1906, his text was published in *Folke Vennen*, an independent Norwegian-language periodical published in Chicago, and edited at the time by Ferdinand Alexander Sandgren.[24]

---

19. T. B. Barratt, "Glimt fra Vesten," *BP*, August 18, 1906, 69–70; T. B. Barratt, "Glimt fra Vesten," *BP*, September 8, 1906, 78.

20. T. B. Barratt, "Amerikafærden," *BP*, July 28, 1906, 66–67.

21. Barratt, *Minner*, 75.

22. T. B. Barratt, "Glimt fra Vesten," *BP*, October 6, 1906, 85–86; T. B. Barratt, "Glimt fra vesten. Da jeg fik min pinstedaab," *BP*, November 3, 1906, 93.

23. T. B. Barratt, "Pintsefest paany," *BP*, October 6, 1906, 86–87.

24. T. B. Barratt, "Pintsefest paany," *Folke-Vennen* (*FV*), November 22, 1906, 2.

This is likely the first account of the Azusa Street revival published in a Scandinavian-language periodical in America. A few weeks later this account was published in *Evangelisten*, a Norwegian-language, Norwegian Evangelical Free Church periodical in Chicago, thus further proliferating the news among Scandinavians in America.[25]

After reading reports of the revival in *The Apostolic Faith*, and corresponding with leaders at the Azusa Street Mission, Barratt began to seek the baptism of the Spirit, through prayer and fasting. After a spiritual battle and tears, he wrote that he had been baptized in the Spirit, on October 7, 1906.[26] He testified widely about his experience at meetings and conventions, and wrote that at one meeting, many Methodist ministers had gone to the altar to seek Spirit baptism.[27] Barratt wrote accounts of his experience and they were published in, among others, *The Christian Alliance* and *Folke-Vennen*, in America, and in *Byposten*, *Krigsraabet* (The Salvation Army), and *Kristelige Tidende* (Methodist) in Norway.[28] The latter two were also read by Norwegians in America, so his testimony was spread widely.

Barratt also sent his account to the Apostolic Faith Mission on Azusa Street but received a response that said he should also have spoken in tongues, and that he would have done so if "he had gone all the way."[29] After studying Scripture, he concluded that they were correct, and so he started again to seek the baptism of the Spirit, but this time with the sign of tongues.[30] Barratt continued to publish the content from different issues of *The Apostolic Faith* and recommended that readers subscribe to it, saying that every issue was like "reading a new chapter in the Book of Acts."[31]

Shortly after Barratt's decision to seek Spirit baptism followed by tongues, Lucy Leatherman arrived at A. B. Simpson's Alliance House.

25. T. B. Barratt, "Pintsefest paany," *Evangelisten*, December 12, 1906, 5–6.

26. T. B. Barratt, "Glimt fra vesten. Da jeg fik min pinstedaab," *BP*, November 3, 1906, 93.

27. T. B. Barratt, "Glimt fra Vesten," *BP*, November 17, 1906, 97–98; T. B. Barratt, "Glimt fra Vesten," *BP*, December 1, 1906, 101–4.

28. T. B. Barratt, "Glimt fra Vesten," *BP*, December 1, 1906, 103; T. B. Barratt, "Da jeg fik min Pintsedaab," *FV*, December 13, 1906, 1, 5.

29. David Bundy, "Spiritual Advice to a Seeker: Letters to T. B. Barratt from Azusa Street, 1906," *Pneuma* 14 (1992) 164; Barratt, *When the Fire Fell*, 124.

30. Barratt, *When the Fire Fell*, 124; T. B. Barratt, "Glimt fra Vesten," *BP*, November 3, 1906, 93–94.

31. T. B. Barratt, "Vækkelsen i Los Angeles," *BP*, December 22, 1906, 106–7.

When Barratt learned that she had been at Azusa Street he asked to speak with her. Leatherman recommended that he attend the Pentecostal meetings led by Maud Williams on 14th Street in New York. On November 15, 1906, he was baptized in the Spirit while at a meeting, and according to his own testimony he spoke and sang in tongues in eight different languages. Leatherman and a Norwegian man prayed for him. Leatherman claimed that "a crown and cloven tongue of fire" was over his head while they prayed.[32] This was a transformational experience which Barratt later characterized as a "love baptism," that gave him a strong fervor for evangelism and desire to spread the Pentecostal revival in Norway, Europe, and around the world.[33] An account of his experience was published in *The Apostolic Faith* in December 1906. Thus, even more Scandinavian-American Pentecostals became aware of him through this testimony.[34]

The Impact of the Revival in Christiana and Barratt's Testimony

Shortly after his Pentecostal experience, Barratt abandoned his fundraising efforts and returned home to Norway. During the last days of December 1906, a revival broke out in Christiania (Oslo). Several people were baptized in the Spirit and spoke in tongues, and the newspapers started reporting the revival. In January 1907, news spread both in Europe and among Scandinavian-Americans, and visitors came from countries such as Sweden, Denmark, Germany, and England to witness the revival in Norway and to speak with Barratt. Soon he was invited to preach in these respective countries. Due to his role in the revival in these and other countries, he became known as "the Apostle of Pentecostalism in northern and western Europe."[35]

Revival and Barratt's Publishing

Many Scandinavian-Americans read about Barratt's Spirit baptism in Scandinavian and/or American Christian periodicals, and quite a few

---

32. Barratt, *When the Fire Fell*, 129; Barratt, "Baptized in New York," *Apostolic Faith*, December 6, 1906, 3. Cf. Barratt, *Da jeg fik min pintsedaab og tungemaalsgaven*, 20.

33. Barratt, *When the Fire Fell*, 130–32.

34. Barratt, "Baptized in New York," *AF*, December 6, 1906, 3.

35. Synan, *Holiness-Pentecostal Tradition*, 131.

followed his regular accounts in *Byposten*. In fact, Barratt sent issues of *Byposten* not only to subscribers, but as gifts to many of the Scandinavian pastors and preachers that he had met in America. However, Barratt really came to the attention of Scandinavian-Americans when the Scandinavian secular press in both Scandinavia and the U.S. started reporting on the revival in January 1907. For Scandinavians, he soon became the most well-known face and articulator of the Pentecostal revival.

Apart from preaching and traveling, Barratt was productive as a writer and filled a role as apologist and theologian of the early Pentecostal movement. In 1907, he produced literature in Norwegian and English that was published in periodicals and as pamphlets, explaining the Pentecostal beliefs and practices. He also responded to critiques of the revival and many of his booklets were distributed internationally.[36] Most issues of *Byposten* contained theological texts on issues such as Spirit baptism, sanctification, and speaking in tongues, as well as testimonies and descriptions of the progress of the revival. In 1909, he published one of the first full-length books on Pentecostal theology titled, *In the Days of the Latter Rain*.[37]

Barratt was able to consolidate the Pentecostal revival in Norway relatively quickly through his early cooperation with other Pentecostal leaders such as Erik Andersen Nordquelle, Carl Magnus Seehuus, and Oscar Halvorsen, and through the spread of his periodical *Byposten*. By 1910, he changed its name to *Korsets Seir* (The Victory of the Cross) and announced that this was the official organ of Norway's Pentecostal movement.

The Impact of Barratt's Testimony and the Revival on Scandinavian-Americans

After Christian periodicals in Norway and the U.S. published Barratt's testimony of Spirit baptism, he started receiving letters from America. *Folke-Vennen* published his first account of being baptized in the Spirit (without tongues) on December 13, 1906.[38] The impact of his testimony

---

36. Some of his early English pamphlets that were spread internationally were: Barratt, *"Tongues": A Reply to Critics*; Barratt, *A Friendly Talk with Ministers and Christian Workers on the Baptism in the Holy Ghost*; Barratt, *The Truth about the Pentecostal Revival*.

37. Barratt, *In the Days of the Latter Rain*.

38. T. B. Barratt, "Da jeg fik min Pintsedaab," *FV*, December 13, 1906, 1, 5.

on several readers was immediate. The following month *Folke-Vennen* published a letter by a John. J. Anderson of Tacoma, Washington, who wrote: "May all of us who are God's children be baptized with this Pentecostal baptism . . . I ask you, all my brothers and sisters in the Lord, to pray for me that I also will be baptized with the Pentecostal baptism like brother Barratt."[39] *Folke-Vennen* continued to publish accounts by Barratt and about the revival in Christiania during 1907 and 1908. In February 1907, the Chicago-based paper *Evangelisten* also published an account of Barratt's Spirit baptism, as well as the news about the revival in Christiania, reaching many Scandinavians in America.[40] It followed up by publishing sympathetic reports of the "Barratt-revival," based on accounts from Norway.[41]

Several Norwegian-Americans wrote letters to Barratt to inform him of the impact that his testimony had on them. Many began to seek Pentecostal baptism and the gift of tongues, and others testified to having already had this experience. From the first weeks of 1907, these types of letters started to appear in *Byposten*. A Norwegian man in Butte, Montana, wrote:

> While I read it tears streamed down my cheeks and there was a shout in my soul to receive the same Baptism in the Spirit. I have worked in the Lord's vineyard in my own strength . . . Oh, how I desire and pray to be filled by the Holy Spirit so that I, in the power of God and not my own, could labor for the salvation of souls . . . pray for me and my wife.[42]

Methodist pastor C. Christophersen, who Barratt met in Forest City, Iowa, also wrote that he was seeking Spirit baptism.[43] The nearly eighty-year-old Norwegian immigrant L. Kristoffersen of Pennock, Minnesota, wrote that after reading Barratt's account of the Azusa Street revival in LA he had asked *Folke-Vennen* for more information.[44] He then received an issue of *The Apostolic Faith* and started spreading its

39. John J. Anderson, "Tacoma, Wash," *FV*, January 17, 1907, 5.

40. "Den religiøse Bevægelse i Kristiania," *Evangelisten*, February 6, 1907, 2–3.

41. "Den nye Vækkelse," *Evangelisten*, February 27, 1907, 2, 4. This account was taken from the Norwegian Periodical *Missionæren*. Bloch-Hoell, *Pinsebevegelsen*, 181.

42. "Forbønner begjæres," *BP*, January 12, 1907, 4. The letter is dated November 28, 1906.

43. "Korrespondance: Amerika," *BP*, March 23, 1907, 38.

44. Barratt's account of the revival in Azusa Street was: T. B. Barratt, "Pintsefest paany," *FV*, November 22, 1906, 2.

testimonies in Minnesota, Wisconsin, and the Dakotas. Shortly after Kristoffersen was baptized in the Spirit.[45] Bertine Jensen, a mother of six who lived in Calfox, also read Barratt's testimony in *Folke-Vennen* in 1907.[46] In a letter she described the effect that his testimony had on her: "I heard the gentle voice of the Spirit within me say, 'You can receive the same experience as brother Barratt if you let God have his way, but you must go through the refining fire and be willing to do all that God asks, since only those who lose their lives will find it.'"[47]

After a period of "tarrying," during which Jensen often read one of the letters that was sent to Barratt from Azusa Street, she was baptized in the Spirit. She began subscribing to Barratt's periodical in 1910, and wrote "[I have a] deep gratitude for you for the blessing you have brought to me and many others."[48] The spreading of Barratt's testimony also led others who had had similar experiences prior to the Azusa Street revival to connect with him and to interpret their experience in a new light. An example is Mr. Barratt Walle of Roanoke, Virginia. He had read Barratt's testimony in *Byposten* and in a letter in 1907, he explained that he also had experienced the Pentecostal baptism a few years earlier.[49]

Scandinavian-American Communities Connected to the "Barratt-revival"

The Northeast

From early 1907, Barratt received many letters from America with testimonies of Spirit baptisms, healings, and information about different Scandinavian Pentecostal revivals. Many Norwegian immigrants had settled in the Northeast, and Pentecostal communities were formed early in Brooklyn, New York, and Hartford, Connecticut. The Norwegian evangelist Oscar Halvorsen from Nøtterøy, Norway, known in the United States as Oscar Hall, played a key role in the early Norwegian Pentecostal community in Lincoln Hall in Brooklyn. Halvorsen met Barratt several

---

45. "Pennok," *BP*, June 15, 1907, 63–64.
46. Bertine Jensen, "Aandsdaab med ildtunger: Brev fra Amerika," *Korsets Seir* (*KS*), March 15, 1910, 41–43. She read T. B. Barratt, "Da jeg fik min pintsedaab," *FV*, December 13, 1906, 1, 5. Calfox likely refers to Colfax, Minnesota.
47. Jensen, "Aandsdaab med ildtunger," *KS*, 41–43.
48. Jensen, "Aandsdaab med ildtunger," *KS*, 42–43.
49. Barratt Walle, "Hilsen fra Virginia," *BP*, February 9, 1907, 19–20.

times in New York during the fall of 1906, and became interested in Pentecostal baptism when he read about the Azusa Street revival. On January 29, 1907, he read an account in a Norwegian periodical of the revival happening in Christiania, and while reading it, he was baptized in the Spirit and began to speak in tongues.[50] The day after, he visited Theodor "Tom" Christensen, leader of the Norwegian free congregation in Lincoln Hall in Brooklyn. Upon entering Christensen's home, Halvorsen began speaking in tongues. Murmurings of this soon spread and many came to the next meetings at Lincoln Hall to observe what had happened to Halvorsen. At the meetings several people were baptized in the Spirit, and the Pentecostal revival spread among the Scandinavians in the area.[51] According to Halvorsen's account, Scandinavian pastors came from the region to observe the meetings and several carried the Pentecostal revival movement with them back to their congregations. Among them was Gabriel Nilsen (Nelson), pastor of a Danish free church in Hartford, and Ludvig Johnsen, of Newhaven, Connecticut.

Shortly afterward, Oscar Halvorsen left Brooklyn to minister in Connecticut. There he held tent meetings in Greenwich, and revival meetings in Hartford at pastor Gabriel Nelson's Norwegian-Danish Evangelical Free Church. Several were baptized in the Spirit.[52] In November 1907, a letter from Nelson appeared in *Byposten*. He confirmed that a Pentecostal revival had started in their Scandinavian church, and that several of the members had been baptized in the Spirit. He thanked Barratt for the books and periodicals he received from Norway. It is evident that the connection between Barratt and Pentecostal leaders in Brooklyn and Hartford was strong from the beginning.[53]

This connection was further strengthened when the Norwegian evangelists Dagmar Gregersen and Agnes Thelle came from Christiania to the Northeast to study at A. B. Simpson's mission school, in 1908.[54] They were part of the "Barratt-revival" and important in pioneering the Pentecostal revival at several places in Europe. They were by then preparing to become missionaries in India, and became the first Norwegian missionaries sent by the Pentecostals in Norway. While studying in America, they ministered regularly among the Scandinavian

50. Skibsted, *Oscar Halvorsen*, 32–33. *The Apostolic Faith* (*AF*), May 1907, 1.
51. Skibsted, *Oscar Halvorsen*, 34–36.
52. Skibsted, *Oscar Halvorsen*, 40–49.
53. "Amerika (Hartford, Conn)," *BP*, November 16, 1907, 102.
54. Skibsted, *Oscar Halvorsen*, 56–57; Engstrøm, *Ha Tro Til Gud*, 43–48.

Pentecostals, especially in Hartford. They sent several letters to *Byposten* with reports from their ministry in the U.S.

During the spring of 1908, Oscar Halvorsen held revival meetings in Black Rock in Bridgeport, Connecticut. Dagmar Gregersen and Agnes Thelle participated, and Pentecostal Scandinavians from Hartford, Newhaven, Brooklyn, and other places in the Northeast joined the meetings.[55] In the summer, these communities arranged the first Norwegian-American Pentecostal convention, which was also held in Bridgeport and led by Halvorsen and Nelson. In 1908 Halvorsen returned to Norway where he served as an evangelist and pastor.

In July 1913, Dagmar Gregersen's husband, Henrik Engstrøm, was invited to preach at a large Scandinavian Pentecostal convention in Hartford, demonstrating the strong connection between the Norwegian Pentecostals in Norway and in the Northeast U.S.[56] Engstrøm wrote that the convention was held at the Scandinavian Mission at 49 Charter Oak Ave., in Hartford, which by then had Norwegian, Swedish, and Danish members.[57] "Pentecostal friends" came from places like Brooklyn, Providence, Worcester, Gardner, and New Britain to attend the conference and several were baptized in the Spirit at their meetings. Engstrøm visited several of the other Scandinavian Pentecostal congregations in the Northeast after the conference, and commented: "Yes, in truth the Lord is visiting our dear countrymen over here in his own way. Now there are congregations in several places that stand entirely for the baptism of the Spirit!"[58]

The Northwest

The Pentecostal revival broke out in several Scandinavian cities and towns along the Northwestern coast in the fall of 1906, and some leaders soon contacted Barratt when they read his testimony and heard about the revival in Christiania. Henrik Langeland from the Norwegian town Poulsbo in Washington, was one of the first Norwegian-Americans to contact Barratt. He had been baptized in the Spirit and spoken in tongues in Ballard in Seattle on November 6, 1906, when a Pentecostal revival broke out at

---

55. Skibsted, *Oscar Halvorsen*, 56.
56. "Fra missionsmarken," *KS*, July 15, 1913, 110.
57. Henrik Engstrøm, "Amerika," *KS*, August 15, 1913, 126–27.
58. Henrik Engstrøm, "Amerika," *KS*, October 15, 1913, 158–59.

a small Scandinavian mission. On January 30, 1907, Langeland wrote to Barratt after reading about the revival in Christiania in *Folke-Vennen* and said that he had read his testimony about Spirit baptism with great interest.[59] In later letters Langeland wrote that he had received several copies of *Byposten*. He informed Barratt that there were quite a few Scandinavian Pentecostals in Seattle and Tacoma, and that they also had a small group in Poulsbo.[60] The next year, Langeland said that he got a hold of Barratt's pamphlet, *A Friendly Talk to Ministers*, and was blessed by it, thinking it should be sent to all Norwegian priests in America.[61] By 1909, Langeland started publishing his own Norwegian Pentecostal periodical from Poulsbo—*Sanhedens Tolk*.[62] Although it is difficult to assess the impact and spread of this periodical, Bertine Jensen wrote that she was distributing it, and Barratt referred to the periodical several times, including at least one of its accounts in his periodical.[63]

One of the strongest connections between Barratt and the early Norwegian-American Pentecostals in the Northwest came through Bernt Berntsen, the Norwegian-American missionary to China who visited Norway. The Pentecostals in Norway began supporting Berntsen and other Norwegian-American missionaries to China, and several letters from the Berntsens were published in *Byposten* between 1908 and 1915. It seems that Bernt and Magna Berntsen were the first missionaries to receive substantial economic support from Pentecostals in Norway.

The Midwest

Scandinavian Pentecostals in the Midwest also contacted Barratt after reading his testimony and reading about the revival in Christiania. By February 1907, he received a copy of *Evangelisten* that included information about the revival in Chicago. Barratt published this report in

---

59. Henrik Langeland, "Korrespondance: Amerika," *BP*, March 23, 1907, 38; Henrik Langeland ,"Udlandet: Amerika" *BP*, May 18, 1907, 56.

60. H. Langeland, "Udlandet: Amerika," *BP*, May 18, 1907, 56; Henrik Langeland, "Poulsbo, Wash," *BP*, October 19, 1907, 94.

61. H. Langeland, "Amerika: Poulsbo, Wash.," *BP*, March 21, 1908, 23.

62. H. Langeland, "Amerika (Poulsbo, Wash)," *BP*, October 1, 1909, 79. It appears that *Sanhedens Tolk* runs to 1914.

63. Bertine Jensen, "Aandsdaab med ildtunger: Brev fra Amerika," *KS*, March 15, 1910, 41–43; "Glimt fra andre blade," *KS*, March 15, 1912, 47; T. B. Barratt, "Fra observations taarn," *KS*, September 15, 1913, 141.

Byposten with the title "Wonderful Revival in Chicago" and said news of this should be spread to as many people as possible.[64] The Swedish pastor J. W. Hjertstrom also wrote to Barratt, telling him of a spiritual renewal in his church in Chicago, and that they were joyous and praising God for the revival in Christiania.[65]

Both Loth Lindquist and L. Kristoffersen informed Barratt of the Pentecostal revival among Scandinavians in Minneapolis.[66] In 1908, Lindquist wrote that the revival was continuing in the city and that "a door had opened in St. Paul." He extended an informal invitation to Barratt writing, "It is for many a dear wish to see Brother Barratt in these Twin Cities."[67] Similar sentiments were expressed regularly by Scandinavian Pentecostals in America over the following years.[68]

Gerhard Olsen Smidt, a Norwegian Pentecostal pastor in Minneapolis, also sent interesting letters to Barratt. Smidt had been an officer in the Salvation Army, first in Norway and then two years in the U.S. He had received a copy of *Byposten* from his sister and said Barratt's letters "shook him to the core."[69] Smidt informed Barratt that there were three Pentecostal missions in Minneapolis: an American, a Swedish, and a Norwegian. He said he was leading the latter two, and the "American" mission he referred to was likely the Apostolic Faith Mission led by Jackson White. Smidt led the Christian Assembly, which seems to be an offshoot of the Apostolic Faith Mission, with both starting in 1907. Smidt's congregation eventually settled at 1817 Minnehaha Avenue South.[70] "The American mission" also had many Scandinavian members and thus the three early Pentecostal churches in Minneapolis were attended by Scandinavians.

Smidt embarked on a Pentecostal preaching tour in the Midwest in 1910 with pastor G. F. Fink from Denver, Colorado. In Lincoln, Nebraska, they held meetings in the opera house that seated 700, where

---

64. T. B. Barratt, "Herlig vækkelse i Chicago," *BP*, February 23, 1907, 25–26.

65. J. W. Hjertstrøm, "Chicago," *BP*, April 6, 1907, 43.

66. L. L. "Minneapolis," *BP*, October 19, 94. It was signed L. L. The same account was republished in December. L. L. "Minneapolis," *BP*, December 28, 1907, 114.

67. L. Lindqvist "Amerika," *BP*, February 8, 1908, 11.

68. *KS*, January 1, 1910, 6; "Glimt fra breve," *KS*, February 15, 1914; "Fra flere hold," *KS*, September 1, 1915.

69. Gerhard Smidt, "Amerika," *KS*, April 15, 1910, 63–64.

70. Gerhard Smidt, *Sanningens Vittne* (*SV*), July 1911, 3.

they prayed for healing among the sick.[71] In 1911, Smidt said that the Pentecostal work in Minneapolis was going forward, and that during a six-month period many souls were saved and healed, and around 100 people at the Minnehaha Avenue Mission had been baptized in the Spirit. The mission now had 300 to 400 members, of whom about half were Spirit baptized. Smidt said that there were "wonderful opportunities" in Minnesota but few workers.[72]

In 1911, Smidt returned to Norway, and arranged for Fink to lead the Minnehaha Avenue Mission while he was away.[73] However, during the following year, Smidt took up work in Finland rather than return to the U.S.[74] Smidt was one of the cases to demonstrate that many Norwegian Pentecostals in America felt a strong connection to the Barratt-revival, even though they had not met him personally but joined his movement when they returned to Norway.

The Reach of Barratt's Publications among Scandinavian-Americans

The Reach of *Byposten/Korsets Seir*

In 1913, *Korsets Seir* published 6,000 copies of the periodical. It is difficult to know how many ended up in America, but it is evident that the periodical reached many readers.[75] In the early years (1907–1918) of the Pentecostal revival in Norway, *Byposten/Korsets Seir* received letters from readers in nineteen different states in the U.S., and from several cities in Canada.[76] In 1910, Pastor Loth Lindquist of Minneapolis commented on the impact of Barratt's periodical, which by then was renamed *Korsets Seir*, saying, "*Korsets Seir* goes forth victoriously and unhindered, across land and water, and brings provisions to hungry hearts so that the victorious can continue the battle in the footsteps of

---

71. Smidt, "Amerika," *KS*, April 15, 1910, 63–64.
72. Gerhard Smidt, "Minneapolis, Minn.," *KS*, June 15, 1911, 92.
73. *SV*, July 1911, 3.
74. Gerhard Smidt, "Nyeste nyt fra Finland," *KS*, March 15, 1912, 48.
75. "Viktige oplysninger," *KS*, April 15, 1913, 63.
76. Letters came from the following states from 1907 to 1916: Alaska, California, Colorado, Connecticut, Illinois, Iowa, Maine, Minnesota, Montana, New Hampshire, New York, Nebraska, North Dakota, Oregon, Virginia, Vermont, Washington, and Wisconsin.

the chief." Lindquist ordered additional copies of Barratt's Norwegian pamphlets *The Truth about the Pentecostal Revival*, and *Jesus' Program—Ours*, to be sent to Minneapolis.[77]

Several Norwegian-Americans actively recruited new subscribers to *Byposten*, such as Jacob Paulsen of Brooklyn, New York.[78] Some also informed Barratt that after reading their own copy of *Byposten* they would circulate it among their friends, especially to people they thought might be open to its contents. Thus, it is likely that the paper's readership was higher than the number of subscribers.[79] Martha Skipple, a Norwegian immigrant from Chicago, said that when she received *Byposten* she would take it with her to read to others.[80] A Methodist reader in Forest City, Iowa, even sent copies to his family in Helgeland, Norway. In most cases, however, it was families in Norway that were sending copies of *Byposten* to their relatives and friends in the U.S.[81] In 1910, a woman in Kansas wrote to Barratt, saying, "We have long thought to write and thank you for the good news that *Byposten* brings, and its edifying content. We circulate it among the Norwegians here; we ourselves are Swedish but we can read Norwegian clearly."[82] By 1912, *Korsets Seir* had so many subscribers and readers in America that an advertisement for a Scandinavian Pentecostal convention appeared in the paper. It was for a week-long convention at pastor Thomas Thompson's mission in New Rochelle, New York, in April of 1912.[83]

Some subscribers in America also read or wrote letters to *Korsets Seir* hoping to get in contact with other Scandinavian Pentecostals nearby. An example of this is a letter from Paul Paulsen in Elba, Nebraska. He had read in *Korsets Seir* about Gerhard Olsen Smidt who mentioned a Pentecostal mission in Lincoln, Nebraska, and a sister Booker. Paulsen went to search for it but could not find it, and so he provided his name and address in *Korsets Seir* and asked the Pentecostals in Lincoln to write to him. Several similar letters were written where Norwegians in

---

77. Loth Lindqvist, "Amerika: Minneapolis," *KS*, November 15, 1910, 173.
78. Jacob Paulsen, "Amerika (Brooklyn)," *BP*, December 28, 1907, 114.
79. "Fra brevmappen," *KS*, May 15, 1913, 80; Albertine Jansen and Aagot Winberg, "Amerika, Chicago," *KS*, November 1, 1913, 167; "Fra flere hold," *KS*, May 1, 1915; June 1, 1915; August 15, 1915.
80. Martha Skipple, "Chicago," *KS*, August 10, 1907, 74.
81. "Forest City," *KS*, March 15, 1911, 47.
82. "Amerika," *KS*, January 1, 1910, 6.
83. "Specielle Pinsemøter," *KS*, April 1, 1912, 56.

America found other Norwegian Pentecostals by reading *Korsets Seir*, or by publishing letters in the periodical with their information and asking any Pentecostals nearby to contact them.[84]

Norwegians in the U.S. also sent letters to Norway to ask for assistance for their churches or missions. An example of this is "a sister" in Dorchester, Massachusetts, who sent a letter to Barratt asking if there was anyone in Norway that could come and open a Pentecostal mission among the Norwegians in Boston. She wrote that there had been activity there earlier but then someone came and taught "Russel's doctrine" (Russellism) and it stopped. Now they were six, but none of them were preachers. She explained further, saying, "Many Pentecostals have lately come from different missions in Christiania and joined different free churches in Boston since there is no Pentecostal preacher here."[85] Shortly afterwards, Mrs. M. Hansen in Waltham, Massachusetts, wrote requesting that the sister in Dorchester contact her.[86]

In 1912, Barratt began publishing *Korsets Seir* (*Korsets Seger*) in Swedish and in Finnish (*Ristin Voitto*). These had some distribution among Swedes and Finns in the U.S. An example is a letter from Br. Selh. Hagen of Astoria, Oregon, who was baptized in the Spirit in Portland. He wrote saying: "*Korsets Seir*, *Korsets Seger*, *Ristin Voitto* and *Brendende spørsmål* reach us regularly through sister Tytti (Lagersedt) in Karis (Finland) and we are very grateful."[87] Thus, Barratt's writings reached not merely Norwegians, Danes, and Swedes, but also Finns.

Several Norwegian-Americans who visited Norway during the early decades of the revival, participated in Pentecostal meetings there in different places. This also strengthened their connection to the Norwegian Pentecostal movement and in many cases to Barratt's leadership. Some came to Barratt's meetings at Møllergaten 38 in Christiania, where he began conducting regular meetings in 1910.[88] A brother known simply as "M. R.," visited Nordfjord in western Norway and conducted Pentecostal meetings there. When he returned to the U.S., he ordered fifty subscriptions of *Korsets Seir* so that he could distribute

---

84. "Verdensvækkelsen," KS, December 15, 1911; December 1, 1914; "Fra flere hold," KS, August 1, 1915.

85. "Aapne døre i Boston," KS, September 1, 1915, 136.

86. "En søster i Amerika," KS, January 15, 1916, 16.

87. "Astorien, Origon," KS, September 1, 1913, 136.

88. A. O. Bergsteen, "Brooklyn," KS, November 15, 1914, 175–76; Jacob Paulsen, "Brooklyn," KS, September 1, 1914, 136.

them freely at the mission where he ministered.[89] Several prominent American, English-language ministers also visited Barratt's mission in Christiania, demonstrating that he was known outside of Scandinavian circles. Among the American preachers were J. H. King (1912),[90] Frank Bartleman (1913),[91] and Robert and Marie Burgess Brown (1914).[92] The Browns spoke with Barratt about the Scandinavians at their mission in New York, and Barratt preached at their church in 1927.[93]

The Songbook *Maran Ata*

Barratt also influenced Norwegian Pentecostals in America through his songbook first published in 1911. It was called *Maran Ata* and included about 600 hymns and songs, many of which Barratt wrote or translated from English. He said, "It is our hope that by the grace of God this [songbook] will advance the spiritual life, both here in Norway and among the Norwegian population in America."[94] The songbook was offered for sale in large quantities. It soon became the standard songbook for Norwegian Pentecostals. Most would buy personal copies and bring them to meetings, along with their Bibles. *Maran Ata* sold thousands of copies and was regularly updated with new editions. In the first four years, there were already three editions and a total of 17,000 copies in print.[95]

In August 1911, the first orders for *Maran Ata* had already started coming from the U.S.[96] A man in Tacoma wrote that he joined the Pentecostal revival on the West Coast around the end of 1906. He was anticipating the new songbook that Barratt was about to publish and hoped that they would use it at their meetings in Tacoma. In October 1911, a letter from Olav Fjermedal in Tacoma thanked Barratt for sending three copies of *Maran Ata*, and in turn, he ordered 100 copies for

---

89. "Der hvor ilden brænder," KS, December 15, 1914, 186.
90. T. B. Barratt, "Fra min dagbok," KS, May 15, 1912, 80.
91. Frank Bartleman, "Kristiania, Norge 14 juni, 1913," KS, July 15, 1913, 112.
92. T. B. Barratt, "Fra min dagbok," KS, July 1, 1914, 102.
93. T. B. Barratt, "Fra min dagbok," KS, July, 1914, 102; T. B. Barratt, "Amerikareisen," KS, November 26, 1927, 7.
94. "Maran ata," KS, June 1, 1911, 88.
95. Bloch-Hoell, *Pinsebevegelsen*, 228.
96. "Syng af Maran ata," KS, August 1, 1911, 120; "Venner i Amerika," KS, February 1, 1912, 22.

their Scandinavian meetings.⁹⁷ By 1916, the work in Tacoma hosted four Scandinavian meetings, and used *Maran Ata* as their standard songbook.⁹⁸ Barratt continued to receive orders during the following years,⁹⁹ and when he toured America in 1927–1928, he observed that many Norwegian-language congregations used it.

Left to right: Lewi Pethrus, Laura Barratt, T. B. Barratt, Anna Larssen Bjørner, and Sigurd Bjørner, Courtesy of Norwegian Pentecostal Historical Archive

Theological works

During the first years of the Pentecostal revival, Barratt wrote many pamphlets in English and Norwegian and most of them seem to have had some distribution among Pentecostals in North-America. In 1913, his book titled *In the Days of the Latter Rain* (*I Sildigregnets Dager*) was translated into Danish, making his apologetic writings accessible to a wider audience of Scandinavians. His texts from the early years focused primarily on describing and defending core Pentecostal teachings and practices such as Spirit baptism, speaking in tongues, prophecy, sanctification, and physical manifestations.¹⁰⁰ From letters in *Byposten/*

97. Olav Fjermedal, "Amerika: Tacoma," *KS*, October 1, 1911, 150. Olav Fjermedal (1880–1942) was originally from Vegusdal, Norway.
98. M. Kvam, "Tacoma, Wash," *KS*, June 15, 1916, 96.
99. An example of this is B. Saudvik, "Cleveland, Ohio," *KS*, April 1, 1915, 55.
100. For greater detail, see Alegre, "Pentecostal Apologetics of T. B. Barratt."

Korsets Seir, it is evident that Scandinavian-American Pentecostals met opposition in their local communities and in many churches, and they found Barratt's resources helpful.

Two of Barratt's texts that seem to have been appreciated across the Atlantic were his responses to critiques from the Swedish-American K. G. Johanson and the American Baptist pastor A. C. Dixon. Johanson had argued in *Nya Wecko-Posten* that Satan was behind the revival and deceiving people. Barratt responded to his objections by addressing them point by point in *Korsets Seir*.[101] In 1914, A. C. Dixon held meetings in Christiania and Barratt went to hear him. Dixon's message was against speaking in tongues—similar to the content of a pamphlet he had written.[102] Barratt produced a detailed response in a pamphlet, titled, "The Gift of Tongues: What Is It?" and published it in both Norwegian and English.[103] He also published it as serial articles in *Korsets Seir* in the fall of 1914, commenting that he knew Dixon had been opposing the Pentecostal movement in America.[104] A. E. Arnesen, who pastored an English-speaking church in Ronneby, Minnesota, wrote that he had read Barratt's responses with great interest. He had heard Dixon speak many times, and was hurt by his attack on the Pentecostal movement.[105]

In several letters from America, writers also mentioned divisions among American Pentecostals, and were saddened by this. The divisions they experienced were especially related to the "Finished-work" doctrine, Oneness Pentecostalism, the "Russellites," and the "new light" teachings of Adolf Ödman.[106] N. G. Nielsen of Hartford, Connecticut wrote to warn Norwegians about the "new light" teachings of Ödman, and said that their "blossoming" mission in Hartford had been divided over the issue and

---

101. T. B. Barratt, "De mange sprok som taltes paa pinsedagen i Jerusalem," *KS*, August 1, 1913, 115–17; August 15, 1913, 122–24.

102. A. C. Dixon, *Speaking with Tongues*; T. B. Barratt, "Svar til Dr. Dixon," *KS*, July 15, 1914, 105.

103. Barratt, *Gift of Tongues: What Is It?*

104. T. B. Barratt, "Svar til Dr. Dixon," *KS*, July 15, 1914, 105–12; T. B. Barratt "Svar til Dr. Dixon," *KS*, August 1, 1914, 113–14.

105. "Bud over hav og land: Minnesota, Ronneby," *KS*, December 15, 1914, 192–94. Another example is sister Snartemo in Tacoma: "Tacoma," *KS*, August 15, 1915, 128.

106. Examples are: Two letters from Tacoma about the divisions caused by Oneness-Pentecostalism: Olav Fjermedal, "Amerika," *KS*, March 1, 1917, 38; "Tacoma," *KS*, August 15, 1915, 128. A letter concerning conflicts related to "Russelism": "Aapne døre i Boston," *KS*, September 1, 1915, 136.

that some left to start a new mission.[107] Barratt strongly warned against these teachings, writing several articles in *Korsets Seir* on these issues.[108] He lamented the confusion and division these matters caused but rejoiced in reports that these aberrant teachings were on the decline.[109]

Emigration of Norwegian Pentecostals and Barratt's Tour of America, 1927–1928

When the Pentecostal revival first started, Barratt envisioned a revival that would permeate all denominations and congregations. He did not have any intention of starting a new church, and certainly not a new denomination. In Christiania, he worked with Erik Andersen Nordquelle to hold meetings in the hall that Nordquelle rented, at Torvgaten 7. Barratt spent most of his time between 1907 and 1909, as a traveling evangelist in Norway and abroad. The opposition that the Pentecostal revival faced in many denominations gradually dampened his optimism about the revival permeating every local church. In 1910, he organized an assembly, similar to other Pentecostal missions, at Møllergaten 38. People from a variety of ecclesial backgrounds attended his assembly.

In 1913, Barratt and his wife, Laura, were baptized by Lewi Pethrus in Stockholm, and he gradually began to propagate the Baptist view of water baptism in addition to the classical Pentecostal five-fold gospel of salvation, sanctification, Spirit baptism, healing, and Jesus' return. His acceptance of water baptism by immersion caused some division but eventually it further consolidated the movement.[110] In 1916, Barratt officially started a church (named Filadelfia in 1921) that was modeled after Baptist congregational churches, and strongly encouraged Pentecostals to organize their communities as independent Pentecostal churches, following the example of his own church. Following this, many new Pentecostal churches were established, and the movement further consolidated

---

107. N. G. Nielsen, "Hartford," *KS*, October 1915, 151.

108. On the salvation of all: T. B. Barratt, "Alles frelse," *KS*, October 15, 1916, 159. On Oneness Pentecostalism, see T. B. Barratt "Vær paa vagt," *KS*, February 15, 1917, 25–26; T. B. Barratt, "Hvad vi tror," *KS*, November 15, 1918, 145–47. Barratt also stopped promoting the missionary ministries of Gunstad (Chile) and Berntsen (China) due to their embrace of "New light" and/or Oneness Pentecostalism.

109. T. B. Barratt, "Det 'nye lys' saakaldet paa retur," *KS*, October 15, 1916, 159.

110. Bloch-Hoell, *Pinsebevegelsen*, 226–27.

with Filadelfia as "the mother church."[111] From 1916 to 1933, the church grew from 200 to 1,700 members.[112]

Emigration of Norwegian Pentecostals

The Pentecostal movement in Norway expanded rapidly and by 1933 there were at least 130 Pentecostal churches in the country.[113] At the same time, the high emigration rate from Norway to America continued.[114] Norwegian Pentecostal emigrants who aligned with Barratt were very likely to bring with them his theology, a copy of *Maran Ata*, issues of *Korsets Seir*, and strong ties with Pentecostal churches in Norway. They often established themselves in largely Norwegian towns in rural areas, or neighborhoods in cities such as Minneapolis, St. Paul, Chicago, Seattle, and New York City. Brooklyn had the largest Norwegian community with roughly 100,000 first- and second-generation Norwegian residents between 1940 and 1950.[115] When new Pentecostal immigrants arrived they often tried to evangelize other Scandinavians and establish new Pentecostal churches. Their connection to their homeland led to an increase in requests for evangelists to travel in America and pastor their new Norwegian congregations. Arne Dahl, Sverre Gustavsen, and Joseph Ystrøm are examples of this.

In February 1926, a group of Norwegian Pentecostals gathered to pray together at Pulcifer Institute, 5111 Fifth Avenue in Brooklyn. This was the beginning of the church that would be known as Salem Gospel Assembly. In March, they organized the church with twenty-four members, and soon elected three elders: Abraham Hansen, T. Gabrielsen, and Jacob Larsen.[116] In the first year, Pastor Sundstrom and Mikael Hansen came from Staten Island to preach, as well as other preachers passing through Brooklyn, but they soon felt the need for a full-time minister. They called evangelist Arne Dahl of Larvik, Norway, and he arrived in October 1926.

111. Bloch-Hoell, *Pinsebevegelsen*, 237–39.
112. Bloch-Hoell, *Pinsebevegelsen*, 237.
113. Bloch-Hoell, *Pinsebevegelsen*, 240.
114. Between 1901 and 1930 there were almost 340,000 registered emigrants from Norway to North-America. Østrem, *Norsk Utvandringshistorie*, 33–35.
115. Inger-Marit Knap Sæby, "Dette var "Lapskaus Boulevard," *NRK*, January 19, 2014. https://www.nrk.no/kultur/dette-var-_lapskaus-boulevard_-1.11423642.
116. Richardsen, "Review," 7–8.

Salem Gospel Assembly, New York City, 1936. Harry Ring, standing at left.
Courtesy of the Ring Family.

Arne Dahl was a protégé of T. B. Barratt, and Barratt's sister, Mary Ball Barratt, was a member of the Brooklyn congregation for several years. Stanley Johannesen, writes, "Certainly Pastor Dahl established in Salem a regime of pastoral authority and a manner of worship and other church activity and usages modeled on the great Pastor Barratt."[117] Membership cards of charter members of Salem Gospel Tabernacle showed that nearly all were former members of the Filadelfia Church in Oslo, or one of the related churches in southern Norway.[118] The church's anniversary booklet confirms that "many dear friends arrived from Norway, who requested membership in the church."[119] In providing a description of the Brooklyn congregation, Johannesen further said: "Salem was in the deepest self-understanding a missionary church. In the most immediate sense, it was a missionary enterprise of Norwegian Pentecostals to the mission field represented by young Norwegian men adrift in New York. It was also, or at least became, a mission of the Barratt Pentecostals to the Holiness and Pentecostal 'brothers and sisters' already in Brooklyn."[120]

117. Johannesen, "Holy Ghost in Sunset Park," 557.
118. Johannesen, "Holy Ghost in Sunset Park," 557.
119. Richardsen, "Review," 8.
120. Johannesen, "Holy Ghost in Sunset Park," 557. Apparently, the Scandinavian Assembly Eben-Ezer led by T. Christensen was not as evangelistic and missions-minded as the new church led by Dahl. Donn Ring, "Impressions of a Pentecostal Ministry: Harry Christian Ring 1906–1963," unpublished manuscript, 1988, 16.

Arne Dahl pastored the church until 1936, when he returned with his family to Norway to become pastor of Tabernaklet in Bergen.[121]

In 1927, Sverre Gustavsen wrote from Chicago where he was ministering in the Scandinavian Mission Eben Ezer, located at 2838 West North Avenue, saying,

> People who have come from Scandinavia have not found any Scandinavian Pentecostal churches in this part of the city and therefore went to other places where they have not been able to worship God according to their own light and have thus regressed in their spiritual life. So now, God has wonderfully arranged it so that the wonderful Pentecostal gospel that the first Christians held onto, is also heard in the Scandinavian languages in this part of the city. The brothers wish to use the *Maran Ata* songbook and request that I order 100 copies which I hope can be sent as soon as possible.[122]

After ministering in Chicago, Sverre Gustavsen ministered in the Norwegian Pentecostal church, Salem, in Brooklyn while their pastor Arne Dahl was on vacation. In one of his letters, he concluded with a sentiment often expressed in letters from Norwegians in America: "May the Lord send revival among the Scandinavian people in this large country."[123] Gustavsen soon returned to work among Norwegians in Chicago, and after two years in the U.S. he went home to Norway to serve a congregation.[124]

Josef Ystrøm was a Norwegian Pentecostal preacher who emigrated from Norway in 1923 and located in San Francisco where he ministered in a Scandinavian Pentecostal congregation.[125] He told the readers of *Korsets Seir* about a large Scandinavian Pentecostal four-day convention at Mount Hermon, California, in June 1927, which he believed was the first of its kind in that part of the country. Scandinavian-Americans came from Tacoma, Turlock, Los Angeles, Kingsburg, Oakland, San

---

121. Richardsen, "Review," 8; Rødland, *Glede i Gud*, 125.

122. Sverre Gustavsen, "Chicago," *KS*, March 26, 1927, 2. The location appears to be the annex of the original North Avenue Mission located at 2836 West North Avenue, Chicago.

123. Sverre Gustavsen, "Brooklyn," *KS*, August 13, 1927, 3-4.

124. Hjalmar Ruud, "På reisefot i Amerika," *KS*, January 28, 1928, 6; Arne Dahl, "Fra den aandelige arbeidsmark i Brooklyn," *KS*, November 3, 1928, 3-4.

125. Josef Ystrøm, "Fra Fjern og nær: San Fransisco," *KS*, August 13, 1927, 3-4.

Jose, Santa Cruz, and San Francisco to attend.[126] They planned to arrange a large national convention there the following year and invited Barratt to preach.[127] In 1924, Ystrøm started to invite Barratt to visit them, and his repeated invitations seem to have motivated Barratt to visit America from 1927 to 1928.[128]

Barratt's Tour of America 1927–1928.

Barratt had regularly received invitations to preach in America since 1908, and in 1927 he dedicated a year to touring and preaching in the U.S. and Canada with his wife, Laura.[129] News of their trip was met with great excitement from Norwegian Pentecostals. He received invitations to hold revival campaigns in many parts of America. In preparation for his journey, Barratt wrote his autobiography in English which he advertised for sale in his periodical.[130] Laura was also a prominent leader of the Pentecostal movement in Norway, and had an especially key role in their publishing work, in foreign missions, and as a co-leader with her husband of the Filadelfia church. In most churches they visited in North America, Laura spoke before her husband preached.

The Barratts arrived in New York in October 1927. They were received at the harbor by family, several Pentecostal pastors and evangelists, and a journalist from the major Norwegian-American newspaper, *Nordisk Tidende*.[131] The Barratts' arrival was a grand event, with a welcome party arranged by Arne Dahl and held in his church in Brooklyn. A lengthy report of Barratt's interview by a journalist was published, titled, "The Englishman Who Became Norway's Most Talked about Man." The article began by saying:

> There are few, if any, Norwegian men who the waves have splashed higher around than pastor Barratt. . . . Nonetheless, despite the mocking and ridicule, pastor Barratt appeared to grow during the storms. Most people would have given up all activity

126. Ystrøm, "Fra Fjern og nær," *KS*, August 13, 1927, 3.
127. Ystrøm, "Fra Fjern og nær," *KS*, August 13, 1927, 3.
128. Lange, *T. B. Barratt*, 268; Barratt, *Erindringer*, 230.
129. Barratt, *Erindringer*, 230.
130. T. B. Barratt, "Amerikareisen," *KS*, October 29, 1927, 4–7.

131. Barratt, "Amerikareisen," *KS*, October 29, 1927, 4–7. Barratt's sister Mary, their daughter Esther, their son Alexander, and daughter-in-law, Astri, all lived in Brooklyn. Some of the pastors that met him were Arne Dahl and Tom Kristensen.

under such conditions but pastor Barratt persevered... Barratt possessed what most people lack; he had faith in his cause.... And if you look at his life's work today, it cannot be denied that the soil he began to cultivate decades ago in the Scandinavian countries, indeed everywhere in the world, is beginning to sprout and grow. Something strange has happened—the storm has stopped... If his name is mentioned today, it is with reverence and admiration for his life's self-denying and faithful work ... Barratt is no ordinary man, but with his immense intelligence, his knowledge in all areas, and his gift of speech, he turns an hour-long conversation into an experience.[132]

This report published by a secular newspaper was surprisingly positive, showing the respect that Barratt had among many Norwegians and Norwegian-Americans, as well as the importance of his role when the Pentecostal movement faced strong opposition.

The Barratts stayed the first months of their journey with his sister, Mary, in Brooklyn. While in New York, Barratt conducted revival meetings at Glad Tidings Tabernacle, and at a Scandinavian Pentecostal church on Staten Island, led by Mikael Hansen. Revival meetings were held also at pastor Helmer Lindblad's Swedish Pentecostal Church in New York City, at pastor Tom Christensen's Eben Ezer in Brooklyn, and at the Norwegian Pentecostal Church in Brooklyn, led by Arne Dahl.[133] Dahl rented the South Reformed Church in Brooklyn for the revival campaign in order to accommodate the crowds.[134]

During this time, the Barratts met many Norwegians, Danes, Swedes, and even Finns whom they had met in Scandinavia earlier. Some had emigrated after the Pentecostal revival began in Norway. Barratt also saw many people who he met during his visit in 1905 and 1906. Many Scandinavians attended Glad Tidings Tabernacle, and pastor Robert Brown told the congregation that he and Barratt were together the night Barratt was Spirit baptized in New York.[135]

After their stay in Brooklyn, the Barratts traveled to Akron, Ohio, and then to Chicago. There he held meetings in a newly-formed

132. "Engelskmanden, som blev Norges mest omtalte Mand," *Nordisk Tidende*, October 20, 1927, 1.

133. For Lindblad, see "Helmer Lindblad hemma hos Herren," *SV*, February 1936, 5.

134. T. B. Barratt, "Amerika-reisen," *KS*, October 29, 1927, 4–7; November 26, 1927, 7; December 3, 1927, 1–2; January 7, 1928, 2–3.

135. T. B. Barratt, "Amerika-reisen," *KS*, November 12 1927, 2–3.

Norwegian congregation named Ebenezer Pinsemission on the west side where Sverre Gustavsen served as pastor. The meetings were hosted in the hall of the Full Gospel Assembly on Mozart Avenue.[136] Barratt commented that he wished he could have stayed six months in Chicago to help Gustavsen raise up a strong Norwegian congregation and encouraged his readers to pray for the Pentecostals of Chicago.[137] Barratt also held an eight-day revival campaign at pastor Efraim Fraim's Philadelphia Church, a Swedish Pentecostal congregation, and taught at the church's Bible school.[138] After this he held meetings at Humboldt Park Swedish Baptist Church led by Victor Norlin, and at the Methodist Episcopal Church on Kedzie Avenue.[139]

The Barratts thereafter traveled to Minneapolis where they held meetings at G. Algot Wikstrom's church, as well as with pastor Frank J. Lindquist's congregation, The Assembly of God Tabernacle, on 13th Street.[140] Then they went to Duluth, and afterwards to Fargo, North Dakota, where Barratt preached in the church of Henry H. Ness. They knew Ness well since Ness had attended their church in Christiania with his parents before emigrating from Norway to America. While in Fargo, Ness told them of the Pentecostal-type revivals in North Dakota and Minnesota that happened before the Azusa Street revival, and Barratt informed the readers of *Korsets Seir* of these occurrences.[141]

On their way to Kansas City, the Barratts attended a revival campaign of Aimee Semple McPherson in Des Moines, Iowa. In Kansas City, Barratt preached at the church led by Arthur F. Johnson, chairman of the Scandinavian Assemblies of God. Thereafter, the Barratts went to Springfield, Missouri, where they stayed with Stanley Frodsham. They continued from there to Denver where they held meetings at an Assemblies of God congregation led by pastor S. H. Patterson and spoke on

---

136. T. B. Barratt, "Amerika-reisen," *KS*, February 11, 1928, 2–3. In 1927, Sverre Gustavsen's address was listed as Den skandinaviske mission Ebenezer, 2838 West North Avenue, Chicago. It seems that permission was given to use "Bethel Full Gospel Assembly" on Mozart Avenue. An evangelist named Harding led the congregation.

137. T. B. Barratt, "Amerika-reisen," *KS*, February 25, 1928, 4.

138. T. B. Barratt, "Amerika-reisen," *KS*, February 11, 1928, 2–3.

139. T. B. Barratt, "Amerika-reisen," *KS*, February 18, 1928, 1–2; February 25, 1928, 4. For Norlin, see *SV*, April 1, 1928, 4.

140. Watson Argue, "The Get Acquainted Page," *Latter Rain Evangel*, January 1934, 8–9.

141. T. B. Barratt, "Amerika-reisen," *KS*, April 21, 1928, 1. The following references from *Korsets Seier* are Barratt's account of his travels in America.

his radio station. From Denver, they went by train to Los Angeles where Barratt preached in the well-known Angelus Temple. He also held meetings for Scandinavians at the Bethel Temple.

In June 1928, the Barratts arrived in San Francisco to participate in the Scandinavian Convention organized by Joseph Ystrøm. While there, he preached in Ystrøm's church, Scandinavian Full Gospel Assembly, located at 3249 Mission Street. He also visited Oakland on the other side of the bay and preached at the Swedish Assembly led by pastor David Nordling.[142] Barratt made further use of his time in the Bay Area, holding a two-week campaign at the English Pentecostal congregation in San Francisco, Glad Tidings Temple, led by pastor Robert J. Craig. Barratt also visited with Carrie Judd Montgomery in Oakland.[143] Together, they participated in the Scandinavian Pentecostal Convention held at Mount Hermon.

Before leaving California Barratt held meetings among Scandinavians in Turlock, Escalon, and Kingsburg.[144] Travelling north they were able to visit and preach in Scandinavian Pentecostal churches in Portland, Oregon, and then in Selah, Tacoma, Aberdeen, and Seattle, Washington. In Seattle, three Pentecostal churches arranged for him to hold tent meetings.[145] After this, they crossed the border into Canada, where they held meetings in Vancouver, Edmonton, Weldon, Parkside, and Winnipeg. From Canada, they traveled to Minot, North Dakota, and again to Minneapolis and St. Paul. They also returned to Chicago and New York City before returning to Europe in October 1928.[146]

During his tour Barratt observed that many Scandinavian-American Pentecostals still read *Korsets Seier* and used *Maran Ata* as their songbook.[147] In several places he was asked to speak about how they had organized Filadelfia Church in Oslo, and he hoped that many new Norwegian Pentecostal churches would be established in the U.S.[148] Barratt observed that there were few Norwegian Pentecostal preachers

142. *KS*, June 30, 1928, 3–4, 7.
143. *KS*, July 7, 1928, 3; August 4, 1928, 2–3.
144. *KS*, August 4, 1928, 3–4, 7; August 11, 1928, 1–3; August 18, 1928, 1–2.
145. *KS*, August 18, 1928, 2–3; September 15, 1928, 3–4; September 1, 1928, 3–4, 6; September 8, 1928, 2–3; September 15, 1928, 3–4; September 22, 1928, 2–3.
146. *KS*, September 22, 1928, 3–4; September 29, 1928, 2–3; October 6, 1928, 2–3; October 13, 1928, 2; October 20, 1928, 2; November 10, 1928, 3–4.
147. *KS*, September 22, 1928, 2–3; November 10, 1928, 4.
148. *KS*, January 28, 1928, 1.

in the U.S.—maybe only ten to twelve. He wrote that there were more Swedish preachers, and some of them pastored congregations with mostly Norwegian members.[149] Several Scandinavian preachers described America as "a difficult field," and were greatly encouraged by Barratt's visit from Scandinavia.[150]

Conclusion

The impact of Norwegian Pentecostals, and especially that of T. B. Barratt on early Scandinavian Pentecostalism, has received little attention in American Pentecostal history. From primary sources, it is evident that Barratt's testimony of his Spirit baptism and the revival in Christiania (Oslo) motivated many Scandinavian-Americans to join the Pentecostal movement. It is also evident that Barratt was effective as an author and defender of Pentecostal doctrine, and that many looked to him for guidance, even though they lived across the Atlantic Ocean.

Furthermore, through Barratt's periodical, *Byposten/ Korsets Seir*, a network of Norwegian Pentecostals in both Norway and America was established early on and continued, which kept their trans-Atlantic connection strong. The Pentecostal movement in Norway grew rapidly, and Norwegians in America looked to Norway to supply evangelists and pastors to help build Scandinavian Pentecostal churches in the U.S. and Canada.

When Barratt toured America, he visited places and people who had sent him letters and subscribed to *Byposten* for years. This further strengthened the ties across the Atlantic. Their connection remained strong for decades until the Norwegian language was no longer used by Norwegian-Americans. Nevertheless, it is important to recognize both the roots and the trans-Atlantic influence of this Norwegian Pentecostal during the first half of the 20th century.

---

149. *KS*, September 1, 1928, 3.
150. Efraim Fraim, "Brev," *KS*, July 7, 1928.

Bibliography

Primary Sources

NEWSPAPERS USED

Aftenposten, Kristiania (Oslo), Norway, 1860–
The Apostolic Faith (*AF*), Los Angeles, 1906–1908
Byposten (*BP*), Kristiania (Oslo), Norway, 1904–1910
Evangelisten, Chicago, 1891–1955
Folke-Vennen (*FV*), Chicago, IL, 1879–1933
Korsets Seir/ Seier (*KS*), Kristiania (Oslo), Norway, 1910–
Kristelig Tidende, Kristiania (Oslo), Norway, 1878–1998
Latter Rain Evangel, Chicago, 1908–1939
Minneapolis Tidende, Minneapolis, 1895–1935
Missionæren, Larvik, Skien, Norway, 1889–1957
Nordisk Tidende, Brooklyn, NY, 1891–1983
Sanningens Vittne (*SV*), Minneapolis, 1911–1939
Svenska Amerikanska Posten, Minneapolis, 1885–1940

OTHER PRIMARY SOURCES

Barratt, Thomas Ball. *A Call to Pentecost*. Sunderland, 1907.
———. *A Friendly Talk with Ministers and Christian Workers on the Baptism in the Holy Ghost*. Sunderland, 1907.
———. *The Gift of Tongues: What Is It?: Being a Reply to A. C. Dixon*, 1914.
———. *In the Days of the Latter Rain*. London: Elim, 1909.
———. *Da jeg fik min pintsedaab og tungemaalsgaven*. Christiania: Bypostens forlag, 1907.
———. *"Tongues": A Reply to Critics*. Sunderland, 1907.
———. *The Truth about the Pentecostal Revival*. London, 1909.
———. *When the Fire Fell, and an Outline of My Life*. Oslo: Alfons Hansen & Sønner, 1927.
Dixon, A. C. *Speaking with Tongues*. Chicago: The Bible Institute Colportage Association, n.d.
Engstrøm, Dagmar. *Ha Tro Til Gud: Alt Er Mulig for Den Som Tror*. Oslo: Filadelfiaforlaget, 1980.

Secondary Sources

Alvarsson, Jan-Åke. "Pingstväckelsens Etablering i Sverige: Från Azusa Street till Skövde På Sju Månader." In *Pingströrelsen: Del 1: Händelser Och Utveckling under 1900-Talet*, edited by Claes Waern, 10–45. Örebro, Sweden: Libris förlag, 2007.
Barratt Lange, Solveig. *T. B. Barratt: Et Herrens Sendebud*. Oslo: Filadelfiaforlaget, 1962.
———, ed. *Thomas Ball Barratt, Erindringer*. Oslo: Filadelfiaforlaget, 1941.
Barratt, Laura. *Minner*. Oslo: Filadelfiaforlaget, 1946.

Bloch-Hoell, Nils. *Pinsebevegelsen: En Undersøkelse Av Pinsebevegelsens Tilblivelse, Utvikling Og Særpreg Med Særlig Henblikk På Bevegelsens Utforming i Norge.* Oslo: Universitetsforlaget, 1956.

Bundy, David. "Spiritual Advice to a Seeker: Letters to T. B. Barratt from Azusa Street, 1906." *Pneuma* 14 (1992) 159–70.

———. *Visions of Apostolic Mission: Scandinavian Pentecostal Mission to 1935.* Uppsala: Uppsala Universitet, 2009.

Dyer, Anne E. "Introduction." In *European Pentecostalism*, edited by William K. Kay and Anne E. Dyer, 1–15. Leiden: Brill, 2011.

Janøy, Jostein. *Tabernaklet Skien: 100 År i Pinsens Tegn.* Skien: Pinsekirken Tabernaklet, 2008.

Lie, Geir. "Oneness Pentecostalism in Norway." *Journal of European Pentecostal Theological Association* 40 (2020) 46–59.

Linderholm, Emanuel. *Pingströrelsen: Dess Förutsättningar Och Uppkomst: Ekstas, under Och Apokalyptik i Bibel Och Nutida Folkereligiositet.* Stockholm: Albert Bonniers Förlag, 1924.

Lovoll, Odd S. *Norske Aviser i Amerika.* Oslo: Scandinavian Academic Press, 2012.

Meier, Ralph. "Fra Kristiania Til Kassel: Pinsebevegelsens Begynnelse i Tyskland Og Forholdet Til Gemeinschaftsbevegelsen." In *Pentekostale Perspektiver*, ed. Knut-Willy Sæther and Karl Inge Tangen, 91–110. Bergen: Fagbokforlaget, 2015.

Richardsen, George. "A Review." In *Salem Pentecostal Assembly 15th Anniversary: 1925–1941.* Brooklyn: n.d. 1941.

Rødland, Kjartan. *Glede i Gud: Pinsekirken Tabernaklet Bergen 1920–2010.* Bergen: Pinsekirken Tabernaklet, 2010.

Skibsted, Werner. *Oscar Halvorsen, liv og virke; skildring fra denne kjente predikants liv og virke, like fra de bevegede vekkelsestider i begynnelsen av dette århundre og til vår tid.* Oslo: Filadelfiaforlaget, 1947.

Strand, A. E. ed. *A History of the Norwegians of Illinois.* Chicago: John Anderson, 1905.

Synan, Vinson. *The Holiness-Pentecostal Tradition: Charismatic Movements in the Twentieth Century.* Grand Rapids: Eerdmans, 1997.

Ystebø Alegre, Rakel. "The Pentecostal Apologetics of T. B. Barratt: Defining and Defending the Faith 1906–1909." PhD diss., Regent University, 2019.

———. "Women in Pentecostalism in Europe." In *Global Renewal Christianity: Spirit-Empowered Movements Past, Present and Future, Vol. IV: Europe and North America*, edited by Vinson Synan and Amos Yong, 259–75. Lake Mary, FL: Charisma House, 2017.

Østrem, Nils Olav. *Norsk Utvandringshistorie.* 2nd ed. Oslo: Det Norske Samlaget, 2014.

Chapter Five

Scandinavian-Americans and the General Council of the Assemblies of God (AG), 1906–1952

DARRIN J. RODGERS

THE GENERAL COUNCIL OF the Assemblies of God (AG) was organized in April 1914, in Hot Springs, Arkansas, in order to provide accountability, structure, and unity so that Pentecostals could better carry out the mission of God in their communities and around the world.[1] This vision transcended the racial and social divides, and the Assemblies of God grew to become a multi-ethnic and international movement. While most other U.S. Pentecostal denominations were regionally defined, the AG claimed a broad nationwide constituency. The approximately 300 men and women who came together in Hot Springs

---

1. Assemblies of God (AG) founders, in their "Call to Hot Springs," laid out five purposes for organization: 1) to encourage unity in doctrine; 2) to "conserve the work" 3) to provide support and accountability for missions; 4) to establish a legal foundation for congregations; and 5) to "establish a general Bible Training School with a literary department." *Word and Witness*, December 20, 1913, 1.

organized a fellowship that would become one of the largest families of Christian churches in the world.²

Participants at the organizational general council represented a variety of independent churches and networks of churches. Almost all participants were white, and most if not all spoke English as their primary language. A few African-Americans were in attendance. Church of God in Christ Bishop Charles H. Mason preached and brought a black gospel choir from Lexington, Mississippi, but they did not join the newly-formed AG. Two Cherokees from Oklahoma—Watt Walker and William H. Boyles—were in attendance and were founding AG ministers.

At least one of the AG founders—R. L. Erickson—had a Scandinavian heritage. Rasmus Lee Erickson (1874–1944), born in Minnesota to Norwegian immigrants, was pastor of the prominent Stone Church in Chicago. He left the AG in 1915 but remained active as an independent Pentecostal evangelist. His daughter married A. G. Garr, the pioneer Pentecostal missionary from the Azusa Street revival.³

The AG quickly expanded across the ethnic divides. The AG ordained its first known Hispanic minister in 1914 (Antonio Ríos Morin) and its first African-American in 1915 (Ellsworth S. Thomas). It created a conference for Hispanic churches in the US in 1918 (later known as the Latin American District). The German Branch formed in 1922 to serve German speakers in the US, and in the 1940s and 1950s eight additional language branches in the US formed (Greek, Hungarian, Italian, Philippine, Polish, Russian, Ukrainian, and Yugoslavian). Language branches functioned similar to English-language geographic districts.⁴

While the AG did not form a language branch for Scandinavians in the US, Scandinavian ministers and Scandinavian-majority churches were scattered among the geographic districts. This chapter shows that districts located primarily in the Midwest and Northwest included large numbers of Scandinavian ministers and churches, and that many leading AG church leaders and educators came from Scandinavian backgrounds. Scandinavian AG ministers started three AG ministerial training schools (North Central Bible Institute, Minneapolis, MN; Northwest Bible Institute, Seattle, WA; and Southwestern Bible Institute, Enid, OK). Furthermore, based on comparative research of the same

---

2. In 2022, the AG claimed just under 3 million U.S. adherents and 85,393,883 adherents in affiliated national fellowships around the world.

3. "Minister Dies of Injuries," *The Charlotte Observer*, January 2, 1945, 5.

4. Rodgers, "Fully Committed," 11–12.

Scandinavian surnames, this chapter argues that between 1935 and 1952, the AG had four to five times the number of ministers and missionaries with the same Scandinavian surnames as those who affiliated with the Independent Assemblies of God (IAG), indicating that a large majority of Scandinavian-American Pentecostals belonged to the AG.

Certain Scandinavian AG leaders and churches have received attention in historical and scholarly literature, but little has been written about Scandinavians in general in AG history. This is partly because information on Scandinavians as a group in the AG is difficult to obtain, as they were not organized into a separate language branch and instead blended in with other churches and ministers. Histories have been written of Germans, Italians, and various eastern Europeans in the AG, but not about Scandinavians, even though Scandinavians may have been more numerous than some of the other ethnic groups in the AG.

Early Scandinavians in the Assemblies of God (AG)

While only one Scandinavian is known to have attended the April 1914 organizational general council, word spread quickly about the newly-organized Pentecostal fellowship. The AG ministerial roster from November 1914 included at least 10 Scandinavians: Carrie P. Anderson (Norwegian-born minister in Detroit Harbor, WI); Bernt and Magna Berntsen (Norwegian-American missionaries to China); Charles O. Carlson (Norwegian-born minister in Stephen, MN); Rasmus L. Erickson (Norwegian-American minister in Chicago, IL); Harold E. and Margaret Hansen (Norwegian-American ministers in West Berkeley, CA); J. G. Emil Lindstrom (Swedish-American minister in Chicago, IL); Beda Magnussen (Norwegian-American minister in Chicago, IL); and Niels C. Sorensen (Danish-born missionary in Argentina).

Additional Scandinavian Pentecostal ministers and missionaries, mostly from independent churches, began to affiliate with the AG. Not surprisingly, most stateside ministers were located in regions with large Scandinavian populations—the Midwest, Washington, California, and the Northeast. Some ministers were the product of a spiritual awakening in the late 1890s and early 1900s among Scandinavians that birthed a number of congregations, primarily in Minnesota and the Dakotas, that practiced speaking in tongues and healing. This awakening predated the Topeka (1901) and Azusa Street (1906–1909) revivals, often considered the focal points of the emerging Pentecostal movement in America. Many leaders in these early revivals later joined the AG, including Carl M. Hanson, a Norwegian-American evangelist who witnessed a glossolalic revival in Grafton, North Dakota in 1895, and John Thompson, pastor of the Swedish Free Mission in Moorhead, Minnesota, which experienced several protracted revivals in the late 1890s and early 1900s.[5]

Several Scandinavians who affiliated with the AG in 1914 had a call to missions work. Veteran missionaries Bernt and Magna Berntsen received their Pentecostal baptism and transferred from the non-denominational South Zhili Mission to the AG, which provided opportunities to network with and receive support from likeminded Pentecostals.[6] Harold and Margaret Hansen had missionary experience in Hawaii for almost six years prior to ministering in California when they joined the AG. They became AG missionaries to China in 1915.[7] Carrie P. Anderson was serving as a minister in Wisconsin when she joined the AG, and she became the AG's first missionary to South China, arriving in late 1914.

The number of Scandinavians in the AG continued to grow. The 1920 AG ministerial roster included at least 32 Scandinavians: Paul J. Andreasen (Danish-born missionary to India); Christian and Agnes Beckdahl (Danish and Norwegian-born missionaries to India); Edwin and Jennie Bendiksen (Norwegian-born missionaries to Belgian Congo); Gideon A. Dahlstein (Swedish-born missionary to China); Elmer C. and Emma Erickson (Swedish-American ministers in Duluth, MN); Harold E. and Margaret Hansen (Norwegian-American missionaries to China); Carl M. Hanson (Norwegian-American minister in Dalton, MN); Arthur F. and Beatrice F. Johnson (Swedish-born missionaries to Europe); Ruth Amanda Johnson (Swedish-American missionary to Japan); Segrid A. Johnson (Swedish-American minister in Los Angeles, CA); Frank Lindblad (Swedish-American minister in Seattle, WA); J. G. Emil Lindstrom (Swedish-American minister in New York, NY); Albert and Ella Moseid (Norwegian-American ministers in Colfax, WI); Niels G. Nielsen (Danish-born minister in Hartford, CT); Ingeborg Norli (Norwegian-born missionary to China); Carolina Nylander (Swedish-born minister

---

5. Rodgers, *Northern Harvest*, 4–17; Rodgers, "Rediscovering Pentecostalism's Diverse Roots," 50; Rodgers, "Pentecostal Origins in Scandinavian Pietism on the Great Plains," 301–29.

6. Iap, "Bernt Berntsen," 91–106.

7. "Brother and Sister Hansen, North China," *Pentecostal Evangel*, February 13, 1915, 4.

in Seattle, WA); Oscar Olsen (Norwegian-American minister in Thief River Falls, MN); James E., Anna C., and Rasmus S. Rasmussen (Danish-American ministers in Egeland, ND); Niels C. and Annina Sorensen (Danish-born missionaries in Argentina); Niels P. and Ellen K. Thomsen (Danish-American missionaries to India); and Ketil and Gertude Timrud (Norwegian-born missionaries to India).

The number of Scandinavian missionaries is remarkable. Thirty percent of Scandinavians on the November 1914 AG ministerial roster (3 of 10 ministers) were missionaries. This increased to 56 percent of Scandinavians on the 1920 roster (18 of 32 ministers) who were missionaries. The large number of Scandinavians who served as missionaries underscores the emphasis on missions among Scandinavian Pentecostals. The fact that more than half of Scandinavian AG credential holders were missionaries also suggests that missionaries were more likely than stateside ministers to affiliate with the AG. Scandinavian pastors and evangelists may not have perceived the need to associate with the AG, while missionaries saw the advantage of affiliating with a larger organization for the purpose of supporting their missionary call.[8]

It is possible to track the growing presence of Scandinavian ministers in the AG by researching the background of ministers on the annual AG ministerial lists, which began publication in November 1914. The lists provide names of ministers and missionaries and the cities where they resided. Applications for AG credentials, which have been deposited at the Flower Pentecostal Heritage Center (the archives of the AG), required that applicants state "Race and Nationality." Applicants from Scandinavian backgrounds sometimes stated their national background, but others simply stated "white" or "American." Census and genealogical records can shed further light on a minister's ethnic identity. A comprehensive statistical analysis of the growing number of Scandinavian AG ministers would be valuable, but it is beyond the scope of this study.

Another approach to tracking the increase in the number of Scandinavian AG ministers is to tally the number of ministers and missionaries with surnames common among Scandinavians from the annual AG ministerial lists. Charts 1 and 2 document the number of ministers with nine common Scandinavian surnames from the ministerial lists from 1914 through 1925. Some people with these surnames were Scandinavian,

---

8. Historian David Bundy noted that some early Scandinavian AG missionaries also claimed affiliation with other groups. Bundy, *Visions of Apostolic Mission*, 323–24.

others were not. These charts indicate likely growth of the number of Scandinavians among the ranks of AG ministers.

Chart 1

AG Ministers + Missionaries	1914	1915	1916	1917	1918	1919
Andersen/Anderson	3	4	4	4	5	7
Carlsen/Carlson	1	1	0	0	0	0
Erickson/Ericson	1	0	0	1	1	2+1
Hansen/Hanson	2	3	1	3	3+3	3+3
Johnsen/Johnson	5	4	1	5+2	8+2	5+5
Nelson/Nilsen	1	1	1	4	3	2+2
Olsen/Olson/Olsson	1	1	0	0	1	1
Petersen/Peterson	0	0	0	1	2	2
Rasmussen	0	0	0	0	2	3
Total	14	14	7	18+2	25+5	25+11

Chart 2

AG Ministers+ Missionaries	1920	1921	1922	1923	1924	1925
Andersen/Anderson	4+2	4+3	9+3	10+3	9+3	9+4
Carlsen/Carlson	0+1	0+1	0+1	0+1	0+1	0+1
Erickson/Ericson	2+1	2+1	0+1	0+1	0+2	0+3
Hansen/Hanson	3+3	5+2	3+3	3+3	3+2	?+?
Johnsen/Johnson	6+5	5+5	5+4	7+2	10	9
Nelson/Nilsen	3	3	4	3	2	3
Olsen/Olson/Olsson	1	1	1	2	2	3
Petersen/Peterson	2	2	1	1	3	4
Rasmussen	3	2	2	2	2	2+1
Total	24+12	24+12	25+12	28+10	31+8	32+11

Chart 1 lists 14 ministers with the surnames in 1914 and 1915. The number dropped to seven in the 1916 list, presumably due to the AG's adoption of the Statement of Fundamental Truths, which affirmed the Fellowship's Trinitarian and evangelical witness. The adoption of the statement of faith resulted in the departure of Oneness advocates, as well as those who opposed what was perceived as "creedalism." Missionaries Bernt and Magna Berntsen had embraced the Oneness movement and were among those who left the AG in 1916.

However, in 1917 and 1918 the number of ministers with the surnames grew significantly. This growth may have been party due to the Selective Service Act of 1917, which allowed people to claim conscientious objector status if they were members of a "well recognized sect" that was on record as being opposed to killing in war. Pentecostals tended to be pacifist in World War I, and many Pentecostal ministers affiliated with the AG, which took a pacifist position, in order to secure their right to be conscientious objectors.[9] Independent Scandinavian ministers were among those who joined the AG for this reason. Elmer C. Erickson, a Scandinavian minister from Duluth, Minnesota, according to a 1975 interview, "declared himself a pacifist but was spared active duty only because of his Assembly of God ordination papers."[10]

Organization of Districts

At the AG's organizational general council in April 1914, delegates voted to recommend that "Local Assemblies in the various fields establish District or State Councils, and that the Presbytery be authorized to appoint Elders or Evangelists to assist the local Assemblies of God in the recognition and establishing of the District or State Council."[11] Within a year, the Arkansas, Southern Missouri, Texas, and West Central (consisting of Iowa and northern Missouri) districts were organized.

Ministers and congregations, scattered and far-between, had few structures for cooperation prior to the formation of districts. When districts formed, they more aggressively promoted cooperative ministries, such as district camp meetings, church planting, missions, formal ministerial training, and evangelism. These district ministries helped bring

9. Alexander, *Peace to War*.
10. Tuttle, "Pentecostal Foundations Project."
11. *Assemblies of God General Council Minutes*, April 1914, 6.

more people into the Pentecostal and AG folds and led to the formation of new AG churches.

Most Scandinavian Pentecostals lived in the Upper Midwest, Northeast, and Northwest. Districts in these regions were formed in the late 1910s and early 1920s. The Northwest and North Central districts had the largest number of Scandinavian ministers and churches.

The Northwest District (consisting of Alaska, Idaho, Oregon, Washington, and western Montana) was formed in June 1919. There were no Scandinavian AG ministers present at the organizational meeting in Seattle, but Swedish-born minister Carolina Nylander affiliated shortly after the meeting. The second superintendent, Samuel Swanson, who served from 1930 until 1935, was an immigrant from Sweden. Most early Scandinavians in the AG in the Northwest District were in Washington. A number of independent Scandinavian Pentecostal churches existed in the Northwest, several of which came into the AG: Ballard Pentecostal Tabernacle in Seattle (pastored by Arvid Ohrnell), Evangel Temple in Seattle (founded by Martin J. Hagli); Christ Memorial Church in Poulsbo (founded by Henrik Langeland in 1909), and Pentecostal AG in Spokane (led by pastor James E. Rasmussen from 1919 until 1944). Scandinavian AG evangelists started additional churches. Frank Lindblad started what became Fremont Pentecostal Tabernacle in Seattle in the 1920s, and Edwin Swanson founded what came to be known as First Assembly of God in Kelso in 1923.[12]

The Northwest produced many Scandinavian Pentecostal missionaries. B. P. Wilson compiled a scrapbook, "Early Pentecostal and Assemblies of God Missionaries of the Northwest District," in which he identified 115 family units from the Northwest that served overseas as missionaries. The scrapbook included missionaries who departed for the mission field between 1907 and 1953 and included mostly AG missionaries from the Northwest, but also some who were not AG or who belonged to other districts, but who had some influence in the Northwest District. The scrapbook included 24 Scandinavian family units: Arthur Ahlberg, Levone Katherine Dahl, Agnes Hammarberg, Signe Alice Hanger, Harold E. Hansen, Wesley Daniel Hansen, Hazel Irene Haugland, Clara Jensen, Helen Louise Johnson, Marie Johnsrud, Martin Kvamme, Martine (Marthina) Kvamme, Algot R. Mattson, Edna O. Pearson, Dagny Marie Peterson, Kari S. Rønnestad, Arthur Helmer Segerquist, Harold Maynard Skoog, John

---

12. Tanneberg, *Let Light Shine Out*, 14–27.

and Carri (Romenstad) Stokkan, Robert Ball Tangen, Magnus Emanuel Udd, Ragnar E. Udd, and Adolph C. Wingard.[13]

The North Central District (consisting of Minnesota, North Dakota, South Dakota, and Wisconsin) was formed in November 1922. Seventeen people were at the organizational meeting, nine of whom were Scandinavian: Niels G. Nielsen; Ragnar S. Peterson, Chrest and Amanda Knudsen, Carl M. Hanson, Frank J. Lindquist, Hjalmer M. and Olga Johnson (Norwegian-American ministers in Osseo, Wisconsin), and Carl Walblom. Participants unanimously elected Norwegian Pentecostal pioneer Carl M. Hanson to serve as the first District Chairman. Hanson had been Spirit-baptized in about 1899 and had been a leader in the early Scandinavian Pentecostal awakening in the 1890s and early 1900s in Minnesota and the Dakotas. In 1923, the District Council elected Frank J. Lindquist to succeed Hanson, and Herman G. Johnson to serve as Secretary-Treasurer. Lindquist and Johnson were both Swedes. At the time, Lindquist was pastor of the AG in Minot, North Dakota, and Johnson, a charter member of the AG in Regan, North Dakota, was an evangelist in North Dakota.[14]

The North Central District grew rapidly as evangelists canvassed the region. The district also grew in territory, adding Montana in 1925. The District's Lake Geneva campgrounds near Alexandria, Minnesota, attracted thousands of people to its summer camp meetings. Services in the large tabernacle were held in English, while German and Scandinavian speakers gathered in separate tents to hear the gospel in their tongues.[15] A North Central District directory, published in 1930, listed the number of congregations in each state: Minnesota (18); Montana (11); North Dakota (20); South Dakota (4); and Wisconsin (12).[16] In the early decades of the district, about half of the churches and ministers were Scandinavian, although most of the Scandinavian churches conducted services in English. The North Central District was the closest the AG came to having a Scandinavian branch. AG churches and ministers

---

13. Wilson, "Early Pentecostal and Assemblies of God Missionaries of the Northwest District."

14. *Minutes of the North Central District Council of the Assemblies of God, 1922–1926 combined.*

15. *North Central District Council of the Assemblies of God Minutes, 1926.*

16. "Directory of Assemblies in North Central District," *Gospel Broadcast*, February 1930, 6.

in the Dakotas, Wisconsin, and Montana withdrew from the North Central District Council and formed separate state districts in 1936.[17]

Several regional centers of revival in the North Central District emerged. The Egeland Free Mission, an independent Scandinavian congregation in Egeland, North Dakota, accepted the Pentecostal message in 1915 and became a focal point of revival in north central North Dakota. The Egeland congregation included the large Rasmussen family, consisting of Danish and Norwegian immigrants, some of whom became active in ministry in North Dakota, Montana, and Washington. The Noonan AG, organized in 1918, quickly grew and launched outreaches into surrounding communities in northwest North Dakota. By the 1920s, the early enthusiasts had established Pentecostal churches or outstations in most towns in Divide, Burke, and northern Williams counties. Most members of these churches were Norwegian, reflecting the ethnic makeup of the counties. G. Raymond Carlson, a Norwegian-American from Crosby, went on to serve as superintendent of the North Central District (1945–1961), president of North Central Bible College (1961–1969), Assistant General Superintendent of the AG (1969–1985), and General Superintendent of the AG (1985–1993).[18]

In south central North Dakota, a 1920 revival among the Swedes in the Regan and Wilton communities spread to the Swedes at Kulm, and later to Bismarck. Herman G. Johnson, raised as a Swedish Baptist and a charter member of the Regan AG, went on to become the first superintendent of the North Dakota District (1936–1951). Free Pentecostalism took root among Scandinavians in southwestern North Dakota in the 1920s. Fear of organization was gradually overcome and strong AG churches developed at Scranton, Rhame, and Hettinger. In Fargo, Norwegian immigrant Henry H. Ness pioneered Gospel Tabernacle in 1926, which grew to 500 adherents by his departure in 1933. The Fargo church helped establish or strengthen churches throughout eastern North Dakota and western Minnesota.

In South Dakota, Norwegian-American Arthur F. Berg served as pastor in Sisseton (1926–1930) and Sioux Falls (1930–1959), as well as superintendent of the South Dakota District from 1936 to 1944. Before coming

---

17. Rodgers, *Northern Harvest*, 51.

18. Hall, "G. Raymond Carlson, The Early Years in the Upper Midwest," 5–8; Hall, "G. Raymond Carlson," 11–15.

to South Dakota, he served as a missionary in Belgian Congo (1922–1926). Berg's wife, Anna, was the daughter of Carl M. Hanson.[19]

C. M. Hanson and daughter Anna Hanson Berg, Used by permission of Flower Pentecostal Heritage Center, Springfield, Missouri.

Wisconsin also boasts a large number of Scandinavians in the AG. Edwin A. Beck, an immigrant from Finland, served as superintendent of the Wisconsin-Northern Michigan District from 1944 to 1946. Swedish-American David M. Carlson also served in the role from 1947 to 1948.[20]

Scandinavians were in the minority in other districts, but still played important AG leadership roles. Swedish-American Arthur G. Osterberg served as superintendent of the Southern California District from 1923 to 1938. His parents, Cenna and Louis, had roots in the Swedish Baptist Church before becoming leaders at the Azusa Street Mission.[21] Victor G. Greisen, a Danish immigrant, served as superintendent of the Kansas District from 1938 to 1955.[22] Norwegian-American

19. "Arthur F. Berg with Christ," *Pentecostal Evangel*, March 11, 1984, 25.

20. Wisconsin-Northern Michigan District history files, FPHC.

21. Gustafson, "Pentecostal Evangelist Cenna Osterberg and the Azusa Street Mission," 16–18.

22. "Former District Superintendent with the Lord," *Pentecostal Evangel*, August 31, 1980, 25; Victor G. Greisen, Autobiography, unpublished manuscript, FPHC; Greisen, *Fra skibsdreng til biskop*.

Oscar C. Arneson served as superintendent of the Southern Idaho District from 1945 to 1952.[23]

Scandinavian Contributions to AG Education and Scholarship

Scandinavians made significant contributions to AG ministerial education and theological scholarship. Perhaps the strongest enduring evidence of this is that three prominent AG universities were founded by Scandinavian-Americans: P. C. Nelson (Southwestern Assemblies of God University, Waxahachie, Texas), Frank J. Lindquist (North Central University, Minneapolis, Minnesota), and Henry H. Ness (Northwest University, Kirkland, Washington).

P. C. Nelson

Southwestern Bible Institute (Enid, OK), now known as Nelson University (Waxahachie, TX), was started in 1927 by Danish immigrant Peter Christopher Nelson (1868–1942). Nelson was a leading Baptist evangelist, pastor, and writer. Following his Spirit baptism in 1920, he joined the AG. He emerged as one of the most articulate Pentecostal theologians of his era.

Born into a Baptist family in Denmark, Nelson and his family immigrated to America in 1872 and settled in Iowa. Nelson felt a calling to preach at age 20 and prepared for the ministry at the Baptist Theological Seminary in Chicago, Illinois, Denison College in Granville, Ohio, and Rochester Theological Seminary in Rochester, New York. He studied theology, languages, and became editor of the missionary department of *The Baptist Record* magazine. Nelson studied under Dr. Augustus Strong, one of the most notable Baptist theologians of the era. Nelson adopted Strong's belief that the Bible was the inspired word of God, and that a Christian needed the Holy Spirit to understand Scripture.[24]

Following graduation from seminary in 1902, Nelson accepted a pastorate in Iowa. In 1904, he launched into evangelistic ministry and became a leading Baptist evangelist in the Midwest. He assembled an

---

23. Brueggemann, *Assemblies of God of Southern Idaho*, 2.

24. Burke and Holder, "Daddy Nelson," 21; Burke and Holder, *Whole Gospel for the Whole World*, 31–43.

entourage of evangelists and musicians known as the Nelson Evangelistic Party and held large, extended revival campaigns in churches, city auditoriums, opera houses, and tents in dozens of states. In 1919, Nelson returned to local church ministry and became pastor of Conley Memorial Baptist Church in Detroit.[25]

Nelson's bedrock belief in the authority of scripture, which he imbibed from his Baptist background, led him to eventually embrace Pentecostalism. A group of Baptist elders, interviewing Nelson as a pastoral candidate, once asked him, "Would you stay with the Baptists or stand on the Bible?" Nelson responded, "I will stick with the Bible, no matter what becomes of the Baptists!" At that time, of course, Nelson had no intention of leaving the Baptist church.[26]

Two experiences in 1920 challenged Nelson's assumptions about how he read the Bible. Like many evangelicals at the time, Nelson read his own experiences (or lack of them) onto Scripture, assuming the cessation of certain biblical spiritual gifts and that miracles rarely, if ever, still occurred. At dinner with friends in 1920, Nelson for the first time heard someone speaking in an unknown tongue. Nelson began to search Scripture and concluded that he could not biblically support his belief that such gifts had ceased.[27]

Several months later, an automobile struck Nelson and severely injured him. Following a miraculous healing, Nelson made a promise to God that he would tell the world about what happened to him. Nelson kept his promise. Within a few weeks, he was Spirit-baptized, resigned his pastorate, and went back into evangelistic ministry. He held his first campaign in Wichita, Kansas, in March and April 1921, and hundreds of people accepted Christ or were healed. Nelson received widespread support from Baptists, Pentecostals, and people from many other churches.

After engaging in energetic ministry as an independent evangelist for several years, Nelson recognized the value of belonging to an organization that could provide networking opportunities and structures to help advance the young Pentecostal movement. He joined the AG in 1925 and, almost immediately, began to provide leadership within the young fellowship.[28]

25. Burke and Holder, *Whole Gospel for the Whole World*, 43–82.
26. Burke and Holder, "Daddy Nelson," 21.
27. Burke and Holder, *Whole Gospel for the Whole World*, 83–86.
28. Burke and Holder, *Whole Gospel for the Whole World*, 121–32.

A long-standing advocate of solid biblical training for ministers, Nelson started Southwestern Bible School in Enid, Oklahoma, in 1927. He also operated a publishing house, Southwestern Press, that churned out numerous theological books for his students and the broader Pentecostal movement.[29]

Nelson's linguistic abilities were legendary. He learned English and several Scandinavian languages at a young age. In college and seminary, he concentrated on the study of foreign languages. He believed that studying languages would help him get close to immigrants and provide opportunities to share the gospel. According to a 1915 biographical sketch, Nelson had a reading knowledge of twenty-five languages (primarily biblical, classical, and European) and could conduct religious services in several of them.[30]

Nelson's prolific pen yielded seven major theological works and another half dozen smaller booklets. His 1934 translation of Eric Lund's *Hermeneutics* from Spanish into English remained a standard Bible college text for decades.[31] Nelson's book which achieved the greatest influence, *Bible Doctrines* (1934), was a commentary on the Statement of Fundamental Truths. The volume has been translated into numerous

---

29. Burke and Holder, *Whole Gospel for the Whole World*, 133–51.

30. According to a 1915 biographical sketch, written when he was still a Baptist minister: "As a student he especially distinguished himself in the languages, acquiring a good knowledge of Latin, Greek, French, German, Dutch, Spanish, Italian, Portuguese, Japanese, Hebrew, Aramaic, the Scandinavian languages, and others. He has a reading knowledge of twenty-five languages and can conduct religious services in several of them. While at Rochester he was translator for the Vick Seed Company, which all pioneers of Shelby County will remember and which at that time did a large business necessitating the use of fifteen foreign languages. He was tutor in Latin and Greek at Denison University and conducted a school of modern languages in one of the New York universities. For a number of years, he took regularly more than a dozen foreign periodicals, receiving these in exchange for a paper in which he conducted the department of missions." "Rev. P. C. Nelson," in White, *Past and Present of Shelby County, Iowa*, 1:549–50. This claim about Nelson's linguistic expertise is repeated in a self-published promotional tract from the same era, stating that he was a "natural linguist, being able to speak several languages and to read twenty-five. "Fifteenth Season," tract, Southwestern Assemblies of God University archives. Nelson's academic prowess was legendary. Hugh Jeter recalled, "According to one report, the *Literary Digest* classified him as one of the very top men worldwide in the field of theology." Jeter, "P. C. Nelson I Knew," 14. While the article from the *Literary Digest* has not been located, the story has been widely repeated and is firmly etched in Nelson lore.

31. Lund, *Hermeneutics*.

other languages, making it one of the most widely-read AG theological textbooks around the world.³²

Nelson worked long hours and slept little, dedicating himself to preaching, teaching, writing, and carrying out his administrative duties. Nelson's labors took their toll on his health, and he literally worked himself to death. P. C. Nelson died on October 26, 1942, but his influence continues through the people he touched, through his writings, and through Southwestern Assemblies of God University, named today Nelson University.³³

Frank J. Lindquist

North Central Bible Institute (Minneapolis), now known as North Central University, was started in 1930 by Frank J. Lindquist (1898–1989). Lindquist, raised in the Swedish Free Mission, became a leading AG pastor, educator, and district superintendent.

Lindquist was born into a Swedish-American community in McKeesport, Pennsylvania. His parents immigrated from Sweden in the 1880s and were active in the Swedish Free Mission, where his father was a deacon. About thirty members of the church, including the Lindquist family, were swept up in a Pentecostal revival in 1914 and formed a new independent Pentecostal congregation.³⁴

---

32. Nelson, *Bible Doctrines*.
33. "With the Lord," *Pentecostal Evangel*, November 7, 1942, 3.
34. Frank J. Lindquist, "Pioneering in the Midwest," *Pentecostal Evangel*, October 30, 1966, 13.

Frank J. Lindquist, Used by Permission of the Flower Pentecostal Heritage Center, Springfield, Missouri

Lindquist was a studious young man and felt called to the ministry, but he had no formal ministry training. Nevertheless, in 1920 he joined with two young evangelists, James Menzie and Ben Hardin, who were holding tent meetings for several weeks in Gary, Indiana. In 1921, Lindquist ventured further into ministry, when he and Menzie traveled to Minnesota, where they evangelized in Staples, Brainerd, Pillager, Motley, Crosby, Ironton, and Casino. They helped start new AG churches in these mostly-Scandinavian communities.[35]

In 1922, Lindquist became a founding member of the North Central District. He served short stints as pastor in Brainerd, Minnesota, and Minot, North Dakota. He was elected to serve as North Central District superintendent in 1923. In 1924, he became pastor of Minneapolis Gospel Tabernacle, which originated in 1907 as an outgrowth of the Azusa Street Revival. The building had seating for 500 people but had declined to only 41 members. The congregation boomed under Lindquist's leadership and, in 1930, erected a new brick building and established North Central Bible Institute. In 1930, the congregation had 262 adult

---

35. Gohr, "Harvest in Minnesota," 10.

members, the majority of whom were Scandinavian. Numerous Scandinavian members of Minneapolis Gospel Tabernacle went on to serve as pastors and evangelists across the US and missionaries in other nations. Lindquist served as district superintendent until 1945, as president of the school until 1961, and as pastor of the congregation until 1967.[36]

Henry H. Ness

Northwest Bible Institute (Seattle, WA), now known as Northwest University (Kirkland, WA), was started in 1934 by Norwegian immigrant Henry H. Ness (1894–1970). Ness was an influential AG pastor, educator, and writer.

Ness was born in Oslo, Norway, where his parents were members of the Filadelfia Church, where T. B. Barratt served as pastor. Like many of his friends, Ness felt the lure of America. In 1911, when Ness was only 17 years old, he left Norway and set sail for America. Ness initially settled in Chicago and then moved to Minneapolis, where he married and became a successful businessman. In his rush to achieve success, Ness neglected his spiritual life. He replaced the heart-felt Christian faith of his Norwegian upbringing with American materialism. One Sunday evening in the early 1920s, his wife, Anna, attended a Pentecostal service in Minneapolis and committed herself to God. She came home with a radiant countenance, which caused Ness to recommit his life to God. The Nesses joined Minneapolis Gospel Tabernacle.[37]

Ness felt called to the ministry and, in 1925, he accepted the pastorate of a small AG church in Brainerd, Minnesota. The following year, he moved to Fargo, North Dakota, where he pioneered Fargo Gospel Tabernacle, an AG congregation. During the seven years of his Fargo pastorate, the church grew to 500 members. He united several groups of Pentecostals in the region, including a group of former members of the Swedish Free Mission in neighboring Moorhead, Minnesota, where people began experiencing the gift of speaking in tongues in the 1890s.[38]

---

36. Armstrong, *Why Not?*, 33–53, 87–114. See also *Historical Sketches of the Minneapolis Gospel Tabernacle, 1907–1930*.

37. "Biography of Our Principal, Rev. Henry H. Ness," 11.

38. Rodgers, *Northern Harvest*, 139.

Ness documented the story of this early Scandinavian-American Pentecostal revival in his book, *Demonstration of the Holy Spirit*.[39]

In 1933, Ness accepted a call to pastor another congregation of Scandinavian immigrants—Hollywood Temple, located in Seattle, Washington. The congregation emerged from a Pentecostal revival among Baptist churches in Seattle in the early 1920s. Founded in 1927 by former members of Elim Swedish Baptist Church, the new congregation was initially called Hollywood Temple Full Gospel Baptist Church.[40]

Ness led the congregation to affiliate with the AG in January 1934. Later that year, he founded Northwest Bible Institute, which was initially located on the church property. The college flourished, and the church planted several daughter congregations in the region. He served as pastor and college president until 1948, when he was appointed by the Governor to be chairman of the Washington State Board of Prison Terms and Paroles, a position he held for six years. Ness was a respected minister and community leader. He authored several books, including the widely-read *Dunamis and the Church* published in 1968. When Henry H. Ness died in 1970, he left behind numerous institutions and countless people impacted by his ministry.[41]

AG Ecclesiological Vision

AG founders envisioned a fellowship that would both protect the sovereignty of the local church and provide accountability and structures that would serve the broader church (such as schools, a publishing house, and a missions agency) that local congregations could not easily provide by themselves. In 1914, the AG was a very loose network of Pentecostal ministers. There was no statement of faith, no constitution and bylaws, and churches could not affiliate. The AG gradually became more centralized, adopting a statement of faith in 1916 (in response to the Oneness movement), creating structures for accountability, and developing numerous national ministries. The AG changed its polity to allow churches to affiliate in 1917 so that local church members could claim to be members of

---

39. See Ness, *Demonstration of the Holy Spirit*.
40. "Biography of Our Principal, Rev. Henry H. Ness," 11.
41. "Henry H. Ness," *Pentecostal Evangel*, March 22, 1970, 28.

the AG and take advantage of the AG's conscientious objector status.[42] The AG adopted a constitution and bylaws in 1927.[43]

The AG, from its outset, departed from strict congregationalism when the founding general council authorized the appointment of twelve representatives "to act in all necessary matters on behalf of this General Council as a Home and Foreign Missionary and Executive Presbytery." The AG developed a polity that was a hybrid of congregationalism (affirming the "sovereignty of the local church") and presbyterianism (providing for governance by ministers elected at the district and national levels).[44]

The AG developed its ecclesiology partly as a response to a tendency toward heresy and authoritarianism that existed in some quarters of the Pentecostal movement. Pentecostals, since the beginning of the twentieth century, have grappled with how to respond to these problems, as well as how to create educational and accountability structures that would prevent or mitigate against the development of new problems.

Early American Pentecostals were painfully aware of faith leaders within their own traditions who embraced heresies and authoritarianism. Two founders of utopian communities who made substantial impacts of the emerging Pentecostal movement—John Alexander Dowie (Zion City, Illinois) and Frank Sandford (Shiloh, Maine)—made frequent headlines with their eccentricities and illegal activities. Dowie claimed to be Elijah the Restorer in 1901, and Sandford was convicted of manslaughter in 1911, resulting from his abusive discipline.[45]

Pentecostal pioneer Charles F. Parham taught various problematic doctrines, including annihilationism (the belief that God will destroy the wicked rather than allow them to endure eternal conscious torment) and Anglo-Israelism (the belief that European peoples descended from the lost tribes of Israel). Parham tried to assert control over the Azusa Street revival and other early Pentecostals, but his influence was significantly diminished following publicity about his alleged homosexual conduct.[46]

Scandinavian-American Pentecostals were not immune to controversies over false doctrine or extreme practices. Frank J. Lindquist

42. "The Pentecostal Movement and the Conscription Law," *Weekly Evangel*, August 4, 1917, 6–7; Pacifism/War Correspondence.

43. McGee, *People of the Spirit*, 104.

44. Brumback, *Suddenly from Heaven*, 178.

45. See Nelson, *Fair, Clear, and Terrible*.

46. See Goff, *Fields White unto Harvest*.

recalled his experience in the 1910s in the independent Scandinavian Pentecostal congregation in his hometown in Pennsylvania:

> In the early days of the Pentecostal meetings in McKeesport, we generally didn't have regular pastors. We depended a great deal on traveling evangelists who came to our Mission. Sometimes there were those who were not doctrinally correct, and that made for problems. I can remember one evangelist who it seems got into modernism. He started to teach this, but we recognized the error, and told him not to preach for us anymore. In those days we had such problems on many issues.[47]

Lindquist realized the need for greater accountability and solid ministerial education, so he affiliated with the AG and eventually started a ministerial training school.

Many early Pentecostals understood the need for accountability and cooperation among churches. Yet their backgrounds and circumstances often prompted resistance to centralized authority. These Pentecostal pioneers often worshipped in independent churches, storefront missions, gospel tents, and homes. Many had been kicked out of mainline churches, and they chafed at again subjecting themselves to another authority outside the local church. Others came from traditions that emphasized local church sovereignty, such as Baptist or Plymouth Brethren, and they brought their ecclesiology into the Pentecostal movement.[48]

Some Scandinavian-American Pentecostals joined the AG, seeing value in its ecclesiological vision of a cooperative fellowship for world evangelization. Others advocated strict congregationalism and critiqued the AG's ecclesiology. The most prominent Pentecostal leaders in Scandinavia—Lewis Pethrus of the Filadelfia Church in Stockholm, Sweden, and Thomas B. Barratt of the Filadelfia Church in Oslo, Norway—both advocated strict congregationalism and actively discouraged Scandinavian-Americans from affiliating with the AG. Pethrus and Barratt worked closely with the Independent Assemblies of God (IAG), the Scandinavian-American group that held to strict congregationalism.

---

47. Armstrong, *Why Not?*, 40.

48. American Pentecostal scholars have largely concentrated on Pentecostal origins in the Wesleyan and Baptist wings of the Holiness movement. Norwegian historian Geir Lie rightly observed that the Plymouth Brethren tradition also made significant contributions to the Pentecostal and charismatic movements, particularly in Scandinavia. See Lie, *Plymouthbrødrene, hellighetsbevegelsen, pinsebevegelsen og moderne karismatikk*.

Relations between the AG and the IAG

The divergent ecclesiological visions of the AG and the IAG, in many ways, set the trajectory for the development of Scandinavian-American Pentecostalism. The AG and the IAG each provided homes to large numbers of Scandinavian-Americans. Each group developed its own identity, traditions, and leaders, and distinguished itself from the other. The IAG was a relatively small ethnically-defined group that, in some ways, tried to organize around an anti-organizational principle. The AG was a much larger multi-ethnic group that aimed to organize for the purpose of fulfilling the mission of God at home and abroad.

The AG, in its early decades, was primarily a fellowship of ministers. While churches could begin affiliating with the AG in 1917, many remained independent even while fully participating in district ministries. By the 1930s and 1940s, many AG districts began making greater effort to officially charter these independent churches.

In some instances, IAG churches joined the AG because the AG was better able to provide ministers to serve their increasingly diverse congregations. Gospel Tabernacle in rural Swede Township, Kulm, North Dakota, was organized in 1923, following a revival where over 50 people accepted Christ. The congregation consisted almost exclusively of Swedish-Americans and identified with the IAG. In 1939, the congregation started an outstation in the town of Kulm, Glad Tidings Mission, which included some non-Scandinavians. In the 1940s the congregations, which shared a pastor, were primarily served by AG ministers, which were more plentiful in the state. When the rural group merged into the church in town in 1949, the church affiliated with the AG.[49]

IAG historian Warren Heckman noted that numerous IAG "pastors and local churches had joined the Assemblies of God" over the years, which was "always a sore spot" for the IAG.[50] Heckman tells of an instance in which Gospel Tabernacle in Two Harbors, Minnesota, switched affiliation from the IAG to the AG in the 1943, which "heightened" the "reaction against organization" by IAG leaders.

> Because of a unique mailing error out of the Minneapolis District Office of the Assemblies of God, a letter fell into the hands of E. C. Erickson. It outlined a plan for taking over one of the [IAG] churches in northern Minnesota. E.C., known as one

---

49. Rodgers, *Northern Harvest*, 184–85.
50. Heckman, *History of the Fellowship of Christian Assemblies (HFCA)*, 66.

who never backed off from a good fight, jumped into his car and drove all the way from Duluth to Minneapolis to face his adversarial brother. After that incident, he made sure the Fellowship never forgot Two Harbors, Minnesota, which had been another Fellowship church lost to the Assemblies of God with documented strategy for its overthrow.[51]

Archived correspondence between North Central District officials and Two Harbors Gospel Tabernacle board members provides another perspective. Board members first contacted the North Central District in January 1943, stating that there was conflict between the pastor and the board and inquiring about affiliating with the AG. Board members stated that very few converts had been made during the previous eight years, and they wanted a pastor who was more evangelistic. The pastor was opposed to joining the AG, and the board members were determined to fire the pastor and join the AG, which they perceived as more evangelistic than the IAG. District officials expressed caution, as they did not want to get into the middle of a church fight. District leaders asked national AG leaders for guidance about the situation. AG General Secretary J. Roswell Flower responded: "I hope that no division will occur in the church as a result of this vote." He advised that "it would be better to permit the church to remain independent than to split it into two. But each case must be decided on its own merits." The church board decided to go ahead and to take a congregational vote to affiliate with the AG, which passed.[52] There are usually differing interpretations of church conflicts, and it is understandable that each side would feel its actions were justified. Ultimately, multiple instances of churches leaving the IAG for the AG ended up reinforcing negative feelings among IAG leaders toward the AG.

Debate over ecclesiology sometimes spilled over into IAG and AG publications. A 1944 article by H. A. Gross in the *Herald of Faith*, an IAG magazine, critiqued the AG for its "man-appointed, unscriptural leadership." Gross stated, "we in the other school of thought firmly believe that no higher authority than the local church can be found in the Bible, which after all must be the basis and foundation for the Christian church." Gross further accused the AG of erecting "sectarian walls" that are a barrier to Pentecostal revival.[53]

---

51. Heckman, *HFCA*, 66–67.

52. Correspondence, Gospel Tabernacle (Two Harbors, MN).

53. H. A. Gross, "Whither Are We Bound, Brethren?" *Herald of Faith*, June 1944, 2, 20.

J. Roswell Flower responded to Gross's article in the quarterly AG ministers' newsletter. Flower wrote, "Our independent Pentecostal brethren are a denomination whether they do or do not so recognize themselves," asserting that they cultivated a distinct group identity by which they are denominated. He further suggested that many independent churches are not actually self-governing, but ruled by dictatorial pastors who lack sufficient accountability. He appealed to the biblical text, arguing that the early church did not hold to an ideal of completely sovereign, independent local churches.[54] Flower outlined and justified the AG's ecclesiological vision:

> When the Assemblies of God were called together in Hot Springs, Arkansas in April of 1914, all the assemblies represented there were independent and sovereign. When the articles of association were drawn up, the independence and sovereignty of the local assemblies were fully recognized and there has been no change throughout the years since. Each church is still sovereign and has authority to conduct its own affairs, to elect its own officers, to call or dismiss its own pastor, etc. The choice of district and general officers was for the purpose of serving the churches, not to govern them. If any district or general officer has a different idea, he is unconstitutional in his attitude and should be so instructed. The purpose of the association of independent assemblies in the General Council was to establish doctrine and practice through mutual agreement, plus certain activities which can be promoted co-operatively but which would be impossible of accomplishment if left to local assemblies. The setting up of a publishing house to be owned by the whole fellowship, to supply literature for the use of all on a scale which could never be duplicated by local churches. The foreign mission cause to be advanced on a co-operative basis. The Assemblies of God missionaries are now operating in over fifty different foreign mission fields. The supply of the needs of the missionaries and the promotion of the mission program would be utterly impossible if left to the local independent churches. And then, the promotion of home missions. Do you know that through co-operative effort there has been added to the fellowship through evangelistic effort an average of more than one new church per day for the past eight years. Can the so-called Independent Assemblies of God duplicate that record through their self-centered, independent policy? In our estimation, the

---

54. Flower, *AG Ministers Letter*, Dec 20, 1944.

results fully justify the organization into a fellowship of the independent, sovereign Assemblies of God, known now as The General Council of the Assemblies of God.[55]

New revival movements brought new challenges that impacted both the AG and the IAG. The Latter Rain and Healing movements of the 1940s and 1950s led to the rise of independent evangelists who developed large international platforms through their use of radio, television, and publishing. While these evangelists helped introduce many people to the Pentecostal message, some of the evangelists exhibited a troubling lack of accountability on doctrine and morals. Some evangelists, such as O. L. Jaggers, promoted eccentric doctrines about UFOs, space aliens, miracle healing oil, and the possibility of physical immortality for Christians on earth. William Branham, who claimed to be a prophet with the anointing of Elijah, was known for his healing ministry and for his unique doctrinal views at odds with most Pentecostals.

The IAG experienced division over the Latter Rain and Healing movements. The IAG came to a crisis point in the early 1950s when some IAG leaders—including Joseph Mattsson-Boze, who served as pastor of the prominent Philadelphia Church in Chicago and editor of the *Herald of Faith* magazine—promoted the ministries of Branham, Jaggers, and other controversial figures. The IAG, because of its polity, had limited denominational publications or institutions. Instead, it depended on strong local churches to develop ministries that would serve the broader fellowship. Limited denominational structures gave an outsized voice to pastors of large congregations, such as Mattsson-Boze. Under this polity, when a leading congregation struggled or proposed controversial ideas, it impacted the broader fellowship.[56] The IAG divided and the segment that critiqued the controversial evangelists eventually adopted the name Fellowship of Christian Assemblies.

The AG condemned the Latter Rain movement and also distanced itself from healing evangelists who lacked accountability.[57] Because the IAG was linked to the Latter Rain movement and certain controversial evangelists, and because the IAG critiqued ecclesiologies that would provide more accountability to these errant ministers, additional distance was created between the AG and IAG.

55. Flower, *AG Ministers Letter*, Dec 20, 1944.
56. Heckman, *HFCA*, 80–83; Ring, "Impressions of a Pentecostal Ministry."
57. *Assemblies of God General Council Minutes*, 1949, 26–27.

AG and IAG: Two Expressions of Scandinavian-American Pentecostalism

Scholarly treatment of Scandinavian-American Pentecostalism often deals primarily with the IAG and only tangentially with the AG or other groups.[58] The IAG certainly had a strong Scandinavian-American identity and close links to Pentecostals in Scandinavia, particularly in the first half of the twentieth century. However, the numbers of Scandinavian-American ministers, churches, and members in the AG have probably been larger than those in the IAG.

In 1952, the IAG ministerial directory listed 111 ministers and 53 affiliated churches in the US.[59] In the same year, the AG claimed 7,600 ministers and 6,362 churches. In 1954 North Dakota and Minnesota were home to 202 AG churches, many of which were located in small towns populated primarily by Scandinavians. If only a quarter of AG churches in those two states in 1952 were majority-Scandinavian (which is probably an accurate estimate), they would be roughly equal to the total number of IAG congregations in the US. At least that many more Scandinavian-majority AG churches probably existed in the rest of the nation.

Another way to measure the relative strength of the AG and IAG among Scandinavians is to compare the numbers of ministers in each group with surnames common among Scandinavians. In 1935 the AG had 76 ministers and 18 missionaries who had surnames common among Scandinavians. The IAG had 20 ministers and 2 missionaries with these surnames. In 1952, the AG numbers increased to 182 ministers and 41 missionaries with these surnames. The IAG had 23 ministers and 19 missionaries with these surnames. The AG has provided a home to large numbers of Scandinavian churches and ministers.

Chart 3

IAG Ministers+ Missionaries	1935	1952
Andersen/Anderson	2	2+6
Carlsen/Carlson	2	1+3
Erickson/Ericson	2	2

58. For example, see Alvarsson, *Varför reste Lewi Pethrus just till Chicago?*
59. *Official Ministerial List of the Independent Assemblies of God*, 1952.

Hansen/Hanson	0	0
Johnsen/Johnson	9+2	12+2
Nelson/Nilsen	1	1+4
Olsen/Olson/Olsson	1	0+1
Petersen/Peterson	2	1+1
Rasmussen	1	4+2
Total	20+2	23+19

Chart 4

AG Ministers+ Missionaries	1935	1952
Andersen/Anderson	19+1	32+9
Carlsen/Carlson	5+1	13
Erickson/Ericson	2+4	4+2
Hansen/Hanson	3+2	12+2
Johnsen/Johnson	22+6	63+9
Nelson/Nilsen	8+2	17+2
Olsen/Olson/Olsson	8	22+13
Petersen/Peterson	7+1	17+4
Rasmussen	2+1	2
Total	76+18	182+41

Conclusion

Scandinavian-Americans have played important roles in the AG since its founding. They have served as AG pastors, evangelists, missionaries, denominational leaders, theologians, and educators. Not only have they built the AG and the broader Church, their contributions constitute a distinct ecclesiological vision within Scandinavian Pentecostalism. Their stories, beliefs, and traditions emerged from their Scandinavian religious and cultural background and developed in conversation with broader Pentecostal and evangelical traditions. Scandinavian-Americans and their contributions to the AG should be valued and studied as one of the expressions within Scandinavian Pentecostalism.

Bibliography

Primary Sources

Newspapers Used

The Charlotte Observer, Charlotte, NC, 1886–
Herald of Faith, Duluth, MN, Chicago, 1936–1950
Pentecostal Evangel, Plainfield, IN, Springfield, MO, 1913–2014
The Weekly Evangel, St. Louis, MO, 1915–1918
Word and Witness, Malvern, AR, 1912–1915

Other Primary Sources

From Archival Materials, Flower Pentecostal Heritage Center (FPHC)
Assemblies of God General Council Minutes, April 1914, 6.
Assemblies of God General Council Minutes, 1949. Springfield, Missouri.
Correspondence, Gospel Tabernacle (Two Harbors, MN).
Flower, J. Roswell. *AG Ministers Letter*, December 20, 1944.
Greisen, Victor G. Autobiography, unpublished manuscript.
Historical Sketches of the Minneapolis Gospel Tabernacle, 1907–1930. Minneapolis, MN: The Church, 1930.
Minutes of the North Central District Council of the Assemblies of God, 1922–1926 combined.
North Central District Council of the Assemblies of God Minutes, 1926.
Official Ministerial List of the Independent Assemblies of God, 1952.
Ring, Donald Harry. "Impressions of a Pentecostal Ministry: Harry Christian Ring 1906–1963," unpublished manuscript, 1988.
Tuttle, John. "Pentecostal Foundations Project: Reverend E. C. Erickson," Evangel College, 1975.
Wisconsin-Northern Michigan District history files.
Yearbook. Seattle, WA: Northwest Bible Institute, 1938.

Secondary Sources

Alexander, Paul. *Peace to War: Shifting Allegiances in the Assemblies of God*. Telford, PA: Cascadia, 2009.
Armstrong, Hart Reid. *Why Not? The Life and Ministry of Frank J. Lindquist*. Wichita, KS: Christian Communications, 1993.

Alvarsson, Jan-Åke Alvarsson, ed. *Varför reste Lewi Pethrus just till Chicago? Relationer mellan Sverige och USA inom ramen för pentekostalismen*. Skellefteå, Sweden: Artos, 2019.

Brueggemann, Helen, ed. *Assemblies of God of Southern Idaho: A History*. Nampa, ID: Artcraft, 1993.

Brumback, Carl. *Suddenly from Heaven: A History of the Assemblies of God*. Springfield, MO: Gospel Publishing House, 1961.

Bundy, David. *Visions of Apostolic Mission: Scandinavian Pentecostal Mission to 1935*. Uppsala, Sweden: Uppsala Universitet, 2009.

Burke, Bob, and Viola Holder. "Daddy Nelson." *Assemblies of God Heritage* 29 (2009) 20–25.

———. *The Whole Gospel for the Whole World: The Life of P. C. Nelson*. Oklahoma City, OK: Commonwealth Press, 2008.

"Directory of Assemblies in North Central District." *Gospel Broadcast*, February 1930, 6.

Gardiner, Gordon P. *Out of Zion into all the World*. Shippensburg, PA: Companion, 1990.

Goff, James R. *Fields White unto Harvest: Charles F. Parham and the Missionary Origins of Pentecostalism*. Fayetteville, AR: University of Arkansas Press, 1988.

Gohr, Glenn. "A Harvest in Minnesota: The Story of A/G Pioneer Frank J. Lindquist: Evangelist, Church Planter, Pastor, Bible College President, and Friend." *Assemblies of God Heritage* n.d. (1990) 10–13.

Greisen, Victor G. *Fra skibsdreng til biskop*. Denmark: Randers bogtrykkeri, ca. 1950.

Gustafson, David M. "Pentecostal Evangelist Cenna Osterberg and the Azusa Street Mission." *Pietisten* 35 (2020) 16–18.

Hall, Fannie Mae. "G. Raymond Carlson: The Early Years in the Upper Midwest." *Assemblies of God Heritage* n.d. (1993) 5–8.

———. "G. Raymond Carlson: The Executive Years in Springfield, 1969–1993," *Assemblies of God Heritage* n.d. (1993) 11–15.

Heckman, Warren. *The History of the Fellowship of Christian Assemblies*. Beaverton, OR: Good Book, 2011.

Iap, Sian-Chin. "Bernt Berntsen: a Prominent Oneness Pentecostal Pioneer to North China." In *Global Renewal Christianity: Spirit-empowered Movements Past, Present, and Future,* edited by Vinson Synan and Amos Yong, 1:91–106. Lake Mary, FL: Charisma House, 2016.

Jeter, Hugh P. "The P. C. Nelson I Knew." *Assemblies of God Heritage* 13 (1993–1994) 13–14, 29–31.

Lie, Geir. *Plymouthbrødrene, hellighetsbevegelsen, pinsebevegelsen og moderne karismatikk: en bibliografisk introduksjon*. Oslo: Refleks, 2005.

Lund, Eric. *Hermeneutics; or, The Science and Art of Interpreting the Bible*. Translated by P. C. Nelson. Enid, OK: Southwestern, 1941.

McGee, Gary B. *People of the Spirit: The Assemblies of God*. Springfield, MO: Gospel Publishing House, 2014.

Nelson, P. C. *Bible Doctrines: Studies in the Statement of Fundamental Truths as Adopted by the General Council of the Assemblies of God*. Enid, OK: Southwestern, 1934.

Nelson, Shirley. *Fair, Clear, and Terrible: The Story of Shiloh, Maine*. Latham, NY: British American, 1989.

Ness, Henry H. *Demonstration of the Holy Spirit as Revealed by the Scriptures and Confirmed in Great Revivals of Wesley, Finney, Cartwright, Whitfield, Moody, etc.* Seattle: Hollywood Temple, c. 1940.

Rodgers, Darrin J. "Fully Committed: 100 Years of the Assemblies of God." *Assemblies of God Heritage* n.d. (2014) 11–12.

———. *Northern Harvest: Pentecostalism in North Dakota.* Bismarck, ND: North Dakota District Council of the Assemblies of God, 2003.

———. "Pentecostal Origins in Scandinavian Pietism on the Great Plains." In *A Light to the Nations: Explorations in Ecumenism, Missions, and Pentecostalism*, 301–29. Eugene, OR: Pickwick, 2017.

———. "Rediscovering Pentecostalism's Diverse Roots: Origins in Scandinavian Pietism in Minnesota and the Dakotas." *Refleks* 5 (2006) 50–64.

Tanneberg, Ward M. *Let Light Shine Out: The Story of the Assemblies of God in the Pacific Northwest.* Walnut Creek, CA: Moore, Mayhew and Fick, 1977.

White, Edward S. *Past and Present of Shelby County, Iowa*, Volume 1. Indianapolis: B. F. Bowen & Co., 1915.

Wilson, B. P. "Early Pentecostal and Assemblies of God Missionaries of the Northwest District." Unpublished manuscript, ca. 1983.

Chapter Six

Scandinavian-American Independent Assemblies of God (IAG), 1914–1952

Jan-Åke Alvarsson and David M. Gustafson

Not all Scandinavian-American Pentecostals agreed with the decision of the American, English-speaking Assemblies of God (AG) of Springfield, Missouri, to adopt its form of church government. When the AG passed a resolution that authorized the appointment of twelve representatives "to act in all necessary matters on behalf of this General Council as a Home and Foreign Missionary and Executive Presbytery," it was deemed by some Scandinavian Pentecostals to be a departure from a congregational form of church government.[1] Those who disagreed with the AG's denominational structure—particularly those with strong Baptist views of church governance—preferred a congregationalism with no possible threat of ecclesial authority over the local church.[2] This prompted them to form loosely-organized fellowships of independent churches.

---

1. Brumback, *Suddenly from Heaven*, 178.
2. Colletti, "Lewi Pethrus," 27.

This chapter examines the *independent* Scandinavian Pentecostals who chose not to affiliate with the English-language Americans (AG) which led them on a different path of development. As this chapter argues, the development of the independent churches was not only ecclesial but cultural. This structure gave them freedom to function as *Scandinavian* Pentecostals. This path of development as a loosely-organized body of churches, however, presented theological challenges, especially when the Independent Assemblies of God (IAG) faced disagreements over the Latter Rain Movement (LRM), but also cultural as the generations moved toward an English-speaking, American identity.

This chapter is divided into four sections. The first section examines the years 1914 to 1922, when two independent fellowships began, both separate of the AG. The two groups were the Scandinavian Assemblies of God (SAG, incorporated) and the Independent Assemblies of God (IAG, unincorporated). The second section focuses on the years 1922 to 1935, highlighting a few congregations and leaders of the SAG and IAG in the U.S., and describes the merger of these two bodies in 1935, under the common banner of the IAG (unincorporated). The third section looks more closely at IAG congregations in Chicago, Minneapolis-St. Paul, New York City, Seattle-Tacoma, and Los Angeles, demonstrating Chicago as the center of the IAG. The final section describes developments within the IAG as it faced the Latter Rain Movement (LRM).

Fellowships of Independent Pentecostal Assemblies, 1914–1922

Between 1914 and 1922, Arthur F. Johnson and E. C. Erickson led informally a group of Pentecostal churches in the Upper Midwest. Both men were born in America, fluent in English and Swedish, and organized conferences for English- and Scandinavian-language speakers. In 1915, a headline in *The Duluth Herald* read: "Conference Will Meet on Saturday: Pentecostal Denomination Will Have Second Annual Convention."[3] The meeting was held at the Bricklayer's Hall at 19th Avenue and First Street in Duluth. Fourteen evangelists and pastors spoke during the sessions between October 30 and November 8, including Edward Armstrong of

---

3. *Duluth Herald*, October 26, 1915, 4. Cf. "This week, Brother Vingren of Para, Brazil, will preach in the Scandinavian language . . . Rev. Edw. Armstrong." *Weekly Evangel*, December 4, 1915, 1.

Chicago; A. A. Holmgren of Minneapolis; F. A. Graves of Zion City, Illinois; Arthur F. Johnson of Duluth; John Moseid of Thief River Falls, Minnesota; Gunnar Vingren of Brazil; and Gust A. Edwards of St. Paul. Services were held in English and Scandinavian languages.

Scandinavian Pentecostal meeting, 1915. Vingren (seated left), B. M. Johnson (seated right); standing left Arthur F. Johnson, C. M. Hanson, others not identified.

Courtesy of Gunnar Vingren Memorial Archives, CPAD, Rio de Janeiro, Brazil

This fellowship which held its first conference in 1914, demonstrated the unity of the Pentecostal movement in the Upper Midwest which included Scandinavians. While some of the speakers were ordained by or affiliated with the AG, others such as A. A. Holmgren were not.

In 1918, A. A. Holmgren and Scandinavian-American Pentecostal ministers incorporated in Minneapolis as the "Scandinavian Assemblies of God in the United States of America, Canada and Foreign Lands."[4] This fellowship was known simply as the Scandinavian Assemblies of God (SAG). B. M. Johnson of Chicago served as chairman, Gust A. Edwards

4. Heckman, *History of the Fellowship of Christian Assemblies* (HFCA), 14.

of St. Paul as treasurer, and A. A. Holmgren as secretary. Additional officers were Theodor "Tom" Christensen of Brooklyn, New York, and C. M. Hanson of Dalton, Minnesota.[5] Gunnar Vingren of Brazil promoted international missions. The periodicals *Sanningens Vittne* (The Witness of Truth) in Minneapolis and *Pingst-Rösten* (The Pentecost Voice) in Chicago served as the periodicals of the SAG.

In the meantime, Arthur F. Johnson and E. C. Erickson led their fellowship of English- and Scandinavian-language churches. They also promoted the idea that their fellowship of Pentecostal churches should remain independent of the AG. While their churches cooperated with one another, they would not compromise their autonomy.

Already, in January 1922, E. C. Erickson called for a meeting in St. Paul, Minnesota, to discuss the idea of establishing an informal fellowship of independent Pentecostal churches. A report stated: "The Pentecostal brethren in the Northern part of the U. S., seeing councils and organizations springing up in the Pentecostal movement, causing division and misunderstanding among the ministering brethren and saints, felt the need of coming together for conference and consultation and searching the word of God, to see in the light of God's word, what the word says about such organizations and councils."[6] When the group of twenty-five pastors met to discuss the idea, they concluded, "We find it unscriptural in these gatherings to form permanent organizations with articles of faith and by-laws. These human methods cannot take the place of spiritual discernment and do not bring spiritual results nor unity."[7]

This matter came to a head in November 1922, when the AG of Springfield, Missouri, organized churches and ministers in Minnesota, Wisconsin, and the Dakotas into its North Central District. Some of the Scandinavians supported this move by the AG, but the independents opposed it. At a meeting organized by the AG, delegates of the meeting elected C. M. Hanson to serve as the district's first chairman, and he was followed by Frank J. Lindquist.[8]

Although E. C. Erickson, like others, was ordained by the AG, he opposed the AG's organization of this district which included a

---

5. Letter to Division of Passport Control, Washington, D.C., from B. M. Johnson, Council of the Scandinavian Assemblies of God, October 4, 1921.

6. *Herald of Faith* (*HF*), February 1950, 6.

7. *HF*, February 1950, 14.

8. *Pentecostal Evangel* (*PE*), December 9, 1922, 11.

superintendent, area presbyters, and oversight of local churches and pastors.[9] Such an arrangement combined congregational and presbyterian forms of church government. In response, Erickson and those who held to a strict congregationalism decided to function as an unincorporated fellowship of autonomous churches under the common banner of the Independent Assemblies of God (IAG).[10]

Thus, in 1924, when Lewi Pethrus, the prominent leader of the Pentecostal movement in Sweden, visited Minneapolis, he described the fallout of the AG in its formation of the North Central District, and the IAG and SAG resisting it. Pethrus supported the independents, saying,

> "There are several kinds of Pentecostals here. We have spoken in the various locations on two occasions. One is the original Pentecostal church that first began here [in Minneapolis]. God worked there wonderfully for several years. But then a mission's committee (*missionskommitté*) was formed among the Pentecostal people who had previously been independent, and through this, together with other difficulties, tensions and conflicts arose. The original congregation [here in Minneapolis] joined the General Council of the Assemblies of God, which the spoken-about missions committee is called."[11] Pethrus opposed the formation of a denomination, seeing such a move as a chance for the devil to divide those who are united by "one and the same spirit."

Pethrus was invited to Minneapolis by the Philadelphia Church, the newly organized independent congregation, which according to him was ordered according to the New Testament.[12] He said that this congregation was a "small group of about 40 people" and that it had struggled "in a difficult fight, on the one hand, against disorder and confusion, and on the other hand, against the [General] Council's structure."[13] Despite the struggle, Pethrus affirmed that the new church was free and would "organize its activities according to the Word of the Lord."[14] A. A. Holmgren joined this new independent congregation, and by 1927, it was named the Philadelphia Scandinavian Pentecostal

---

9. Heckman, HFCA, 55, 66.
10. Colletti, "Lewi Pethrus," 22.
11. *Evangelii Harold* (*EH*), May 29, 1924. Cf. *Brev-Duvan*, April 1924, 4.
12. Colletti, "Lewi Pethrus," 19–20.
13. *EH*, May 29, 1924.
14. *EH*, May 29, 1924.

Church (*Skandinaviska pingstförsamlingen Filadelfia*). The building was located at 26th Avenue and Taylor Street N. E., and the congregation was led by G. Algot Wikstrom, originally of Överluleå, Sweden.

Despite sporadic tensions between the AG and independent churches, there was generally brotherly regard for one another. Although C. M. Hanson served with the AG, in 1927, when traveling in Colorado, he wrote to *Sanningens Vittne* "asking for the prayers of all believers" because of his weakened health condition. In response, A. A. Holmgren wrote, "Brother Hanson is one of the older pioneers in the Pentecostal revival. In his company, the publisher of this periodical [Holmgren] made his first missionary journey as a Pentecostal preacher. In recent years, Brother H.[anson] has worked mostly among the [AG] Americans. Everyone who knows him, please pray for him to recover soon."[15]

Moving toward a Merger of the Independents, 1922–1935

A third group of independent Scandinavian Pentecostals emerged. This informal group was comprised mainly of Swedes who had immigrated to America in the 1920s and 1930s, and had close ties with the Swedish Pentecostal movement in Sweden led by Lewi Pethrus.[16] The leader of Sweden's Pentecostal movement had a profound influence upon Scandinavian-American Pentecostals, especially after his first visit to Chicago in 1924.

Shortly after Pethrus's visit, a new church began in Chicago. The work was led by Arvid Ohrnell (1891–1963) who came to Chicago from Sweden in 1925.[17] The following year, the new congregation took the name Filadelfiaförsamling (Philadelphia Church), and a year later, it incorporated as the Philadelphia Swedish Pentecostal Church.[18] This congregation also launched a periodical in 1926, titled *Trons Härold* on the pattern of *Evangelii Härold*, the organ of the Pentecostal movement in Sweden.

The Philadelphia influence came further as Pentecostal ministers from Pethrus's orbit arrived to America in the 1920s and 1930s to lead IAG churches. A prime example is Carl Hedeen (1863–1950) who began in Sweden as a "Pentecostal friendly" Baptist pastor and later joined

---

15. *Sanningens-Vittne* (*SV*), November 1928, 8
16. Heckman, *HFCA*, 54.
17. *Philadelphia Church 35th Anniversary*, 1.
18. *Philadelphia Church 35th Anniversary*, 2.

the Pentecostal movement.[19] He was originally from Undersåker—the younger brother of Olof Hedeen of the Swedish Baptist Theological Seminary of Chicago. With close ties to Lewi Pethrus, Carl Hedeen served as pastor of the Filadelfia Church of Jönköping, Sweden. When he immigrated to America in 1930, Hedeen became the pastor of the Philadelphia Church of Chicago.[20]

In 1934, a conference was held at the Philadelphia Church in Minneapolis to discuss the idea of merging the IAG and SAG. The periodical *Svenska Amerikanska Posten* announced that Carl Hedeen of Chicago would come to Minneapolis, along with "preachers, evangelists, missionaries, and visitors from congregations in various parts of the country" to the annual conference of the Scandinavian Pentecostal Assemblies.[21] Services were held in English, Swedish, Norwegian, and Danish.

In the following year, two events brought the IAG and SAG to merge. At the annual meeting of the Scandinavian Assemblies of God (SAG), held October 6–13, 1935, in Minneapolis, SAG ministers voted unanimously to dissolve their corporation and join the Independent Assemblies of God (IAG).[22] The final arrangement to merge took place at a general gathering of ministers of the two fellowships. This happened two weeks later, at the annual convention of the IAG held at the Bloomington Temple in Minneapolis, from October 21–22, 1935. With both fellowships agreeing to merge, the united fellowship continued under the name, the Independent Assemblies of God (IAG), unincorporated.

Another motion was made and carried that the pastors, evangelists, and missionaries who were not present, but whose names appeared on the SAG's list, would be notified of the merger by letter and an announcement in *Sanningens Vittne*. Arthur F. Johnson, A. A. Holmgren, and Carl Hedeen were appointed to convey the decisions of the two conventions to those who were not present.[23] At the time of the merger

---

19. Davidsson, *Lewi Pethrus' Ecclesiological Thought, 1911–1974*, 61n33. Cf. *Folke-Vennen* (FV), January 16, 1908, 2; *Chicago-Bladet*, March 10, 1931, 3.

20. Carl Hedeen started the periodical *Brudgummens Röst* in 1911, and invited Pethrus to join the editorial staff. Alvarsson, "Relationer mellan Sverige och USA inom ramen för pentekostalismen," 61.

21. *Svenska Amerikanska Posten*, September 5, 1934, 1.

22. *HF*, January 1936, 8.

23. *HF*, January 1936, 8.

in 1935, the fellowship of the IAG numbered 54 pastors and evangelists, and 21 foreign missionaries.[24]

In the following year, the first conference of the united IAG was held in Brooklyn, New York, at the Salem Gospel Tabernacle hosted by Arne Dahl, with plenary speakers E. C. Erickson, Joseph Mattsson-Boze, and Helen Jepsen.[25] In the same year, Erickson launched the English-language periodical, Herald of Faith. Then, in 1939, the periodicals *Sanningens Vittne* of Minneapolis and *Trons Härold* of Chicago merged into a single periodical named *Sanningens Vittne och Trons Härold*. This combined periodical was published in Chicago by Philadelphia Church.

National Convention of Independent Assemblies of God at Philadelphia Church, Chicago, October 5–10, 1943. Philadelphia Church, Chicago. Photo by David M. Gustafson.

Development of IAG Congregations in the U.S.

The founding of several Scandinavian Pentecostal churches in Chicago made it the center of Scandinavian-American Pentecostalism. This movement began with the Pentecostal revival in the Windy City on February 5, 1906, at Second Swedish Baptist Church,[26] and the Pentecostal revival at the North Avenue Mission on January 14, 1907,[27] followed by the Pentecostal-baptism of William Durham on March 2, 1907, in Los Angeles

---

24. Heckman, *HFCA*, 15, 57, 59.
25. *HF*, April 1936, 12.
26. *Nya Wecko-Posten*, February 6, 1906, 4; March 13, 1906, 4.
27. *PE*, June 23, 1923, 10.

at the Azusa Street Mission, after which he returned to his mission and held Pentecostal meetings with hundreds of Scandinavians attending.[28]

Scandinavian Pentecostal Church on Barry Avenue, Chicago

The Full Gospel Assembly, known as the Scandinavian Pentecostal Church (*Skandinaviska Pingst Församlingen*), and commonly as the "Barry Avenue Church" began in 1908.[29] Oscar Frizen recalled, "Pastor [William] Durham had just returned from California filled with the Holy Spirit and his soul was ablaze for God . . . I heard about meetings that were being held at the 'Old North Avenue Mission,' and I had such a hunger for God and for a deeper spiritual life that I attended some of the meetings. The Spirit was manifested in a wonderful way, and the testimonies of the people with the shining faces, went right to the heart. . . . The Lord filled me with His wonderful Holy Spirit on the 24th day of November, 1907. A group of us started prayer meetings in different homes."[30]

Soon after, Nels Anderson invited Oscar Frizen and the others to hold meetings in his tailor shop at 944 West Barry Avenue, rent-free. At first, various preachers ministered to the small congregation including Durham, F. A. Sandgren, C. M. Hanson, P. A. Dahlman, and laymen Juehl Sjoli and John Frizen.[31]

By the spring of 1910, Bengt Magnus Johnson became the resident pastor.[32] Johnson held worship services on Sunday afternoons and evenings, with street meetings between these events, often held at the corner of Belmont and Wilton avenues near the elevated train stop.[33] Monday night was the missionary meeting, Tuesday was choir, Wednesday was a Swedish meeting, and Friday was an English meeting for the youth.

---

28. *The Apostolic Faith*, February-March, 1907, 4. *FV*, March 26, 1908, 4; *Pentecostal Testimony*, July 1912, 3.

29. *Word and Work*, May 1910, 155; *SV*, July 1911, 4. The church was also called The Apostolic Faith Assembly. *SV*, September 1929, 8; *HF*, October 1944, 28.

30. *Lake View Chimes*, November 1, 1951, 1.

31. *Lake View Chimes*, November 1, 1951, 1.

32. Although the call was extended around Easter 1908, Johnson arrived later. *Lake View Chimes*, November 1, 1951, 1. Johnson's daughter Violet Elenar Johnson died on April 25, 1910, in Norway, Michigan, indicating that the family likely had not yet relocated to Chicago.

33. Nybakken, "History of Barry Avenue Church, Chicago," 1–2.

Full Gospel Assembly (Barry Avenue Church), Chicago,
Courtesy Nybakken-Anderson Family

In 1910, a revival took place at the Montana Street Mission at the corner of Montana Street and Sheffield Avenue, where Durham came to hold evangelistic meetings.[34] For two weeks, B. M. Johnson closed the doors of Barry Avenue Church so that members could attend Durham's meetings. Several of the youth of the church received Pentecostal-baptism including three of Nels Anderson's children.

In the same year, Aimee Semple—nearly twenty years old at the time—visited Barry Avenue Church on her way to New York City where she was to meet her husband, Robert Semple. The young couple would soon leave as missionaries for China. After an evening sermon, the congregation stood at the doors to bid her farewell, singing, "God Be with You till We Meet Again."[35]

---

34. Nybakken, "History of Barry Avenue Church, Chicago," 2. Durham's meetings were held in the Persian Pentecostal Mission at Sheffield Avenue and Montana Street. *SV*, April 1912, 4.

35. Nybakken, "History of Barry Avenue Church," Chicago, 3.

Despite the fact that B. M. and Pauline Johnson had a large family, they welcomed visiting missionaries on furloughs to stay with them.[36] Thus, their home at 1125 West Barry Avenue became known as "the Missionary Home."[37] One of the visiting missionaries was Carrie P. Anderson, AG missionary born in Kristiansand, Norway, who converted to faith in 1910 under Durham's ministry, and four years later was commissioned to south China, serving later in Singapore and Malaysia.[38]

In 1924, when Lewi Pethrus visited Chicago, he was hosted by the Johnsons. He wrote: "On March 23, we began our meetings with Brother B. M. Johnson on Barry Ave. During the first half of the day, we had a meeting in the large auditorium of an elementary school. The room was crowded, and God's Spirit showed himself glorious. Then we had meetings for the next three days, both mornings and evenings, in the Barry Ave. church which, as it turned out, to be far too small."[39]

B. M. Johnson's congregation continued to meet at 944 Barry Avenue until a new church building at 1331 North Racine Avenue was ready for occupancy. In 1928, a "parade of saints" walked from the old church to the new building.[40] The first service was held in Swedish with the congregation singing from the songbook that Johnson compiled, *Lovsångstoner* (Songs of Praise).[41] When Johnson resigned from the church in 1935, he was succeeded by John A. Westman who led the congregation, known then as Lake View Gospel Church, for the next decade.

---

36. *EH*, March 4, 1920.

37. Nybakken, "History of Barry Avenue Church, Chicago." 3.

38. *Latter Rain Evangel*, September 1914, 12. Similarly, Beda Maria Magnusson Stone was a missionary to Hong Kong. She was born in 1883 in Ockelbo, Sweden, immigrated to Chicago in 1903, joined the Pentecostal movement in the Windy City, became a minister of the Assemblies of God, Springfield, Missouri, in 1914, and commissioned the following year to China.

39. *EH*, May 8, 1924.

40. Heckman, *HFCA*, 125.

41. See Johnson, *Lovsångs-toner*. This songbook was published in two editions around the years 1924 to 1927. Swedish-language songs were composed by Oscar Ahnfelt, Lina Sandell, J. Blomqvist, Nils Frykman, Lewi Pethrus, and C. M. Holm. Ten songs were written or composed by Lotten (Tenman) Sjoli (1877–1967) originally of Sillerud, Sweden, and resident of Chicago with her husband Juhl Sjøli. Norwegian-language songs were composed by T. B. Barratt and Fred Christoffersen. No. 187 is Pethrus's "Löftena kunna ej svika" (The Promises Cannot Fail).

North Avenue Mission / Ebenezer Pentecostal Mission of Chicago

In 1911, when William Durham left Chicago to move to Los Angeles, the North Avenue Mission (then named the North Avenue Full Gospel Assembly), underwent an obvious change in leadership. In addition to C. M. Hanson, the congregation was led by F. O. Price. When Price left in 1915, to serve the nearby Humboldt Park Pentecostal Assembly, the North Avenue Mission was served by itinerant preachers.[42] At other times, the pulpit was filled by visiting missionaries such as W. W. Simpson and his wife, Alma (Ekvall), who served in China, and Thomas and Emily Griffin, evangelists from Santa Barbara, California.[43] Nevertheless, the church struggled to find a resident pastor.

Then in 1920, the congregation called Adolph Petersen to lead the storefront mission. Petersen, a native of Tønder, Denmark, brought new life to the congregation. *The Latter Rain Evangel* reported, "Pastor Peterson of the North Avenue mission is aggressive and filled with the Spirit and the crowds that have attended nightly have taxed the mission hall to its limit."[44] Thus, in 1923, Petersen closed the old North Avenue Mission at 2836 W. North Avenue and moved the congregation one block north on the side street to 1665 N. Mozart Street.[45] He wrote:

> Many of the saints throughout the world will undoubtedly remember the old North Avenue Mission, where the rain fell in such copious showers in the early outpourings of Pentecost. It was on the fourteenth day of January, 1907, when the fire first fell in this humble mission and people flocked from all over the city and surrounding places to see this new thing which the Lord was doing. Hundreds of people were saved and baptized in the Spirit and many of our leading Pentecostal ministers of today received their baptism in the old North Avenue Mission. Among them are Brother E. N. Bell of Springfield, Mo., chairman of the General Council, and Brother A. H. Argue of the Canadian evangelistic trio; Mrs. Aimee Semple McPherson received her first healing in this mission, and many of the leading missionaries on the foreign field were saved or baptized here, then went out to the uttermost parts of the world

---

42. *Pentecostal Herald*, July 1915, 4; *Word and Witness*, August 1915, 8.
43. *Latter Rain Evangel*, January 1916, 8; *PE*, June 15, 1918, 13.
44. *Latter Rain Evangel*, April 1921, 29.
45. Adolph Petersen, "Chicago, Ill. Full Gospel Assembly," *PE*, June 23, 1923, 10.

with the Full Gospel message. Dear Brother W. H. Durham, who was the first pastor of the Full Gospel Assembly, has gone to glory and is awaiting the final ingathering of precious souls won through his ministry.[46]

The new building opened on July 15, 1923, with A. H. Argue and his children, Watson and Zelma, conducting revival meetings.

When Petersen left the church, he was succeeded by Sverre Gustavsen.[47] With several Norwegians from the neighborhood attending services, the church took the name Eben Ezer Pinsemission (Ebenezer Pentecostal Mission).[48] In 1927, Gustavsen reported: "Pastor T. B. Barratt and Evangelist Hjalmar Ruud from Oslo, Norway, have just concluded a series of meetings with us here on the west side of Chicago, which were a great blessing to us.... We prayed with souls who sought salvation, and many also sought the baptism of the Spirit and a deeper life in God."[49]

Gustavsen was followed by pastors Morten J. Hagli, Joseph Ystrom, Jens Pettersen, and August A. Andersen. During this time, the church affiliated with the AG. In 1952, Paul S. Bredesen led Ebenezer Full Gospel Assembly.

West Auburn Park Pentecostal Assembly of Chicago

The West Auburn Park Pentecostal Assembly located at 70th and S. Elizabeth streets in Chicago, was founded in 1910, and served subsequently by J. W. Hjertstrom and Petrus Swartz.[50] In 1926, Swartz was succeeded by Arthur F. Johnson.[51]

Prior to Johnson's first term as pastor, he and his wife, Beda, traveled to Sweden on their way to serve as missionaries in Russia.[52] While in Malmö and Västerås, Sweden, they were recognized for their gifts of singing and preaching.[53] They were held in such high regard that in 1921, Arthur was invited to speak at the building dedication of

46. *PE*, Jun. 23, 1923, 10.
47. *HF* April 1941, 26; June 1941, 21, 29.
48. *SV*, February 1928, 8.
49. *SV*, February 1928, 6.
50. *EH*, May 8, 1924. Petrus Swartz later served as pastor of the Grand Crossing Evangelical Mission in Chicago, located at 813 E. 75th Street. *SV*, September 1928, 5.
51. See also, Alvarsson, "Relationer mellan Sverige och USA," 34.
52. *EH*, April 14, 1921.
53. *EH*, March 11, 1920, 39.

Filadelfia Church in Stockholm.[54] In the following year, they planned to enter Russia but since it was closed, they went to Tallin (Reval) in Estonia. Their time was short there, however. In 1924, when they communicated plans to return to America, they coordinated the last leg of travel with Lewi Pethrus, meeting him in Youngstown, New York, on their way to Chicago.

Back in Minnesota, Arthur F. Johnson began working immediately as an itinerant evangelist, holding meetings in twelve states.[55] At the start of 1926, he began the pastorate at West Auburn Park Pentecostal Assembly in Chicago.[56] After three years, he left to become pastor of the Westport Scandinavian Assembly of God in Kansas City, Missouri, but returned to West Auburn Park in 1932, for a second term.[57]

When the West Auburn Park Assembly merged with Grand Crossing Evangelical Mission, the new congregation acquired property at 5850 South Halsted Street and changed its name to the Swedish Assembly of God.[58] S. Paul Carlyss (1895–1979) served as pastor of this church from 1937 to 1947. Just prior, Carlyss had pastored the Scandinavian Evangelical Free Church on 25th Avenue in Minneapolis.[59]

Philadelphia Church of Chicago

Although the Barry Avenue and West Auburn Park churches were older, the center of Chicago's Scandinavian Pentecostal churches shifted to the Philadelphia Church on North Clark Street. As mentioned above, Philadelphia Church began as a mission under the ministry of Arvid Ohrnell. When Ohrnell came to Chicago in 1924, he set out to reach young Swedes, and soon met a small group that gathered regularly for prayer. Some of the members had experienced Pentecostal baptism when visiting Sweden,

54. *EH*, August 25, 1921. Cf. *EH*, November 10, 1921.
55. *EH*, May 29, 1924.
56. *Chicago-Bladet*, December 15, 1925, 8.
57. Heckman, *HFCA*, 128.
58. Heckman, *HFCA*, 126–27.
59. *Evangelical Beacon*, December 14, 1937, 10; *HF* April, 1943, 29; *PE*, November 11, 1944, 14; Alvarsson, "Relationer mellan Sverige och USA", 34. Carlyss's church in Minneapolis (Scandinavian Evangelical Free Church at 25th Avenue and 8th Street South) supported missionary Nils H. Hanson who converted to faith at the Apostolic Faith Mission of Minneapolis in 1916. Hanson served as a missionary to India with the Scandinavian Mission Society ("Free-Free"). *Bref-Dufvan*, April 1929, 7–8; Halleen, *Golden Jubilee*, 139.

and others were inspired by one of the "Pentecostalized churches" in Chicago.[60] Ohrnell and others rented a room at 3315 North Clark Street where they began public meetings in November 1925, and simply called themselves "Philadelphia" after Lewi Pethrus's church in Stockholm. In addition to Ohrnell, Victor Norlin, pastor of the Humboldt Park Swedish Baptist Church, spoke often at Philadelphia's Sunday afternoon meetings.[61] Efraim Fraim also assisted in the new work.

Efraim Fraim (1897–1978)—a lawyer and pastor who had studied at the Örebro Mission School in Sweden—held a Bible course at the West Auburn Park Pentecostal Assembly. When the Bible course ended, he was asked to become Philadelphia Church's pastor.[62] Philadelphia Church held its first baptismal service in 1926, at a small lake in West Auburn Park where nine believers were baptized. Later that summer, baptismal services were held on the shore of Lake Michigan. The church soon organized musicians into a string orchestra according to the pattern in Sweden. In November 1927, the congregation purchased a facility at 3300 North Sheffield Avenue, where services were held for the next fourteen years.

In 1930, Carl Hedeen arrived from Sweden, as mentioned above.[63] When he came to Chicago, he succeeded Fraim. Hedeen stayed four years when he accepted the pastorate of the Scandinavian Pentecostal Church in Tacoma, Washington.[64] In the autumn of 1933, Philadelphia Church contacted a young pastor in Sweden named Josef Mattsson (1905–1989), known later as Joseph Mattsson-Boze. When Lewi Pethrus visited Chicago in November 1936, he said: "The Philadelphia Church was organized about 10 years ago and currently has about 275 members.... The number, who understand Swedish, has in recent years decreased significantly, due partly to a large number of Swedes having to return to Sweden because of the economic depression in America and partly due to virtually no Swedes immigrating in recent years.... It has, with Brother Mattsson at the helm, done its utmost to prepare our meetings in the best possible way."[65]

60. Alvarsson, "Relationer mellan Sverige och USA," 36.
61. *Philadelphia Church 35th Anniversary*, 2.
62. Alvarsson, *Svenskt frikyrkolexikon*, 131.
63. Alvarsson, "Relationer mellan Sverige och USA," 37.
64. Pethrus, *Västerut*, 227.
65. Pethrus, *Västerut*, 31.

Joseph Mattsson-Boze served the church in his first term as pastor from 1933 to 1939. When he moved to New York, Lewi Pethrus's son, Oliver Pethrus (1915–1982), was called to become the assistant pastor and conductor of the string orchestra. In September 1939, Harry Lindblom was called to become Philadelphia Church's pastor. Having resigned from the Lake View Evangelical Free Church, Lindblom served as the interpreter of the European Pentecostal Conference in Stockholm with Lewi Pethrus before returning to Chicago to become pastor of Philadelphia Church.[66]

Due to the increased attendance, the building on Sheffield Avenue was too small. When a bank building at 5437 North Clark Street became available, the congregation purchased the property and held the dedication service in March 1940.[67] Due to illness, Lindblom's time as pastor of the Philadelphia Church was short; he died in the summer of 1940.[68]

Through contacts with Sweden, likely mediated by Oliver Pethrus, the congregation learned that the successful pastor of Filadelfia Church in Stockholm was considering resigning and pursuing another ministry. Therefore, in September 1940, Lewi Pethrus was called to be the pastor of the Philadelphia Church in Chicago.

After consideration, Pethrus agreed to a three-year term.[69] Due to World War II, however, he could not arrive until March 1941. Even then, he could not bring his wife, Lydia, and the other children who had remained in Sweden. Thus, he worked in the Chicago church only until July 1941, when he asked to be relieved of his duties. Shortly before leaving Chicago, he arranged tent meetings with Einar Waermo, a (1901–1983), a well-known vocalist, composer, and, former opera tenor from Grängesberg, Sweden, who had come to live in Los Angeles.[70] In September, Pethrus returned to Sweden.

In November 1941, Philadelphia Church called Andrew W. Rasmussen (1905–1996), editor of *Trons Härold* to become the next pastor. When finances fell short at the Philadelphia Book Concern, the church's publishing arm, the church borrowed money from Filadelfia Church

---

66. Gustafson, "Dr. Harry Lindblom," 65–68.
67. *Philadelphia Church 35th Anniversary*, 3.
68. Gustafson, "Dr. Harry Lindblom," 70.
69. Heckman, *HFCA*, 71.
70. *HF*, April 1936, 3–5; Pethrus, *Den anständiga sanningen*, 57.

in Stockholm.⁷¹ Rasmussen remained as pastor until 1944, when he started a new work in Edmonton, Canada.

Since Mattsson-Boze returned to Chicago from New York in April 1943, and resumed his office, the congregation had co-pastors briefly. When Mattsson-Boze took over from Rasmussen as editor of *Trons Härold*, Harry Ring was hired to join the pastoral staff to assist in various ministries, including teaching classes at Philadelphia's Annual Bible Study Course, a means to train pastors, lay people, and missionaries of the IAG.

Harry C. Ring (1906–1988) was born in New Jersey to Norwegian-immigrant parents. He was a proven fiscal manager, and when he arrived in Chicago, he learned that the Philadelphia Book Concern and *Herald of Faith* were on the verge of a bankruptcy. While Mattsson-Bose was able to inspire the congregation with a word from the Lord, he lacked the practical business savvy that Ring provided.

Other Pentecostal Churches in Chicago

In addition to these four congregations, there were several other Scandinavian assemblies in Chicago.⁷² These included Christ Church Pentecostal at 6309 Yale Avenue, led by Gordon P. Swartz (1903–1972), son of Petrus Swartz.⁷³ Another was Swedish Pentecostal Mission that met at 814 West 59th Street in the Englewood neighborhood.⁷⁴ This congregation later took the name Bethany Pentecostal Assembly (*Betania pingstförsamling*).⁷⁵ For several years, J. August Edgren, originally from Ölme, Sweden, served the church as the pastor.

The Humboldt Park Scandinavian Pentecostal Assembly of God at Ballou (later St. Louis Avenue) and Wabansia streets was led by Magnus

---

71. Pethrus, *Den anständiga sanningen*, 72–73.

72. By 1911, the Swedish Apostolic Church (*Svenska Apostolisk Församling*) met at 1208 59th Street in Chicago's Englewood neighborhood on city's southside. *SV*, July 1911, 4. Moreover, by 1913, another Swedish Pentecostal mission opened in the Edgewater neighborhood at Rosehill Drive and Paulina Street. *SV*, May-June 1913, 8. It is not known whether these congregations relocated, merged, renamed, or closed.

73. *HF*, April 1936, 10; May, 1941, 28–29; April 1943, 29. Christ Church was renamed Wittich Memorial Church, and later renamed Christian Hills Full Gospel Church. *HF*, September 1942, 16–17; October 1942, 7–8; November 1942, 15.

74. *Pentecostal Herald*, July 1915, 4.

75. *SV* September 1922, 8; December 1926, 8; January 1927, 8.

A. Hydéhn.[76] This church held combined services with B. M. Johnson's congregation when missionaries George and Sophie Hansen visited from China, as well as combined meetings with the Full Gospel Assembly (old North Avenue Mission) on Mozart Street to host Smith Wigglesworth.[77] The Humboldt Park Assembly also hosted evangelists John J. Ashcroft of Merchantville, New Jersey, and C. M. Hanson of Dalton, Minnesota.[78]

In 1926, the Scandinavian Pentecostal Church at Greenleaf and Elmwood Streets in Evanston, Illinois, was led by David Nordling, the former pastor of Filadelfia Church in Skövde, Sweden. Nordling immigrated to New York in 1923, and after serving the Scandinavian Pentecostal Church in Evanston, left for Oakland, California. In 1929, the church in Evanston—then named Assembly of God (Pentecostal)—was led by F. A. Sandgren and C. A. Anderson. When Sandgren accepted the role of associate pastor alongside Carl Hedeen at the Philadelphia Church in Chicago, he orchestrated a merger of the Evanston congregation with the Philadelphia Church.[79]

While Chicago, more than any other city, had the largest number of Scandinavian Pentecostal churches, others were established in the Upper Midwest, Northeast, and Northwest. Churches in Minnesota also affiliated with the IAG.

Philadelphia Church of Minneapolis

As mentioned above, Philadelphia Church of Minneapolis began when the earlier established Scandinavian Christian Assembly joined the North Central District of the AG.[80]

In 1927, when F. A. Sandgren visited nearby St. Paul, he recalled being there more than a decade earlier, in 1912 and 1913, when construction was underway to build the tabernacle of the Full Gospel Assembly (*Full Evangelisk Församling*) at 700 Jenks Avenue East. At the time, Sandgren reported: "At last the fire is beginning to fall in our tabernacle at

---

76. *Pentecostal Herald*, July 1915, 4; March 1917, 1.

77. *Pentecostal Herold*, August 1918, 4; *PE*, September 27, 1924, 14.

78. *PE*, February 14, 1925, 14. Cf. *PE*, October 19, 1935, 20; *Bridegroom's Messenger*, June 1935, 8.

79. Heckman, *HFCA*, 133; "Rev. Sandgren Dies, Evangelist, Editor," *La Grange Citizen*, January 19, 1933.

80. Frank J. Lindquist became pastor of the Minneapolis Gospel Tabernacle in 1924.

Jenks and Greenbrier. Many are seeking God for the baptism with the Holy Ghost. The place is filled and some have come through the past two weeks. Bro. Webster I. Horton, of Los Angeles, has been with us for the past two weeks and God is using him."[81]

However, when Sandgren visited St. Paul fourteen years later, in 1927, he expressed his disappointment over the church's lack of Pentecostal activity and how the congregation, which had joined the AG, did not seem to live up to its name as before. In his musings over how congregations select their names, he said: "So, one begins to ask: 'Why do they not call this or that church 'Laodicea' or add in parentheses under the auspicious name, 'Ichabod,' when the glory, which was there before, has departed?"[82]

In contrast, Sandgren spoke highly of the new IAG congregation in Minneapolis, saying, "Philadelphia means brotherly love. . . . When the brothers in the Philadelphia Church in Minneapolis found out that I was in St. Paul, they called me by phone and invited me to come and share a message with them in Swedish and English. It was such a joy to go there and see how this group of believers has such love for one another, and it was not difficult to speak in such a congregation because the Spirit was free and the freedom was felt." Sandgren commented positively about the ministry of the "free-spirited brother" Algot Wikstrom, and his visit with A. A. Holmgren.[83]

Bethel Temple of St. Paul

In St. Paul, another church affiliated with the IAG, namely, Bethel Temple. This congregation was birthed from the vision of Almeda M. Engquist (1882–1943), originally from Algutsboda, Sweden.[84] After she arrived in Minneapolis, she met her future husband, Charles Engquist (1880–1959). While he owned a wholesale meat company, they ministered together in St. Paul with Almeda as an evangelist and Charles as a pastor.[85] By 1927, Bethel Temple met in a storefront at the corner of

---

81. *Word and Witness*, November 20, 1913, 3.
82. *SV*, November 1927, 5–6; *PE*, January 2, 1932, 12.
83. *SV*, November 1927, 6.
84. Heckman, *HFCA*, 145.
85. *HF*, April 1943, 30.

Snelling and Juno avenues.[86] Almeda led the weekly services, including a Tuesday morning prayer and praise meeting, and a Sunday evening service that aired over WMIN. Her constant theme was: "Send a revival and save St. Paul."[87] When Almeda died in 1943, Charles continued as pastor but invited students from North Central Bible College in Minneapolis to assist him.[88]

In 1951, the evangelist Helen Jepsen came to speak at the church, she was invited to stay and served as the next pastor. Years earlier, Helen Jepsen (1895–1977) led the Full Gospel Tabernacle in Clarkfield, Minnesota, west of Minneapolis, and conducted a broadcast radio program on KWLM. As a Pentecostal evangelist, she was billed as the "tiple [a ten-string ukulele] playing preacher" who converted to faith when she was a "'Sahara, Oriental and Hula dancer' for clubs, stags and smokers."[89]

Duluth Gospel Tabernacle

In Duluth in 1920, a year after E. C. Erickson took over the mission of Arthur F. Johnson, the congregation purchased a building occupied earlier by Presbyterians. Seven years later, Erickson's congregation began to erect a new building on the same site.[90] The church's name was changed to Duluth Gospel Tabernacle. In 1924, when Lewi Pethrus visited Duluth, he described the young pastor, saying, "Brother Elmer Erickson, despite his youth, is a clear-sighted church leader."[91] Pethrus mentioned that the church's attendance was between 200 and 300. In 1937, when he visited the city again, he commented that Duluth Gospel Tabernacle "is probably the largest Scandinavian-oriented Pentecostal church in the United States with a membership of about 600."[92]

---

86. *HF*, January 1936, 6.
87. Heckman, *HFCA*, 146.
88. *HF*, July 1943, 6.
89. Heckman, *HFCA*, 147.
90. Alvarsson, "Relationer mellan Sverige och USA," 45.
91. *EH*, June 5, 1924, 265–66.
92. *EH*, December 9, 1937, 995; Pethrus, *Västerut*, 55.

E. C. Erickson and Harry Ring. Summer Camp in northern Minnesota in 1935. Courtesy of the Ring Family.

In turn, E. C. Erickson visited Sweden several times.[93] In 1931, he participated in Bible study week in Kölingared and spoke at the dedication of Filadelfia Church on Rörstrand Street in Stockholm.[94] Erickson was among Pethrus's favorite interpreters, along with Arthur F. Johnson and Harry Lindblom.[95] In 1949, when Kristian Nielsen visited Duluth, he reported: "The congregation [has] a choir of 40 people" and "an orchestra,

---

93. Interview with Paul Zettersten by Jan-Åke Alvarsson, Uppsala, Sweden, October 10, 2016.

94. *EH*, June 18, 1931.

95. *EH*, November 19, 1936, 954–55. Cf. *EH*, May 12, 1949, 330.

consisting of all conceivable instruments, with 35 musicians" and "every Sunday evening the congregation broadcasts on the radio."[96]

Erickson's visibility from the publishing of *Herald of Faith*, his leadership role in the IAG, and his contacts with leaders in Sweden, contributed to him becoming a prominent figure in the Pentecostal movement. As a gifted Bible teacher, he taught at a Bible school in Mexico in 1944, and two years later, co-founded Immanuel Christian Assembly in Los Angeles.[97]

In addition to these churches in Minnesota, congregations affiliated with the IAG were located in the Upper Midwest in the states of Wisconsin, Michigan, North Dakota, South Dakota, Iowa, and Nebraska. As for the Northeast, several independent missions and local churches formed in New York City.

Swedish Pentecostal Church of Madison Avenue, New York City

After the initial work of Emil Lindstrom with the Apostolic Faith Mission (*Den Apostoliska Trons Mission*) in New York City, the mission moved to 56th Street.[98] Lewi Pethrus described this ministry as "one of the oldest [Pentecostal missions] in the country."[99] The ministry had been through a difficult crisis because of "some brothers' [Ödman's and Newman's] involvement in 'new light' [Oneness Pentecostal] activities" but the mission survived the storm and despite the turmoil was "wonderfully blessed."[100] The mission held meetings in Swedish, except for Saturdays when they were in English.[101]

In 1924, when Pethrus visited there, he held "large Swedish meetings" in cooperation with A. F. Hedlund, originally from Åmål, Sweden.[102] Already, there were discussions of organizing the mission into a local church. Three years later, the Swedish Pentecostal Church (*Svensk*

---

96. *EH*, May 12, 1949, 330.
97. Heckman, *HFCA*, 81–82.
98. *SV*, July 1920, 5.
99. Pethrus, *Västerut*, 74–75.
100. *EH*, November 13, 1919.
101. *EH*, January 22, 1920.
102. *EH*, April 24, 1924; *SV* April 1935, 4–5.

pingstförsamlingen) held worship services at 624 Madison Avenue, led by a new pastor, Helmer Lindblad, originally from Frinnaryd, Sweden.

In 1939, Joseph Mattsson-Boze moved to New York from Chicago to lead the Swedish Pentecostal Church, and remained until 1943, when he returned to the Windy City. The Swedish Pentecostal Church in New York changed its name then to Rock Church. The new pastor was Nicolai J. Pöysti, a Russian-born, Swedish-speaking Finn who came to New York City from Vyborg in western Russia.[103] Earlier, Pöysti had served with the Russian and Eastern European Mission.[104]

Salem Gospel Tabernacle of Brooklyn

Several Norwegian families attended the Scandinavian Assembly Eben-Ezer, a church comprised of *Frie Venner* (Free Friends) that met at 415 53rd Street in Brooklyn. The congregation was led by Theodor "Tom" G. Christensen (1865–1931), originally from Risør, Norway.[105] Christensen was introduced to the Pentecostal movement by his friend, Oscar Halvorsen, in January 1907, mentioned in chapter 4. When Christensen became a Pentecostal, he engaged with other Scandinavian Pentecostals and eventually served as an officer of the SAG. In 1926, however, a new Norwegian Pentecostal church began in Brooklyn when some Pentecostal friends more oriented toward T. B. Barratt and the Filadelfia Church of Oslo, along with some Free Friends from Eben-Ezer church, gathered for a prayer meeting at Pulcifer Institute Hall located at 5111 5th Avenue in Brooklyn.

A few weeks later, the Scandinavian Pentecostal Church (*Den skandinaviske pinsemenigheten*) was organized with twenty-four charter members. This was the beginning of Salem Gospel Tabernacle. In October of that year, the church called Arne Dahl to be the pastor. In 1931, when the congregation outgrew Pulcifer Hall, they purchased a theater at 7th Avenue and 52nd Street. Five years later, Salem called Harry Ring to assist Dahl.

After ten years of serving the congregation, Dahl returned to Norway, and A. W. Rasmussen succeeded him as pastor. Church attendance grew to nearly 500 at the time.

---

103. *HF*, April 1943, 31.
104. See Poysti, *With Christ in Russia and Siberia*.
105. *EH*, November 13, 1919.

Andrew W. Rasmussen (1905–1996) was originally from Pennock, Minnesota.[106] He was the son of Scandinavian immigrants; his father came from Denmark and his mother from Sweden. In 1923, Rasmussen attended Moody Bible Institute in Chicago, and during this time came into contact with Pentecostals, and soon experienced Spirit-baptism. When he returned home to Minnesota, he preached the Pentecostal message in the Lutheran, Salvation Army, and Mission Covenant churches.[107] After ministering in Chicago, he came to Brooklyn.

In 1941, Harry Ring became pastor of Salem Gospel Tabernacle, which then met at 5322 Fourth Avenue in Brooklyn. Ring led the Norwegian-language services and Arthur M. Johnson (1903–1968) conducted English services. In the fall of 1942, Salem purchased a nearby Jewish synagogue from the B'nai Israel congregation. Ring was trained in architecture and finance, and insisted that to upgrade "old Salem" was too expensive. When he found the synagogue for sale during the middle of World War II, the only condition that the synagogue's rabbi made was that no cross should be mounted on the outside of the building until the Nazis were defeated.[108] Ring agreed to his request but insisted that they put the name "Jesus" in front of the sanctuary, since after all, Jesus was a Jew. The rabbi agreed and so B'nai Israel on 4th Avenue became Salem Gospel Tabernacle. Ring served for three years, resigning to become pastor of Elim Gospel Tabernacle, a new branch church on Staten Island.

Scandinavian Pentecostal (Philadelphia) Church of Seattle

In the Pacific Northwest, Scandinavian Pentecostals of the IAG continued to establish and develop congregations. The regional center was Seattle-Tacoma.

The flagship church in Seattle began as the Jones Avenue Mission of Ballard, which underwent several name changes including the Scandinavian Pentecostal Church (*Skandinaviska pingstförsamlingen*), and later Philadelphia Church of Seattle.[109] In 1920, Einar J. Holm, an evangelist

---

106. *SV*, June 1932, 5.

107. Rasmussen, *Last Chapter*, 28, 64–65, 76–77.

108. "Our Humble Beginnings: Sunset Park Community Church," http://www.sunsetparkchurch.org/Our-Humble-Beginnings; Donn Ring, email correspondence, May 25, 2022.

109. *SV*, February 1927, 8.

from Canada, came to minister.[110] Two years later, Karl G. (Staalesen) Stolsen (1887–1940), originally of Kristiansand, Norway, served the congregation and was asked by the church board to become the "elder in charge" with renumeration.[111]

In 1925, after Stolsen gave notice of his intention to resign so that he could minister nearby in Tacoma, Ernst L. Nilsson of Jönköping, Sweden, accepted the pastorate, beginning a month after his arrival to America. While in Tacoma, Nilsson published a periodical titled *Pingst-Vittnet* (The Pentecostal Witness) that served as the organ for Norwegian Pentecostal churches in the Pacific Northwest. When C. M. Hanson was traveling in Washington, he wrote about his cooperation with Nilsson, saying, "I have been to Spokane, Seattle, Ballard and Tacoma. Will have a baptism here tomorrow. Then travel back to Ballard for the Bible conference with Br. Nilsson."[112] When Nilsson left for another ministry, he was succeeded by Arthur F. Johnson who arrived to Seattle in 1930.[113] When Arthur F. Johnson returned to his passion as an itinerant evangelist, the church called Arvid Ohrnell.

Arvid Ohrnell had come to Seattle when he was offered the opportunity to become a prison chaplain in the State of Washington.[114] However, after meeting with Pentecostal friends at the Scandinavian Pentecostal Mission in 1933, they persuaded him to lead the church which he did for the next three years. Ohrnell came to the point, however, when he needed to focus entirely on his ministry as a prison chaplain which he did for the next sixteen years.[115] He served as the first National Prison Chaplain for the Assemblies of God.

Ohrnell was followed by B. M. Johnson who came from Chicago as the interim pastor for seven months. In 1937, Pethrus visited the church and reported: "In Seattle, Washington, the Scandinavian Pentecostal Church and the congregations of Fremont Tabernacle and Hollywood Temple [two AG churches] have invited us. . . . We had our first meeting on Sunday morning in the Scandinavian Pentecostal Church on Jones

---

110. Heckman, *HFCA*, 115.

111. Heckman, *HFCA*, 116. K. G. Stolsen also served at Philadelphia Church of Chicago in 1934 and 1935. *Philadelphia Church 35th Anniversary*, 3.

112. *SV*, Mar 1927, 6.

113. *EH*, September 29, 1932, 664; Heckman, *HFCA*, 116.

114. Alvarsson, "Relationer mellan Sverige och USA," 60.

115. Carl R. Garrett, "His Converts Are in Jail," *PE*, February 3, 1952, 5–6.

Avenue, where Brother B. M. Johnson is pastor. It was dear to see so many old friends after so many years."[116]

Pethrus reminisced about his visit to the church, saying, "During my travels here, I have had many encouraging memories about how kind and beloved is the song "The Promises Cannot Fail" (*Löftena kunna ej svika*) and from here I have a new example of this. Brother B. M. Johnson, who led this Swedish meeting, suggested to the congregation that they sing "The Promises Cannot Fail." No one had a songbook with the song but he said that it was so well-known that everyone could just sing along. I think I have never heard it sung louder than on this occasion."[117]

Later in 1937, Morten J. and Bergine (Engen) Hagli, who had been missionaries to China, were welcomed to Seattle from nearby Tacoma.[118] During this time, the name of the Seattle church was changed to Ballard Pentecostal Tabernacle, and twelve years later became Philadelphia Church.

Scandinavian Pentecostal Church of Tacoma

Scandinavian Pentecostals held tent meetings in Tacoma as early as 1907. For the next decade, the small fellowship met at the Free Mission Hall. In 1920, the Norwegian "Bro. Paulsson" led the work.[119] With more immigrants arriving from Norway and Sweden, in 1926, Anton Nilsen called a meeting of the congregation and adopted the name, Scandinavian Pentecostal Church (*Skandinaviska Pingstförsamlingen*). In addition, the congregation called Karl G. Stolsen as pastor, and elected three deacons, John Kvamme, Ole Snartemo, and K. J. Konsmo.[120]

In the following years, the independent church flourished as it ministered in the Norwegian language. After Stolsen, the church was served by David F. Lundquist, Jens Gustafsen, and A. W. Rasmussen. During Rasmussen's pastorate, the church changed its name to Bethel Pentecostal Assembly and began holding services in English in order to reach

---

116. *EH*, April 29, 1937, 356–57; Heckman, *HFCA*, 117.

117. *EH*, April 29, 1937, 356–57. For the lyrics of "The Promises Cannot Fail" in Swedish and English, see the periodical of the Scandinavian Missionary Society ("Free-Free"). *Brev-Duvan*, November 1926, 2.

118. Heckman, *HFCA*, 117.

119. *EH*, April 22, 1920.

120. Heckman, *HFCA*, 121.

English-speaking neighbors in addition to Scandinavian immigrants.[121] Rasmussen was succeeded by Carl Hedeen.

Immanuel Christian Assembly of Los Angeles

Despite the fact that 312 Azusa Street was at the center of the Pentecostal movement from 1906 to 1909, there were no flagship Scandinavian Pentecostal churches in LA. In 1913, the Scandinavian Mission at 8th and Wall streets, a daughter mission of the Azusa Street Mission, organized as a local church and joined the Swedish Evangelical Free Church of America, keeping ties with its Pentecostal missionaries, nevertheless.[122] Arthur Osterberg changed the name of his congregation from the Full Gospel Tabernacle to Full Gospel Assembly Church. However, this congregation was never uniquely Scandinavian. He later served as superintendent of the Southern California-Arizona District of the Assemblies of God.[123]

By 1927, Emil Lindstrom, who had pioneered the Scandinavian Pentecostal work in Brooklyn, New York, moved to LA, where he began the Scandinavian Pentecostal Mission (*Skandinaviska Pingstmissionen*) at 128 Main Street in Los Angeles. However, Lindstrom faced the challenge of bi-vocational work, planting a church while employed as a gardener. When he died in 1932, the mission ended.

In 1946, however, E. C. Erickson helped to establish Immanuel Christian Assembly.[124] As he became aware of the need for a Scandinavian Pentecostal church in LA, he along with friends from Duluth and some members of the Evangelical Free Church of Los Angeles, began Immanuel Christian Assembly.[125] A leader in the congregation was Einar Waermo, the well-known vocalist of the IAG who toured extensively with Einar Ekberg.[126] Two years after the church's founding, Immanuel Christian Assembly named Paul Zettersten (1922–2021) of Uppsala, Sweden, as the pastor.

---

121. *EH*, April 19, 1937, 356; Pethrus, *Västerut*, 227; Heckman, *HFCA*, 121.
122. Gustafson, "Scandinavian Mission of the Azusa Street Revival," 192–95.
123. Alvarsson, "Relationer mellan Sverige och USA," 56–57.
124. Heckman, *HFCA*, 81–82.
125. Alvarsson, "Relationer mellan Sverige och USA," 29.
126. Alvarsson, *Svenskt Frikyrkolexikon*, 476.

IAG and the Latter Rain Movement

In Canada, in 1944, Ole Forseth invited A. W. Rasmussen to conduct meetings at the Bethel Pentecostal Church in the Peace River area of Alberta. Rasmussen saw the need to gather small groups of Pentecostals in Canada, and so in 1945, he and his family moved to Edmonton to establish the Edmonton Gospel Temple.

In 1947, William Branham, an American Pentecostal minister and faith healer, promoted teachings which led eventually to the Latter Rain Movement (LRM) which began at the Sharon Bible Institute in North Battleford, Saskatchewan. Both A. W. Rasmussen and Joseph Mattsson-Boze were stirred by Branham's teaching and this new Pentecostal revival.[127] Rasmussen invited LRM leaders George Hawtin and Percy Hunt to speak at IAG meetings but when pastors became divided over Branham's teachings, controversy resulted within the IAG. While some joined Rasmussen and Mattsson-Boze who promoted LRM doctrine, others like E. C. Erickson opposed it, speaking against its excesses and what he determined were unscriptural teachings.[128] Erickson along with others like Arthur F. Johnson were disturbed by the teaching of the "New Order of the Latter Rain" that held to the restoration of apostles and prophets, which in effect undermined the IAG's view of local church leadership and autonomy. Erickson held that no congregation was to become subject to outside authorities including those recognized as modern-day apostles and prophets.

In 1949, when the General Council of the Assemblies of God met in Seattle, the AG warned its ministers about the "New Order of the Latter Rain."[129] Among the visitors to the AG's General Council meeting was Arthur F. Johnson.[130] During the same year, Mattsson-Boze traveled to Sweden and spoke enthusiastically about the LRM to churches there. He referred to phenomena with which Pentecostals in Sweden felt at home—phenomena that included praying, fasting, seizing (*gripenhet*), and healing.[131] This prompted Lewi Pethrus to travel to the U.S. and Canada in order to form

---

127. Alvarsson, "Relationer mellan Sverige och USA," 40–41. For the view of apostleship, see *HF*, July 1950, 5, 13; August 1950, 5, 8.

128. Colletti, "Lewi Pethrus," 27.

129. On April 20, 1949, the Assemblies of God sent out a six-page *Special Edition of the Quarterly Letter*. In 1953, AG openly withdrew support from Branham. Blumhofer. *Restoring the Faith*, 211.

130. *PE*, October 22, 1949, 8.

131. Alvarsson, "Relationer mellan Sverige och USA," 41.

his own opinion of the movement. When in Chicago, he urged the IAG to "buy the whole field in order to get the treasure" (Matt. 13:44).[132] However, many pastors of the IAG opposed him. Erickson prophesied to Pethrus: "When this movement, as we have seen it here, arrives in Sweden, you will be the first man to shut the door on it."[133]

Although Pethrus initially endorsed the LRM, by 1950, he expressed reservations.[134] Needless to say, the reputation of the esteemed mentor by many Scandinavian-American Pentecostals was tarnished and his influence among them waned.[135] Ironically, during Pethrus's same visit to America, he was awarded an honorary doctorate from Wheaton College, near Chicago.[136]

In October, 1951, at the IAG's annual convention held at Immanuel Christian Assembly in Los Angeles, a rift had clearly started to form between the two groups over the LRM. Rasmussen and Mattsson-Boze, along with those who embraced Branham's teachings and the LRM were moving in a different direction and split the IAG into two groups. See Appendix.

Conclusion

Scandinavian-American Pentecostals developed relationships along ecclesial, regional, and ethno-linguistic lines. Congregations of the IAG spanned the U.S. and Canada with flagship churches in the metropolitan areas of Chicago, Minneapolis, St. Paul, Duluth, New York City, Seattle, and Tacoma. As this chapter shows, Chicago was at the center of Scandinavian-American Pentecostalism, both chronologically, beginning in February 1906, and numerically, by virtue of the number of Norwegian- and Swedish-language congregations in the Windy City.

For the Scandinavian Assemblies of God (SAG), from 1918 to 1935, this fellowship's identity was both theological as Pentecostals and ethno-linguistic as Scandinavians. For the IAG, from 1922 to 1935, this

---

132. Colletti, "Lewi Pethrus," 27.

133. Heckman, *HFCA*, 81.

134. Carlsson, "American Influences on the Swedish Pentecostal Movement," 161.

135. "Lewi Pethrus Renounces So-Called 'Latter Rain' Revival," *Herald of Pentecost*, February 1952, 2, 12, cited in Colletti, "Lewi Pethrus," 28.

136. Pethrus was awarded the honorary Doctorate of Divinity at Wheaton College on October 11, 1949. Lundgren, "Lewi Pethrus and the Swedish Pentecostal Movement," 169–170.

fellowship's identity was primarily ecclesial. Churches that associated with the IAG saw themselves as a voluntary body of self-governing congregations, in contrast to the larger, dominant Assemblies of God (AG). Nonetheless, most IAG congregations were comprised of Scandinavian immigrants and their children. For both the SAG and IAG, the idea of joining the larger, English-speaking AG churches would demand a compromise (real or perceived) of their ecclesial convictions, as well as a forfeiture of their ethno-linguistic function and identity (which eventually came). Despite this "ecclesial boundary," relations between IAG and Scandinavian leaders of the AG were generally cordial, with some ministers moving back and forth between IAG and AG congregations.

By 1935, the decision of the SAG and IAG to merge under the common banner of the IAG (unincorporated), signified a desire to maintain an ecclesial identity and to expand as a fellowship of churches. The decision *not* to include the word *Scandinavian* in the name marked the beginning of movement away from an immigrant cultural identity. This occurred increasingly at the congregational level too. Local churches adopted English names like "Rock Church" as they sought to open doors to English-speaking Americans.

Thus, with the merger in 1935, came the English-language periodical, *Herald of Faith*, which began in 1936. As younger generations of Pentecostals entered IAG congregations and these congregations sought to reach their neighborhoods, use of the Scandinavian languages decreased.[137] The flow of Filadelfia-formed Pentecostal ministers from Scandinavia in the 1920s and 1930s was a trickle by the 1940s.

By 1950, the number of contacts and exchanges between Scandinavian-American Pentecostals and Pentecostals in Scandinavia decreased as well. Nevertheless, Scandinavia-America relations continued on a limited basis. While surnames of conference leaders and pastors of IAG congregations remained largely Scandinavian, there were increasingly more non-Scandinavians names,[138] and references to anything Scandinavian decreased, except to acknowledge the heritage.

In 1952, the Swedish-language periodical *Sanningens Vittne och Trons Härold* ceased publication, signifying the end of a *functional*

---

137. Westerberg, "Ethnicity and the Free Churches," 235. Cf. Heckman, *HFCA*, 17–18.

138. Examples are Adolpho C. Valdez in New York City and Milwaukee; Sophie Pfankuchen in Madison, Wisconsin; and George Milobratovich in Detroit. *HF*, February 1950, 6.

Scandinavian Pentecostalism in America. Though the Scandinavian element faded, the passion for Spirit-led evangelism remained, even taking such ministries to the airwaves on local radio stations. Moreover, the IAG continued to emphasize Pentecostal spirituality with Spirit-baptism and speaking in tongues, educating young women and men in church-based education, planting new congregations, coordinating national and regional meetings, and commissioning missionaries for overseas work. Clearly, between 1918 and 1952, the IAG found its niche in America among the Scandinavian-American free-church bodies and American Pentecostal denominations. However, its loosely-organized nature left it open to theological and ecclesial threats, in particular, when presented by the Latter Rain Movement (LRM) which led to its split.

Bibliography

Primary Sources

Newspapers Used

The Apostolic Faith, Los Angeles, 1906–1908
Brev-Duvan, Buffalo, MN, 1909–1933
Bridegroom's Messenger, Atlanta, GA, 1907–1970
Chicago-Bladet, Chicago, IL, 1877–1952
Duluth Herald, Duluth, MN, 1910–1982
Evangelical Beacon, Minneapolis, 1931–2003
Evangelii Harold (*EH*), Stockholm, Sweden, 1915–1993
Folke-Vennen (*FV*), Chicago, IL, 1879–1933
Herald of Faith (*HF*), Duluth, MN, Chicago, 1936–1950
La Grange Citizen, La Grange, IL, 1905–1963
Lake View Chimes, Chicago, IL
Latter Rain Evangel, Chicago, 1908–1939
Nya Wecko-Posten, Chicago, 1884–1918
Pentecostal Evangel (*PE*), Plainfield, IN, Springfield, MO, 1913–2014
Pentecostal Herald, Chicago, 1915–1923
Pentecostal Testimony, Chicago, 1909–1912
Sanningens-Vittne (*SV*), Minneapolis, 1911–1939
Svenska Amerikanska Posten, Minneapolis, 1885–1940
Weekly Evangel, St. Louis, MO, 1915–1918
Word and Witness, Malvern, AR, 1912–1915
Word and Work, Framingham, MA, 1919–1940

Other Primary Sources

Johnson, Bengt Magnus. *Lovsångs-toner*. Chicago: B. M. Johnson, n.d.
Letter to Division of Passport Control, Washington, D.C., from B. M. Johnson, Council of the Scandinavian Assemblies of God, October 4, 1921.
Nybakken, Pearl. "History of Barry Avenue Church, Chicago." Chicago. Unpublished paper.
Philadelphia Church 35th Anniversary. Chicago: Philadelphia Church, 1961.
Ring, Donn. Correspondence with David M. Gustafson, May 25, 2022.
Zettersten, Paul. Interview by Jan-Åke Alvarsson, Uppsala, Sweden, October 10, 2016.

Secondary Sources

Alvarsson, Jan-Åke. *Varför reste Lewi Pethrus just till Chicago?: Relations mellan Sverige och USA inom ramen för pentekostalismen*. Uppsala: Artos, 2019.
———, ed. *Svenskt frikyrkolexikon*. Stockholm: Atlantis, 2014.
Blumhofer, Edith W. *Restoring the Faith: The Assemblies of God, Pentecostalism, and American Culture*. Urbana: University of Illinois Press, 1993.
Brumback, Carl. *Suddenly from Heaven: A History of the Assemblies of God*. Springfield, MO: Gospel Publishing, 1961.
Colletti, Joseph R. "Lewi Pethrus: His Influence upon Scandinavian-American Pentecostalism," *Pneuma: Journal of Pentecostal Studies* 5 (1983) 18–29.
Davidsson, Tommy H. *Lewi Pethrus' Ecclesiological Thought, 1911–1974: A Transdenominational Pentecostal Ecclesiology*. Boston: Brill, 2015.
Erickson, Scott E., ed. *American Religious Influences in Sweden*. Uppsala: Tro & Tanke, 1996.
Gustafson, David M. "Dr. Harry Lindblom: Swedish Evangelical Free Churchman and Co-laborer with Pentecostal Churchman Lewi Pethrus, 1924–1939." *Theofilos* 13 (2021) 51–78.
———. "The Scandinavian Mission of the Azusa Street Revival of Los Angeles, 1907–1913," *Swedish-American Historical Quarterly* 72 (2021) 165–208.
Heckman, Warren. *The History of the Fellowship of Christian Assemblies (HFCA)*. Beaverton, OR: Good Book, 2011.
Lundgren, Ivar. "Lewi Pethrus and the Swedish Pentecostal Movement." In *Essays on Apostolic Themes*, edited by Paul Elbert, 158–71. Peabody, MA: Hendrickson, 1985.
"Our Humble Beginnings: Sunset Park Community Church." http://www.sunsetparkchurch.org/Our-Humble-Beginnings.
Pethrus, Lewi. *Den anständiga sanningen*. Stockholm: C. E. Fritze, 1953.
———. *Västerut: En resenärs erfarenheter*. Stockholm: Förlaget Filadelfia, 1937.
Rasmussen, A. W. *The Last Chapter*. Monroeville, PA: Whitaker, 1973.
Westerberg, Wesley M. "Ethnicity and the Free Churches." *Swedish-American Historical Quarterly* 24 (1973) 231–37.

Chapter Seven

Between Multiple Worlds
Emerging Scandinavian-American
Pentecostal Theology, 1907–1919

Tommy Davidsson

THIS CHAPTER EXPLORES THE emerging theology of first-generation Scandinavian-American Pentecostals from 1907 until the formation of the Scandinavian Assemblies of God (SAG) and the publication of Andrew August Holmgren's (1866–1949) "Summa Theologica Pentecostalis," *Pingströrelsen och dess förkunnelse* (The Pentecostal Movement and its Preaching) in 1919.[1] The purpose is to show how the theology of early Scandinavian-American Pentecostals was formed by being an immigrant community in the United States with strong ties to their home countries, and especially to influential Scandinavian Pentecostal leaders such as Thomas Ball Barratt (1862–1940) and Lewi Pethrus (1884–1974).[2] The

---

1. Holmgren's book is a compilation of a wide variety of sources, including works from 19th century evangelical revivalists, Pentecostal pioneers, and his own theological writings. His aim was to provide a balanced picture of Pentecostalism as opposed to the many negative portrayals at the time. Cecil M. Robeck notes that Holmgren believed it to be "the first substantial study of this global movement." This article tries to show that it also reflects the end product of a decade long theological process. Robeck, "Origins of Modern Pentecostalism," 17.

2. Even if Danish Pentecostals belong in this category, they have not been included in this study.

chapter also demonstrates that the immigrants were neither insulated from theological developments in their native American context nor from discussions raging in broader theological circles on both sides of the Atlantic. Douglas Jacobsen suggests that an "accurate and helpful way of understanding the emergence of [. . .] various subtraditions within the rubric of larger Pentecostalism [is] to see them as part of the necessary process of clarifying and codifying pentecostal values, practices, and beliefs as the movement advanced."[3]

Aligned with Jacobsen's suggestion, this chapter examines four themes of particular importance for Scandinavian-American Pentecostals in the early development of their theology, which also incorporate many of their "values, practices, and beliefs," namely (1) the full gospel and the "finished work of Calvary," (2) radical congregationalism, (3) the intermediate state and eternal punishment, and (4) the oneness debate.[4] These four themes are not randomly selected, but they generated tension and conflict as seen in A. A. Holmgren's periodical *Sanningens Vittne* [The Witness of Truth],[5] other Scandinavian-American journals, and the abovementioned *Pingströrelsen och dess förkunnelse*. Even though the information from these sources is scant, complementing information from Scandinavian Pentecostal periodicals such as *Brudgummens röst* [The Voice of the Bridegroom] (Swedish), *Evangelii härold* [The Gospel Herald] (Swedish), and *Byposten/ Korsets seier* [The City Post/ The Victory of the Cross] (Norwegian) provide additional information to paint a clearer picture of their emerging theology, due to the trans-Atlantic discussions between Scandinavian ministers in America and their colleagues in Scandinavia.

This chapter argues that Scandinavian-American Pentecostal theology was formed in the interaction between the "multiple worlds" of 19th century Evangelicalism with its pietist, revivalist and holiness streams, American Pentecostalism, Scandinavian Pentecostalism, and debates in the broader theological sphere of the Western world. It will

3. Jacobsen, *Thinking in the Spirit*, 134.

4. Since a lot has been written about topics 1, 2, and 4, these sections will be given less attention than topic 3, which has never been properly researched before.

5. Scandinavian-American Pentecostals published additional journals such as B. M. Johnson's *Pingst-Rösten* [The Voice of Pentecost], H. Langeland's *Sandhedens tolk* [The Interpreter of Truth] and the devotional *Eben-Ezer*. These magazines are most likely lost to history, but excerpts can be found, for example, in *Brudgummens röst* vol. 2, issue March 1, 1912 and *Sanningens Vittne*, January 1, 1914, 4. See also, Holmgren, *Pingströrelsen och dess förkunnelse*, 42.

also show that Norwegian and Swedish American Pentecostal theology was not monolithic but contained slight variations in emphasis. The examples will further demonstrate that the final emergence of a "Scandinavian-American Pentecostal theology" was built on a tense and decade-long process of what doctrines should, or should not, belong to the "Apostolic Faith."

The Full Gospel and the "Finished Work of Calvary"

Scandinavian-American Pentecostals came from a variety of religious backgrounds,[6] but what united them was not only a common linguistic and cultural heritage but also a deep conviction and experience of the Full Gospel. As Donald Dayton has shown in his seminal work in the *Theological Roots of Pentecostalism*, the Full Gospel can be traced to theological developments in the Methodist and Holiness Movements of the 18th and 19th centuries. Despite Dayton's claim that Puritanism and Pietism "are to a large extent parallels rather than direct or actual sources,"[7] more recent studies have shown that Dayton limits Pietism's role too much.[8] In fact, Darrin Rodgers has convincingly demonstrated that "Early Scandinavian Pentecostals in Minnesota and the Dakotas, recent immigrants to America whose primary tongue was not English, maintained significant connections to their roots in Scandinavian Pietism."[9]

Moreover, Scandinavian Pentecostals experienced pre-Azusa street revivals at the end of the 19th century that included manifestations of glossolalia. Rodgers argues that it is possible "that early Pentecostals in Chicago first became aware of contemporary tongue-speech, not from news of Azusa Street, but from news of prior glossolalic revivals in Minnesota and the Dakotas."[10] A quick perusal of their earliest Pentecostal publications also shows that Scandinavian Pentecostals were heavily influenced by the British and American revivalist tradition. Reports from the ministries of C. G. Finney, D. L. Moody, A. J. Gordon, R. A. Torrey, C. H. Spurgeon, William and Catherine Booth, Evan Roberts, among

6. Alvarsson, "Relationer mellan Sverige och USA," 12–17.
7. Dayton, *Theological Roots of Pentecostalism*, 38.
8. See Rodgers, "Rediscovering Pentecostalism's Diverse Roots: Origins in Scandinavian Pietism in Minnesota and the Dakotas"; Bundy, *Vision of Apostolic Mission*; Reed, *"In Jesus' Name."*
9. Rodgers, *Northern Harvest*, 15.
10. Rodgers, *Northern Harvest*, 16.

others, frequently appear.[11] In addition, Scandinavian immigrants frequently visited and participated in Holiness missions such as A. B. Simpson's mission in New York and J. A. Dowie's Zion City north of Chicago. The fact that many Scandinavian immigrants felt perfectly at home in the evangelical revivalist tradition, lacked established networks, and came from a cultural context where racism was not a problem, might also explain why "a disproportionate number at the Azusa Street revival" were Scandinavians.[12] The Swede, Andrew Johnson-Ek, for example, was part of the first missionary band—the Palestine Missionary Band—that was sent out from Azusa Street and reported about the revival to William Durham and T. B. Barratt.[13] Considering all these influences, it is understandable that early Scandinavian American Pentecostals shared Pietism's emphases on heartfelt religion, the devotional reading of Scripture,[14] and its anti-organizational and anti-creedal attitude. They also adhered to Methodism's and the Holiness movement's stress on the necessity of being born-again, inner and outer holiness, divine healing, and Christ's imminent Second Coming.[15]

What stands out in the earliest writings of Scandinavian-American Pentecostals, however, is their emphasis on the baptism of the Holy Spirit as a subsequent experience to salvation, and speaking in tongues as the initial evidence of Spirit baptism.[16] These descriptions are not only biblical expositions of the Pentecostal position, but they also stress the

---

11. See for instance, *Sanningens Vittne (SV)*, July 1, 1912, 6; *SV*, November 1, 1920, 77, *Brudgummens röst (BR)*, September 1911, 18; *BR*, November 15, 1915, 167; *SV*, January 1914, 1.

12. Alvarsson, "Pingstväckelsens etablering i Sverige," 16–17; Alvarsson, "Relationer mellan Sverige och USA," 24.

13. Alvarsson, "Relationer mellan Sverige och USA," 25.

14. Holmgren's pithy statement perfectly sums up Scandinavian Pentecostals' approach to Scripture: "Read it and become wise, believe it and be saved, practice it and become holy." Holmgren, *Pingströrelsen och dess förkunnelse*, 184.

15. *SV*, March-April 1913, 1, 3, 8; May-June 1913, 1, 4–5; January 1914, 1; January 1919, 2; Holmgren, *Pingströrelsen och dess förkunnelse*, 180–183. It is telling that the available Pentecostal tracts for Swedish-American Pentecostals in 1913 dealt with the following topics: 1) Salvation, Spirit Baptism, and Healing. 2) The Baptism in the Holy Spirit. 3) The Church of Christ. 4) After the Rapture of the Bride—What? 5) Prophetic Message. 6) Full redemption. 7) The Sealing of the Spirit. 8) An Opposer's Testimony by Pastor J. H. King. 9) The Great Crisis. 10) "Behold, I Am Coming Soon." A Presentation of the End Times. 11) The Lost, a Revelation. 12) The Pentecostal Revival. 13) A Personal Testimony by Wm. H. Durham. *SV*, May 1, 1913, 8.

16. *SV*, May-June 1913, 1–2; January 1920, 2; *BR*, April 1911, 16; Holmgren, *Pingströrelsen och dess förkunnelse*, 108–31, 226–46.

movement's special place in God's redemptive plan to restore the Full Gospel before the End Times.[17] The Pentecostal movement is, for example, portrayed as the small and despised, but divinely anointed, "David" who stands up against the mighty, but apostatized, "Saul," of other churches.[18] The acceptance of speaking in tongues as the initial evidence of Spirit baptism is therefore viewed as an important identity marker, which distinguishes them as people who are willing to obey the Bible's teaching despite personal or denominational objections.[19] This understanding of Pentecostalism in general, and Spirit baptism and glossolalia in particular, was nothing new, but something that Scandinavian Pentecostals shared with all other Pentecostal sub-traditions.

The first major crack in the Pentecostals' united theological front happened in the wake of "the finished work of Calvary" controversy in 1911. The background of the controversy has been traced to the theological musings of William H. Durham (1873–1912), the pastor of the North Avenue Mission in Chicago. The story of William Durham's rise to fame in early Pentecostalism has been retold elsewhere, so our focus here is only on his impact on Scandinavian Pentecostalism.[20] Durham has been designated as the author of the "finished work of Calvary," a doctrine that opposed the prevailing Holiness notion that "separated the negative aspects of salvation (pardon) from its positive aspects (holiness) into two distinct works of grace."[21] Durham disagreed with this view and rather emphasized that sanctification entailed a continuous identification with Christ's Finished Work on the cross, nullifying the need for a second work of grace.[22]

Durham's key role in the development of Finished Work theology has been questioned by Christopher Richmann, who argues that Durham was more of the doctrine's promoter than its sole inventor, a role he rather shared with A. S. Copley. Richmann further argues that the doctrine was more soteriological than Christological in nature, which should remove some of the blame Durham has received for being the fountainhead of Oneness theology. Even if Durham's role as inventor of the doctrine has been exaggerated, his eager promotion of it, from 1911

17. Holmgren, *Pingströrelsen och dess förkunnelse*, 8–12.
18. *SV*, July 1, 1911, 1–3.
19. *SV*, March-April 1913, 2–3.
20. Blumhofer, "William Durham," 123–42; Jacobsen, *Thinking in the Spirit*, 136–45.
21. Richmann, "William H. Durham and Early Pentecostalism," 230.
22. Reed, *"In Jesus' Name,"* 88.

to his untimely death in 1912, ensured that it also affected Scandinavian-American Pentecostals. It is a well-known fact that the issue created a divide between Wesleyan and Finished Work Pentecostals that remains to this day, but it also became an issue where a difference of belief arose between Swedish and Norwegian Pentecostals.

The Swedish adoption of the Finished Work position can largely be explained by the geographical proximity of prominent Swedish Pentecostal leaders to William Durham's North Avenue Mission. The Pentecostal-friendly periodical *Folke-Vennen*, with ties to the North Avenue Mission, reported on early Pentecostal activities from 1904 to 1912 and promoted the development of Swedish, Norwegian, and Danish Pentecostal churches in Chicago. Durham's mission was also the sending church for the well-known missionaries to Brazil, Daniel Berg (1884–1963) and Gunnar Vingren (1879–1933).[23] The local Swedish pastor, B. M. Johnson, the editor of the Pentecostal journal *Pingströsten*, was "one of them who were inspired by William H. Durham."[24] A. A. Holmgren was inspired by Durham too, attending his meetings and conferences when visiting Chicago.[25]

Andrew August Holmgren at the Office of *Sanningens Vittne*,
Courtesy of the Holmgren Family

23. Berg and Vingren also retained close contacts with Sweden. See, Josefsson, *Liv och över nog*, 83.
24. Alvarsson, "Relationer mellan Sverige och USA," 34.
25. Heckman, *History of the Fellowship of Christian Assemblies*, 49.

This is not to say that the doctrine did not cause divisions as it spread among Swedish Pentecostal congregations, yet it seems to have prevailed quickly. A report from Colorado Springs in the May-June 1913 issue of *Sanningens Vittne* states: "The teaching that sanctification is a separate work of grace has also caused here division in the camp of the saints."[26] In the same issue, N. A. Martinson of Moorhead, Minnesota, announces victoriously: "I am so glad that many of the saints have realized that the Bible does not teach sanctification as a 'second work of grace.' I was caught up in this teaching for a while, but I never got it to really fit with the Bible's teaching."[27] David Reed sums up the effective spread of the doctrine in subsequent years, saying: "By 1930 three of every five Pentecostals had embraced the Finished Work teaching. The deep South, mostly rural, had largely resisted the new movement. But in the West, Midwest and Canada, Durham's teaching had swept in a fully eighty percent of the Pentecostal movement."[28]

An exception to these statistics, at least initially, was Norwegian Pentecostalism. As a staunch Wesleyan Pentecostal, T. B. Barratt opposed the doctrine. Barratt writes in *Korsets seier*, which was read by Norwegian Pentecostals in America:

> We do not believe in the Durhamian theory that everyone, the moment they are regenerated, is *completely sanctified*. That many over there [in America] have received enough light in the question about the old man's crucifixion, [that one] can perhaps reach complete cleansing of the heart at the same time as regeneration should not be questioned. We do not want to limit God's power. But God's Word and experience show us, that *most do not reach into the higher life at regeneration*. They must therefore go through a *cleansing process* whereby this happens. Some experience it *before* their Spirit baptism, some *after*. It *must* be experienced afterwards, unless one has reached it already, otherwise one will slide into pride, partiality, unlovingness, judgmentalism, worldliness, and carnality so that the spiritual power one has received will not be fully realized. [...] We do not believe therefore that the work is unconditionally finished in us, because it is finished at Calvary [italics in original].[29]

---

26. *SV*, May-June 1913, 6.
27. *SV*, May-June 1913, 6.
28. Reed, *"In Jesus' Name,"* 97.
29. *Korsets Seier* (*KS*), October 15, 1913, 154.

In a later article, Barratt did not hesitate to call the doctrine "a heresy."[30] Karl Inge Tangen makes the important observation, however, that although Norwegian Pentecostals could be considered as "Wesleyan" until Barratt's death in 1940, Barratt did not let the issue hinder him from having fellowship with Pentecostals of the "Finished Work" tradition, such as Carl Magnus Seehuus and Lewi Pethrus. Tangen therefore surmises, "The division between Wesleyan and Baptist ('Reformed') Pentecostals was not as strong in Scandinavia as in the North American context."[31] The same gracious attitude marked the relationship between Scandinavian-American Wesleyan and Finished Work Pentecostals as well. What this brief survey shows more clearly, however, is that "Finished Work" Pentecostals had "realized" or "received light" that sanctification did not belong to the Full Gospel. The Full Gospel was therefore considered to be "open" for amendments by contingents of (Finished Work) Pentecostals, which more historically anchored Methodist-Holiness Pentecostals, like T. B. Barratt, resisted.

Radical Congregationalism

Radical congregationalism is probably the most well-known distinctive of early Scandinavian Pentecostalism. This form of church structure rejects any type of organization above or between local churches. The idea of the local church's independence has its roots in Anabaptism and Separatist Puritanism, which merged in the theology of Baptist pioneer John Smyth (1554–1612). The belief in the autonomy of the local church was combined with several other features of Baptist ecclesiology, such as the separation of church and state, regenerate church membership, individual and corporate purity, and church discipline.[32] European Baptists retained the importance of the local church's independence throughout the 18th and 19th centuries, even though tendencies of a greater degree of centralization started to become visible toward the end of the 19th century.[33]

The roots of radical congregationalism among Scandinavian-American Pentecostals have been traced to Baptist ecclesiology and the

30. *KS*, November 1, 1915, 162.
31. Tangen, "Healing in the Pentecostal Tradition," 129.
32. Davidsson, *Lewi Pethrus' Ecclesiological Thought 1911–1974*, 22–24.
33. Struble, *Den samfundsfria församlingen*, 22–24.

teaching of William Durham.[34] However, recent research has shown that the true source of inspiration might rather have been the Evangelical Free Church of America (EFCA), or simply "the Free" as they were also called. The EFCA originated from a split among Swedish Mission Friends in America when the majority decided to form the Covenant that was perceived by the Free to be a return to denominationalism.[35] A radical branch of the EFCA, the Scandinavian Mission Society USA or commonly referred to as "Free-Free," incorporated in 1898.[36] This radical branch of the EFCA believed in "congregationalism, the priesthood of all believers, women's right to preach, few pastors, many elders that led the free churches, as well as an emphasis on sanctification, healing, and speaking in tongues."[37] An important link between these groups and the burgeoning Pentecostal movement in Chicago was Carl M. Hanson (1865–1954), who initially belonged to the "Free," but was ordained as a minister with the North Avenue Full Gospel Assembly by William Durham in September 1909.[38] Hanson later transferred his ministerial credentials to the Assemblies of God in 1917.[39] Another link between Durham and the Free could have been John Gustav Princell (1845–1915).[40] William Durham's radical congregationalism might therefore not have been his own, but something he imbibed from the "Free" and the "Free-Free."[41] It is perhaps therefore more correct to view Durham's importance in Pentecostal historiography as someone who effectively propagated new doctrines than authored them.[42]

---

34. Struble, *Den samfundsfria församlingen*, 71, 80.

35. Alvarsson, "Relationer mellan Sverige och USA," 18.

36. Gustafson, "Mary Johnson and Ida Anderson," 57. The Society formed in 1887 but incorporated later.

37. Alvarsson, "Relationer mellan Sverige och USA," 19–20.

38. "Religion och vansinne," *Svenska Folkets Tidning*, March 15, 1905, 5.

39. Rodgers, *Northern Harvest*, 11.

40. A comparison between J. G. Princell's and Durham's views regarding religious denominations demonstrates many similarities and supports the idea that Durham borrowed from Princell, who was a leader among the Free. Since Durham does not admit borrowing from Princell, his indebtedness cannot be stated with certainty. See Josephine Princell, *Memoirs of J. G. Princell*, 76–79; *Folke-Vennen*, February 17, 1910, 3.

41. W. Durham, *Folke-Vennen*, February 17, 1910, 3.

42. A reworked edition of Durham's article about organizations was first published in *Brudgummens röst* in August 1913, and later in *Evangelii härold* in January 1916. See BR, August 1913, 13–16; *Evangelii härold* (EH), January 1916, 9–10.

Swedish American Pentecostals adopted radical congregationalism from the "Free" and the "Free-Free." However, a big issue for early Pentecostals related to the question of whether it was better for Pentecostals to stay in their old denominations and be a positive influence, or to leave them and find freedom elsewhere. The earliest extant accounts of *Sanningens Vittne* testify to a deep resentment of the established denominations and clear preference for the latter: "The denominations have more or less fallen away from God's plan. They are not part of God's order, and the worst of all is, they neither want to be."[43] Those who had left the denominations were viewed as "David's heroes."[44]

The issue became especially acute on April 29, 1913, when Lewi Pethrus and the Filadelfia church of Stockholm were excluded from the Baptist Union. Obviously unaware of the latest developments in Sweden, Holmgren published an article on May 1 in *Sanningens Vittne* entitled: "Should the Spirit-baptized Organize Themselves into Congregations?" Using a well-known biblical metaphor, he explained that Pentecostalism and the old denominations were as incompatible as "new wine" in "old wineskins."[45] Holmgren's remedy was to plant churches based on the "ideal pattern" of Scripture.[46] He gave explicit details of what an ideal church should look like, but he also took a swipe at T. B. Barratt, whom he accused of wanting to create an "unscriptural" denomination similar to the one that the Covenant Church in America had established. The background of this accusation goes back to a dream Barratt had had since July 1908, which was to create a Pentecostal Missionary Union that was supposed to be "an 'alliance' between independent congregations so that support for missionaries could be pooled and efforts coordinated [. . .]."[47] Holmgren joined here several other critics from both inside and outside Norway who had interpreted Barratt's use of "alliance" in the same fashion.[48]

Having come across Holmgren's article during a trip to Finland, Barratt responded to Holmgren's accusation in *Korsets seier* in July 1913, and reiterated that he had never had such an intention. He objected to Holmgren's notion that if a Pentecostal remained with their

43. *SV*, July 1, 1911, 1.
44. *SV*, July 1, 1911, 2.
45. *SV*, May 1, 1913, 4.
46. *SV*, May 1, 1913, 4.
47. Bundy, *Vision of Apostolic Mission*, 230.
48. Bundy, *Vision of Apostolic Mission*, 230.

denomination, they would lose their anointing. On the contrary, there were enough cases to prove that Pentecostals could still minister effectively within their denominations, and there was no reason to despise their efforts and endurance.[49] In fact, Barratt viewed it as unrealistic to believe that one could gather all Pentecostals into churches established according to Holmgren's model. He rather proposed, just like he had done in 1908, that a more realistic aim was to establish an informal alliance where Pentecostals, who longed for fellowship with other Pentecostals, could meet. The conferences and gatherings would be open for all Pentecostals, both for those in established denominations and for those in independent (isolated) churches.[50] In follow-up articles over the summer, Barratt stressed that the alliance should not exclude anyone, and not even be based on belief in Spirit baptism and glossolalia, but based on the "cross and the blood."[51] By fall 1913, the fallout of the Baptist Union's decision to excommunicate the Filadelfia church in Stockholm, a decision Barratt regarded as fanaticism,[52] and Lewi Pethrus's adoption of radical congregationalism,[53] ended any hope of an informal alliance in Scandinavia. Despite Barratt's objections to radical congregationalism, Norwegian Pentecostals adopted the same view by 1916.[54]

Independent Scandinavian-American Pentecostals maintained their stance for radical congregationalism in the following years. They opposed the formation of the Assemblies of God (AG) in 1914, and its decision to formalize a creed (Fundamental Truths) in 1916. That their position had changed little by 1919, is clear from Holmgren's repetition of it in *Pingströrelsen och dess förkunnelse*, although B. M. Johnson's more favorable assessment of the Assembly of God's presbyterian church government was included as well.[55]

It is important for our discussion here that independent Scandinavian-American Pentecostals adhered to the doctrine even more radically than Lewi Pethrus himself. Joseph Colletti has shown that when the Latter-Rain revival appeared in 1949, Pethrus did not oppose it even though it contained elements that went against a radical congregational

49. *KS*, July 15, 1913, 106.
50. *KS*, July 15, 1913, 105–7.
51. *KS*, August 1913, 122; September 1913, 134–35.
52. *KS*, July 1913, 101–2.
53. Davidsson, *Lewi Pethrus' Ecclesiological Thought 1911–1974*, 87–94.
54. Struble, *Den samfundsfria församlingen*, 71.
55. See Holmgren, *Pingströrelsen och dess förkunnelse*, 246–61.

ecclesiology.⁵⁶ Even if Pethrus's reaction must be understood in light of the conflict he was facing with Sven Lidman at the time,⁵⁷ the fact that they maintained their ecclesiological convictions more steadfastly than their Pentecostal "hero" testifies to the degree they perceived radical congregationalism as part of Apostolic faith. Even if it was never mentioned explicitly as a fifth element of the Full Gospel, the same restorationist methodology was used when it was explained and defended. Biblical arguments were given for its validity and church history was used to show that revivals died as soon as they were organized.⁵⁸ Thus, in light of the tenacity by which the doctrine was believed and implemented, it is fair to say that radical congregationalism belonged to the Full Gospel for Independent Scandinavian-American Pentecostals.

The Intermediate State and Eternal Punishment

Premillennial dispensational eschatology was an integral part of the Full Gospel and a core aspect of early Scandinavian-American Pentecostals' theological outlook.⁵⁹ Premillennial dispensationalism was not the only aspect of eschatology, however, that affected early Scandinavian-American Pentecostals. At the turn of the 19th century, a theological debate was raging on both sides of the Atlantic concerning the state of believers and unbelievers after death.⁶⁰ The discussion centered not only on the eternality of the soul but also on the doctrine of eternal punishment and related topics such as materialism, universalism, annihilationism (conditional immortality), and soul sleep. That the discussion was extensive can be seen in William Cochrane's (1831–1898) attempt to summarize the ongoing debate in nine points, yet for our purposes it is sufficient to mention three:

> *The Materialistic*—Man is nothing but a material organism, whose conscious existence is terminated at death. [. . .] *The Annihilationist*—The soul is not naturally immortal, and can only be made immortal by union with the Saviour. [. . .] *The Orthodox*—Future punishment is everlasting. At death the state is

56. Colletti, "Lewi Pethrus," 27–29.
57. Davidsson, *Lewi Pethrus' Ecclesiological Thought, 1911–1974*, 110–11.
58. Holmgren, *Pingströrelsen och dess förkunnelse*, 246–55.
59. SV, March-April 1913, 8; January 1914, 1. For a thorough discussion, see Faupel, *Everlasting Gospel*.
60. Cochrane, *Future Punishment, or, Does Death End Probation?*, 5.

fixed for eternity. No man who dies impenitent will, after death, change his character and obtain pardon [italics mine].⁶¹

The issue of the future state of believers and unbelievers came to the fore for Scandinavian-American Pentecostals in 1914.⁶² The issue began as an in-house matter when one of the local pastors, Adolf Ödman (1871–1941) from Manchester, New Hampshire, published an article in *Sanningens Vittne*, where he argued for soul sleep in the intermediate state and the annihilation of the unregenerated after the Final Judgment.⁶³ In order to understand why the issue impacted the nascent Scandinavian-American Pentecostal movement the way it did, we need first to understand Ödman's role in the early movement.

Alfred Ödman was born in Ödenäs, Sweden, in 1871, and emigrated as an unmarried Baptist preacher to America in 1907. His initial contact was pastor Albin Holmer at Crozer (Baptist) Theological Seminary in Chester, Pennsylvania. Moving to Concord, Massachusetts, Ödman was ordained in the local Swedish Baptist church in November 1907.⁶⁴ As an ordained Baptist preacher, he was frequently invited to speak at conferences,⁶⁵ weddings,⁶⁶ anniversaries,⁶⁷ and church services in the New England area.⁶⁸ That his parishioners took a liking to his ministry is evident from a statement in *Svea* in September 1908: "Pastor Ödman is

---

61 The other views Cochrane mentions are: the Universalist or Restorationist, the Optimistic, the Probationist, the Romish, the Dantean, and the Agnostic. Cochrane, *Future Punishment, or, Does Death End Probation?*, 18–19.

62. The issue had been addressed earlier, but it did not cause a major controversy until 1914. Up until that time, "Russellism" was almost exclusively viewed in a negative light. See, *SV*, March-April 1913, 4; *SV*, May-June 1913, 3. Since the controversy surrounding the Future State and the Oneness debate both arose in 1914, the two issues are often conflated in the sources even though they had different origins. The conflation is because advocates of the doctrines used the same designation for them, i.e., "the New Light."

63. This specific issue of *Sanningens Vittne* is no longer available, but Lewi Pethrus quotes from it verbatim in *Brudgummens Röst*, so there is no doubt as to Ödman's views. See further below.

64. The report from the meeting stated that, "Many and profound were the questions, that were presented to the candidate, and who was deemed to possess a thorough knowledge in what belongs to the preaching ministry, he was warmly recommended to be ordained to this call." *Svea*, November 20, 1907, 5.

65. *Svea*, June 1, 1910, 5.

66. *Svea*, April 28, 1909, 4.

67. *Svea*, June 8, 1910, 3.

68. *Svea*, January 8, 1908, 6; *Svea*, February 5, 1908, 4.

becoming more and more appreciated by our Scandinavian people as a particularly gifted preacher."[69]

However, this positive impression took a drastic turn for the worse in 1911. Having accepted the Pentecostal message (most likely in 1910), he became an eager and uncompromising Pentecostal preacher to the dismay of the Baptist Union, who dismissed him from the denomination.[70] The reason for his dismissal is unknown, but that it had to do with his Pentecostal convictions and methods is likely based on the stern criticism he received in local newspapers. For instance, in February 1911, the Swedish-American periodical *Svea* wrote a devastating report of Ödman's ministry, as well as that of his fellow Pentecostal preacher, Emil Lindström. The paper accused them of influencing the pastor of the Swedish-Finnish Mission Covenant Church in Worcester, Massachusetts, H. Grönlund, with their Pentecostal doctrines to the point that he lost his mind and threw himself out of a second store window, barely escaping the ordeal alive.[71] The article did not only limit itself to blaming Ödman and Lindström for the accident, but included blatant character assassinations as well:

> Former Baptist preachers Adolf Ödman, Manchester, N. H., and Emil Lindström, Portland, Me., have resided for a while here in town and preached in pastor Grönlund's church or chapel, where they distributed their newly discovered teachings. Believing themselves to be filled with the Holy Spirit they preached about Spirit baptism, sinlessness, speaking in tongues, holiness etc. The new teachings made him ponder, with the consequence that he lost his mind. [. . .] On our part we believe very little in "apostles" of this kind and evangelists, since they are in most cases people, with whom something is lacking, occasionally quite a lot, and their unlimited self-confidence and complete lack of self-criticism and in most cases their great ignorance do not set any limits at all to their ministry but is hysterically driven forward, as far as possible, and therefore there are occasionally—like here—sad consequences.[72]

Another report in *Nordstjernan* [The North Star] portrayed the two ministers as proselytizing, sectarian fanatics, whose teachings resembled

69. *Svea*, September 23, 1908, 4.
70. *SV*, April 1, 1912, 4.
71. *Svea*, February 1, 1911, 8.
72. *Svea*, February 1, 1911, 8.

"freshly baked pancakes from Satan."[73] Despite these disturbing testimonies and his dismissal from the Baptist Union, Ödman still enjoyed favor with the Scandinavian-Pentecostal movement. As Alvarsson and Gustafson have shown in Chapter 3, Ödman's ministry was very much appreciated, and he was regarded as a "brother and teacher" in the newly formed Pentecostal churches.[74] His theological writings were also frequently published in *Sanningens Vittne*.[75] Ödman's good standing in the movement explains why he had such a receptive audience when he introduced his "New Light" teaching in 1914. It is difficult to say why Ödman shifted his focus from preaching classical Pentecostal doctrines to annihilationism and soul sleep at this particular time,[76] but the example of Swedish Holiness preacher, Nelly Hall, shows that he was not the only Scandinavian who promoted "Russellism" on the East Coast at this time.[77] It is also difficult to pinpoint when Ödman first adopted his views.[78] Even if it cannot be determined with certainty when he first adopted his views and why he began preaching them in 1914, his new preaching created deep rifts among Scandinavian-American Pentecostal churches and got him both friends and foes in America and Europe.

His most prominent friend turned out to be Herman August Newman (b.1880), who zealously joined him in propagating the "New Light" among Swedish and Norwegian congregations along the East Coast. A. A. Holmgren also gave him initial support. His foes became none other than T. B. Barratt, and particularly, Lewi Pethrus, as well as

73. *Nordstjernan*, February 7, 1911, 3.

74. *SV*, March 1, 1913, 7.

75. *SV*, July 1, 1911, 1–3.

76. *Svea* retells of an incident at a Swedish ecumenical meeting in Brockton, MA, in early 1914 where Ödman "had acted disruptively" and was "escorted out of the meeting and rebuked." The article also states that he eventually "gave up" and left the city. The negative experience can perhaps shed some light on why he changed from preaching classical Pentecostal doctrines to annihilationism and soul sleep in 1914. *Svea*, February 11, 1914, 5.

77. "Russellism" refers to the teaching of Charles Russell (1852–1916), who advocated annihilationism and soul sleep, and whose teachings later influenced the theology of Jehovah's Witnesses and Adventists. Russell's headquarters was situated in Pittsburgh, Pennsylvania, from where much of the teaching disseminated. See, Gunner, *Nelly Hall*, 195–210.

78. Ödman preached "a comforting eulogy about rest and resurrection" at a funeral in August 1908. The sermon focused on John 11:11: "Our friend is sleeping, but I go and wake him from his sleep." Even if this could allude to a belief in soul sleep, the evidence is too limited to say so confidently. *Svea*, April 15, 1908, 4.

missionary to Brazil, Gunnar Vingren and the editor of *Pingst-Rösten*, B. M. Johnson of Chicago.[79]

The beginning of the controversy started in 1914, when Ödman launched his beliefs in an article in the 36–37 issue of *Sanningens Vittne* entitled "The Six Foundational Truths." The issue ended up in the hands of Lewi Pethrus, who wrote a rebuttal in the December issue of *Brudgummens röst*. Pethrus did not take exception to the whole article, but only to the last part, where Ödman argued that only Jesus had gone up to heaven based on John 3:13 and Acts 2:29, 34, and that souls were sleeping until the resurrection, as well as to point out Ödman's "hard [and] judgmental tone." Pethrus also did not understand why A. A. Holmgren had not omitted the last part when it was published.[80] Pethrus's counterarguments centered on Ödman's neglect of other biblical texts such as 2 Kings 2:11, John 14:1, 2 Cor. 12:2, and Eph. 4:10, and that nothing in the Acts passage, or any other passage Ödman quoted, proved that "'all the dead sleep . . . unconscious sleep until their resurrection day appears.'"[81] On the contrary, Jesus' promise to the thief on the cross that he should be with him in paradise (Luke 23:43) showed that souls are not sleeping after death.[82] Pethrus argued further that, "Paul does not say as Ö.[dman] claims, that spirit, body and soul lay in the tomb, but instead he says that when we are away from the body, we are home with the Lord."[83] Nor could it be argued that the unrighteous were sleeping until the resurrection as the story of Lazarus (Luke 16:19–31) demonstrated.[84]

In his first response to Ödman's article, Pethrus zeroed in on his view of soul sleep. In a follow-up article in February 1915 entitled "An Eternal Punishment," he went after Ödman's annihilationism: "It is not enough for brother Ödman to preach the soul's unconsciousness in the intermediate state, but he also seeks to prove the final annihilation of

---

79. *KS*, November 1, 1915, 162; *EH*, January 20, 1916, 11.

80. *BR*, December 1914, 13. That Pethrus was sincerely upset over Holmgren's editorial neglect can be seen in an article in *Evangelii härold* over two decades later where he stated: "We who have been part of the Pentecostal revival for many years, know, what damage 'Sanningens Vittne' caused many years ago, when it gave room for the Ödmanian delusions and subsequent writings. Since the newspaper and its editor had many of the Pentecostals' confidence, this course of action caused untold damage." *EH*, November 12, 1936, 937.

81. *BR*, December 1914, 14.

82. *BR*, December 1914, 14.

83. *BR*, December 1914, 14.

84. *BR*, December 1914, 14.

the unregenerate."⁸⁵ According to Ödman, the eternal torment of the unregenerate was a "God-denying, barbaric, unreasonable, meaningless, tyrannical, reprehensible and unscriptural doctrine, based on another serious delusion, namely the natural man's immortality."⁸⁶ The doctrine of the immortality of the soul "is as little taught in Scripture as infant baptism, confirmation, purgatory, celibacy, and other serious delusions. It is therefore time for this Babylonian leaven to be cleansed from the 'apostolic faith.'"⁸⁷

From these quotes it is evident that for Ödman annihilationism and soul sleep ("the New Light") accompanied the restoration of the Full Gospel along the same line as divine healing and Spirit baptism. Moreover, the "Catholic" or "Orthodox" doctrines of the eternality of the soul and the eternal punishment of the unregenerate were to be removed from it. Pethrus's reply to Ödman's "murderous delusions" did not engage in this fundamental question as to whether the Full Gospel was still "open." Rather, his reply centered on three logical and exegetical misconceptions: (1) Death is not annihilation, but a "divorce" of soul and body. The person lives on even after death and the final resurrection (Gen. 1:2, Eccl. 12:7, Luke 15:23–24, Rev. 20:12, 15). (2) A life without God before death is as reasonable as an eternity without God after death. (3) The Bible speaks about "eternal punishment" for those who reject him (Matt. 5:22, 29, 25:46; Luke 16:23; Rev. 14:11).⁸⁸

Even if Pethrus did not reply to this fundamental problem if the Full Gospel was open or not, T. B. Barratt did. In an article entitled "Deceiving and Strange Doctrines," Barratt noted that the times were full of the influence of evil spirits that demanded discernment.⁸⁹ He further explained that the problem was worse for "Pentecostals when they appear within the movement that we believe in and know for sure is from God."⁹⁰ The remedy was to be aware of all teaching "that was not orthodox, namely: [which] *is not biblical and evangelical*" [italics

---

85. *BR*, February 1915, 23.

86. *BR*, February 1915, 23.

87. *BR*, February 1915, 24.

88. *BR*, February 1915, 24–26. Even in his later book *En evig dom*, where he addressed annihilationism and soul sleep extensively, Pethrus never mentioned this fundamental problem.

89. *KS*, November 1, 1915, 162.

90. *KS*, November 1, 1915, 162.

in original].⁹¹ The point was "to move forward toward the Lord, and not be tied down by old Catholic teachings, but to follow the blueprint that the Lord had revealed to us by His Spirit."⁹² However, "*the foundation should not be destroyed or undermined* [italics in original]," and any doctrine must be "built on Christ and his Word," and withstand Scripture's cleansing fire.⁹³ Barratt then proceeded to argue that many false teachings that were now circulating like "the New Light" was "nothing new but has been fought against by the Church for centuries" as well as lacking any Scriptural foundation.⁹⁴ Consequently, for Barratt, any additions to the Full Gospel had to square with Scripture *and* evangelical tradition for it to be accepted among Pentecostals.

We do not know if Pethrus's and Barratt's articles ever reached Ödman and Newman, but even if they did, they did little to change their course of action. In fact, Ödman wrote a pamphlet entitled "Are the Dead Alive?," which he used to promote his views even further.⁹⁵ Newman went to an even greater length and started a journal called *Tidsåldrarnas ljus* [The Light of the Ages] that advocated "the New Light."⁹⁶ N. G. Nielsen's report from Hartford, Connecticut tells of their impact:

> [T]here has come a lot of strange teachings among the Spirit-baptized here in the Eastern parts of America. There are several Swedish brothers who preach it, but especially one person, his name is Ødman, and he has written the pamphlet I am now sending. Because of this teaching there have been great divisions among the Spirit-baptized. Hartford is one of the places that has had to suffer from it. We had a flourishing congregation and the Lord blessed us. Then came this brother with his "new light" as they call it, that there is no eternal punishment, that the soul is not immortal, etc. We discovered that this did not correspond with the teaching of Scripture and therefore we forbad the brother to talk anymore about this matter among us. From that came the split. Many left and started a new mission. Now I understand that this brother Ødman shall travel to Sweden in

91. *KS*, November 1, 1915, 162.
92. *KS*, November 1, 1915, 162.
93. *KS*, November 1, 1915, 162.
94. *KS*, November 1, 1915, 162.
95. *EH*, January 13, 1916, 7.
96. *EH*, November 2, 1916, 179. Newman seems to have added the notion around this time that Christ's Second Coming had already taken place spiritually, and only those who were spiritual would see him. See *BR*, March 15, 1920, 44.

a month and will surely preach the "new light" there also [. . .]. The other brother Newman goes even further in his teaching. It will be a good idea to warn the brothers in Sweden and Norway to not open the door for him.[97]

As Nielsen's report shows, Ödman did not limit his teaching to the East Coast of America, but soon planned a campaign in Sweden and Norway as well. Ödman left on October 28, 1915, but before he arrived, Pethrus managed to publish a book-length response to Ödman's views entitled *En evig dom* [An Eternal Punishment]. Its release, as well as notifications in *Evangelii härold* and T. B. Barratt's articles in *Korsets seier*, made sure that Ödman's teachings never got a foothold in Scandinavia.[98] A. A. Holmgren also withdrew his support at this time by making a public statement in *Evangelii härold*. Having seen Ödman drifting "further and further away [from the truth]," he refused to have his pamphlet published in *Sanningens Vittne*, and "dragged into a doctrinal camp he did not endorse."[99] The purpose for his public statement was to ensure that "nobody needed to think that [he] in some way supported Ödman's ministry in Sweden,"[100] a decision that Gunnar Vingren praised.[101] Ödman returned to America September 14, 1916, and it seems like his meager success in Sweden dampened his enthusiasm dramatically.[102] Newman did not give up completely, however, and promoted the "new light" occasionally,[103] but the combined efforts of Pethrus, Barratt, Vingren, Johnson, and eventually Holmgren ensured that the doors for annihilationism and soul sleep were also closed in Scandinavian-America Pentecostal churches.[104] Holmgren's omission

97. *KS*, October 1, 1915, 151.
98. *KS*, November 1, 1915, 162; *EH*, January 20, 1916, 11.
99. *EH*, January 13, 1916, 7.
100. *EH*, January 13, 1916, 7.
101. *EH*, January 20, 1916, 11.
102. *Korsets seier* reports on October 15, 1916, 159: "Brother Lewi Pethrus told us, that one of the most eager proponents of the 'New Light' that has come from America, to confuse our friends in Norway and Sweden, is now walking around like a drunkard in one of the big cities in Sweden." It is impossible to know what Pethrus meant by this controversial statement, but that it indicates an unsuccessful trip is likely, especially since he largely disappears from Pentecostal records after he returned to America.
103. B. M. Johnson writes from Chicago in November 1916 that "H. A. Newman has now come here to Chicago again if possible to get his heresy going again, because it has been rather quiet about this teaching for a long time." *EH*, November 2, 1916, 179.
104. See for instance, *EH*, November 2, 1916, 180; *KS*, October 15, 1916, 157, 159; *EH*, August 1, 1918, 123; January 22, 1920, 11.

of any other perspective than Lewi Pethrus's in *Pingströrelsen och dess förkunnelse* is indicative of how thoroughly the doctrine of annihilationism and soul sleep were rejected among Scandinavian-American Pentecostals by 1919.[105] Newman returned to the Baptist Union and became a pastor in the Second Baptist Church in Bridgeport, Connecticut.[106] Pethrus and Newman likely reconciled later considering that the two traveled together to the United States in 1936.

The story of Ödman's and Newman's attempt to introduce annihilationism and soul sleep among Scandinavian Pentecostals shows that they were aware of and affected by the larger theological discourse in the world. The branding of their new belief as "the New Light" further demonstrates that they intentionally tapped into the restorational mindset of Finished Work Pentecostals to legitimize their claims. The fact that Pethrus emphasized scripture and reason, whereas Barratt stressed scripture, experience (spiritual discernment), and *tradition* highlights the difference in development between the Finished Work and Wesleyan Pentecostal traditions. As a more historically anchored Wesleyan Pentecostal, Barratt could appeal to the Church's historical fight against the doctrines, which proved that "the New Light" was nothing new at all but an age-old heresy. Pethrus, on the other hand, as a leader of a Finished Work sub-tradition, was more limited to analytical expositions of Scripture and rational arguments. Although the issue addressed a larger theological discourse in the world, the issue remained an in-house matter and left other North American Pentecostal denominations virtually untouched.[107] Therefore, the emergence of Scandinavian-American Pentecostal theology cannot be reduced to a particular interpretation of common Pentecostal distinctives. They faced their own challenges, where answers were not easily borrowed from other Pentecostal traditions.

The Oneness Controversy

The Oneness controversy arose in the context of Finished Work Pentecostalism. The controversy followed the decline of both William

105. See Holmgren, *Pingströrelsen och dess förkunnelse*, 309–317.
106. *EH*, March 9, 1922, 39.
107. Charles F. Parham advocated an annihilationist position, but most classical Pentecostals adhered to the traditional orthodox view, including William Seymour, who strongly opposed Parham's annihilationism. See, Nel, "Rethinking Hell from a Classical Pentecostal Perspective," 1–7; Robeck, *Azusa Street Mission and Revival*, 50.

Seymour's Azusa Street mission in Los Angeles and Charles Fox Parham's ministerial failures in Texas in 1910,[108] as well as Durham's sudden passing in 1912. David Reed describes the situation in American Pentecostalism at the outbreak of the controversy as one of "spiritual entropy, doctrinal confusion, and struggle to work out the implications of the Finished Work teaching for unity among Pentecostals, the nature of the church, and the meaning of full salvation within the context of the Pentecostal experience."[109] Far from being a sudden theological development, Reed explains that its historical roots can be traced to Pietism's, Methodism's and the Holiness Movement's Christocentric, experiential, and restorationist (anti-creedal, anti-institutional) emphases.[110] The immediate catalyst of the movement was the Canadian evangelist, Robert E. McAlister (1880–1953), whose baptismal sermon at an international camp meeting at Arroyo Seco, California, in April 1913, spawned its development in 1914. McAlister was an adamant Finished Work proponent, who vigorously disseminated the doctrine through his publication *The Good Report*.[111]

At the Arroyo Seco meeting, McAlister's preoccupation with Christology explains his reflection on the discrepancy between Jesus' command in Matt. 28:19 and the Apostles' practice in the Book of Acts to baptize in the name of the Lord Jesus Christ.[112] Even if McAlister never intended to reject the Trinitarian formula, his explanation that the Apostles understood "'Lord Jesus-Christ' to be the Christological equivalent of 'Father-Son-Holy Spirit'"[113] caused an immediate stir in the audience.[114] Frank J. Ewart (1876–1947), an associate of William Durham in Chicago, studied this new "revelation" in depth, and on April 15, 1914, preached a sermon on Acts 2:38, and was rebaptized "in Jesus' name," together with Glen A. Cook.[115]

By summer 1915, two key developments had taken place. First, Ewart arrived at the conclusion that only the "in Jesus' name" formula was to be used at baptisms, based on the "radical oneness of God" (modalism),

108. Reed, "Oneness Seed on Canadian Soil," 192–93.
109. Reed, *"In Jesus' Name,"* 110.
110. Reed, *"In Jesus' Name,"* 7–42.
111. Reed, "Oneness Seed on Canadian Soil," 193.
112. Reed, "Oneness Seed on Canadian Soil," 194.
113. Reed, "Oneness Pentecostalism," 937.
114. Reed, "Oneness Seed on Canadian Soil," 194.
115. Reed, "Oneness Pentecostalism," 937.

whereby he also deemed the orthodox doctrine of the Trinity as unscriptural. Secondly, the "New Issue" was spreading rapidly, seriously influencing the newly established Assemblies of God as well as influential ministers like E. N. Bell, G. T. Haywood, and F. Small.[116] However, even if McAlister was rebaptized in December 1915, and contemplated the issue seriously, there is "no indication that he fully embraced the Oneness doctrine of God."[117] Only through the uncompromising work of J. Roswell Flower (1888–1970), who summoned the third General Council of the AG in October 1915 to particularly address the issue, did the tide slowly turn back in favor of classic Trinitarian teaching. At the fourth General Council in fall 1916, a decision was taken to appoint a five-person committee to formulate a "Statement of Fundamental Truths" of which David W. Kerr (1856–1927) was the main contributor. Reed describes him as "the hero for the orthodox Trinitarian faction."[118] The meeting ended with victory for the Trinitarian group, meaning that the Oneness group was, in effect, excluded from the fellowship. The subsequent 17-point statement particularly emphasized classical Trinitarian teaching and underlined that the Trinitarian formula of Matt. 28:19 was the only one to be invoked at future baptisms.[119]

The Oneness controversy that shook North American Pentecostalism in 1914–1916 hardly made a ripple in Scandinavia.[120] Lewi Pethrus ignored it completely, and it did not find its way into any issue of *Evangelii härold* before 1920. The controversy was only briefly mentioned in a letter from Texas published in *Brudgummens röst* in March 1920.[121] T. B. Barratt addressed it a bit more, but only after having been specifically asked to by Olav Fjermedal in Tacoma, Washington. Fjermedal writes:

> Here on the [West] Coast there have lately been a lot of doctrines up for discussion in the different Pentecostal churches. [. . .] Some want to be baptized in the name of the Father, the Son and the Holy Spirit, others in Jesus' name [only . . .], and so they let themselves be baptized several times, which is without doubt harmful for God's cause. You brother Barratt, if you feel

---

116. Reed, "Oneness Seed on Canadian Soil," 196.
117. Reed, "Oneness Seed on Canadian Soil," 198.
118. Reed, "In Jesus' Name," 163.
119. Reed, "In Jesus' Name," 165.
120. Andersen, "Hvordan taklet pinsebevegelsen i Norge svermeriet?," 95.
121. *BR*, March 15, 1920, 44–45.

led to write in 'K. S.' [*Korsets Seir*] an article about these things it would be read with interest by many.[122]

Barratt's first response in November 1915 is so cursory that he combines it with other "made in America" heresies like "Finished Work" and Ödman's "Russellism." The only aspect of the Oneness controversy he addressed was the confusion surrounding the baptismal formulations in Acts and Matthew 28:19.[123] Only about a year and a half later, possibly when the Trinitarian implications of the controversy had become clearer, did he address it in any length.[124]

Even if Oneness Pentecostalism did not affect Scandinavian Pentecostals for several decades,[125] the situation for Scandinavian-American Pentecostals was much more acute. As Fjermedal's report shows, it divided Norwegian-American Pentecostal churches and broke spiritual bonds. Holmgren's considerable attention to the issue also shows that it influenced Swedish-American Pentecostals. Pethrus's lack of theological direction forced Holmgren to draw on sources closer to home for guidance, relying on texts from D. W. Kerr, R. E. McAlister, and especially the Assemblies of God's description of the Godhead as outlined in its Statement of Fundamental Truths.[126] The inclusion of the Assemblies of God's description of the Godhead in the section dealing with "foundational truths" is telling, since it shows that Swedish-American Pentecostals were in essential agreement with their North-American

---

122. *KS*, July 15, 1915, 111–12.

123. For Barratt, the mentioning of "baptism in Jesus' name" in Acts 10:48 and 19:5 did not preclude a trinitarian understanding but was emphasized because Jesus was the most controversial of the three divine persons in Luke's time. It was also inconceivable that Luke would have done away with Jesus' command in Matthew 28:19. Moreover, those who were baptized with the trinitarian formula were by default baptized in Jesus' name, making it unnecessary to baptize them over again. *KS*, November 1, 1915, 162. The article notes that adherents of both Oneness theology and annihilationism used the epithet "New Light" for their teaching at this time. See also, *KS*, October 15, 1916, 159; February 15, 1917, 25.

124. Barratt critiques Oneness's modalism as an affront to the Father's and the Spirit's honor. The doctrine of the Trinity was a "foundational" doctrine, without which there would be no "real Christianity." Having made these initial remarks, Barratt proceeds by listing numerous biblical passages where the Father, the Son, and the Spirit are seen as distinct persons, yet sharing one essence. *KS*, February 15, 1917, 25–26.

125. Evangelist Torsten Severin Austring (1886–1978) brought Oneness Pentecostalism to Norway in October 1962, but the movement has never had any real impact. See, Lie, "Ikke-trinitariske pinseretninger i Norge," 19.

126. Holmgren quoted the entire AG statement on the Godhead verbatim. See Holmgren, *Pingströrelsen och dess förkunnelse*, 176–79, 188–98.

counterpart regarding the doctrine of the Trinity. However, the inclusion of D. W. Kerr's, and especially R. E. McAlister's articles, may imply that it was not unreserved. The first meeting at Hot Springs, Arkansas, in 1914, and the third General Council in 1915, were marked by a conciliary attitude, appealing for unity despite theological differences.[127] Kerr's text in Holmgren's book is a Swedish translation of his article "We All Agree," published in *The Weekly Evangel*, March 4, 1916. As opposed to the harsh demarcations that followed the publication of the Statement of Fundamental Truths, Kerr's article stressed areas of agreement between the two camps:

> Under present conditions of disagreement, it might be interesting to those of us who disagree, to know some of the things in which we all agree. We venture therefore to suggest to the large body of truth-loving people of the Pentecostal Movement, some of the points on which we are of one accord. As to the points on which we seem to disagree, we may find when we come to understand each other better, that we are not so far apart as some of our observing friends and critics suppose us to be.[128]

Kerr's article proceeded to list eight areas where agreement existed.[129] Even more interesting is Holmgren's decision to include R. E. McAlister's article entitled "Great Is the Mystery of the Godhead" and adding it right after Kerr's article as if they were meant to complement each other. The date of the article is unknown,[130] but it is likely that it was published at least a year or so after McAlister's rebaptism in December 1915. It is important to underline here that rebaptism in Jesus' name did not imply agreement with Oneness doctrine, but primarily "to

---

127. Reed, *"In Jesus' Name,"* 164.

128. D. W. Kerr, "We all Agree," *The Weekly Evangel*, March 4, 1916, 6.

129. The eight areas of agreement were: (1) God's lordship, (2) Jesus as the true witness who was sent to reveal the true God, (3) Jesus being fully qualified to witness to his identity, character and competency, (4) belief in Jesus' teaching concerning the Unity of the Being of God, (5) that there could not be an image without an object, (6) the believer's eternal citizenship in Heaven, Christ's Second Coming, and bodily resurrection, (7) the believer's inheritance in Christ, and (8) that because of the last seven, "we are not hopelessly divided." *The Weekly Evangel*, March 4, 1916, 6–7.

130. The article was not published in the Assembly of God periodicals *Word and Witness* or *The Weekly Evangel*. Holmgren retrieved it from an unknown edition of B. M. Johnson's *Pingst-rösten*. As far as I can tell, it is only in Holmgren's book that it survives. It is unlikely, however, that *Pingst-rösten* was the first place it was published, considering its primarily Swedish readership.

conform to apostolic practice."[131] The article supports Reed's claim that McAlister was the lone exception of the "early pioneers," G. T. Haywood, Frank Ewart, and Franklin Small, who did not become one of the "primary architects" of Oneness doctrine.[132] In fact, in one of his opening statements, he rejected modalism: "I have believed that Jesus is God in a relative sense, but I cannot see that he is God in the absolute sense, so that the Father should lose his identity to the degree, that he should become synonymous with the Son. When I say that Jesus is God in a relative sense, I mean in regard to redemption [. . .]."[133] Thus, McAlister advocated a differentiation between the divine persons as to the economy rather than to the ontology of the Trinity. However, he left the question open as to whether the Father, the Son, and the Spirit should be ascribed personality in the fullest sense of the word. To speculate about "the very essence of the Godhead, and make comparisons here, would only confuse us."[134] Rather than to speculate about the different personalities of the Trinity, McAlister (still faithful to his Christological preoccupation) admonished his readers to look to Christ who perfectly revealed the Father. Yet, he underlined that, "the Father's identity is never lost in the Son and the Son's identity is never lost in the Father. Three identities [are] in regard to relation, but one in regard to essence and substance."[135] McAlister concluded the article by reducing the Oneness controversy to the "difference between the *relative* and the *absolute* with respect to Christ as God." He claimed both sides had strong biblical arguments, but no consensus could be reached if the original starting point was wrong. If a biblically correct starting point could be found, "all the arguments would fall, and the battle would be over."[136]

It is difficult to guess what reasons Holmgren might have had to incorporate D. W. Kerr's and R. E. McAlister's articles in his book, but it might point to the fact that he, and other Swedish-American Pentecostals, did not perceive "the New Issue" to be so detrimental in 1919 that it necessitated a severing of spiritual fellowship. In fact, taken together, they point to a desire for future reconciliation if a common theological ground could be found. The stark contrast between the need for theological

131. Reed, *"In Jesus' Name,"* 144.
132. Reed, *"In Jesus' Name,"* 3.
133. Holmgren, *Pingströrelsen och dess förkunnelse*, 194.
134. Holmgren, *Pingströrelsen och dess förkunnelse*, 196.
135. Holmgren, *Pingströrelsen och dess förkunnelse*, 196–97.
136. Holmgren, *Pingströrelsen och dess förkunnelse*, 198.

direction for Scandinavians living in America as opposed to Pentecostals in Scandinavia proves that Scandinavian-American Pentecostals cannot be lumped together with all other Scandinavian Pentecostals. At certain times they had to look to other sub-traditions, like the Assemblies of God, and in the end, find their own path.

Conclusion

This study has shown that early Scandinavian-American Pentecostals were in essential agreement with all other Pentecostals as to the fourfold Gospel. However, in terms of the Finished Work doctrine, Swedish and Norwegian Pentecostals held opposite views due to Swedish Pentecostal leaders' proximity to William Durham and T. B. Barratt's insistence on sanctification as a separate work of grace. A slight difference can also be seen in the movement's most distinctive belief, radical congregationalism. Here the Norwegian branch was for a period less dogmatic about the local church's independence than their Swedish counterpart. Yet, radical congregationalism set Scandinavian-American Pentecostals apart from other sub-traditions within the larger Pentecostal family, including the Assemblies of God of Springfield, Missouri, and sometimes even more so than Pentecostal leaders in Scandinavia. Although difficult to say with certainty, they might have also taken their own path in relation to Oneness Pentecostals. On the other hand, Scandinavian-American Pentecostals experienced internal issues that only impacted their Scandinavian side, such as during the Ödman conflict. The context of this issue was much broader than a peculiar Pentecostal distinctive, which shows that they were also aware and impacted by global theological trends. Scandinavian-American Pentecostals found themselves therefore between multiple worlds, a combination of American, Scandinavian, and international contexts that shaped their theology and identity.

The four themes covered in this chapter demonstrate that the underlying factor that fueled the emergence of a Scandinavian-American Pentecostal theology related to the unsettled problem of what doctrines should or should not belong to the Full Gospel. The strong belief in the Pentecostal movement's restoration of lost biblical truths, and their anti-organizational, anti-creedal, and anti-traditional convictions, led to an openness for new revelations or "New Light." Richmann correctly notes that this problem specifically affected Finished Work Pentecostals:

If interpreters are looking for reasons why the Oneness movement emerged from the finished-work camp of Pentecostalism, this thirst for new revelation may be a powerful clue. Having rejected the 'new' teaching of Durham, Wesleyan Pentecostals established themselves as preservers of heritage, even within the innovative Pentecostal community. For those in the finished-work camp who had accepted Durham's teaching as an end-times revelation, a precedent of openness to new doctrine was established, making them more receptive to the Oneness message.[137]

Even if Richmann only mentions the Finished Work and Oneness controversies here, the same dynamic can be observed in the controversy over annihilationism and soul sleep, as well as the arguments for radical congregationalism. By 1919, the theological controversies that had marked 1911–1917 were over. It is therefore no coincidence that Holmgren was able to publish the first account of Pentecostals' history and beliefs at this time since the doctrinal controversies among Scandinavian-American Pentecostals had finally been settled.

Bibliography

Primary Sources

NEWSPAPERS USED

Brudgummens Röst (*BR*), Stockholm, Sweden, 1911–1922
Evangelii Härold (*EH*), Stockholm, Sweden, 1915–1993
Folke-Vennen, Chicago, IL, 1879–1933
Korsets Seier (*KS*), Kristiania (Oslo), Norway, 1910–
Nordstjernan, New York City, 1872–1966
Sanningens Vittne (*SV*), Minneapolis, 1911–1939
Svea, Worcester, MA, 1897–1966
Svenska Folkets Tidning, Minneapolis, 1881–1927
The Weekly Evangel, St. Louis, MO, 1915–1918

OTHER PRIMARY SOURCES

Cochrane, William. *Future Punishment, or, Does Death End Probation? [Microform]: Materialism, Immortality of the Soul, Conditional Immortality or Annihilationism.* Brantford, Ont.: Bradley, Garretson, 1886.
Holmgren, A. A. *Pingströrelsen och dess Förkunnelse.* Minneapolis: S. V. Publishing House, 1919.

137. Richmann, "William H. Durham and Early Pentecostalism," 241.

Secondary Sources

Alvarsson, Jan-Åke. "Pingstväckelsens etablering i Sverige: Från Azusa Street till Skövde på sjumånader." In *Pingströrelsen: Händelser och utveckling under 1900-Talet*, 1:11–43. Örebro: Libris förlag, 2007.

———. "Relationer mellan Sverige och USA inom ramen för pentekostalismen: En översikt av nittonhundratalets kontakter." In *Varför reste Lewi Pethrus just till Chicago?: Relationer mellan Sverige och USA inom ramen för pentekostalismen*, 9–79. Artos & Norma bokförlag, 2019.

Andersen, Øyvind Gaarder. "Hvordan taklet Pinsebevegelsen i Norge svermeriet?" In *Pinse for alle: Pinsebevegelsen gjennom 100 år, 93–100*. Skjetten, Norway: Hermon forlag, 2007.

Blumhofer, Edith L. "William Durham: Years of Creativity, Years of Dissent." In *Portraits of a Generation: Early Pentecostal Leaders*, 123–42. Fayetteville, AR: University of Arkansas Press, 2002.

Bundy, David. *Vision of Apostolic Mission: Scandinavian Pentecostal Mission to 1935*. ActaUniversitatis Upsaliensis. Studia Historico-Ecclesiastica Upsaliensia 45. Uppsala: Uppsala University Library, 2009.

Davidsson, Tommy. *Lewi Pethrus' Ecclesiological Thought 1911–1974: A Transdenominational Pentecostal Ecclesiology*. Leiden: Brill, 2015.

Dayton, Donald W. *Theological Roots of Pentecostalism*. Grand Rapids: BakerAcademic, 2011.

Faupel, David W. *The Everlasting Gospel: The Significance of Eschatology in the Development of Pentecostal Thought*. Journal of Pentecostal Theology. Supplement Series. Blandford Forum, UK: Deo, 2019.

Gunner, Gunilla. *Nelly Hall: Uppburen och ifrågasatt: predikant och missionär i Europa och USA 1882–1901*. Studia Missionalia Svecana XCII. Uppsala: Swedish Institute of Mission Research, 2003.

Gustafson, David M. "Mary Johnson and Ida Anderson: 'Free-Free' Missionaries of the Scandinavian Mission Society USA to Natal, South Africa." *Pneuma* 39 (2017) 55–77.

Heckman, Warren. *The History of the Fellowship of Christian Assemblies*. Beaverton, OR: Good Book, 2001.

Jacobsen, Douglas G. *Thinking in the Spirit: Theologies of the Early Pentecostal Movement*. Bloomington, IN: Indiana University Press, 2003.

Josefsson, Ulrik. *Liv och över nog: Den tidiga pingströrelsens spiritualitet*. Skellefteå, Sweden: Artos, 2005.

Lie, Geir. "Ikke-trinitariske pinseretninger i Norge. En historisk og teologisk kontrastering." *Baptist* 5 (1998) 19–30.

Nel, Marius. "Rethinking Hell from a Classical Pentecostal Perspective: Some Ethical Considerations." *Stellenbosch Theological Journal* 7 (2021) 1–24.

Olson, Roger E. "Pietism and Pentecostalism: Spiritual Cousins or Competitors?" *Pneuma* 34 (2012) 319–44.

Princell, Josephine. *Memoirs of J. G. Princell*. Translated by David M. Gustafson. Gustafson, 1916, 1999.

Reed, David A. *"In Jesus' Name": The History and Beliefs of Oneness Pentecostals*. Blandford Forum, UK: Deo, 2008.

———. "Oneness Pentecostalism." In *The New International Dictionary of Pentecostal and Charismatic Movements*, 936–44. Grand Rapids: Zondervan, 2003.

———. "Oneness Seed on Canadian Soil: Early Developments of Oneness Pentecostalism." In *Winds from the North: Canadian Contributions to the Pentecostal Movement*, 191–213. Leiden: Brill, 2010.

Richmann, Christopher J. "William H. Durham and Early Pentecostalism: A Multifaceted Reassessment." *Pneuma* 37 (2015) 224–43.

Robeck, Cecil M. *The Azusa Street Mission and Revival The Birth of the Global Pentecostal Movement*. Nashville: Thomas Nelson, 2006.

———. "The Origins of Modern Pentecostalism: Some Historiographical Issues." In *The Cambridge Companion to Pentecostalism*, 13–28. Cambridge: Cambridge University Press, 2014.

Rodgers, Darrin J. *Northern Harvest: Pentecostalism in North Dakota*. Bismarck, ND: North Dakota District Council of the Assemblies of God, 2003.

———. "Rediscovering Pentecostalism's Diverse Roots: Origins in Scandinavian Pietism in Minnesota and the Dakotas." *Refleks* 5 (2006) 50–64.

Struble, Rhode. *Den samfundsfria församlingen och de karismatiska gåvorna och tjänsterna: Den svenska pingströrelsens församlingssyn 1907–1947*. Stockholm: Almqvist & Wiksell International, 1982.

Tangen, Karl Inge. "Healing in the Pentecostal Tradition: A Scandinavian Perspective." *Journal of the European Pentecostal Theological Association* 41 (2021) 124–40.

Chapter Eight

Scandinavian-American Pentecostal Mission to Brazil

Gunnar Vingren and Daniel Berg, 1910–1962

ISAEL DE ARAUJO AND JOEL WRIGHT

PERHAPS, MOST BRAZILIANS PRESENT in the port city of Belém, the capital of Pará, Brazil, on the mouth of Amazon River, on November 19, 1910, would not have been impressed by the two Swedish-American adventurists wearing wool suits and carrying simple suitcases as they disembarked a ship named, the Clement.[1] They began their missionary careers with a Brazilian meal at a local restaurant, sat on a bench in the central park, cried out to God for help, and wondered where they would spend the night.[2] Little did they know that over one hundred years later, their work would multiply to become the *Assembléias de Deus* (AD) of Brazil, with over 200,000 local congregations and over 22 million members, contributing in the shift of Christianity towards the Global South.[3]

---

1. Araujo, *100 Acontecimentos*, 1–6.

2. *Sanningens Vittne* (*SV*), August 1936, 4. Swedish-language sources were translated by David M. Gustafson.

3. Johnson and Zurlo, *World Christian Encyclopedia*, 138; Jenkins, *Next Christendom*, 80–81, 115.

Gunnar Vingren (1879–1933) and Daniel Berg (1884–1963) were not the first Pentecostal missionaries to arrive in Brazil, however. Louis Francescon (1866–1964) arrived earlier in 1910, working further south, in São Paulo. Prior to Brazil, Francescon launched Italian Pentecostal congregations in Los Angeles, St. Louis, and Philadelphia. He engaged mainly in itinerant evangelism to Italian immigrants, moving in and out of Brazil eleven times.[4] In contrast, Vingren and Berg remained in the country and focused on evangelism and multiplying Portuguese-speaking Brazilian leaders, a strategy that over time far exceeded Francescon's results. The Swedish-American missionaries introduced Pentecostal spirituality to the Brazilian nationals. This form of Christianity that included phenomena of Spirit-baptism, glossolalia, divine healing, and prophesying resonated with Brazilians. Vingren's and Berg's mission practice recognized over time the importance of indigenous agency to expand the number of Brazilian evangelists, pastors, churches, and missionaries to lead the movement.[5] A century later, millions of Brazilians heralded Vingren and Berg as "torchbearers of the Pentecostal fire to Brazil."[6]

This chapter argues that Vingren's and Berg's mission practice in Brazil not only introduced the Full Gospel with Pentecostal spirituality, but came to recognize the role of indigenous agency to empower Brazilian converts to become leaders. The chapter begins with a brief background of the early lives of Vingren and Berg. It examines events that led to their partnership to go as missionaries to Brazil. This is followed by their arrival to Belém where they established their missionary work. The chapter then describes their missionary work as they partnered with Scandinavian-American churches and Brazilian converts. This is followed by a description of the development and expansion of the national leadership of the Assemblies of God in Brazil.

---

4. Louis Francescon (1866–1964) established Congregação Cristã do Brasil which in 2007, had three million members. Araujo, *Dicionário do Movimento Pentecostal*, 321.

5. For indigenous Pentecostal missiology, see Yong, "Many Tongues, Many Practices," 47–48.

6. Raiol, *1911—Missão de Fogo no Brasil*, 77–84; Araujo, *100 Acontecimentos*, 537.

Daniel Berg (left) and Gunnar Vingren (right) before traveling to Brazil (1910), Courtesy of the Gunnar Vingren Memorial Archives, CPAD, Rio de Janeiro, Brazil

Early Lives of Gunnar Vingren and Daniel Berg

Adolph Gunnar Vingren was born August 8, 1879, in Östra Harg, Sweden.[7] His parents were active there in the Baptist Church, considered a free-church in the context of the Church of Sweden—the Lutheran state church. When Gunnar was nine years old, he sensed God's call upon his life. During his teen years, however, he met spiritual challenges as well as victories, writing in his diary: "I fell deeply into sin until I was 17, when the Lord called me again."[8] His return to God happened on New Year's Eve, 1896, when he attended a New Year's Eve service at the Baptist Church with his father, and purposed to start his spiritual life afresh.

---

7. Födelse och dop bok, Östra Harg, Östergötland, 1867–1892, 155 (ArkivDigital). Gunnar Vingren's biography says he was born in Östra Husby. Originals of Gunnar Vingren's diary (12 volumes) are at Casa Publicadora das Assembléias de Deus (CPAD), Rio de Janeiro. Vingren's diary was been published in Swedish and Portuguese. Vingren, *Pionjärens dagbok*, 14.

8. Vingren, *Diário do Pioneiro*, 19.

Seven months later, the young Gunnar was baptized in water by immersion at a Baptist church in Vråka, Småland.

Vingren followed his father's example of leading Bible studies. Moreover, His interest in missions ignited after he read an article in a missionary publication about the needs of people in other parts of the world. The fact that his uncle, Carl Vingren, was the first Baptist missionary commissioned to China by the Swedish Baptist Mission (Svenska Baptist Missionen), brought the reality of global missions even closer, prompting him to pray for the nations, and he did so with tears.[9]

After praying with others for divine wisdom, he attended the Bible school in Götabro, with ties to the holiness movement and an emphasis on healing, directed by Emil Gustavsson and C. J. A. Kihlstedt.[10] The session of Bible school lasted just a month but was of great benefit spiritually to the young Vingren. After completing compulsory military service, he returned home and worked in the gardens of Drottningholm, the royal palace, near Stockholm.

In June 1903, Vingren was struck with "American fever." He soon boarded a steamship at Gothenburg for the U.S. When he arrived in Boston, he traveled by train to Kansas City, Missouri, to stay with his uncle, Carl Vingren, then a local pastor, who was there at the time, away from his mission work in China.[11]

Early in 1904, Gunnar traveled to St. Louis, Missouri, where he worked at the Botanical Gardens. While attending a Swedish church, members encouraged him to pursue theological studies at the Swedish Baptist Theological Seminary in Chicago.[12] Agreeing to do so, he began courses in the fall term at this seminary in Morgan Park affiliated with the University of Chicago.

Vingren graduated from the school on May 11, 1909, after nearly five years of study. He wrote a thesis titled: "The Tabernacle and It's Lessons," which offered a Christological reflection of Israel's Tabernacle in the Old Testament.[13] Clearly, his time as a student in seminary provided

9. Vingren, *Diário do Pioneiro*, 24.

10. Vingren, *Diário do Pioneiro*, 20.

11. Carl Vingren (1865–1947) would return to China (Shandong Province) as a missionary during 1906 to 1907 with the Southern Baptist Convention.

12. Vingren, *Diário do Pioneiro*, 24.

13. A copy of Vingren's thesis at Bethel Seminary in St. Paul, with assistance from archivist, Diana Magnuson, was hand-delivered to CPAD in Brazil by Joel Wright, and translated into Portuguese for the 100 Year Anniversary of the *Assembleias de Deus*. See Vingren, *O Tabernáculo e Suas Lições*.

a theological foundation for his future missionary work. During his summer breaks, he engaged in interim preaching and pulpit supply in Swedish Baptist churches in Chicago, Sycamore, and Blue Island, Illinois. He also began to consider missionary work, submitting an application to the General Convention of American Baptists. In the meantime, he accepted the call to the pastorate of First Swedish Baptist Church in Menominee, Michigan, beginning in June 1909.

Daniel Gustav Berg (Höberg) was born April 19, 1884, in Västra Tunhem, Sweden, south of Vargön. During his childhood years, he became a close friend of Lewi Pethrus, also from Västra Tunhem. As teenagers, Berg and Pethrus worked in the same factory and were baptized by immersion on the same day, February 12, 1899, at the Rånnum Baptist Church in Vargön.[14] Pethrus later became Sweden's leading Pentecostal pastor.

Daniel Berg's parents were Baptists, and the family's reputation with the local Lutheran priest was strained. On one occasion the priest said that neither the young Daniel Berg nor any of the unbaptized Berg children would ever leave Vargön.[15] Daniel defied the priest's words when he not only left Vargön but traveled to Brazil, and later Portugal, as a career missionary.[16] Berg learned early in life the value of his Baptist, free-church tradition, saying, "Already at that time I could observe the disadvantage and danger of a people having a directed [or determined] faith, without freedom."[17]

Daniel Berg caught "American fever" too, leaving for the U.S. at age 18. He embarked from Gothenburg, Sweden, on March 5, 1902. When he landed in Boston, he traveled to Providence, Rhode Island, where he found work on a farm. Later he was employed at a foundry in a trade that he would later find helpful.

In 1909, Berg returned to Sweden to see his family and friends. While there, he met with Lewi Pethrus, "his best childhood companion."[18] By then, Pethrus had assumed leadership of the Baptist Church of Lidköping. Pethrus testified to Berg that he experienced the baptism of the Holy Spirit. Of course, such a spiritual experience—Pentecostal baptism—was a new concept to Berg. When he returned to the U.S. in early February

14. Pethrus, *Ett sagolikt liv*, 30–31.
15. Berg, *Enviado Por Deus*, 15.
16. Berg, *Enviado Por Deus*, 13.
17. Berg, *Enviado Por Deus*, 15.
18. Berg, *Enviado Por Deus*, 28.

1909, having been deeply impacted by Pethrus's testimony, Berg began to study the Bible more deeply on the topic. He also began to pray and seek God earnestly for the Pentecostal baptism. During this time, he moved from Providence, Rhode Island to Chicago, Illinois.

Pentecostal Prophesy and Partnership to Pará

In the spring of 1909, when Berg arrived in Chicago, he found work at a produce house that sold fruits and vegetables. With interest in the growing Pentecostal revival in Chicago, he began to seek the Pentecostal baptism for himself. He attended meetings at the Second Swedish Baptist Church and the North Avenue Full Gospel Mission, and his prayer for Pentecostal baptism was soon answered—on September 15, 1909.[19]

After Vingren accepted a pastorate in Menomonie, Michigan, he planned to attend a spiritual edification conference, hosted by Swedish Baptists in Chicago, from November 17–21, 1909. A large attendance was expected at Second Swedish Baptist Church.[20] An advertisement in *Nya Wecko-Posten* read, "Visitors are registered from various states within the country from Maine to Missouri."[21] At this conference Vingren and Berg met and soon became good friends.[22] While Berg had already experienced Pentecostal baptism, Vingren came to Chicago in November seeking this experience and soon testified that he received what he sought. He wrote:

> The conference began on a Wednesday evening, and I registered as someone seeking the baptism of the Spirit. On Thursday and Friday, the Spirit of the Lord led me to spend more time in prayer. On Saturday the Spirit of the Lord fed my soul as usual. On Saturday night, after the meeting was over, many of us lingered, waiting on the Lord. I felt something strange in my jaw bones and was thrown to the floor by the power of God, and under the same power I lay motionless on my back until four

---

19. Berg, *Enviado Por Deus*, 33, 55; Araújo, *Dicionário do Movimento Pentecostal*, 122–23.

20. The five-day conference was held at Second Swedish Baptist Church. *Nya Wecko-Posten* (*NWP*), November 9, 1909, 5; November 23, 1909, 4. See A. A. Holmgren's account: *SV*, May 1934, 5. Vingren wrote later in his diary that the conference was held at First Swedish Baptist Church. Vingren, *Diário do Pioneiro*, 25. Leaders of First Swedish Baptist and Second Swedish Baptist led in the event.

21. *NWP*, November 9, 1909, 5.

22. Vingren, *Diário do Pioneiro*, 2011, 28; Berg, *Enviado Por Deus*, 34.

o'clock in the morning when the power released me and I could stand up. On Sunday afternoon, I again felt God's power but in a different way. I thought that I was lifted off the floor while I stood and testified. I felt God's power too when I sat down, realizing later that I was close to speaking in tongues. The hunger for the baptism of the Spirit became so great that I thought I could not live if I was not baptized with the Spirit of God.[23]

Although the edification conference ended on Sunday evening, on Monday night, November 22, Vingren joined a private prayer meeting at the home of Otto and Hannah Mellquist in the Humboldt Park neighborhood that lasted past 3 a.m. on Tuesday, November 23. When the others got up from prayer to go home, Vingren asked them to stay and pray for him for another five minutes. He said that when his friends again knelt down, the Holy Spirit fell upon him. Vingren recalled: "A brother then saw a tongue of fire above me, and he exclaimed, 'I see it now!' I saw it myself—the glow of fire over my chest—and then I began *to speak with new tongues* [emphasis original] and praised God. Now, what had happened in the past when those in the house of Cornelius received the Holy Spirit was repeated. It was said, 'For they heard them speaking in tongues and praising God' (Acts 10.46). This blessed experience cannot be described in words; it can only be experienced. Glory to Jesus, hallelujah!"[24] Thus, after five days of attending the edification conference, as well as the prayer meeting, Vingren experienced Pentecostal baptism, saying, "the Lord Jesus baptized me with the Holy Spirit and fire!"[25]

Following these events in Chicago, Vingren returned to Menominee and remained there until February 1910.[26] When he returned to his church with a flood of excitement filling his soul, he began to preach the need for Pentecostal baptism. However, the response from everyone in the congregation was not entirely positive. Half accepted this teaching and half resisted it.[27] Those who did not support Vingren's

---

23. Gunnar Vingren, "Min erfarenhet av Andens dop," *Brudgummens Röst*, September 1916, 129–30.

24. Vingren, "Min erfarenhet av Andens dop," 130.

25. Vingren, *Diário do Pioneiro*, 25, cited in Palma, *Grassroots Pentecostalism in Brazil and the United States*, 38–39. Cf. Gonçalves, *A Glossolalia e a Formação das Assembleias de Deus*, 234–35.

26. Gunnar Vingren, Diary, "1912 Agenda," Gunnar Vingren Memorial Archives, CPAD, Rio de Janeiro, Brazil.

27. The history of the Swedish Baptist church of Menominee states that during the pastorate of William Ritzen who replaced Vingren in 1910, there were 31 members

Pentecostal message asked him to leave the church. Thus, he resigned in February of that year.

During this period of his life, Vingren seriously considered two other major life decisions. First, he was serious about a young woman whom he had asked to marry him. Second, he became serious about pursuing missionary work with the General Convention of American Baptists, as already mentioned. A decision came from the Conference that he should go as a missionary to Assam, India, along with his fiancée. However, Vingren soon felt uneasy about this plan and wondered if this was truly God's leading. As he faced inner turmoil, he decided that he would not go forward with plans to India. He wrote to the Convention saying that he had decided, under God, not to pursue this field of service.[28] The change of plans landed hard with his fiancée. This prompted their painful decision to break off their engagement and go their separate ways. Later he wrote to her saying that his decision was a necessary step to follow God's leading.

In the spring of 1910, Vingren returned to Chicago and attended two of the newly-formed Pentecostal churches, the North Avenue Full Gospel Mission led by William H. Durham, and the Swedish Pentecostal Church (Svenska Pingst Församlingen) led by B. M. Johnson.[29] In the early part of the summer of 1910, he became friends with F. A. Sandgren who then accepted him as a co-pastor in South Bend, Indiana, at the Swedish Baptist Church on Napier Street. When Vingren arrived in South Bend, he found housing with the Uldin family that lived on Catalpa Street.[30]

This Swedish Baptist Church of South Bend proved to be a place of refuge for Vingren. The congregation had received Sandgren's ministry and his Pentecostal teaching. In the first week of Vingren's arrival, the church reported that ten people were baptized in the Holy Spirit. In total, nearly twenty people were Spirit-baptized that summer.[31] Besides these

---

who became Pentecostals and left the church. 75th Anniversary, 1887–1962, Thirteenth Street Baptist Church, Menominee, Michigan, August 31–September 2, 1962, 5.

28. Almeida Baptista, *História das Assembleias de Deus*, 14.

29. Araujo, *Dicionário do Movimento Pentecostal*, 900. For more details on the contrasting voices of Chicago area Pentecostalism of Durham, Hjerstrom, A. A. Holmgren and others, see Gonçalves, *A Glossolalia e a Formação das Assembleias de Deus*, 231–38.

30. In the early 1900s, Adolph Uldin's address is listed at 1402 Catalpa Street in South Bend.

31. Vingren, *Diário do Pioneiro*, 26.

two men, the congregation welcomed another Pentecostal-Baptist pastor from Chicago, Henry Nelson.[32]

In addition to the teaching of Pentecostal baptism and speaking in tongues, the Baptist Church of South Bend practiced the gift of prophesy. An important person in this regard was Olof Adolf Uldin (1857–1944), originally a native of Övre Ullerud, Sweden. Uldin was one of the founding pillars of the Swedish Baptist Church in South Bend, and an important member of the community. On one occasion, during a summer prayer meeting at the Uldin home, Uldin spoke to Vingren under the influence of the Holy Spirit, saying, "God has called you to go to Pará."[33] Vingren recalled:

> Brother [Uldin] received one day, by the Holy Spirit, wonderful words and hidden mysteries, which were revealed. Among other things, the Holy Spirit spoke through this brother that I should go to Pará, where the people for whom I would give testimony of Jesus were of a very simple social level. I should teach them the first rudiments of the Lord's doctrine. We also heard through the Holy Spirit the language of that people, the Portuguese idiom. We should eat very simple food, but God would give us all which would be necessary . . . God had now spoken and I understood that I had received a divine calling for my future missionary field. Glory to Jesus![34]

One of the hidden mysteries (and humors) of these prophetic words to go to "Pará" was that no one at the prayer meeting knew where Pará was located. Thus, the next day Vingren and Uldin went to the local library in South Bend to research the location of Pará. They soon discovered that Pará was a state in northeastern Brazil, with Belém as its capital port city.[35]

---

32. F. A. Sandgren came from Durham's Full Gospel Assembly to First Swedish Baptist Church of South Bend as an evangelist from April to May 1910. During this time, he held "Pentecostal services" multiple times each week. Henry Nelson was the pastor until the third week of May 1910. From mid-May of 1910 through October of 1911, Sandgren was listed in the *South Bend Tribune* as pastor of First Swedish Baptist Church.

33. Vingren, *Diário do Pioneiro*, 27. The name Pará was indigenous; "pa'ra" meaning in Tupi-Guarani, "River-Sea."

34. Vingren, *Diário do Pioneiro*, 25, cited in Sinner, *Churches and Democracy in Brazil*, 245.

35. Vingren, *Diário do Pioneiro*, 25, 27–28. For an explanation Pará being familiar to the people in South Bend, see Sinner, *The Churches and Democracy in Brazil*, 245.

Later that summer, Uldin again spoke words of prophesy in the Spirit, this time saying that both Berg and Vingren should go to Pará.[36] Vingren had invited Berg, who was working on a farm in Chicago, to move to South Bend to join in the ministry of the church.[37] Uldin's prophesy happened on a Saturday afternoon as the two young men were entering Uldin's home and Uldin had arrived home from work. As they all entered the kitchen, the power of the Spirit came over Uldin who said that Berg should accompany Vingren to Brazil.[38]

On another occasion, Uldin prophesied that the day for them to depart from New York City was November 5, 1910.[39] Moreover, he prophesied that Vingren would marry a woman by the name of Strandberg.[40] With these words of prophesy, the two young men accepted with full assurance that God had called them as missionaries to Brazil.

With connections in Chicago to the North Avenue Mission and the Swedish Pentecostal Church, Vingren and Berg sought their affirmation, as well as prayer and financial support.[41] Earlier, the aspiring missionaries had collected $90 for travel expenses to Brazil.[42] When they arrived to the North Avenue Mission, they were offered prayer support only. The church had recently taken on other missionaries such as George and Sophie Hansen and Robert and Aimee Semple (McPherson) to China.[43] While Durham could not guarantee the Swedes financial support, on October 2, 1910, he ordained them as ministers of the gospel.[44] While at Durham's mission, Vingren was led to give an offering of $90 to support the North Avenue Mission's periodical, *Pentecostal Testimony*.[45]

Thankfully, when these two aspiring missionaries went to the Swedish Pentecostal Church, led by B. M. Johnson, they received an offering

---

36. Vingren, *Diário do Pioneiro*, 26, cited in Sinner, *Churches and Democracy in Brazil*, 245.

37. Vingren, *Diário do Pioneiro*, 2011, 28.

38. Vingren, *Diário do Pioneiro*, 28. Cf. *SV*, March 1937, 5.

39. Vingren, *Diário do Pioneiro*, 29.

40. Vingren, *Diário do Pioneiro*, 27. See also Isael de Araujo, *Frida Vingren*.

41. Vingren, *Diário do Pioneiro*, 27–29. Cf. Vingren, *Despertamento apostolico no Brasil*, 9.

42. Berg, *Enviado Por Deus*, 2011, 37.

43. *Pentecostal Testimony*, July 1, 1910, 10.

44. "We [Berg and Vingren] were ordained October 2, 1910, by Brother Durham in the Full Gospel Assembly at North Ave. in Chicago." *Word and Witness*, March 20, 1914, 7.

45. Vingren, *Pionjärens dagbok*, 29.

that far surpassed the $90 they had given to Durham's publication.⁴⁶ Johnson said, "Those who want to help our brethren on their journey can do so privately."⁴⁷ After the service, Vingren and Berg greeted others to say goodbye. When they left the church and searched their pockets, the two men found more money than was necessary for the journey. They soon left by train for New York City.

When Vingren and Berg went to purchase tickets to Brazil, they were told that no ship was scheduled to leave on November 5, 1910.⁴⁸ However, after waiting a few minutes, the ticket master informed them that, indeed, a ship named Clement, which had been undergoing repairs in dry dock, was just listed and would depart that day for Brazil. Thus, they bought two third-class tickets, and fourteen days later landed in Brazil.

Vingren and Berg arrived in Belém on November 19, 1910. When they disembarked, there was no one to receive them. They had no contacts, little funding, and no skills to speak Portuguese. However, they prayed and soon found a Methodist missionary, Justus Henry Nelson, who spoke English.⁴⁹ When they inquired about housing, he directed them to the First Baptist Church of Belém on a street named Rua João Balby. The Baptist church offered them a room in the church basement for a reasonable amount per night.⁵⁰

Berg soon found employment at a foundry called the Port of Pará Company where he received a monthly salary of 12,000 réis. With most of his earnings used for living expenses, extra money helped pay for Vingren to take Portuguese lessons from a private tutor. At the end of every day, Vingren would teach Berg all the Portuguese he had learned. The rest of Berg's income was used to buy Portuguese Bibles that came from a U. S. Bible society.

In early February 1911, the pastor of the Baptist Church of Belém, Eric Nelson, left for mission work in the State of Piaui, leaving the congregation under the leadership of moderator José Batista de Carvalho but soon he was replaced by deacon José Plácido da Costa. In Vingren's

---

46. *The Lake View Chimes*, November 1, 1951, 1. Heckman, *History of the Fellowship of Christian Assemblies (HFCA)*, 124.

47. Burgess and Van der Maas, *New International Dictionary of Pentecostal and Charismatic Movements*, 1177.

48. González and González, *Christianity in Latin America*, 282.

49. Palma, *Grassroots Pentecostalism in Brazil*, 75.

50. Berg, *Enviado por Deus*, 49–50. See also Chesnut, *Born Again in Brazil*, 26.

diary, he wrote that the Baptists hoped that once he had learned Portuguese that he could become their pastor.[51] Needless to say, Vingren and Berg neither remained quiet about the Pentecostal message nor the "Pentecostal flame" that kindled within them.[52] Their insistence on Pentecostal baptism and the gift of speaking in tongues soon raised concerns among the church leaders.[53]

For several months, Vingren led prayer meetings with groups of ten to fifteen members of the Baptist church. As they increasingly received requests for prayer from people in Belém, as well as members of the congregation, conflicts arose. José Plácido da Costa, a man described as spiritual, alien to contention, was one of the first to accept the Pentecostal doctrine of Vingren and Berg.[54] The church secretary was Manoel Maria Rodrigues and the treasurer was José Batista de Carvalho. They too became sympathetic to the Pentecostal doctrine taught by Vingren and Berg. Moreover, Celina Albuquerque and Maria de Nazaré, also active members, believed in the Pentecostal message and received the baptism of the Holy Spirit.[55]

Threatened by Vingren's and Berg's teaching, a debate over theological distinctives of Baptists and Pentecostal-Baptists (or Baptist-Pentecostals) ensued.[56] The matter came to a head on June 13, 1911, during a special session called by Raimundo Nobre after a prayer service. Thirteen members, plus Vingren and Berg, were expelled from the church.[57] In the wake of this action by the church leadership, those expelled soon gathered around Vingren and Berg. Of course, these two Swedish missionaries were familiar with such debates and divisions, having experienced them earlier in Chicago and Menomonie.[58]

Five days later, on Sunday, June 18, 1911, with 18 people present, plus Vingren and Berg, the Missão de Fé Apostólica (Apostolic Faith

51. Vingren, *Diário do Pioneiro*, 37–38.
52. Vingren, *Diário do Pioneiro*, 39.
53. Palma, *Grassroots Pentecostalism in Brazil*, 75.
54. Vingren, *Diário do Pioneiro*, 40.
55. Vingren, *Diário do Pioneiro*, 36, 40–41; *SV*, July 1911, 4.
56. For a critique of Vingren's and Berg's early ministry and Pentecostal practices, see Price, "A Comparative Analysis of the Growth of the Brazilian Baptists and the Assemblies of God in Metropolitan São Paulo, 1981–1990," 122–128.
57. Araujo, *100 Acontecimentos*, 15. For Eric Nelson's view, see *NWP*, September 26, 1911, 8.
58. *NWP*, May 21, 1907, 4, stated, "Speaking in tongues was never given to all believers." Gonçalves, *Glossolalia e a Formação das Assembleias de Deus*, 236.

Mission) was formed at the home of Henrique and Celina Albuquerque, located at Rua Siqueira Mendes 67, Cidade Velha, in Belém.[59] The reason for meeting initially at the Albuquerque home was because an earlier healing of Celina. Vingren recalled, "We had prayer meetings every night in a sister's home who had an incurable illness on her lips. We felt sad. We were saddened because she could not attend services at the church. The first thing I did was to ask her if she believed that Jesus could heal her. She said yes. So we told her to get rid of all the medicine she was taking. We prayed for her, and the Lord Jesus healed her completely."[60] After Celina's healing, Vingren and Berg continued to have meetings in the Albuquerque home. The new church soon conducted water baptisms for several new converts to faith.[61]

Moreover, some of the believers there experienced Pentecostal baptism. Vingren related that one woman spoke in tongues for several hours after she was baptized in the Holy Spirit.[62] During the following months, both in Belém and throughout the state of Pará, Brazilians received the baptism of the Spirit with the evidence of speaking in tongues. This was important to Vingren who taught: "A strange [unknown] tongue is the most perfect and real manifestation of the evidence of the baptism of the Spirit."[63] Berg said, "I praise God for the wonderful baptism of the Holy Spirit and for the Bible evidence of 'speaking in other tongues.'"[64] Moreover, Berg quoted Vingren who emphasized the unity that comes from Spirit-baptism, saying "If everyone achieved the experience of the baptism with the Holy Ghost, it would give rise to an unshakeable union between one another, and they would be like one family."[65]

From the earliest days of Berg's and Vingren's ministry, stories circulated about the power of God manifesting, even before non-believing

59. For a list of the eighteen members with Vingren and Berg, see *Bíblia do Centenário*, 34–35. Cf. *SV*, November 1930, 7.

60. Vingren, *Diário do Pioneiro* (1991), 36, cited in Chesnut, *Born Again in Brazil*, 27.

61. In 1911, 13 converts to faith were water-baptized and 3 were Spirit-baptized. From 1911 to 1914, a total of 384 were water-baptized and 276 were Spirit-baptized. Peterson and Vásquez, eds. *Latin American Religions*, 175–76.

62. Vingren, *Diário do Pioneiro*, 43.

63. Vingren, *Boa Semente* no. 1, 1919, 1; Gonçalves, *Glossolalia e a Formação das Assembleias de Deus*, 235.

64. *Weekly Evangel*, April 22, 1916, 12.

65. Berg, *Enviado por Deus*, 94, cited in Palma, *Grassroots Pentecostalism in Brazil*, 76.

Brazilians. One such story told of a meeting held in Vila Coroa where a demon-possessed man appeared who jerked and twisted with such force that no one could constrain him.[66] Some people tried to contain him but could not. Then, all of a sudden, Josina Galvão began to prophesy, and filled with the Spirit, went to the demon-possessed man, pointing her finger toward him, and commanded in Jesus' name for the demon to leave. Immediately, the man sat quietly, completely overwhelmed by divine power. Then, people saw something like lightning come out of a window and disappear. The onlookers acknowledged that indeed God was with these Pentecostal people.

As soon as Berg learned enough Portuguese to be understood, he began to evangelize in the cities and towns along the Belém-Bragança Railroad.[67] As the gospel message was little known in rural areas of Pará, he pioneered the work of evangelism in that region. In 1913, he wrote to *Sanningens Vittne*, saying,

> I have just returned from Bragança, where Jesus opened a door for his Word through a family that believes the truth, and the sister in the family is now baptized in water and seeking the baptism of the Spirit. We had a meeting there last Sunday evening and many came and listened to the Word of the Lord. Also, in a village outside Bragança named Quatipuru, the Lord has started to work so that there are now 22 people who have completely given themselves to Jesus, and a few weeks later we baptized 7 of them in water, and 2 more last Thursday. Last night Jesus baptized a sister in the Holy Spirit in our mission here in Pará, and another sister three weeks ago.[68]

After preaching in Bragança, Berg carried out a similar work on Marajó Island, traveling the area by canoe. Wherever he went, he returned to teach the Bible to the small, evangelical groups that formed. On Marajó Island, some opposed his work. New converts to faith were threatened and even stoned. Despite intermittent persecution, Berg's and Vingren's unrelenting evangelistic work won converts to the new Pentecostal assemblies. To avoid open opposition from antagonists and hecklers, they held water baptisms late in the evening in the rivers and igarapés of the area.[69]

66. Conde, *História das Assembléias no Brasil*, 40.
67. *Word and Witness*, November 20, 1913, 2.
68. *SV*, May–June 1913, 5. Daniel Berg's address was Caixa 653, Para, Brazil.
69. Chesnut, *Born Again in Brazil*, 28.

Another story was told that on one occasion, an opponent of Berg shouted a curse at him saying that he would be devoured by a jaguar. The words were spoken near the town of Ipixuma where the thick Amazonian jungle is home to jaguars who often prey near the water's edge. After weeks of evangelism, Berg conducted his first baptisms and a ranch worker, seeing the group, yelled the curse, "May a jaguar attack the missionaries and all those dressed in white!"[70] The baptism concluded peaceably, despite the man's words. As everyone was beginning to disperse, a young man came running and said that he just saw a jaguar dragging off something. The people followed the young man, retracing his steps, worried that it might be an attack on one of the family members who had just witnessed the baptisms. The group found pieces of clothing and scattered human remains. It turned out to be the ranch worker who pronounced the curse. It was said that this incident "struck the fear of God" in the community.

In 1913, Vingren and Berg reported that over 100 converts were baptized in water and over 70 received the Pentecostal baptism. Two months later, Vingren said that over 40 more "received their baptism in the Holy Ghost."[71] Writing to subscribers of the *Word and Witness* he said, "The devil is stirred up. Nearly all the 43 in the interior of whom I wrote to you receiving the baptism have been arrested, some of them for several days; but God did not suffer them to be hurt. One boy got the baptism in prison."[72]

The first Pentecostal believer in Brazil to be consecrated to pastoral ministry was Isidoro Filho. He was ordained by Vingren in 1912, and served the congregation in Soure, on the Island of Marajó.[73] In 1913, José Plácido da Costa was commissioned as a missionary to Portugal.[74] In the same year, a second pastor, Absalão Piano, was ordained by Vingren in Rio Preto, Tajapuru do Norte. A third to be ordained was Crispiniano de Melo, who served on the Paraenses Islands.[75] Vingren and Berg sought to empower the Brazilians to carry on the missionary work.

---

70. Raiol, *1911: Missão de Fogo no Brasil*, 55–63.
71. *Word and Witness*, November 20, 1913, 2.
72. *Word and Witness*, January 20, 1914, 4.
73. Araujo, *Dicionário do Movimento Pentecostal*, 523.
74. Conde, *História da Assembleias de Deus no Brasil*, 62.
75. The fourth to be ordained was Pedro Trajano and the fifth was Adriano Nobre. For Nobre, see *Word and Witness*, March 20, 1914, 7.

Mission Partnership of Scandinavian-Americans and Brazilians

In addition to Berg working at the Port of Pará Company, he contributed to the mission by selling Portuguese Bibles door-to-door. Of course, this ministry helped to raise funds and gave him opportunities to share the Full Gospel—Jesus as Savior, Healer, Baptizer, and Coming King.[76]

Vingren and Berg also received funds from Pentecostals in the United States. Two of their greatest advocates were the pastor-editors, B. M. Johnson of Chicago, editor of *Pingst-Rösten*, and A. A. Holmgren of Minneapolis, editor of *Sanningens Vittne*. In fact, for decades *Sanningens Vittne* became the primary organ in the U.S. to report Vingren's and Berg's missionary news. This periodical was also the means by which they received funds from congregations and individuals in the U.S.[77] In addition to a brief news report about Berg's travel to Sweden, it reported the funds that A. A. Holmgren received for the Brazilian mission, and dispersed to Berg and Vingren. In addition to B. M. Johnson and A. A. Holmgren, Henry Nelson of South Bend was equally active in promoting the Brazilian mission and handling their mission finances.

In 1914, Berg traveled to Sweden where he visited his long-time friend, Lewi Pethrus. The Baptist congregation where Pethrus served—7th Baptist Church of Stockholm—earlier had become a Pentecostal congregation, and 1913 reorganized as Filadelfia Church.[78] As a result of Berg's trip, he and Vingren were added to Filadelfia Church's list of missionaries.[79]

On October 25, 1914, Otto and Adina Nelson arrived in Belém from Chicago to join the mission work.[80] They were commissioned by B. M. Johnson and leaders of the Swedish Pentecostal Church, known commonly as the Barry Avenue Church.[81] Then on August 18, 1916, Samuel and Lina Nyström arrived in Belém as the first missionaries sent by the Filadelfia Church of Stockholm.[82]

---

76. *Word and Witness*, November 20, 1913, 2.
77. For example, see *SV* January 1914, 6.
78. Halldorf, *Pentecostal Politics in a Secular World*, 37–38.
79. Vingren, *Det började i Pará*, 17.
80. Araujo, *Dicionário do Movimento Pentecostal*, 504.
81. Heckman, *HFCA*, 124.
82. Bundy, *Visions of Apostolic Mission*, 401.

In 1915, Vingren traveled to the U.S. where he made visits to several churches, among them the Swedish Apostolic Mission in McKeesport, Pennsylvania. In Chicago, he preached at the Barry Avenue Church. While there, he attended a conference with several pastors in attendance, and preached in one of the services.[83]

When the conference attendees became interested in the mission work in Brazil, they received an offering for Vingren to purchase a boat that could be used by the mission on the Amazon River, especially for Berg as he visited the various evangelistic outposts to reach the Brazilian nationals.

Vingren arrived back in Belém in May of 1917. His time away from the mission field opened doors for financial support, recruiting missionaries, and gaining direction for Brazil's Pentecostal movement. A new missionary to arrive from the Filadelfia Church in Stockholm was Frida Strandberg (1891–1940), who landed in Belém on July 3, 1917.[84] She took up residency in the missionary home of the church at Travessa 9 de Janeiro, 75. Three months later—on October 16, 1917—she and Gunnar Vingren married, fulfilling Uldin's prophecy. Vingren recalled this detail, writing, "The Holy Spirit also said that I would marry a person called Strandberg, which happened later, as I married Frida Strandberg. This prophecy occurred long before I knew her. God also said other things which I had later the opportunity to verify that they were truths."[85]

At the time of their wedding, Gunnar Vingren was 38 and Frida was 26. Over the next several years, the couple had six children: Ivar, Ruben, Bertil, Gunvor, Astrid, and Margit. Sadly, their daughter, Gunvor, died from croup at three years of age.[86]

In 1917 Missão de Fé Apostólica in Belém printed its first hymnal of 194 hymns and songs. Also, in November 1917, the mission published its first periodical, *Voz da Verdade* (Voice of Truth) edited by Almeida Sobrinho and João Trigueiro da Silva. However, this publication was short-lived, ending circulation in the following year. Nevertheless, it was unanimous that there was a need for an organ that would communicate the Full Gospel message and mission news, and so the periodical *Boa*

---

83. *Weekly Evangel*, December 4, 1915, 1.

84. Araujo, *Frida Vingren*, 30, 37.

85. Vingren, *Diário do Pioneiro*, 25, cited in Sinner, *Churches and Democracy in Brazil*, 245.

86. Araujo, *Frida Vingren*, 154.

Semente (Good Seed) began. The first issue was published in January 1919. Vingren was the editor and Samuel Nyström the assistant editor.

Growth of the Mission to the Assemblies of God of Brazil

Earlier, when Vingren traveled in the U.S., the name 'Assembly of God' captured his attention. Although the work in Belém had started as the Apostolic Faith Mission (Missão de Fé Apostólica), on January 11, 1918, Vingren and Berg registered it in the state of Pará as the Assembléias de Deus—the Assemblies of God.[87] Some years later "brothers in Sweden and America" surmised that the work in Brazil had organized as a denomination—a grave concern for Scandinavian Pentecostals who held fiercely to the autonomy of the local church. Thus, Vingren provided a five-point explanation.

He said, first, that he held the same position as when he arrived in Brazil in 1910.[88] He did not believe in formal church membership as a condition for membership in God's church (*Guds församling*). Although he kept a list of addresses to know where people lived, he did not keep a membership roll, noting that the local church is a "community in the Spirit that belongs to the Assembly of God."[89]

Second, he explained, "We call ourselves here 'Assembléia de Deus'= Assembly of God, because we consider that expression biblical."[90] Then, he appealed to the late William H. Durham of Chicago who had ordained him and Berg. Durham referred to his congregation as "an assembly of God" and Vingren and Berg had no intention of establishing a denomination. The reason he registered the work in the state was merely to guarantee legal rights.[91] Vingren reiterated, "If some brothers at home have misunderstood this relationship and said that we are a denomination, then we object and hereby clarify that we are free, only wanting to be led of the Holy Spirit and believe that only the Holy Spirit shall be the leader of the assembly."

87. Araujo, *Dicionário do Movimento Pentecostal*, 41.

88. *SV*, April 1927, 7. Cf. Lewi Pethrus verifying that Vingren and Berg had not organized a Pentecostal denomination but were in line with the free church model. *Evangelii Härold*, October 1930, 23.

89. *SV*, April 1927, 7.

90. *SV*, April 1927, 7.

91. Vingren cited an example in Pará, the socialists, who dissolved because they were not registered in the state.

Third, Vingren emphasized that every congregation in Brazil was independent from the other and none could make a decision for another.

Fourth, he made it clear that there is only one head of the church, namely, Christ. The proper response of believers is to humble themselves before him and one another, exalting only Christ.

Finally, he described that the goal of the Assemblies of God was to work for the salvation of souls and to give the Holy Spirit room for the gifts of the Spirt to manifest in congregations, as happened in the early Christian era.

In 1918, the Swedish-American missionary Joel Carlson and his wife Signe arrived in Brazil, taking up work in Recife (Pernambuco).[92] It did not take them long to see the need there to support the growing number of orphans who lived in the community. Encouraged by those who labored with them, the Carlsons founded Betel Orphanage. In 1919, Nels Julius Nelson joined the work in Brazil. He was commissioned by the Lake View Gospel Church, known earlier as the Barry Avenue Church.

In 1920, Daniel Berg married Sara Ahlberg (1896–1981) in Sweden. She joined him in the work in Pará and then in Afua. In January 1922, Sara Berg wrote from Afua, saying, "The Lord has saved a few here, but it seems quite difficult presently. Nevertheless, the Lord is mighty to break the copper gates and pull apart the iron bars.... We had a baptism ceremony on Sunday when 3 were baptized. Glory to Jesus! We are encouraged by every soul who comes to him. Daniel is now out with the mission boat to the islands.... Thank you very much for the letter with $22.57."[93]

Regarding missionary support, during the first twenty years in Brazil, sources of financial support shifted. At the beginning, Gunnar Vingren, Daniel Berg, Otto and Adina Nelson, and Nels J. Nelson—received support primarily from the U.S. However, Vingren and Berg along with their wives became members of the Filadelfia Church in Stockholm, and were accepted as that congregation's missionaries, with purportedly "full support."[94] Vingren, however, qualified such a claim saying that his financial support came from Filadelfia Church in Stockholm, Pastor Lewi Pethrus, and from the United States. For Otto Nelson and his wife, they received financial support partly through *Sanningens Vittne*, and partly

---

92. Araujo, *Dicionário do Movimento Pentecostal*, 44, 156.
93. *SV*, January 1922, 7.
94. *SV*, November 1930, 7. Cf. Vingren, *Det började i Pará*, 39.

through B. M. Johnson and others. However, they also received funding from Sweden, if only a small amount quarterly.[95]

From August 18–22, 1921, the first Regional Convention of the Assemblies of God took place in the state of Pará. The event was hosted by the congregation of São Luís, with the representation of the churches of Bragança, Catipuru, Tacari, Capanema, Abaeté, Bonito, Burrinho, Cedro, Timboteua, Pau Amarelo, Peixe Verde, Guamá, Belém, and Aramã.[96] Also in 1921, the Assemblies of God in Brazil sent a second missionary to the field, José Matos, to Portugal.[97] Another change came in 1922, when Daniel and Sara Berg moved to Vitória (Victoria), Brazil, to establish the Assembly of God in that state capital city.[98]

In the same year, due to the congregation's position as the first church and as the center of evangelistic activities in Brazil, the Assembly of God of Belém had the responsibility of preparing Christian workers who received a calling to ministry as pastors and evangelists. In response to this, the Assembly of God of Belém organized and carried out the first Bible School for Workers.[99] The classes were conducted by Samuel Nyström from March 4 to April 4, 1922, mostly for Brazilians who were serving as pastors. The second Bible School for Workers took place two years later, and was directed by Vingren.[100] Over 40 students enrolled from the states of Pará, Ceará, and Rio Grande do Norte.

The year 1921 marked the appearance of a hymnbook—*Cantor Pentecostal*.[101] This hymnal contained 44 hymns and 10 choruses. It was compiled by Almeida Sobrinho and distributed by the Assembly of God of Belém. The first edition of *Harpa Cristã* (Christian Harp) was published in Recife in 1922, and became the official hymnbook of the Assemblies of God.[102] The second edition of *Harpa Cristã*, with 300 hymns, was printed in Rio de Janeiro, in 1923.

In 1922, Vingren traveled to Sweden and then to the U.S. During his time in the States, he preached in services of churches in cities such

---

95. *SV*, November 1930, 7.
96. Conde, *História das Assembleias de Deus no Brasil*, 54.
97. Araujo, *Dicionário do Movimento Pentecostal*, 155.
98. *Pentecostal Evangel*, February 3, 1923, 12.
99. Conde, *História das Assembleias de Deus no Brasil*, 55.
100. Araujo, *Dicionário do Movimento Pentecostal*, 282.
101. Conde, *História das Assembleias de Deus no Brasil*, 53.
102. Araujo, *Dicionário do Movimento Pentecostal*, 341.

as Duluth, Minneapolis, Chicago, New York, and in various places in Minnesota.¹⁰³

Meeting of the Scandinavian Assemblies of God, 1922. Front row, left to right: Hedwig Nordlund, her son Herbert Nordlund, A. A. Holmgren, B. M. Johnson (center), Gunnar Vingren, unknown. Middle row (sitting): Theodor "Tom" Christensen, Petrus Swartz, John Feuk. Back standing: Gustav Nordlund, unknown, unknown, unknown, John W. Moseid, C. A. Moseid, unknown. Courtesy of Gunnar Vingren Memorial Archives, CPAD, Rio de Janeiro, Brazil.

In 1922, in St. Paul, Minnesota, 25 pastors gathered to form the Independent Assemblies of God (IAG) and Vingren participated in the event. The basis of the IAG's unity was belief that each local church was free to manage and direct its own affairs, without forming a denominational structure.¹⁰⁴ A similar organization had formed in 1918 in the Chicago area and was called the Scandinavian Assemblies of God (SAG).

In Brazil, Berg and wife Sara remained in Vitória until 1924, when they went to Santos to develop the Assembly of God in the State of São Paulo. Their first daughter named Lisbeth died in Santos about this time,

---

103. Vingren, *Diário do Pioneiro*, 128.
104. *Herald of Faith*, February 1950, 14.

the couple having two other children named David and Debora.[105] As for the Berg family, in 1927, Daniel and Sara relocated to São Paulo.[106]

During 1924, Vingren moved south with his family to Rio de Janeiro, which then was the national capital. Vingren founded the Assembly of God in Rio de Janeiro.[107] In 1925, in the church in Rio de Janeiro, Vingren consecrated Palatino dos Santos as a deacon, and later ordained him as a pastor. Vingren also consecrated Emília Costa as deaconess, the only person who held that position in the church. She was active in evangelism and ministered in several of the city's jails.[108]

From a Scandinavian Mission to a Brazilian Pentecostal Movement

The first Convention of the Missionaries of the Assemblies of God in Brazil was held in 1926, at the Assembly of God in São Cristóvão, Rio de Janeiro. Dr. A. P. Franklin, secretary of foreign missions of the Swedish Free Mission (Svenska Fria Missionen, Missão Livre Sueca) was active in the meetings. During the convention, it was approved that Swedish missionaries would work in Brazil with the Swedish Free Mission of Sweden. In return, the Swedish Free Mission would represent the interests of the work of the Assemblies of God in Sweden. The same agreement was made with the Scandinavian Assemblies of God (SAG) of the United States.

By 1928, the Assemblies of God in Brazil had established congregations in 20 states, with a total of 16,000 members and 150 churches. The names of Brazilian pastors were succeeding the names of Scandinavian missionaries. A new generation of Brazilian leaders were active in the work including: Paulo Leivas Macalão, Francisco Gonzaga, Bruno Skolimowski, Clímaco Bueno Aza, João Pedro da Silva, Antonio Rego Barros, Cícero Canuto de Lima, Manoel Pessoa Leão, José Morais, José Floriano Cordeiro, Manoel Cezar da Silva, and José Marcelino da Silva.[109]

During this time, Brazilian pastors felt increasingly the need to have greater freedom in carrying out the work of the Assemblies of God, especially in the North and Northeast regions of the country. In

105. Berg, *Enviado Por Deus*, 222.
106. Araujo, *Dicionário do Movimento Pentecostal*, 122–124
107. Vingren, *Diário do Pioneiro*, 139.
108. Conde, *História das Assembleias de Deus no Brasil*, 238.
109. Araujo, *Dicionário do Movimento Pentecostal*, 45.

1929, they decided to bring together the national pastors and the Swedish missionaries for a meeting.[110] There was no intention of the nationals to divide the Assemblies of God. They only wanted more autonomy, urging that they not be misunderstood and that the work in Brazil remain united. Nevertheless, when the meeting was scheduled for September 1930, in Natal, the Swedish missionaries feared division.[111] Lewi Pethrus described the events saying,

> In the summer of 1930, missionary Gunnar Vingren arrived [to Sweden] from Brazil. His mission was to take me to the National Convention to be held in September. There were difficulties between the missionaries and the Brazilian pastors, and Vingren considered that if there was no understanding, all the work would be divided. . . . During those 20 years [since 1910] the work had grown a lot and a group of Brazilian preachers considered that they had little influence on the churches. There were strong political splits in the country and nationalism had contributed to create a certain aversion to foreigners. These Brazilian preachers had organized the conference and invited the missionaries, as well as a representative of the mission in the home country.[112]

At this time, missionaries from the U.S. and Sweden held many of the top national and state-wide roles.[113] Since the start of the work in Pará in 1911, the mission had spread to the islands beyond the Amazon River, to the interior of the state of Pará, to the state of Mato Grosso next to the Bolivia border in the west, south to the states of Maranhao, Ceará, Rio Grande Do Norte, Paraíba, Pernambuco, Alagoas, Bahia, Espírito Santo, Rio de Janeiro, São Paulo, and Rio Grande do Sul, the southernmost state.[114]

At the Convention of the Missionaries of the Assemblies of God in 1930, in attendance were 11 Swedish-American and Swedish missionaries

---

110. The pastors present at the preliminary meeting in the Potiguar capital were Cícero Canuto de Lima, Francisco Gonzaga da Silva, Antônio Lopes, Ursulino Costa, José Amador, Napoleão de Oliveira Lima, José Barbosa, Francisco César, Natanael Figueiredo, and Pedro Costa.

111. For the background of their fears, see Araujo, *100 mulheres que fizeram a história das Assembleias de Deus no Brasil*, 10.

112. Nelson and Nelson, *Lewi Pethrus*, 222.

113. For the broader leadership, see Araujo, *Dicionário do Movimento Pentecostal*, 57–78.

114. *SV*, November 1930, 7.

and 23 Brazilian pastors and evangelists.[115] According to the November 1930 edition of the periodical, *Boa Semente*, the missionaries present were: Gunnar and Frida Vingren, Daniel Berg, Otto Nelson, Samuel Nyström, Nels Julius Nelson, Algot Svensson, Anders Johansson, Beda Palma, Joel Carlson, and Nils Kastberg. Present from Sweden was pastor Lewi Pethrus. The Brazilian pastors were: Cícero Canuto de Lima, Francisco Gonzaga, Josino Galvão de Lima, Juvenal Roque de Andrade, José Felinto, José Amador, Napoleão de Oliveira Lima, Manoel Hygino de Souza, Luiz Gonçalves Chaves, Antonio Lopes Galvão, Ursulino Costa, Manoel César (Neco), Manoel Pessoa Leão, and Diomedes Pereira.[116]

It was decided that, because the work had stabilized in the northern states, i.e. the states north of Alagoas, that it would be in the best interest of the mission to turn the ministry over by July 1, 1931, to the Brazilians and to have the missionaries withdraw south and to open new fields.[117] In addition, the convention decided that the general conventions would be held every year, bringing all the pastors, missionaries, and evangelists of the Assemblies of God in Brazil together with the purpose of uniting under one vision.

This was followed by a decision to merge the two periodicals of the Assemblies of God. *Boa Semente* was the oldest of the two periodicals. It circulated in the North and was published by the Assembly of God in Belém and was edited by Samuel Nyström and Nels J. Nelson. *O Som Alegre* (The Sound of Joy) was the newest of the two periodicals. It circulated in the Southeast, was published by the Assembly of God of Rio de Janeiro, and edited by Gunnar and Frida Vingren. In the final analysis, it was decided to end both periodicals and create a new one, *Mensageiro da Paz* (Messenger of Peace).[118] The editorial office would be located in Rio de Janeiro and the editor would be Vingren, assisted by Nyström. The first issue circulated in December 1930.

A point of discussion at the 1930 Convention was women's ministry. Gunnar Vingren defended the role of women in public ministry while Samuel Nyström, for his part, opposed the idea. At the end of the debate, the following resolution was ratified: "Women have every right to participate in the gospel work, testifying of Jesus and his salvation, and

---

115. Antoniazz et al., *Nem Anjos Nem Demônios*, 83.

116. *Boa Semente*, November 1930, cited in Daniel, *História da Convenção Geral das Assembleias de Deus no Brasil*, 27.

117. *SV*, November 1930, 7.

118. Conde, *História das Assembleias de Deus no Brasil*, 354.

also teaching when needed. But it is not considered fair for a sister to have the role of the pastor of a church or teacher, except in exceptional cases mentioned in Matthew 12:3-8 [a reference to the principle of the state of need]. This should happen only when there are no brothers in the church capable of pastoring or teaching."[119]

Vingren pastored the Assembléa de Deus of São Cristóvão, Rio de Janeiro, from 1924 to 1932. Yet, his influence as a respected leader extended broadly to nearly all regions of the country as he traveled to encourage and advise the growing number of churches. This pioneer missionary even presided over the second General Convention of the Assemblies of God in Rio de Janeiro in 1931.[120]

On August 15, 1932, Vingren returned to Sweden. As Vingren departed, he acknowledged how much he loved Brazil, now the land where his daughter, Gunvor, was buried.[121] Under his direction, the church in Rio de Janeiro "grew more than any other in Brazil at that period."[122]

In Sweden, although Vingren was weak and ill from stomach cancer, he attended services at the Filadelfia Church in Stockholm. In fact, he celebrated his last New Year's prayer vigil there. Vingren said that he was "dying happy" (*vou feliz*) and passed on June 29, 1933.[123]

After a period of rest, the Bergs and their son, David, departed Brazil to do missionary work in Portugal, between the years 1932 to 1936, in the city of Porto. After Vingren's passing, and the Berg's leaving, the Assemblies of God of Brazil continued its exponential growth under such leaders as Paulo Leivas Macalão [124] The Pentecostal movement doubled to an estimated 700,000 people in the Assembly of God congregations by 1963.[125] The expansive growth that followed accelerated even more under entirely Brazilian leadership.

---

119. Vingren, *Diário do Pioneiro*, 180.

120. Daniel, *História da Convenção Geral*, 46.

121. Gunvor died July 23, 1932, and the family departed Rio de Janeiro on August 15, 1932. Araujo, *Frida Vingren*, 154.

122. Conde, *História das Assembleias de Deus no Brasil*, 238.

123. Oliveira, *As Assembléias de Deus no Brasil*, 18. For the final words of Vingren, see Araujo, *Dicionario Movimento Pentecostal*, 905.

124. Araujo, *Dicionário do Movimento Pentecostal*, 46-47.

125. Araujo, *Dicionário do Movimento Pentecostal*, 50.

Assemblies of God Conference in Brazil, *Sanningens Vittne*, 1936. Front row: Lídia Rodrigues Nelson, Signe Carlson, Joel Carlson, Samuel Nyström, Daniel Berg, A. A. Holmgren, Nels J. Nelson, Cícero Canuto de Lima, Nils Kastberg, unknown. Public Domain.

In 1936, to commemorate the twenty-fifth anniversary of its founding, the Assembly of God of Belém held the General Convention of the Assemblies of God at its headquarters.[126] Pastors and missionaries who lived abroad and who, directly or indirectly, were linked to its activities, were invited and attended. The General Convention attracted dozens of missionaries, pastors and evangelists including Daniel Berg and Samuel Nyström, who were working in Portugal at the time. A. A. Holmgren, editor of *Sanningens Vittne*, traveled from Minneapolis to attend as a representative of the Independent Assemblies of God (IAG).[127] Holmgren was also part of the committee that read the letter from the North American Assemblies of God Mission (Springfield, Missouri) about sending missionaries to Brazil.

After Daniel and Sara Berg and family served in Portugal, and visited Sweden, the couple returned to Brazil on May 11, 1949.[128] They remained in the city of Santo André (São Paulo) until 1962, when they returned permanently to Sweden. In 1963, Berg was hospitalized. Even

---

126. Daniel, *História da Convenção Geral*, 107.
127. Daniel, *História da Convenção Geral*, 110–11. Cf. *SV*, August 1936, 8.
128. *Evangelii Härold*, June 16, 1949.

while he was there, he distributed tracts and offered to pray for people in his ward. He died on May 27, 1963.[129]

Daniel Berg was buried in Enskede in Stockholm next to Gunnar Vingren, which speaks of their enduring friendship. That many hundreds of Brazilian pastors have visited their gravesides in Sweden speaks also to the enduring love for these two missionaries who founded the Assemblies of God of Brazil.

Lewi Pethrus praised Daniel Berg, saying he had personal qualities as a worker and man of faith. He described Gunnar Vingren as the "main leader" with many qualities and abilities that contributed to the Pentecostal movement growing so rapidly in Brazil.[130]

Conclusion

In 1910, Vingren and Berg purchased one-way tickets to Brazil to begin their work as missionaries. In hindsight, they are considered by many as "apostles of Brazilian Pentecostalism." Like other Pentecostals, their breakthroughs in evangelism came through the "Full Gospel" that included the manifestation of glossolalia, prophesies, and healings. The Pentecostal experience, rooted in the New Testament, gave them greater freedom in the practice of mission than the traditional Swedish Baptist forms, and they more readily addressed needs and cultural expressions of the Brazilian people.

In terms of mission practice, Vingren and Berg were aware of the need individually and collectively for missionaries to empower Brazilians for church leadership as pastors, missionaries, and evangelists. This strategy—even with some growing initiatives from the Brazilians in 1930—encouraged Swedish-American and Swedish missionaries to move to new regions of Brazil that were without local Assemblies of God and to plant new ones. The promptings by the Brazilians, however, were evidence that for two decades Vingren and Berg had understood indigenous agency and empowered Brazilians for leadership roles. The Swedish-American missionaries were intentional in developing partnerships also with the burgeoning Scandinavian-American Pentecostal churches in the U.S., and the Pentecostal movement in Sweden in which Lewi Pethrus and Filadelfia Church of Stockholm played a central role.

129. Araujo, *Dicionário do Movimento Pentecostal*, 124.
130. Vingren, *Diário do Pioneiro*, 16.

Vingren and Berg were not merely missionaries dedicated to go by faith to the mission field for the long-term. They were missionaries who facilitated evangelism, organized prayer meetings, baptized new believers, ordained pastors, commissioned missionaries, launched publications, and taught theological education. Once the local assemblies and even the whole Pentecostal movement—Assembleias de Deus—was established, they moved on.

In Vingren's seminary thesis, he wrote repeatedly the words, "step by step" (*steg för steg*) to describe Yahweh (the Lord) leading the people of Israel, taking one step forward at a time.[131] Vingren and Berg practiced this with the Brazilian nationals, going forward "*steg för steg*," and in Portuguese, "*passo a passo*."

Bibliography

Primary Sources

Newspapers Used

Boa Semente, Belém, Brazil, 1919–1930
Brudgummens Röst, Stockholm, Sweden, 1911–1922
Evangelii Härold, Stockholm, Sweden, 1915–1993
Herald of Faith, Duluth, MN, Chicago, 1936–1950
The Lake View Chimes, Chicago, Illinois
Nya Wecko-Posten (*NWP*), Chicago, 1884–1918
Pentecostal Evangel, Plainfield, IN, Springfield, MO, 1913–2014
Pentecostal Testimony, Chicago, 1909–1912
Sanningens Vittne (*SV*), Minneapolis, 1911–1939
Weekly Evangel, St. Louis, MO, 1915–1918
Word and Witness, Malvern, AR, 1912–1915

Other Primary Sources

Vingren, Gunnar. Diary, "1912 Agenda." Gunnar Vingren Memorial Archives, CPAD, Rio de Janeiro, Brazil.
———. *O Tabernáculo e Suas Lições*. Rio de Janeiro: CPAD, 2011.
Vingren, Gunnar Vingren and Ivar Vingren. *Diário do Pioneiro: Memórias de Gunnar Vingren*. Rio de Janeiro: CPAD, 1985, 2011.
———. *Pionjärens dagbok*. Stockholm: Lewi Pethrus förlag, 1969.

---

131. Vingren, *O Tabernáculo e Suas Lições*, 88.

Secondary Sources

Almeida-Baptista, Douglas Roberto de. *História das Assembleias de Deus: O Grande Movimento Pentecostal do Brasil*. Curitiba, Paraná, Brasil: Editora Intersaberes, 2017.

Antoniazzi, Alberto, et al. *Nem anjos nem demônios: interpretação sociológica do pentecostalismo*. Petrópolis, Brazil: Editora Vozes, 1994.

Araujo, Isael de. *Frida Vingren*. Rio de Janeiro, CPAD, 2014.

———. *100 Acontecimentos Que Marcaram a História das Assembleias de Deus no Brasil*. Rio de Janeiro: CPAD, 2011.

———. *100 mulheres que fizeram a história das Assembleias de Deus no Brasil*. Rio de Janeiro: CPAD, 2011.

———. *Dicionário do Movimento Pentecostal*. Rio de Janeiro: CPAD, 2007.

Berg, Daniel. *Enviado Por Deus: Memórias de Daniel Berg*. Rio de Janeiro: CPAD, 2011.

Bundy, David. *Visions of Apostolic Mission: Scandinavian Pentecostal Mission to 1935*. Uppsala, Sweden: Uppsala Universitet, 2009.

Burgess, Stanley M., and Ed M. Van der Maas. *The New International Dictionary of Pentecostal and Charismatic Movements*. Grand Rapids: Zondervan 2002.

Chesnut, R. Andrew. *Born Again in Brazil: The Pentecostal Boom and the Pathogens of Poverty*. New Brunswick, NJ: Rutgers University Press, 1997.

Daniel, Silas. *História da Convenção Geral das Assembleias de Deus no Brasil*. Rio de Janeiro: CPAD, 2004.

Gonçalves, José. *A Glossolalia e a Formação das Assembleias de Deus*. Rio de Janeiro: CPAD, 2022.

González, Ondina E., and Justo L. González. *Christianity in Latin America: A History*. New York: Cambridge University Press, 2008.

Halldorf, Joel. *Av denna världen?: Emil Gustafson, moderniteten och den evangelikala väckelsen*. Skellefteå: Artos, 2012.

———. *Pentecostal Politics in a Secular World: The Life and Leadership of Lewi Pethrus*. Cham, Switzerland: Palgrave Macmillan, 2020.

Heckman, Warren. *The History of the Fellowship of Christian Assemblies (HFCA)*. Beaverton, OR: Good Books, 2011.

Jenkins, Philip. *The Next Christendom: The Coming of Global Christianity*. New York: Oxford University Press, 2011.

Johnson, Todd M., and Gina A. Zurlo, eds., *World Christian Encyclopedia*. Edinburgh: Edinburgh University Press, 2019.

Nelson, Samuel, and Tommy Nelson. *Lewi Pethrus: A vida e obra do missionário sueco que expandiu a mensagem pentecostal no Brasil e no mundo*. Rio de Janeiro: CPAD, 2005.

Oliveira, Joanyr de. *As Assembléias de Deus no Brasil: Sumário Histórico Ilustrado*. Rio de Janeiro: CPAD, 1997.

Palma, Paul J. *Grassroots Pentecostalism in Brazil and the United States: Migrations, Missions, and Mobility*. Cham, Switzerland: Palgrave Macmillan, 2022.

Peterson, Anna, and Manuel Vásquez, eds. *Latin American Religions: Histories and Documents in Context*. New York: New York University Press, 2008.

Pethrus, Lewi. *Ett sagolikt liv. En självbiografi*. Uppsala: Livets Ords Förlag, 1995.

Price, Donald E. "A Comparative Analysis of the Growth of the Brazilian Baptists and the Assemblies of God in Metropolitan São Paulo, 1981–1990." ThD thesis, University of South Africa, 2004.

Raiol, Rui. *1911—Missão de Fogo no Brasil, A Fundação da Assembleia de Deus.* Belém: Editora Pak-Tatu, 2011.

Sinner, Rudolf von. *Churches and Democracy in Brazil: Towards a Public Theology Focused on Citizenship.* Eugene, OR: Wipf & Stock, 2012.

Vingren, Ivar. *Det började i Pará: Svensk Pingstmission i Brasilien.* Sweden: Ekrö: Missions Institutet-PMU, 1994.

———. *Despertamento apostolico no Brasil.* Rio de Janeiro, Brasil: CPAD, 1987.

———. *O Tabernáculo e Suas Liçõe.* Rio de Janeiro: CPAD, 2011.

Yong, Amos. "Many Tongues, Many Practices: Pentecost and Theology of Mission at 2010." In *Mission after Christendom: Emergent Themes in Contemporary Mission*, edited by Obgu U. Kalu et al., 43–58. Louisville, KY: Westminster John Knox, 2010.

Chapter Nine

Missionary Tongues of Sophie Hansen

Testimonies of Xenolalia in Shanghai: 1908–1923

RUTH MA

SOPHIE HANSEN (1864–1925) WAS a first-generation Pentecostal missionary in China known for her xenolalia (xenoglossy) or "missionary tongues," namely, speaking in a foreign language without prior study of any kind, and understood by others for whom the language is known. This phenomenon is associated with the filling of the Holy Spirit described in the Book of Acts: "All of them [the apostles] were filled with the Holy Spirit and began to speak in other tongues as the Spirit enabled them. Now there were staying in Jerusalem God-fearing Jews from every nation under heaven. When they heard this sound, a crowd came together in bewilderment, because *each one heard their own language being spoken*" (Acts 2:4–6).

Sophie Hansen, Courtesy of the Hansen Family

Sophie Hansen's accounts of xenolalia are mentioned in several Pentecostal histories in the West.[1] In contrast, she has not been mentioned in Chinese church histories until recently.[2] This is partly due to the fact that she was one of several Pentecostal missionaries in China at the beginning of the twentieth century, and a housewife who labored alongside her husband in mission work. Furthermore, several influential Chinese theologians prior to 1949 held less than favorable views toward Pentecostals and excluded many of their stories from church histories. Some Chinese scholars placed Pentecostal phenomena into the category of spirit-possession tied to Chinese folk religion.[3] Consequently, Pentecostals were left in the "historical dust."[4]

1. Anderson, *Spreading Fires*, 63; Lian, *Redeemed by Fire*, 46.
2. 葉先秦 Iab, 晚雨聖靈 *Latter Rain of the Spirit*, 94.
3. Lian, *Redeemed by Fire*, xxx–xxxi.
4. According to 叶先秦/ Iab, the impressions of the Pentecostal-Charismatic movement on Chinese church historians came in part from criticisms by numerous Chinese church leaders such as Zhao Zichen (赵紫宸) and Wang Mingdao (王明道), especially regarding the emphasis on euphoric or ecstatic experiences. 叶先秦 Iab, "华北五旬节运动宣教先驱-贲德新及其思想," *Bernt Berntsen*, 33–58.

In the West, reports in the early twentieth century of Pentecostals speaking an unlearned language were questioned.[5] Often these accounts provided few if any details corroborated by testimonial evidence, and those that did were rare. Theologian Craig Keener says, "Many of Pentecostalism's early exponents understood tongues as a form of missionary xenoglossy, a view attested also among some church fathers. Although some cases of xenoglossy have appeared, most tongues experiences have not functioned this way (either in the New Testament or today)."[6]

In some cases, when missionaries who presumably received the gift of xenolalia arrived on the mission field, they met the stark reality that the indigenous people could not understand them.[7] Their tongues-speech (glossolalia) was unintelligible to their hearers. For example, after arriving in Macao, China, T. J. McIntosh was extremely disappointed when the Chinese people could not understand the words he uttered.[8] Other Pentecostal missionaries such as A. G. Garr in Hong Kong expressed that speaking in tongues would not directly aid in the spreading of the gospel.[9] Such conclusions caused distress for other Pentecostals and evoked criticism from opponents of the movement.[10] Despite the fact that xenolalia did not materialize on the mission field as initially expected, Pentecostals believed that tongues-speech, nevertheless, could manifest through supernatural means in intelligible languages, and reports of xenolalia persisted.

Historian Grant Wacker casts doubt on the veracity of accounts of xenolalia in Pentecostal historiography. While he refers to Sophie Hansen as "a first-generation Pentecostal who claimed a permanent gift of missionary tongues," he adds, "not much is known about Hansen except that about 1907 she was called to China as a missionary."[11] Wacker references a few periodicals which give accounts of Sophie's xenolalia, and then he says:

> The question of origins is particularly intriguing since severe questions of credibility conflicted all reports of missionary tongues, including Hansen's. Granted, Hansen cited a

---

5. Wacker, *Heaven Below*, 46–47.
6. Keener, *Spirit Hermeneutics*, 64. Cf. Minets, *Slow Fall of Babel*, 170–219.
7. Blumhofer, "Revisiting Azusa Street," 60.
8. Melton, "Pentecostalism Comes to China," 45.
9. Melton, "Pentecostalism Comes to China," 49.
10. Anderson, *Spreading Fires*, 61.
11. Wacker, *Heaven Below*, 46–47.

corroborator, but all that survived was Hansen's statement, not the corroborator's. (Moreover, we may reasonably assume that after six months of living in China Hansen might well have unconsciously picked up more of the language than she realized.) I have not located any instance in which a person is affirmed that they heard their *own* natal language spoken at length through xenolalic means.[12]

This chapter argues from period sources that a breakthrough of the Hansens' mission in Shanghai came in July 1908, when Sophie Hansen spoke Mandarin with natal proficiency. The effect was that people in Shanghai began to attend their meetings and accept their message. The chapter begins, first, with Sophie Hansen's life prior to becoming a missionary in China. This section gives an overview of her emigration from Norway to America, her marriage to George (Jørgen), birth of their children in Chicago, call to China as missionaries, and her experiences of Pentecostal-baptism and xenolalia in Chicago.

Second, the chapter examines the Hansens' ties to the North Avenue Mission in Chicago and pastor William H. Durham, and their travel to China with missionaries of the Apostolic Faith Mission of China led by Bernt Berntsen, including eight adults from the Azusa Street Mission in Los Angeles.

Third, this chapter examines Sophie's gift of xenolalia in Shanghai that resulted in Chinese hearers accepting the gospel message. Along with street evangelism and a healing ministry, Sophie and George formed a mission within a year of arriving in Shanghai. This section examines the corroborative evidence of Sophie's xenolalia by her family, native Chinese hearers, and American missionaries.

Finally, this chapter examines how Sophie's xenolalia occurred within a context of planting local missions and churches over a period of fifteen years. Arriving to China at the end of 1907, she and her husband launched their work in Shanghai in 1908, and labored there until 1923, when they returned to the US on furlough. They never returned but nonetheless the work continued to expand under the leadership of their son, Samuel Hansen.[13]

---

12. Wacker, *Heaven Below*, 47. Wacker makes reference to *Bridegroom's Messenger*, May 15, 1911, 3, and October 1921, 3; *Triumphs of Faith*, June 1916, 142, reprinted in *Work and Work*, May 1922, 10, and in *Pentecostal Times* n.d., no. 12 (Adelaide, Australia), 16; and *Pentecostal Evangel*, December 22, 1917, 11; March 18, 1919, 10.

13. *The Bridegroom's Messenger* (*BM*), May 1923, 4.

A Housewife with a Pentecostal Experience

Pauline Sofie Pedersen was born November 11, 1864, in Skinnarbøl, Norway. She immigrated to the United States when she was 23 years old. In Chicago, on May 11, 1889, she married George (Jørgen) Hansen. Since that time, she was known as Mrs. Sophie (or Sophia) Hansen.

Sophie was a housewife who gave birth to nine children. Her husband, George—born as Jørgen Anders Hansen (1868–1928) in Egersund, Norway—came in 1885 to Chicago where he worked as a sailmaker, awning maker, dock worker, and painter.[14] Their first son, Harry, was born in 1890, but died at only five years of age. In the same year of his death, in 1895, their oldest daughter, Jenny, was born. Later, the couple had a second son, Paul, who also died in childhood. Sophie gave birth to six more children. Sophie and George had seven children living at the time when they went to China as missionaries, namely, Jenny, Helga, Samuel, Henry, George, Joseph, and Anna.

During these years, Sophie, who was already a Christian, attended Kedzie Avenue Methodist Church, a Norwegian-Danish congregation on Kedzie Avenue in Chicago. George, however, had the habit of going out at night and drinking with friends. After an evening of drinking, his buddies would stop at a local Christian mission for a free bowl of soup and bread. It was said that "the minister would give them an ear full"—preaching a message of repentance and faith in Jesus.[15] Then, one night while out with his friends, George's life changed dramatically. He fell to his knees and converted to faith. When he stood up, he slammed his fist on the bar and shouted: "Hear the word of the Lord!"

In the same neighborhood lived Bernt and Magna Berntsen. The Berntsens had emigrated from Norway to the US in 1893. Bernt worked as a shopkeeper at a local grocery store on North Avenue. During these years, he got into trouble in his business life and "sank into drinking and came close to falling into hell."[16] However, in a crisis moment, he surrendered his life to Christ. He later testified that the power of God took ahold of him and removed all desires for alcohol. Berntsen then pursued a holy life and opened a bookstore that he operated until he sensed God's call as a missionary to China. He sold the business to the

---

14. Gundersen, "Øybuen som ville frelse kineserne," 126. Credit is given to Rakel Ystebø Alegre and David M. Gustafson for translating Norwegian and Swedish sources.

15. Hansen, "Hansen Stories about Jorgen," 1.

16. *Korsets Seier* (*KS*), June 1, 1910, 92.

Free Friends (*de frie venner*) who continued to operate the bookstore. In 1904, Bernt Berntsen (贲德新), Magna, and their three children left Chicago for China to join the South Zhili Mission (南直隸福音會), an independent, non-denominational, evangelical (Trinitarian) mission with its main goal to bring the gospel to China.[17]

Sophie and George both became active in the Kedzie Avenue Methodist Church during this time. Moreover, George began to sense God's call on his life to become a missionary.[18] Every morning he and Sophie prayed and meditated on the Scriptures which increased their interest in overseas missions. Sofie said, "[My] husband and myself had a calling and a burden for China [in 1904] three years before the Lord sent us."[19] When George told the Methodist church about his interest to go to the foreign field, the congregation refused to support him, thinking that anyone with so little education and seven children must be misguided to consider such a venture.[20]

Nevertheless, George began to write letters to people of wealth such as the Rockefellers and Marshall Fields, asking them to support him and Sophie as missionaries. With nothing to show for this effort, he turned to people on Chicago's streets.

In 1904, George's nephew, Tønnes Hansen of Norway, was working as a seaman. When his ship docked in New Orleans for several days, he traveled north to Chicago to visit his relatives. When he arrived, George was preaching the gospel in a street meeting. George greeted Tønnes, handed him a hat, and asked him to walk through the crowd to receive the offering.[21] George said that the Lord had called him and Sophie to China and that they needed to raise money for the journey.

As Sophie and George began to hear from friends about the Pentecostal experience, they decided to investigate it for themselves.[22] Sophie said: "During that time I was seeking the baptism in the Holy Ghost. The Lord spoke to me on one occasion, 'pray now for the Chinese language to

---

17. *The Apostolic Faith* (*AF*), January 1908, 3. For the South Chihli Mission at Tamingfu, see Tiedemann, "Origins and Organizational Development of the Pentecostal Missionary Enterprise in China," 109.

18. *Latter Rain Evangel* (*LRE*), September 1, 1914, 19.

19. *BM*, May 15, 1911, 3.

20. Hansen, "Letter to Mikal Hovland in Norway," 3. David E. Hansen (1925–2019) was born in Chefoo (芝罘), now the central district of Yantai (烟台市). In 1950, he was ordained as a minister at Wittich Memorial Church in Chicago by Gordon P. Swartz.

21. Gundersen, "Øybuen som ville frelse kineserne," 126.

22. Hansen, "Letter to Mikal Hovland in Norway," 3.

be given thee through the Holy Ghost.' So I did."²³ Sophie testified about her Pentecostal baptism, saying:

> I received salvation many years ago; praise God for the forgiveness of sins. Later on I saw the light for the healing of my body (James 5:14), and then was led into sanctification and the baptism in the Holy Ghost with signs following (Acts 2), which I received March 16, 1907. It is, indeed, wonderful what the Lord can do when we are fully given over to Him. Rivers of living water streamed down from the throne of God upon me. My spiritual vision saw angels walking up and down, and I heard the voice of God so clear and plain through the Holy Spirit.²⁴

Sophie explained that immediately before receiving her Pentecostal baptism, she experienced an intense spiritual battle with the powers of darkness—powers which she had never known before. Then, soon after her Pentecostal baptism she received the gift of xenolalia. She explained: "When I received the baptism in the Holy Ghost I spoke a few words in Chinese which were understood by a missionary who had been in China, and these few words stayed with me for weeks."²⁵ During this time George and Sophie also met with a local Chinese laundryman to render his opinion of her foreign tongue. In correspondence to relatives in Norway, David Hansen wrote: "The laundryman confirmed that grandmother was speaking Chinese but in a different dialect than his."²⁶

Given that Sophie spoke only a few words of Chinese and that these words stayed with her for some weeks, she again prayed to the Lord, saying:

> "Thou knowest I am going to China, and Thou must give me more of the language for this is not enough." The Lord answered, "Wilt thou be faithful in little?" I answered, "Yes, Lord." So one night as I slept, the Lord opened the windows of heaven on my soul and poured out all the blessing and language I was able to stand. Then I sat up in bed a half hour speaking and singing as if I had a congregation. My husband was witness to it and although he did not understand he got a blessing. Since

---

23. *BM*, May 15, 1911, 3; *LRE* August 1911, 13; *KS*, December 1916, 186.

24. *LRE*, August 1911, 13; *Sanningens Vittne* (*SV*), November 1, 1921, 6; *Pentecostal Evangel* (*PE*), April 1, 1922, 4.

25. *LRE*, August 1911, 13; Sofia Hansen, "Underbar tungetale i evangeliets tjeneste," *KS*, February 15, 1912, 30. Cf. *KS*, December 1916, 186.

26. Hansen, "Letter to Mikal Hovland in Norway," 3.

that time I was at rest regarding the Chinese language, and a few months later [in November 1907], the Lord sent us to China.[27]

Missionaries of the Apostolic Faith Mission of China, Commissioned by the North Avenue Mission of Chicago

While Bernt Berntsen was serving as a missionary in China, he received two pieces of information that piqued his interest about the burgeoning Pentecostal movement in America. The first was an issue of *The Apostolic Faith* from the Azusa Street Mission in Los Angeles that described the miracles and signs happening there and in other places of the world. The second was a letter from a woman in Chicago. Berntsen said:

> About December, 1906, I received the Apostolic Faith paper; and as I read it through in the spirit of prayer, I saw it was the thing that I had been looking for, and the first day of January [1907] I asked God as usual for a verse for that year, and He spoke plainly these words, "They shall be endued with power from on high." That gave me such a wonderful faith! After that I went to Shanghai with the intention of finding someone in the Centennial Missionary Conference [April 1907] that had the baptism of the Holy Ghost who could help me out. Instead of that I met opposition from every side, and one from Los Angeles that had attended the meetings denounced the whole thing as of the devil. I went back to my station with a still stronger determination in my heart for the baptism. After I got home I received a letter from Chicago telling about the work going on in Chicago, and the writer herself had received her Pentecost. As my wife read the letter to me, this melting power that I had been praying for came upon me, and I fell down on the floor crying out "God's wonderful mercy!"[28]

With these two pieces of information, Berntsen boarded a ship to Seattle, arriving August 27, 1907. In Seattle, he met a band of missionaries from the Azusa Street revival who were heading to Japan, Korea, India, and China. After visiting with these newly-commissioned Pentecostal missionaries, he traveled to Los Angeles, where on September

---

27. *LRE*, August 1911, 13; *BM*, May 15, 1911, 3. George Hansen said that he was Spirit-baptized in 1907. *LRE* September 1, 1914, 19.

28. *AF*, January 1908, 3.

15, 1907, he received his Pentecostal baptism.²⁹ *The Apostolic Faith* reported, "[Berntsen] went to the altar at Azusa Mission, and soon fell under the power, and arose drunk on the new wine of the kingdom, magnifying God in a new tongue. As soon as he could speak English, he said 'This means much for China.'"³⁰

Berntsen did not identify the woman from Chicago who had received her Pentecostal baptism in the spring of 1907, and who had written to him and Magna to tell them about it. The letter likely came from a woman who knew them from their years in Chicago and had interest in their China mission. It is not certain whether or not the letter was written by Sophie Hansen. The letter told of "the work going on in Chicago, and the writer herself had received her Pentecost." Certainly, much was happening at this time in Chicago. Just before Sophie experienced her Pentecostal baptism, William H. Durham (1873–1912), pastor of the North Avenue Mission, had returned from the Azusa Street Mission where he had received his Pentecostal baptism on March 2, 1907. Upon his arrival home to Chicago in April, he transformed the North Avenue Mission, also known as the North Avenue Full Gospel Assembly, into a center for the Pentecostal revival.³¹

Earlier, in 1906—as noted in chapter two—missionaries from the Azusa Street Mission, such as Lucy Leatherman, had visited the North Avenue Mission. Leatherman had long been a familiar figure on the Chicago storefront mission scene and made the most of her visit by promoting Spirit-baptism followed by tongues-speech in foreign languages.³² (Incidentally, two years later, Lucy Leatherman held evangelistic meetings with the Hansens in Shanghai).³³

What is certain is that within seven months of Berntsen receiving the letter from a woman in Chicago, the Hansens joined the Berntsens in Seattle to board a ship bound for China.³⁴ Moreover, both families were supported financially by the North Avenue Mission.³⁵ Durham's periodical, *Pentecostal Testimony*, under a section titled "Our Foreign Missionaries," reported: "The last missionaries going out from us were

29. *KS*, June 1, 1910, 92; *AF*, January 1908, 3.
30. *AF*, September 1907, 1.
31. Blumhofer, *Aimee Semple McPherson*, 81.
32. Blumhofer, "Portrait of a Generation," 96–97.
33. *BM*, August 15, 1909, 2.
34. 葉先秦 Iab, 晚雨聖靈, 94; Anderson, *Spreading Fires*, 133.
35. *BM*, May 15, 1909, 4.

Mr. and Mrs. R. J. Semple [Aimee Semple McPherson] and Miss Phoebe Holmes, who left us last winter and are now situated in Hong Kong, China, which will be their field of labor for the present or till the Lord leads them elsewhere. Mr. B. Berntsen and family and some other workers are located at Cheng Ting Fu, Chili, North China. Brother George Hanson and family are at Shanghai, China."[36]

The Hansen and Berntsen families knew each other in Chicago before they made arrangements to work together in China.[37] Their common interests in pursuing a holy life (with literature found at Bernt Berntsen's bookstore) and missionary work in China, drew them into the same circles, sooner or later.[38]

Historian Tønnes Gundersen posits that the Hansens left the Kedzie Avenue Methodist Church and joined the Pentecostal movement as early as 1904.[39] This was the year when Durham became the pastor of the North Avenue Mission. News was circulating of Pentecost-like revivals in Topeka, Kansas, and Aberdare, Wales, and within a few years, the North Avenue Mission was at the heart of the Pentecostal movement in Chicago, drawing hundreds of Scandinavian immigrants to revival meetings and worship services.

When Bernt Berntsen became a Pentecostal in 1907, he formed the Apostolic Faith Mission of China (中國使徒信心會), an independent, Pentecostal (Trinitarian) mission society.[40] He recruited eleven Spirit-filled missionaries along with their children to form this new mission society.[41] In addition to Sophie and George Hansen, he recruited six adults from the Scandinavian Mission of Los Angeles, the daughter mission of the Azusa Street Mission.[42] These Scandinavian-born

---

36. *Pentecostal Testimony* (*PT*), July 1, 1910, 10. When the Semples and Miss Holmes were commissioned, the Berntsens and Hansens were already settled in China. R. J. and Aimee Semple were ordained by Durham in Chicago on January 2, 1909. Blumhofer, *Aimee Semple McPherson*, 80.

37. In 1900, Sophie and George Hansen lived at 117 Stave Street (at Attrill Street), later numbered 2117 N. Stave. In 1904, when the Berntsens left for China, they lived at 787 West North Avenue, later numbered 2546 West North Avenue. It was a 15 minute walk from the Hansens to the North Avenue Mission at 943 West North Avenue, later 2836 West North Avenue.

38. *BM*, August 1, 1910, 1; *The Upper Room* (Los Angeles), August 1910, 6.

39. Gunderson, "Øybuen som ville frelse kineserne," 148.

40. *PT*, August 1911, 13.

41. Tiedemann, "The Origins and Organizational Development," 121–22.

42. Gustafson, "Scandinavian Mission of the Azusa Street Revival," 183–85.

immigrants were: Gustaf S. Lundgren, Ellen Carlson (Lundgren), Adolph Johnson, Linda Erickson (Johnson), Mary Bjorkman, and Hanna Holmsten (Axberg). In addition, Berntsen recruited Roy and Lydia Hess, both English-language Americans from the Azusa Street Mission.[43] A young, un-named African-American woman from the Azusa Street Mission accompanied them.[44]

After Berntsen recruited these eight adults from Los Angeles, he traveled back to Chicago to finalize arrangements with the Hansens. At the end of October 1907, on his return to the West Coast and reflecting on his new Pentecostal experience, he wrote: "My wife and children are in China, and I am here in America. I have just left Chicago and am in Denver, Colorado. I have had a blessed time in Chicago and the surrounding area . . . I now know what it means to possess the Holy Spirit. It is an experience I will never forget; it is power. I have always felt satisfied with the Lord, but never like this now. It feels like a spring that comes up from inside me and fills me with praise. . . . I sail from Seattle the 29th of November. There will be more of us in the travel party."[45]

Berntsen also welcomed Emma B. Hansen (Burns), a Norwegian-born, sixteen-year-old from Tacoma, Washington.[46] Miss Hansen decided to join the band of missionaries one week before their scheduled departure.

---

43. *AF*, May 1908, 4; *BM*, November 15, 1908, 1.
44. Gundersen, "Øybuen som ville frelse kineserne," 131.
45. *Evangelisten*, November 13, 1907, 5.
46. *The Pentecost*, June 1909, 4.

Missionaries of the Apostolic Faith Mission of China, 1908. Courtesy of the Hansen Family. Top row, left to right: Hanna Holmsten, Mary Bjorkman, Ellen Carlson, and Emma B. Hansen; Middle row: Magna Berntsen, Roy Hess, Lydia Hess, George Hansen, Sophie Hansen, and an unnamed African-American young woman from Azusa Street Mission.

The missionary band departed on November 29, 1907, and arrived in Shanghai on December 31.[47] After visiting Shanghai and other places, they arrived in Zhengdingfu in the Hebei province (河北省正定府) in early February.

In addition to receiving financial support from the North Avenue Mission, Sophie and George received funding from Scandinavian-American Pentecostals and their newly-formed congregations. In a manner similar to Durham's *Pentecostal Testimony*, the Swedish-language periodical *Sanningens Vittne* under the heading of "Our Missionaries" listed, among others, "Brother George Hansen in Shanghai."[48] In 1912—the second year of the publication—the names and addresses of the Scandinavian-American Pentecostal pastors, evangelists, and missionaries were listed including: F. A. Sandgren, B. M. Johnson, and C. M. Hanson, and missionaries, Gunnar Vingren and Daniel Berg

---

47. *BM*, June 1, 1916, 2. Emma B. Hansen said that the ship was delayed by one day which would have meant it departed November 30, 1907.

48. *SV*, March 1, 1913, 4.

(Brazil), and George Hansen (Full Gospel Mission, Shanghai).⁴⁹ F. A. Sandgren, a native of Sweden, was an elder of the North Avenue Mission, and ministered alongside Durham, focusing on Scandinavian immigrants. Sandgren was fluent in Norwegian, as well as his native Swedish. He was active in his role at the North Avenue Mission when the Hansens were commissioned to China.

The Breakthrough with Xenolalia

For whatever reasons, in June 1908, the Hansens (漢森夫婦) left Zhengding Fu to return to the port city of Shanghai. George said, "We were quite a big band that started out and I followed the crowd because some [the Berntsens] had been in China before. You know how easy it is to lean on other folks, but we must lean on Jesus alone. When I got to China I marched inland and was there four and a half months, but the Lord said, 'You go back to Shanghai.'"⁵⁰ Historian Daniel H. Bays surmises that it was from difficulties of learning the language or physical difficulties of family life in rural Zhengding Fu that George and Sophie and their seven children, and Roy and Lydia Hess and their daughter, returned to Shanghai.⁵¹ Shanghai was a cosmopolitan city and an easier place to launch a Pentecostal mission.⁵²

Sophie and George received their first letter and financial support soon after arriving in Shanghai which strengthened their belief that this was God's plan for them. They settled in the American and Jewish district of Hongkou (虹口), a lower-status area with plenty of low-rent places

---

49. *SV*, April 1, 1912, 4. The name of Full Gospel Mission of Shanghai, followed North Avenue Full Gospel Assembly in Chicago.

50. *LRE* September 1, 1914, 19. The Hess family was in Shanghai five months. *BM*, November 15, 1908, 1.

51. Bays, "Missionary Establishment and Pentecostalism," 55. In Shanghai, Antoinette ("Nettie") Moomau 慕淑德 (1873–1937) already conducted a ministry for women since 1899. In 1906, she visited the Azusa Street Mission in LA, became a Pentecostal, and joined the Apostolic Faith Mission. In 1908, Leola Phillips (1879–1910) arrived in Shanghai and by July 1910, she and Moomau held Pentecostal meetings at the Door of Hope. *The Pentecost*, July, 1909, 12; Mayfield, "Shanghai Brothels, Spirit Baptisms," 135–53.

52. Gundersen, "Øybuen som ville frelse kineserne," 131–32.

for foreigners to stay.[53] The Hansens lived at No. 4 Dent Road, Hongkou district, Shanghai (上海虹口鄧脱路4号).[54]

Sophie and George soon began evangelistic meetings on the street, presumably in a manner similar to what George had done in Chicago. Since they were not able to speak Chinese, George led his children in singing hymns in English—embarrassed as they were at being made a spectacle—while Sophie played her portable organ.[55] All of this was done to draw a crowd. The locals found this scene of Americans rather bizarre, not only as George spoke in English but as he tried to get them to bow in prayer while he prayed in English.[56] The Hansens' landlord was a Chinese professor who apparently stood in the middle of the crowd to observe all that was happening.

Then, something occurred that soon changed the course of the Hansens' ministry in Shanghai. Sophie spoke the gospel in the Chinese language which the people of the neighborhood could understand. She described the event as follows:

> After we had been here [in China] six months the Lord first led me out to speak to the Chinese in their own tongue. On Sunday, July 26, 1908, I was moved by the Holy Ghost to start outside our own home. Wonderful! Wonderful! Many listened with tears in their eyes as I spoke to them on that chapter where Jesus wept over Jerusalem [Matthew 23:37–39]. A Chinese believer there who knew a little English, understood and told us what I said. I was afterwards led to go from street to street and from house to house and speak to them, and Jehovah was with me and held back the powers of darkness, so if any one mocked they either had to give up and listen or go. To God be all the glory! The language has remained ever since; some have denied it, yet it is true. It can be used at any time, but to preach the Gospel only; I cannot read nor write the Chinese language. The Lord is blessing the work here. We have meetings every night except Monday, and four meetings on Sunday. Good attention is paid to the Gospel message; some accept Christ, and some

---

53. Gundersen, "Øybuen som ville frelse kineserne," 130.

54. Gundersen, "Øybuen som ville frelse kineserne," 131. In 1943, the road's name was changed to Dantu Road (丹徒路).

55. Hansen, "Letter to Mikal Hovland in Norway," 3.

56. Gundersen, "Øybuen som ville frelse kineserne," 133.

receive healing in their bodies, and some have also been baptized in the Holy Spirit.[57]

While Sophie's experience of speaking Chinese in Chicago was *inspirational* xenolalia, as it was for many Pentecostal missionaries—inspiring them to travel to overseas mission fields—her experience on July 26, 1908, in Shanghai was *operational* xenolalia, namely, without knowing the Chinese language, she spoke words given to her by the Holy Spirit which were understood by her Chinese listeners as a gospel message in their native tongue.

Sophie's gift of xenolalia was soon confirmed by the testimony of others. One missionary who substantiated her xenolalia was Katherine C. Woodberry (1858–1920).[58] Katherine's account was included in a "Report of Beulah Chapel" published in May 1909, in *The Christian and Missionary Alliance*, the periodical of the mission society by the same name. In her several-page report, she included the account of how the Lord had provided a substitute worker at Beulah Chapel in Shanghai, stating:

> One Friday night, Mr. Wanghow Chang came to the meeting. He is a handsome and prepossessing young man, and can talk English fluently. We learned that he came from the National Institute, and he was a Christian. That was good news, and we inquired farther. Then he told us a most wonderful thing. A few months ago, he said he was walking down a street in Shanghai when he came upon a few missionaries on a street corner preaching and singing, and the lady, Mrs. Hanson, was "speaking in the Mandarin tongue." When he discovered that she did not know what she was saying, but did this by the power of her God, he was convinced and soon converted. His father is a Mandarin in Szechuen, and is well connected. The Hansons gave him the Gospel of John which he read through the same evening, and then came to them for instruction. The result was that, in a short time, he began to interpret for them at their meeting for the Chinese, for they cannot work in Chinese except "as a sign." This man is one in a hundred. We know the Hansons, and were much impressed. Mr. Chang gladly consented to fill the vacant

---

57. *LRE*, August 1911, 13. Despite errors in dates published (*BM*, May 15, 1911, 3; *Confidence*, April 1911, 89), Sophie Hansen reported this happening on July 26, 1908. *KS*, February 15, 1912, 30.

58. In cases of xenolalia, Randal Ackland says, "Ideally, testimonies included some verification of the language. . . . If a native speaker was not present, the next best thing were missionaries who understood the language." Ackland, "Toward a Pentecostal Theology of Glossolalia," 152.

post in the school, and Dr. Wong is free again to translate Dr. [Joseph A.] Seiss, [*The Apocalypse: Lectures on Revelation*] Vol. II. Is it not wonderful how God can work?[59]

This account was reprinted in August 1909 in both *The Bridegroom's Messenger* and *The Pentecost* which popularized Sophie's experience of missionary tongues.[60]

In establishing the credibility of a testimony, the character of the witness is vitally important. Katherine Woodberry and her husband, John Woodberry, were veteran missionaries in China. They arrived in 1895, and settled initially in Tianjin (天津) where they set up the Beulah Chapel for students of Beiyang Medical School and Beiyang Naval Academy.[61] In 1899, during the Boxer Rebellion, Beulah Chapel was destroyed and they moved to Shanghai where they built a new Beulah Chapel on Szechuan Road North. When the Hansens arrived in Shanghai, John Woodberry and George Hansen collaborated at various times. For instance, in 1910, George wrote, "Thursday afternoon I had the privilege of baptizing [new believers] for pastor Woodberry, [of] the Christian Missionary Alliance, as pastor Woodberry is home in America for a while."[62]

Katherine Woodberry provided expert testimony of Sophie's xenolalia. Her description of Wanghow Chang meeting the Hansens was to tell readers how the Lord had provided for the needs of Beulah Chapel. Her account of Sophie's xenolalia was a sidenote within a long report of Beulah Chapel. Katherine knew Wanghow Chang personally, heard his statement of Sophie speaking the gospel in Mandarin, and observed his changed life after the event. She also knew the Hansens and how they conducted their meetings, saying, "for they cannot work in Chinese except 'as a sign.'" Moreover, Katherine was in a position to know the difference between a missionary who had learned Mandarin by arduous study and practice (and often speaking in "broken Mandarin" or with a strong accent) in contrast to a missionary who after a short time in the county explained the gospel message in Mandarin with natal proficiency.

---

59. Mrs. Woodberry, "Report of Beulah Chapel," *The Christian and Missionary Alliance*, May 22, 1909, 134. Compare an independent report published in Danish in *Kirkeklokken* and later reprinted in *Korsets Seir. KS*, December 1916, 186.

60. *BM*, August 15, 1909, 3. Cf. Mrs. Woodbury, "Tongues Heard and Understood," *The Pentecost*, August 1909, 2.

61. Tian, "Modern and Chinese Protestant Revivalism Movement."

62. *BM*, April 15, 1910, 4.

Despite the breakthrough in Shanghai due to Sophie's xenolalia, the Hansens met resistance. On one occasion, late in the summer of 1908, they "had bad words and rotten eggs thrown at them."[63] Resistance also came from those who opposed the idea that the Holy Spirit could speak through Sophie to the Chinese people. Yet, her operational xenolalia continued for years beyond her initial experience on July 26, 1908.

In 1910, *The Upper Room*, a Pentecostal periodical published in Los Angeles, printed an article titled, "Speaking in Chinese." It stated:

> Brother George Hansen writes us from Shanghai July 8 [1910] as follows: "The Lord is working in our midst. The meetings are crowded every night and some of them accept Jesus. We can hardly get them to leave the hall after the service is closed; and so it has kept on for months . . . Regarding the speaking in Chinese, the Holy Ghost does indeed speak through my wife. This has been much opposed, but the Lord Jesus in His mercy has kept us un-moveable. Now I feel clear before the Lord to send in the names of some of those who have understood her in Chinese. Below is a letter written by Bau Yien-Ching of the St. John's Y.M.C.A. School.[64]

The letter from Bau Yien-Ching, dated "Shanghai, China, July 5, 1910," appeared also in *The Bridegroom's Messenger*, and listed the fifteen names of witnesses. Bau Yien-Ching wrote:

> I know it is my duty to tell what God is doing in Shanghai, and what the Holy Spirit is saying to us in our own language through Mrs. George Hansen. The Holy Spirit is saying to us that Jesus died on the cross for our sins and His blood cleanses our hearts. "Believe Jesus and trust Jesus." Telling to us that He is coming very, very soon, and stands with stretched out arms, "Come to me, come to me;" telling us that the idols cannot save, they shall be destroyed. Last night we had prayer meeting [and] He spoke to us in the gospel of St. John 14:27 and so on. Well, God is certainly giving us signs. Praise be unto God our Father. Bau Yien-Ching
>
> Signed:
> Bau Yien-Ching   Boh Knung-Shing   Miss Woo Kune-Z
> Sung Yoon-Tai   Dyung Ong-Vung   Miss Loh Zee-Z

63. *BM*, November 15, 1908, 4.
64. *The Upper Room* (Los Angeles), August 1910, 6.

Dzung Shong-Bay	Woo Yien-Ching	Miss Tsong Vonn-Z
Tsang-Vang-Jan	Wang Tsy-Woo	Miss Yenh-Z
Ong Tsung-Shung	Miss Sung Bon-Z	Miss Ding-Z

These are the Chinese names translated into English. They have been given for the glory of God only. They thereby acknowledge that the Holy Spirit spoke the Chinese language to them through Mrs. George Hanson.

Yours for His kingdom,   Bau Yien-Ching[65]

In 1914, George testified that Sophie's xenolalia continued. He said: "My wife has the gift of the Chinese language and many times when anointed by the Spirit is understood by them [Chinese hearers]. My oldest daughter [Jenny] and I have both understood at different times, and this gift has stood for [over] five years. My two daughters [Jenny and Helga] are with us in the work and speak Chinese fluently. My oldest daughter often interprets for me."[66]

Obviously, Sophie and George learned to speak and comprehend a level of Chinese necessary for daily use.[67] As mentioned above, after five years in Shanghai, George learned enough of the Chinese language to understand Sophie's xenolalic messages. However, he never gained the level of fluency needed to preach a sermon without an interpreter. In the case of Roy and Lydia Hess, they struggled to learn the Chinese language and returned to Los Angeles in 1909.[68] In addition to Jenny and Helga, Samuel Hansen became fluent, speaking three Chinese dialects perfectly—Mandarin (普通話), Ningpo (寧波話), and Shanghainese (上海話).[69]

This wide range of competency to speak the Chinese language highlights the uniqueness of Sophie's ability. No other missionaries in Shanghai claimed this gift for themselves. In 1920, George reported: "Souls are slain under the mighty power of God and come through to

---

65. Bau Yien-Ching, "Witness to the Chinese Language as the Spirit Gave Utterance," *BM*, September 15, 1910, 2. The names of the fifteen witnesses were written in English using a phonetic method, perhaps the Wade-Gile Romanization. It would be difficult, if not impossible, to determine the original Chinese names with Chinese characters.

66. *LRE*, September 1, 1914, 19. Sophie Hansen described her xenolalia as "*denne naadegave*," "this gift of grace." "Aandens gave til at tale kinesisk," *KS*, December 1916, 186.

67. Gundersen, "Øybuen som ville frelse kineserne," 141.

68. Tiedemann, "The Origins and Organizational Development" 127.

69. Gundersen, "Øybuen som ville frelse kineserne," 141.

their baptism, speaking in tongues as the Spirit gives utterance."[70] While his statement, "speaking in tongues as the Spirit gives utterance," referred likely to Spirit-imparted, unintelligible glossolalia, reports of xenolalia by Chinese Christians in Shanghai were rare.[71]

As mentioned above, Sophie's claim to natal proficiency only happened when she spoke words related to the gospel. This was known within Pentecostal circles. In one instance, H. E. Hansen (not related to George), an Assemblies of God missionary in Beijing, was often mistaken as the missionary whose wife had the gift of missionary tongues. He set the record straight, however, stating that George's wife had the gift, not his.[72]

Sophie's xenolalia of gospel messages with native proficiency continued into the 1920s.[73] On September 15, 1921, she reported in *Sanningens Vittne* and *The Bridegroom's Messenger*:

> The Holy Spirit speaks Chinese through me from heaven without learning it, just as clearly as when I received the gift in 1908, July the 26th, and it has remained ever since. Can speak it any time, but the Gospel only. Glory to Jesus. Many have the trials been with it, and many have my enemies been, but Glory to God, He has caused me to triumph gloriously through the precious blood of Jesus, our coming King . . . We find the most results when the glory, and the power and the demonstrations of the Holy Ghost is manifested. Then the heathens come running to the meetings and are astonished.[74]

Aside from eye-witness testimonies, what happened after Sophie's initial experience of xenolalia in Shanghai proved what was expected in the first place. She and George launched the Full Gospel Mission (全備福音堂) in 1908, the first Pentecostal congregation in Shanghai.[75] Her xenolalia was not a singular, isolated event; it occurred multiple times over

---

70. *BM*, October 1920, 3.

71. On July 1, 1909, Nettie Moomau and Leola Phillips reported that a Chinese woman spoke English "clear as could be, though she has never studied it." *PE*, February 24, 1945, 2. Cf. *The Pentecost*, October 1909, 3; *PE*, May 2, 1931, 1.

72. *PE*, March 18, 1919, 10, cited in Wacker, *Heaven Below*, 288.

73. In 1916, Sophie reported in *Triumphs of Faith* that as she traveled to various places in China, she spoke Chinese at will, but when "speaking the 'Gospel only,' not 'earthly things.'" *Triumphs of Faith*, June 1916, 142, cited in Wacker, *Heaven Below*, 47, 288.

74. *BM*, October 1921, 3; *SV*, November 1, 1921, 6.

75. Hansen, *Thirty Years of Service with the Hansens in China*, 1937, 1.

several years within the broader task of establishing a mission congregation that expanded into several missions and local churches.

Expansion of the Full Gospel Mission

In 1908, Sophie and George held evangelistic meetings nightly, sometimes near a local park where they could reach all classes of people with the gospel.[76] They also sought to reach those who lived on the river. They would on some days take a small boat (sampan) and travel up the Huangpu River where thousands of families lived on small boats and preach the gospel.[77] In addition, the Hansens opened a school for boys and hired a Chinese principal. In 1911, the school had 36 students but soon grew to 85.[78]

In addition to these activities, the Hansens prayed for the people of Shanghai. In 1910, George said, "We are expecting the Lord to come upon us in mighty reviving power at any time. He is already moving and drawing upon the people."[79] As previously mentioned, the Hansens rented living quarters from a Chinese professor.[80] One night during a prayer meeting, this landlord came running out of the house, shouting that the house was on fire.[81] After everyone evacuated, he sent his servant through all the rooms of the house to see where the fire was but he found nothing. After all of the commotion, the professor and his servant themselves admitted that "It was God from heaven [who] let fire appear unto them." The professor-landlord became one of the first converts of the Full Gospel Mission.[82]

---

76. *BM*, November 15, 1908, 4.

77. *BM* April 15, 1910, 4; *KS*, December 1916, 186. Before 1914, George rented a sampan (small boat) that was pulled slightly offshore. On occasion, he launched into the Whangpoo River, and preached the gospel to sailors aboard the U.S. and British naval vessels. S. Gordon Hansen, "Back to Our China Boyhood," 1996, 2–3. Courtesy of Anna Hansen-Lane. In 1921, Full Gospel Mission acquired a "gospel wagon" for Christian workers to hold street meetings and distribute gospels and tracts. *BM*, January and February 1921, 3; January 1923, 3; *SV*, November 1, 1922, 7.

78. *LRE*, August 1911, 13; *Confidence*, April 1911, 89.

79. *The Upper Room* (Los Angeles), August 1910, 6.

80. Gundersen, "Øybuen som ville frelse kineserne," 130.

81. *The Upper Room*, August 1910, 6. Cf. Gundersen, "Øybuen som ville frelse kineserne," 138.

82. Hansen, "Letter to Mikal Hovland in Norway," 3.

In 1912, as the ministry progressed, George reported in *Sanningens Vittne*: "A couple of weeks ago we baptized 14 in water and then celebrated the Lord's Holy Communion."[83] With numbers of Chinese hearing the gospel and professing faith in Jesus, the Pentecostal distinctive of Spirit-baptism "with signs following"—referring to speaking in tongues or glossolalia—became an important indicator of genuine faith. George said, "Many times when the Chinese profess salvation we are not sure of their experience, but when they receive the baptism in the Holy Spirit there is no doubt of their salvation."[84]

With increasing numbers of people converting to faith and attending services, the meeting place became too small. Thus, the Hansens relocated the Full Gospel Mission to a larger hall, at 284-8 East Yalu Road (東鴨綠路) in Shanghai.[85] Moreover, George trained Chinese believers in preaching and urged them to start their own churches in Shanghai and other areas of China. By 1914, he reported, "We have three missions; two in Shanghai and one across the big [Whangpoo (黃浦江)] river."[86]

Sophie and George's healing ministry was important to their mission work too. In 1915, George reported: "God is blessing us, saving souls in our midst and baptizing in the Holy Ghost, and healing the sick. In the later part of January, I had the privilege of baptizing thirty-two in water; and in the latter part of April twenty-five more. We have had a miracle of healing."[87] In this case of healing, a child who was near death and speechless for three days was restored to health. It was reported:

> Some of our Christians happened along and told them [the parents] Jesus had the power to heal the sick. So they called for us to pray. When we went there, I felt that before God could answer prayer, the people must give up worshiping the idol. The father said that he would wait and see if the child was healed. We said

83. *SV*, January 1, 1912, 3.

84. *LRE*, September 1, 1914, 20.

85. Gundersen, "Øybuen som ville frelse kineserne," 140. In 1922, Samuel and Minnie Hansen were married at this location. This address later became No. 524–532 Zhoujiazui Road (周家嘴路524号至532号). 孙金富, 吴孟庆, 刘建 Editorial Committee, 上海宗教志 Shanghai Religious Chronicle, 上海市专志系列丛刊 Shanghai Monograph Series (上海社会科学院出版社 Shanghai Academy of Social Sciences Press, 2001), 441.

86. *LRE*, September 1, 1914, 20. Cf. *The Christian Evangel*, June 15, 1918, 10. Ding Pei Seng started the work in Pootung across the Whangpoo River of Shanghai. Hansen, *Thirty Years of Service*, 2.

87. *BM*, August 1, 1915, 3. Cf. *KS*, July 15, 1913, 110.

we could not pray. At once he changed his mind and began to tear down everything belonging to the idol worship and threw them into the river nearby. Then we prayed and laid hands on the child. The child raised up instantly, calling on the father and mother for something to eat. The father jumped, clapped his hands for joy and said, God has raised his child from death. He and his whole house turned to the Lord and also some of the neighbors.[88]

This account, and many others, stands in contrast to Sophie and George's three youngest children—George, Joseph, and Anna—who died of pneumonia and smallpox in 1910. George believed in divine healing and claimed that he himself had the gift of healing.[89] However, he and Sophie did not see their three children healed.[90] Even with miracles, signs, and wonders happening around them and through them—all pointing to the inbreaking of God's kingdom in Christ—they and their congregations were reminded of the effects of sin and death as an enemy.[91]

Another difficult situation came in 1916, when a disruption occurred within the Apostolic Faith Mission of China. Bernt Berntsen left the society which he had organized. Two years earlier, he had affiliated as a missionary of the Assemblies of God, Springfield, Missouri, but in 1916, he left this denomination after embracing Oneness theology.[92] With this shift in his theological position regarding the doctrine of God, the majority of Pentecostals considered him heretical—no longer holding to the orthodox view of the Trinity—and distanced themselves from him.[93] Sophie and George, as well as the other missionaries of the Apostolic Faith Mission of China, maintained the Trinitarian view and parted ways with

---

88. *Word and Witness*, August 1915, 7. Cf. *BM*, August 1, 1915, 3, and the story of Ching Pao San in Hansen, *Thirty Years of Service*, 1.

89. Gundersen, "Øybuen som ville frelse kineserne," 140.

90. Anderson, *Spreading Fires*, 133. Based on George's theology of healing, his three children may not have received medical attention. Gundersen, "Øybuen som ville frelse kineserne," 135.

91. *BM*, May 15, 1909, 4.

92. Bernt and Magna Berntsen were among the first credentialed missionaries of the Assemblies of God. *Combined Minutes of the General Council of the Assemblies of God 1914*, 13. However, Berntsen adopted Oneness theology. Daniels, "Does the Wind Bend or Break the Grass?, 92. In 1912, Berntsen established a Chinese language periodical, *Popular Gospel Truth* (通傳福音真理 報) to spread Pentecostal beliefs. After 1916, this periodical served the Oneness movement.

93. Melton, "Pentecostalism Comes to China," 56–58.

Berntsen.⁹⁴ He relocated to Beijing, and by 1919, affiliated with the Pentecostal Assemblies of the World.⁹⁵ In 1920, Sophie and George Hansen were listed as missionaries in full harmony with the Scandinavian Assemblies of God of the USA that held to the Trinitarian view.⁹⁶

Despite this turn of events, the work in Shanghai continued with the Hansens as before. George reported, "God works in our midst, souls are saved and some filled with the Holy Spirit. We also keep on praying for the sick and many bodies are healed, hallelujah! We just have baptized 33 in water."⁹⁷ Given what the Hansens began with in 1908, much was accomplished. Sadly, George and Sophie were not able to witness everything that others saw. On February 10, 1923, Sophie and George returned to the United States for furlough in order to visit the congregations that financially supported them. Two years later, on February 12, 1925, Sophie died in a tragic vehicle accident near Dunsmuir, California. *The Latter Rain Evangel* reported:

> Friends of Mrs. George Hanson will be pained to learn of her death by accident. She and her husband were taking their last trip prior to sailing to their mission station in Shanghai, traveling by stage [bus] to Oakland, Calif. The steering wheel broke and they were plunged over an embankment. All the occupants of the stage [bus] were injured, among them Brother Hanson. His wife was instantly killed. He is slowly recovering, and asks for prayer for himself and his family to whom this will be a great loss.⁹⁸

---

94. George remained under the auspices of the Apostolic Faith Mission of China. *Directory of Protestant Missionaries in China, Japan, and Corea*, 99, 273. The AG was represented in China by AG missionaries, the AFM, and Pentecostal Missionaries (US). Couling, *Encyclopaedia Sinica*, 31, 36.

95. French, "Early Oneness Pentecostalism," 337. The separation between the Hansens and Berntsens became more complicated in 1920 when Henry Berntsen married Helga Hansen.

96. *SV*, January-February, 1920, 5.

97. *SV*, September 1, 1920, 7–8. Cf. *BM*, January and February, 1922, 3. Additional accounts pertained to divine healings. *BM*, August-September, 1921, 3. In another occasion a Chinese woman experienced a divine visitation, seeing and hearing Jesus, and from this experience, learned how to read the Bible. *BM*, March 1921, 3. As a result of Lucy Fu's healing, the Full Gospel Mission's Cantonese congregation was founded in 1923. *BM*, September-October 1923, 2; Hansen, *Thirty Years of Service*, 2.

98. *LRE*, April 1925, 23–24. Marshall C. Henrichsen of the Pentecostal Assembly in Dunsmuir assisted George after the accident. Subsequently, George traveled to Carrie Judd Montgomery's Beulah Heights in Oakland. Correspondence from George Hansen to his children, Dunsmuir, CA, February 23, 1925. Family Hansen Collection.

George did not return to China. He never fully recovered due to injuries from the accident and died January 18, 1928, in Los Angeles.

When Sophie and George departed China for furlough, Samuel Hansen had assumed leadership of the Shanghai congregation. He along with his wife, Minnie Florence Hansen, continued this work after his parents' deaths.[99] The Chinese affectionately referred to Samuel as the "white Chinese man."[100] In 1932, the Full Gospel Mission began building their own church located at No. 799 East Yuhang Road (東余杭路 799 号) with all of the funding coming from Chinese believers.[101] Samuel Hansen reported, "We outgrew the old mission in Shanghai and then the Lord provided the present tabernacle which accommodates about six hundred. Every Sunday the place is filled to utmost capacity with Christians and the Lord continues to add to our number."[102]

Samuel Hansen (front row, center) with ministerial students in Shanghai, ca. 1941. Courtesy of the Hansen family.

99. Gundersen, "Øybuen som ville frelse kineserne," 142.

100. Gundersen, "Øybuen som ville frelse kineserne," 146.

101. Editorial Committee, 上海宗教志 *Shanghai Religious Chronicle*, 441.

102. Hansen, *Thirty Years of Service*, 4; The address was: 799 East Yuhang Road. S. Gordon Hansen, "Back to Our China Boyhood," 1996, 1.

By 1937, besides the central congregation, known then as the Full Gospel Tabernacle, the work had expanded to four assemblies in and near Shanghai that were connected to the central congregation, and no less than eight congregations that had branched off from it and were independent and self-supporting.[103]

At that time, more than a thousand believers were members of the four congregations, and well over a thousand people in addition were reported to be saved by the gospel and had benefited from the Full Gospel Mission since its beginning.[104] To face the challenging time of World War II, more than ten Pentecostal churches came together in May 1941, and founded Shanghai Federation of Pentecostal Churches. Full Gospel Mission was one of them and acted as the Spiritual Formation Center, and Samuel Hansen conducted classes to train pastors, evangelists, and missionaries.[105] By then, all of the Federation's leaders and preachers were Chinese.[106]

Conclusion

Sophie and George Hansen arrived in China without strong educational backgrounds, with minimal financial support, and no acquired language skills. Despite these deficiencies, they established the Full Gospel Mission within a year of arriving in China. The mission eventually became a self-sufficient Chinese church with branch congregations in other locations, as well as multiple missions around Shanghai. According to eye witnesses, Sophie's xenolalia as a Pentecostal sign played a pivotal role in the Chinese people listening to her message.

While xenolalia practiced by Sophie was extremely rare among Pentecostals during this time, it is acknowledged nevertheless as a historical means of evangelism. Church history describes various and diverse forms of gospel witness. Xenolalia is one of them, beginning on

---

103. Hansen, *Thirty Years of Service*, 1.

104. Hansen, *Thirty Years of Service*, 12.

105. David Hansen estimated that, conservatively speaking, before the start of World War II, over 3,000 people gathered every Sunday at the three branch churches in Shanghai and ten mission stations in the surrounding area. Hansen, "Letter to Mikal Hovland in Norway," 3.

106. 孙金富, 吴孟庆, and 刘建, 上海宗教志 *Shanghai Religious Chronicle*, 456. Iap, "上海靈工團: 戰時發起的五旬節派合一組織 (1941–1949) "Shanghai Federation of Pentecostal Churches," 建道學刊 *Jiandao Academic Journal*, no. 54 (January 1, 2020) 37–69.

the day of Pentecost (Acts 2:4), and affirmed by early twentieth-century Pentecostals.[107]

While Sophie's xenolalia, which came into public use on July 26, 1908, was not the only activity that contributed to the expansion of the Full Gospel Mission, it played a significant role. Witnesses in the public record such as Wanghow Chang, Katherine Woodberry, Bau Yien-Ching, and fourteen additional residents of Shanghai who signed their names to an affidavit, testified to hearing her speak the gospel in Chinese before she learned the language. She exercised xenolalia as one of several means of evangelism embedded within a community of Christians who themselves engaged in proclaiming the Christian gospel in Shanghai and beyond.[108]

Bibliography

Primary Sources

Newspapers Used

The Apostolic Faith (*AF*), Los Angeles, 1906–1908
Bridegroom's Messenger (*BM*), Atlanta, GA, 1907–1970
The Christian and Missionary Alliance, Nyack, New York, 1882–
The Christian Evangel, St. Louis, Springfield, MO, 1913–1919
Evangelisten, Chicago, 1891–1955
Korsets Seir (*KS*), Kristiania (Oslo), Norway, 1910–
Latter Rain Evangel (*LRE*), Chicago, 1908–1939
The Pentecost, Indianapolis, Kansas City, 1908–1910
Pentecostal Evangel (*PE*), Plainfield, IN, Springfield, MO, 1913–2014
Pentecostal Testimony (*PT*), Chicago, 1909–1912
Popular Gospel Truth (通傳福音真理 報), China, 1914–1919
Sanningens Vittne (*SV*), Minneapolis, 1911–1939
The Upper Room, Los Angeles, 1909–1911

---

107. William H. Turner said, "It was also in 1907, that Pentecost was brought to China, where the author is now working, and to which land he came in 1919 as a missionary. Within six months of the falling of Pentecost here some two hundred missionaries and Chinese had received the Baptism." Turner, *Pentecost and Tongues*, 128–41, 149.

108. There were others who went out from the work in Shanghai as missionaries to Honolulu, Hawaii, and South China. Hansen, *Thirty Years of Service*, 3.

Other Primary Sources

Hansen, David. "Letter to Mikal Hovland in Norway." From San Bernardino, CA, n.d., Hansen Family Collection.

Hansen, Samuel. *Thirty Years of Service with the Hansens in China, 1937*. Printed booklet of the Hansen Family Collection.

Hansen, S. Gordon. "Back to Our China Boyhood." 1996. Hansen Family Collection.

Hansen, Tim. "Hansen Stories about Jorgen." Personal correspondence with David M. Gustafson, February 22, 2023.

Secondary Sources

Ackland, Randal H. "Toward a Pentecostal Theology of Glossolalia." PhD Thesis, Bangor University, Wales, 2019.

Anderson, Allan. *Spreading Fires: The Missionary Nature of Early Pentecostalism*. Maryknoll, NY: Orbis, 2007.

Bays, Daniel. "The Protestant Missionary Establishment and Pentecostalism." *Pentecostal Currents in American Protestantism*, edited by Edith W. Blumhofer et al., 50–67. Urbana: University of Illinois Press, 1999.

Blumhofer, Edith L. *Aimee Semple McPherson: Everybody's Sister*. Grand Rapids: Eerdmans, 1993.

———. "Portrait of a Generation: Azusa Street Comes to Chicago." *Enrichment: A Journal for Pentecostal Ministry* 11 (2006) 95–102.

———. "Revisiting Azusa Street: A Centennial Retrospect." *International Bulletin of Missionary Research* 30 (2006) 59–64.

Daniels, Joel D. "Does the Wind Bend or Break the Grass? A Comparative Study of Pentecostal Spirituality and Chinese Religious Thought." PhD diss., Georgetown University, 2020.

Gundersen, Tønnes H. "Øybuen som ville frelse kineserne," *Dalane Folkemuseum Årbok* (2011–2012) 124–49.

Gustafson, David M. "The Scandinavian Mission of the Azusa Street Revival of Los Angeles, 1907–1913." *Swedish-American Historical Quarterly* 72 (2021) 165–208.

葉先秦 Iab, Sian-Qin. 晚雨聖靈：真耶穌教會的再定位與全球五旬節派研究的想像和再現 *The Latter Rain of the Spirit: Reorientation of the True Jesus Church with Special Reference to the Imagination and Representation of Global Pentecostal Studies*, (台湾基督教文艺, Chinese Christian Literature Council Ltd. 2019.

叶先秦 Iab, Sian-Qing. "华北五旬节运动宣教先驱-贲德新及其思想," *Bernt Berntsen: A Prominent Oneness Pentecostal Pioneer to North China*, 建道学刊 *Jiandao Academic Journal* (2012) 33–58.

Iap, Sian-Chin. "上海靈工團：戰時發起的五旬節派合一組織 (1941-1949) "Shanghai Federation of Pentecostal Churches." 建道學刊 *Jiandao Academic Journal* no. 54 (2020) 37–69.

Keener, Craig S. *Spirit Hermeneutics: Reading Scripture in Light of Pentecost*. Grand Rapids, Eerdmans, 2016.

Lian, Xi. *Redeemed by Fire: The Rise of Popular Christianity in Modern China*. New Haven, CT: Yale University Press, 2010.

Mayfield, Alex R. "Shanghai Brothels, Spirit Baptisms: The Door of Hope Women as a Source for Pentecostal Resourcement." In *Sisters, Mothers, Daughters: Pentecostal Perspectives on Violence Against Women*, edited by Michael Palmer et al., 135–53. Leiden: Brill, 2022.

Melton, J. Gordon. "Pentecostalism Comes to China: Laying the Foundations for a Chinese Version of Christianity." In *Global Chinese Pentecostal and Charismatic Christianity*, edited by Fenggang Yang et al., 43–62. Leiden: Brill, 2017.

Minets, Yuliya. *The Slow Fall of Babel: Languages and Identities in Late Antique Christianity*. New York: Cambridge University Press, 2022.

Tian, Esther. "Modern and Chinese Protestant Revivalism Movement and Its Founder, Li Shuqing." *China Christian Daily*, November 14, 2022. http://m.chinachristiandaily.com.

Tiedemann, R. G. "The Origins and Organizational Development of the Pentecostal Missionary Enterprise in China" *Asian Journal of Pentecostal Studies* 14 (2011) 108–46.

Turner, W. H. *Pentecost and Tongues: The Doctrine and History*. Shanghai: Shanghai Publishing, 1939.

Wacker, Grant. *Heaven Below: Early Pentecostals and American Culture*. Cambridge, MA: Harvard University Press, 2001.

Chapter Ten

Formation and Transformation of a Scandinavian-American Pentecostal Congregation in South Bend, Indiana, 1907–1967

BEVERLY C. JOHNSON-MILLER

SCANDINAVIAN IMMIGRANTS TO THE United States in the late 19th and early 20th century, perhaps more than any other immigrant population, had an enduring influence in the birth, growth, and character of the modern Pentecostal movement. Pioneers of the early decades shaped the movement's defining characteristics. Their experiential spirituality, expressive corporate worship, and mission-oriented church life, define Pentecostalism in the 20th century.

Many Scandinavian immigrants who arrived in America were predisposed to join this burgeoning movement, including a number in South Bend, Indiana. On one hand, the immigrants desired to break free from the formalism and nominalism of Scandinavia's state churches. In America, they sought a heart-felt Christian faith, desired spiritual revival with divine encounters, and embraced a passion for evangelizing others. As a result, pioneers of the Scandinavian-American Pentecostal movement engaged in establishing, shaping, and proliferating the movement's spread globally.

While the Azusa Street revival that began in Los Angeles in 1906 was a catalyst of the modern Pentecostal movement, a Pentecostal spirituality had already emerged among Scandinavian immigrants, particularly in Illinois, Minnesota, and the Dakotas. The streams of Scandinavian and American Pentecostal spirituality converged in Chicago and flowed to South Bend's Swedish Baptist Church through "Pentecostalized" Swedish Baptist ministers. Prophetic encounters during home prayer meetings prompted the sending of two missionaries to Brazil which resulted in unprecedented growth of the Pentecostal movement there. Nevertheless, a Pentecostal spirituality, as well as formation of an influential Pentecostal congregation in Indiana resulted too. While the Brazil phenomenon is well-known, the impact in and through the South Bend congregation has been largely overlooked.

The story of the South Bend Gospel Tabernacle (SBGT), and the immigrant story behind and within that story, provides an illustration of Pentecostal spirituality among and through Scandinavian-American Pentecostals. The story documents the origin, nature, and significance of Pentecostal faith-forming and life-transforming practices, and provides a window into a Scandinavian-American congregation that helped shape, and was shaped by, the Pentecostal movement.

With roots in the Pentecostal movement in Chicago from as early as 1906, SBGT has left a lasting mark on thousands of people of Northern Indiana, the Assemblies of God (AG) of Springfield, Missouri, and nations around the globe through its world-wide mission efforts. Its influence was felt even within the Roman Catholic Church and its Charismatic movement.

What began as a Swedish Baptist Church in 1885, this congregation was touched by the Pentecostal revival emanating from Los Angeles and Chicago between the years 1906 and 1910. Although this South Bend congregation weathered doctrinal storms and ecclesial struggles for a decade, in 1920, the Swedish Baptist General Conference closed its doors. However, in 1928 a remnant of Swedes from that congregation, along with others, arranged a series of tent meetings that led soon to the formation of South Bend Gospel Tabernacle (SBGT), and by 1960, this congregation averaged more than 1,400 children and adults in its Sunday

School. SBGT became the largest Assemblies of God congregation in Indiana, and the second largest in the U.S. at that time.

This chapter is a case study of South Bend Gospel Tabernacle (SBGT) of South Bend, Indiana, highlighting the theological vision and spiritual practices that shaped Pentecostal faith-formation. It posits that while SBGT emerged as a flourishing and impactful Pentecostal congregation, it exacted a high cost of its members in terms of time devoted to the church's ministries, often with a heavy sense of obligation. Despite the downside of this, the church engaged its local culture, as well as cross-culturally through short-term and overseas missions.

The first part of this chapter documents the historical formation of the South Bend Gospel Temple (SBGT) with roots in the Swedish Baptist Church of South Bend. O. A. Uldin and his son, G. A. Uldin, played significant roles in this history, as well as pastors such as Henry Nelson, F. A. Sandgren, Gunnar Vingren, and Adolph Petersen. The later part of the chapter examines faith-forming practices within the congregation that have shaped a distinctly Pentecostal spiritual practice and identity, providing a glimpse into this Pentecostal congregation. Thus, this study draws from historical and archival literature, as well as from oral interviews and qualitative analysis.

The Story Behind the SBGT Story

While factors driving immigration from Scandinavia to America were largely economic—land for farming, jobs in manufacturing, and opportunity for social equality and personal advancement—political and religious realities were also significant contributing factors.[1] Many Scandinavians settled in, or transitioned through, Chicago where Sweden-born residents numbered second only to Stockholm, Sweden. Scandinavian churches played a vital role in the settlement experience, preserving homeland priorities and values while "transforming and recreating them into Swedish American identity."[2]

Pre-Azusa Pentecostal phenomena such as speaking in tongues, prophesying, and divine healings had occurred among Scandinavian immigrants since the end of the 19th century under leaders such as August Davis in Chicago and Minneapolis, and Carl M. Hanson in Minnesota

---

1. Ljungmark, *Swedish Exodus*, 31–32.
2. Gustafson, *Swedish Chicago*, 33–49.

and the Dakotas. As early as February 1906, speaking in tongues and supernatural healing occurred at the Second Swedish Baptist Church in Chicago under the pastorate of J. W. Hjertstrom.[3] Historian Edith L. Blumhofer writes: "... in February 1906 Second Swedish Baptist Church became the setting for emotional revival scenes, including speaking in tongues ... Hjerstrom became the chief advocate among American Swedish Baptists for expressive forms of prayer, repentance, and worship and for baptisms with the Holy Spirit."[4]

Later in 1906, Scandinavian immigrants in Chicago, including many from the Swedish Baptist churches, visited revival meetings and services led by William H. Durham at the North Avenue Mission. In 1907, after Durham's visit to the Azusa Street Mission in Los Angeles, where he himself experienced Pentecostal baptism, his mission in Chicago became a leading Pentecostal center in the Windy City. Blumhofer comments: "Durham took a 'clear stand' for the baptism in the Holy Spirit and the North Avenue Mission could not hold the crowds. He moved his family out and opened their living quarters in the rear of the mission for overflow. Meetings ran day and night."[5]

Coming from both directions—the American stream of Pentecostalism from Los Angeles and the Scandinavian-American stream that emanated from Chicago—the Pentecostal revival soon spilled over to other Swedish Baptist congregations. In 1910, Durham reported in *Pentecostal Testimony* that the nearby Humboldt Park Swedish Baptist Church of Chicago had more than one hundred people who "have received the Holy Ghost ... including all the officers ... and a large percentage of the members."[6]

It is important to recognize that Durham shaped not only the early Pentecostal movement theologically with his "finished work" doctrine that placed sanctification at the time of regeneration,[7] but he also shaped the Pentecostal movement practically through his teaching and modeling of experiential spirituality, particularly related to Spirit-baptism. He taught, for instance, that "God did not simply send a revival of religion, but He has sent a genuine Apostolic Pentecostal outpouring of the Holy

---

3. Olson, *Centenary History*, 588.

4. Blumhofer, "Urban Pentecostalism: Chicago, 1906–1912," 161.

5. Blumhofer, "Urban Pentecostalism: Chicago, 1906–1912," 166.

6. William Durham, "How the Work Is Progressing," *Pentecostal Testimony* (*PT*), July 1, 1910, 15.

7. Durham, "The Finished Work of Calvary," *PT*, August 1912, 4–11.

Ghost, exactly like the one described in the Bible . . . The blessed Holy Spirit simply comes upon and into our souls and bodies and takes possession and speaks through us, as a proof that it is the real Bible brand we receive . . . ."[8] Clearly, Durham and the Pentecostal expressions in Chicago gave notable and enduring shape to the larger Pentecostal movement, especially among Scandinavian immigrants.

Scandinavians in South Bend, Indiana, found employment mainly at the Oliver and Studebaker companies. Most were Swedes who lived in a section of South Bend nicknamed "Swede Town," typical of other cities.[9] In 1900, there were approximately 500 Swedish immigrants living in South Bend, part of the city's population of 36,000.[10] Three Swedish immigrant churches had formed, the Swedish Lutheran Church in 1881, the Swedish Baptist Church in 1885, and the Swedish Mission Covenant in 1888. Members of the Swedish Baptist Church lived almost exclusively in two of the city's seven wards; 120 resided in the second ward, and 27 in the northern part of the sixth ward.[11]

Exactly when the Pentecostal revival arrived in South Bend is uncertain. It is certain, however, that it came to South Bend between 1906 and 1907. In September 1907, evangelistic meetings were held there by C. B. Fockler of Mishawaka, Indiana, and F. F. Bosworth, a former band director of J. Alexander Dowie. Meetings were initially held in a "tent tabernacle" at the corner of South and Lafayette streets, but in November 1907, moved indoors to 754 S. Michigan Street with the revival services lasting through June 1908.[12] In September of that year, the revival meetings moved to the nearby town of Plymouth, Indiana, where Bosworth and Fockler were joined by the "girl evangelist," Jeanie Campbell, and "singing evangelist" from Chicago, Albert E. Buss.[13]

Any particular influence of these Pentecostal revival meetings on members of the Swedish immigrant community is not known. However, during these revival meetings, a congregation formed that eventually

---

8. Durham, "The Great Crisis Number Two," *PT*, July 1, 1910, 2–3.

9. Cederoth and Jahnson, "History of the Swedish Baptist Congregation, South Bend, Indiana," 1897, 1.

10. Miceli, "Industrialization and Immigration," 137–39.

11. *Statistics of Population, Indiana, 1910*, 585.

12. C. B. Fockler, *The South Bend Tribune* (*SBT*), September 26, 1907, 5. C. B. Fockler, "Revival Meetings: Fockler and Bosworth," *SBT*, December 7, 1907, 13.

13. C. B. Fockler, "Plymouth Fockler and Bosworth Revival," *The Weekly Republican*, September 3, 1908, 5.

became a temporary church home for several people who left the Swedish Baptist Church following their Pentecostal baptism. With the assistance of Bosworth and Carrie Diltz, C. B. Fockler opened a Pentecostal church in Mishawaka. The name of the congregation changed from "Christian Assembly" in 1907, to "Assembly of God" in 1914.[14]

Swedish Baptist Church of South Bend, Indiana

As for Scandinavian-American Pentecostals, in 1907, Henry Nelson, a Swedish Baptist minister and conference leader in Chicago, returned to South Bend to become the pastor of the Swedish Baptist Church after he himself had experienced Pentecostal revival in Chicago. Along with several other Swedish Baptist ministers, Nelson embraced the Baptist Pentecostal movement led by J. W. Hjertstrom at Chicago's Second Swedish Baptist Church during the early months of 1906.[15]

As for the history of the Swedish Baptist Church in South Bend, it was organized in December 1885, by Henry Nelson and nine charter members. At the time, the congregation shared a kindred vision and values with the Swedish Baptist Church of LaPorte, Indiana, founded the previous year, by Henry Nelson.[16] The first elected trustees of the Swedish Baptist Church of South Bend included two Uldin brothers—Olof Adolph Uldin and Carl Magnus Uldin. It was reported that O. A. Uldin was a "powerful pillar who . . . remained standing in both storm and calm without being shaken."[17] The congregation's building at Laurel and Napier streets was dedicated in October 1891.[18] Within the first 12 years, the congregation grew to approximately 100 members.[19] The South Bend congregation affiliated with the Swedish Baptist Conference of Illinois.[20] As part of this conference, the South Bend congregation looked to church leaders

---

14. The name of the church was changed to Pentecostal Assembly in 1927, and to First Assembly of God of Mishawaka in 1948. Contat et al., *History of First Assembly of God Mishawaka*, 3–9.

15. *Nya Wecko-Posten* (*NWP*), March 27, 1906, 4–5; *NWP*, April 17, 1906, 4; Olson, *Centenary History*, 264–66, 589–91.

16. *SBT*, September 28, 1886, 5.

17. Cederoth and Jahnson, "History of the Swedish Baptist Congregation, South Bend, Indiana," 8.

18. *SBT*, October 16, 1891, 1.

19. *Elkhart Weekly Review*, June 9, 1897, 2; Ericson, *Harvest on the Prairies*, 97, 153.

20. Ericson, *Harvest on the Prairies*, 9.

and seminary students in Chicago for resourcing pastors, evangelists, and other ministry leaders, both visiting and resident.

In May of 1907, the founding pastor, Henry Nelson, re-assumed his role of pastor.[21] As already mentioned, Nelson was at the center of the Pentecostal revival among the Swedish Baptists in Chicago along with Hjertstrom and others such as B. M. Johnson, Martin Carlson, and Petrus Swartz. Later, Nelson took an active role in gathering and handling funds for Gunnar Vingren and Daniel Berg who became missionaries in Brazil.

Henry Nelson had served not simply as pastor of the Swedish Baptist churches of La Porte and South Bend, but for twelve years he was the representative of the American Baptist Publication Society.[22] Since 1907, he served as president of the Scandia Loan and Investment Association, based in Chicago. His bi-vocational role allowed him to travel on weekends by train to South Bend in order to serve the small congregation there. Nelson maintained this role until June 1910. Prior to his departure, he hosted F. A. Sandgren, an evangelist and elder from William H. Durham's North Avenue Mission (also known as the Full Gospel Assembly) in Chicago, for several weeks of revival meetings.[23] Nelson's final sermon was titled "The Holy Ghost and Jesus Christ."[24]

In June 1910, F. A. Sandgren took over as pastor of the Swedish Baptist Church of South Bend, holding "Pentecostal meetings" consistently 3 to 4 times each week.[25] A published testimony reveals the nature of the meetings:

> Sunday, August the 28th [1910], God permitted us to attend the Swedish Baptist Church in South Bend, Indiana where God is baptizing them in the Holy Ghost. Oh, Glory to Jesus. Praise the Lord. What a feast to our souls and bodies the few hours we spent worshiping with these saints. Oh, what unity. Oh, what love and fellowship we had after being for two months away from a Pentecostal assembly. Truly God is good to such as are of a clean heart. The Holy Ghost was with us of a truth [sic], singing in the Spirit and prayer to the edification of those present. It

21. *SBT*, April 20 1907, 11; May 18, 1907, 7; December 19, 1908, 14.

22. Schön et al., *History of the Swedes of Illinois*, 366.

23. *Sanningens Vittne* (*SV*), April 1, 1912, 2–3; *SBT*, April 21, 1910, 5; May 21, 1910, 11; May 28, 1910, 16; April 22, 1911, 13.

24. *SBT*, May 28, 1910, 16.

25. *SBT*, June 11, 1910, 11; F. A. Sandgren, "Pentecostal Meetings in South Bend, Ind.," *PT*, July 1, 1910, 16.

was heaven itself. Brethren pray for us." Leon Geis and wife, 111 Cottage Ave., Goshen Indiana.[26]

Early in the summer of 1910, Gunnar Vingren had become friends with F. A. Sandgren who invited him to be co-pastor of the South Bend congregation. Vingren said that from Menomonie, Michigan, "the Lord led me to the First Swedish Baptist Church in South Bend, Indiana . . . I stayed as their pastor until the last part of September 1910."[27] When Vingren arrived to South Bend, he stayed in the home of Olof and Esther Uldin with Olof's three sons, Manley, Gedion Adolph (G.A.), and Howard, who lived at 1402 Catalpa Street.

During a Saturday evening prayer meeting in the home of the Uldins, it was said that God's Spirit came mightily upon them.[28] Olof Uldin prophesied that Vingren should go to Pará and teach the people there about Jesus Christ. It was after this prayer meeting that the Holy Spirit impressed Daniel Berg to join Vingren in South Bend. Then, on a Saturday afternoon in the Uldin home, again the power of God came over Uldin who prophesied that Berg was to go with Vingren to Pará, Brazil.[29]

---

26. Leon Geis and Wife, "Goshen, Indiana," *The Bridegroom's Messenger*, September 15, 1910, 3.
27. Gunnar Vingren, "Diary, 1912 Agenda."
28. Vingren, "Gunnar Vingren: The Pioneer's Diary," 172.
29. Vingren, "Gunnar Vingren: The Pioneer's Diary," 172.

Olof A. and Esther Uldin, 1944. Courtesy of the Uldin Family.

The Pentecostal ministry of Vingren in South Bend was fruitful. He reported, "On the first week, Jesus baptized ten people with his Holy Spirit and with fire. Praised be his name forever! In the end, almost twenty people were baptized in that summer. Glory to Jesus! In that way, Jesus transformed that Baptist church in South Bend into a Pentecostal church."[30] After Vingren and Berg left South Bend for Chicago, they were ordained by William Durham on October 2, 1910.[31] They arrived by ship in Brazil on November 19, 1910.

Disruption, Conflict, and Dissolution

The impact of the prayer meetings in the South Bend community continued through the pastoral leadership of F. A. Sandgren until October 1911, and beyond that through the lay leadership Olof Uldin.[32] It appeared that the Swedish Baptist Church in South Bend had become a Pentecostal church, as Vingren noted. However, while the Pentecostal

---

30. Vingren, "Gunnar Vingren: The Pioneer's Diary," 172.
31. *Word and Witness*, March 20, 1914, 7.
32. *SBT*, October 21, 1911, 13.

revival brought renewed spiritual life, it also stirred conflict within this Swedish Baptist congregation. From 1911 to 1912, Baptist state missionary John Hedeen, Adolph Olsen of Chicago, and students from the Swedish Baptist Theological Seminary in Morgan Park (Chicago), conducted the worship services and meetings of the church.[33] In 1912, the Swedish Baptist Conference reported "a lot of fighting and unrest; but after a fairly thorough cleaning."[34]

In 1911, the church's membership of 42 dropped to a total 20 in two years. In 1914, the church reported, "Our congregation is small and works under very difficult conditions. However, we want to be faithful."[35] From 1912 to 1920, several Spirit-filled ministers (Baptist-Pentecostal and/ or Pentecostal-Baptist ministers) served as visiting and short-term resident pastors, including Martin Carlson of the Humboldt Park Swedish Baptist Church of Chicago, F. W. Jewell of the Pentecostal Convention Tabernacle of Petoskey, Michigan, Gust Fredrickson of the Pentecostal Mission of St. Joseph, Michigan, and Arthur F. Johnson of the West Auburn Park Church of Chicago.[36]

In 1920, after multiple attempts to restore the congregation had failed, the Swedish Baptist Illinois Conference locked the church's doors and purchased the building for one dollar.[37] Despite this action, the Baptist Conference held Sunday afternoon services from November 1921 to October 1922 under the name of the "Swedish Baptist Mission," located on West Colfax Street.[38] In a final effort to keep a Swedish Baptist Church in South Bend, meetings were held at the home of Mrs. C. M. Anderson but that failed too.

Fresh Pentecostal Winds in South Bend

During the years of conflict and dissolution of the Swedish Baptist Church, Pentecostal prayer meetings continued in the home of Olof and

33. *SBT*, December 11, 1911, 7; November 11, 1911, 13; December 30, 1911, 11; January 27, 1912, 7; March 2, 1912, 9; August 10, 1912, 9; December 28, 1912, 9; Ericson, *Harvest on the Prairies*, 52, 135.

34. *Svenska Baptisternas Årsbok, 1912*, 21; *SBT*, August 10 1912, 9.

35. *Svenska Baptisternas Årsbok, 1913–1914*, 20.

36. *SBT*, August 3, 1912, 9; August 10, 1912, 9; July 30, 1913, 1; July 11, 1914, 11; *SV*, September 1, 1923, 6. Also see *SV*, June 1, 1932, 6.

37. *South Bend News-Times*, May 1, 1920, 4.

38. *SBT*, August 6, 1922, 10.

Esther Uldin. Most who attended the prayer meetings attended worship services at First Assembly in Mishawaka.[39] Former members of the Swedish Baptist Church joined other congregations such as the Swedish Mission Covenant. Interestingly, there were efforts outside the Swedish immigrant community for years to establish a Pentecostal congregation in South Bend but had been without success.[40]

Then in 1927, G. A. Uldin, son of Olof Uldin, invited Adolph Petersen of Chicago to South Bend in order to conduct a tent revival campaign during the summer. It was reported that 18 people received the baptism of the Spirit.[41] Adolph Petersen's revival crusades lasted for as much as seven consecutive weeks.[42]

Born in Tønder, Denmark, Adolph Petersen (1878–1949), a Jewish Dane, was taken in by the Salvation Army when he was kicked out of his parent's home in Chicago, following his conversion to faith in Christ at age sixteen. In Chicago, Petersen helped to establish the Stone Church, another leading Pentecostal congregation in the Windy City.[43] In 1920, Petersen assumed leadership of the North Avenue Mission (Full Gospel Assembly) on North Avenue.[44] Following Durham's departure to Los Angeles in 1911, and sudden death in 1912, this Chicago storefront mission went through "some years of famine and testing." In 1923, Petersen closed the "old North Avenue Mission for lack of space" and moved the congregation to a "brick tabernacle, costing about $24,000, one block from the old location."[45]

---

39. Paul Murray (son-in-law of G. A. Uldin), interview by Beverley Johnson-Miller, South Bend, Indiana; January 14, 2017.

40. Murray, interview.

41. *SV*, February 1, 1927, 5; *SBT*, September 17, 1927, 7; June 18, 1927, 9; January 29, 1927, 11; June 11, 1910, 11.

42. *Pentecostal Evangel (PE)*, January 27, 1934, 12; June 27, 1931, 19.

43. *Sterling Daily Gazette*, May 24, 1929, 3; Carl Halquist (ordained AG minister and grandson of Adolph Petersen), interview, by author; DM620046.

44. Adolph Petersen, "Chicago, Ill., Full Gospel Assembly," *PE*, June 23, 1923, 10. Besides SBGT, Petersen served the Assembly of God of St. Louis, Assembly of God in Turlock, California, and Wood River Assembly in Alton, Illinois.

45. Adolph Petersen, "Danish Evangelist," *The Minden Courier*, October 14, 1920, 12–13; *Latter Rain Evangel*, July 1923, 13. The church located at 1665 Mozart Street (at Wabansia Avenue) in Chicago.

Birth of the South Bend Gospel Tabernacle

In June 1928, G. A. Uldin cooperated with Thomas W. Wellard, a Scottish immigrant and pastor of the Mishawaka Pentecostal Assembly, and several former members of the Swedish Baptist Church of South Bend, to establish a new Pentecostal work.[46] During that summer, G. A. Uldin purchased and erected a tent at the corner of Vernon and Dayton Streets, and on June 24, 1928, Thomas Wellard conducted "Old Fashioned Revival Meetings Under Canvas" which lasted for over a month.[47]

Ada Peterson and Other Evangelists

Evangelist Ada Peterson (later the wife of G. A. Uldin) was also invited to hold an evangelistic crusade.[48] Ada Terés Peterson (1901–1990), born in Hinneryd, Sweden, had immigrated with her family to the United States and lived in Cass County, Minnesota. She and her family experienced Spirit-baptism during the tent revival services in Casino, Minnesota, led by Frank Lindquist, evangelist and district superintendent of the Assemblies of God,[49] and James Menzie, pastor of the Casino Full Gospel Assembly.[50]

Ada Petersen's evangelistic work began as a school teacher in Cass County, Minnesota. Without any church in the township, she began holding worship services and a Sunday School, leading adults and children to faith.[51] Like others, she became known as a "girl evangelist," conducting evangelistic services in Minnesota, Michigan, and Ohio.[52]

46. T. W. Wellard served the Mishawaka Assembly for nine months when he joined G. A. Uldin to establish a Pentecostal congregation in South Bend.

47. *SBT*, June 23, 1928, 4.

48. Uldin, "Calvary Temple History, 1973–1977."

49. Ghor, "A Harvest in Minnesota," *Assemblies of God Heritage*, 10, Murray, interview.

50. *The Brainerd Daily Dispatch*, October 25, 1922, 2; September 24, 1924, 7; June 19, 1926, 5; February 16, 1929, 2. J. Menzie and F. Lindquist became leaders of the Assemblies of God. Menzie married Agnes Peterson, Ada Peterson's sister, and served as a pastor in Northern Indiana.

51. Murray, interview. It was reported that Murray's family came to Christian faith through the bus ministry of SBGT.

52. Services were held at the Casino Full Gospel Assembly, Young People's meeting and at Sauk City. Minnesota. *The Brainerd Daily Dispatch*, January 7, 1927, 2; *The Sauk Centre Herald*, April 28, 1927, 4; Jun. 9, 1927, 2; May, 19, 1927, 10. Ada went to Benton Harbor to serve as pastor *The Herald-Press* (Saint Joseph, Michigan) January 27, 1931, 5; March 1, 1929, 5; *The Herald-Palladium* (Benton Harbor, Michigan) Sep. 7, 1929, 5.

In South Bend, Ada Peterson's tent meetings began August 7, 1928, and were held every night except Mondays and Saturdays. These tent meetings ended Sunday, September 9. The following week, revival meetings resumed in a storefront location at 120 E. Sample Street with the Nankivell Evangelistic Party and the Jubilee Singers of Chicago.[53] This was followed by another three-week revival with "Evangelists Williams and Marker."[54] After a one-week break, the church hosted another three-week revival with Rev. J. W. Merrin of Portland, Oregon, who was "ranked second to Billy Sunday."[55] Revival services resumed on December 26, 1928, with J. H. Bostrom who preached the sermon, "Is Healing for All?"[56]

In November 1928, Wellard described the revival meetings that had begun earlier that summer, saying, "We are shouting the victory at South Bend. Since the work started in June, we have been carrying on a continuous revival with the assistance of other evangelists and have had the blessed privilege of seeing souls weep penitential tears and get real old-time salvation, bodies healed in answer to prayer, and backsliders reclaimed. We have secured a beautiful building that seats several hundred, which we are using for a tabernacle; it is located at 120 Sample Street. We expect to carry our revival services through the entire winter."[57]

While Wellard served as pastor—from August 1928 to March 1931—he hosted at least twenty-one evangelists, 12 men and 9 women, of which thirteen were of Scandinavian descent. Six of the female evangelists held meetings on multiple occasions.[58] Between 1928 and 1933, SBGT hosted more than twenty-five evangelists, many on multiple occasions, with at least 16 from Scandinavian immigrant families, and at least 14 women.

By February 1930, Wellard ended his affiliation with the Assemblies of God, and on March 22, 1931, he resigned from SBGT to assume

---

53. *SBT,* September 15, 1928, 4; August 6, 1928, 4; August 25, 1928, 4; August 18, 1928, 3; September 1, 1928, 4; September 8, 1928, 4; September 15, 1928, 4; September 29, 1928, 6. Howard Uldin, "Calvary Temple History."

54. *SBT,* October 6, 1928, 4; October 13, 1928, 4; October 20, 1928, 4.

55. *SBT,* October 27, 1928, 12; November 3, 1928, 4; November 10, 1928, 14.

56. *SBT,* December 26, 1928, 52; January 2, 1929, 13.

57. Thomas Wellard, "Wanted," *PE,* November 3, 1928, 12.

58. On one occasion, Wellard hosted Lilian Yeomans of Los Angeles who spoke at the Christ Ambassadors Convention that drew 200 delegates. *SBT,* June 9, 1929, 20; January 2, 1930, 8.

the pastorate of the newly organized Grace Fundamental Church of South Bend.[59]

Growth of SBGT

Adolph Petersen, who had conducted multiple SBGT revival campaigns between 1929 and 1931, became pastor of SBGT on March 29, 1931. Earlier, in addition to his ministry at the Full Gospel Tabernacle on Mozart Street in Chicago, he had served as the State Presbyter of Illinois of the Assemblies of God.[60]

After Petersen assumed his role as pastor in South Bend, he and twenty members of the church formally applied for the SBGT to join the General Council of the Assemblies of God (Springfield, Missouri). A letter of application was drafted on May 14, 1931, and Elsie Anderson, niece of Olof Uldin, was elected secretary to oversee incorporation proceedings.[61] Charter members included several Scandinavian immigrant families: Uldin, Anderson, Lankford, (Emil) Johnson, Krussell, Hafstrom, Engstrom, (Eric) Johnson, and Halquist.[62]

With visionary determination and financial sacrifice, several Swedes under Petersen's oversight constructed the first tabernacle. In 1932, during the Great Depression, Swedish-born carpenter and Swedish Mission Covenant member, Eric E. Johnson, attended a Sunday evening service to find out what his wife, Linnea Moberg Johnson, was "mixed up with."[63] Deeply moved, Eric stood during the service and said, "You folks need your own building. I'm not a member here but my wife is, and we need to get you off this side street and on the main street. I'll give

---

59. "General Council Notices," *PE*, February 15, 1930, 14; *SBT*, March 20, 1931, 40.

60. *Sterling Daily Gazette*, January 11, 1929, 8.

61. Adolph Petersen, "Church Set in Order, Application for Incorporation with the Assemblies of God" (General Council of the Assemblies of God, April 9, 1931).

62. Carl F. Halquist, for example, immigrated from Sweden in 1912, married in 1914, had four sons and one daughter. He was a beloved elder, affectionately referred to as "Grandpa Halquist," and highly regarded for his spiritual wisdom, mentoring, and leadership. Four of his five children, as well as numerous grand-children and great-grandchildren, served or are currently serving as AG pastors, evangelists, or missionaries. Several of the Scandinavian church-founding families mentioned have similar histories.

63. Linnea Moberg Johnson, daughter of Swedish Mission Covenant Church pastor, Olaf Kristensen Moberg, served as a Lieutenant in the Salvation Army, led street evangelism efforts, and formed a Swedish women's church band.

the first hundred dollars and since many of you men are out of work, I'll show you how to build it."[64] Within weeks, the church acquired land on the main thoroughfare in South Bend, at 1115 S. Michigan Street. The opening service was held August 29, 1934, with the new tabernacle filled to capacity.[65] Olof Uldin reported in *Sanningens-Vittne*, "We have now built a tabernacle that holds between 3 and 4 hundred and the Lord is at work. Praised be his holy name! Our meetings, which are held in English, are well-visited and Adolph Peters[en] is our pastor, many have been saved and some baptized in the Holy Spirit, for which we praise God."[66]

Scandinavian-American
Preachers and Evangelists at SBGT, 1927–1938[67]

Adolph Petersen	1927, 1929
J. H. Bostrom	1928, 1929
Ada Peterson (Uldin)	1928, 1934, 1938
Hilda Bresch	1929, 1931, 1933, 1934
B. M. Johnson	1929, 1930
H. Johnson	1929
P. C. Nelson	1929
B. Davidson	1930
Frank W. Jewell	1930
Ruth Johnson	1930
Carl Swanson	1932

64. *PE*, June 4, 1932, 12.
65. *SBT*, August 29, 1934, 5.
66. Adolph Petersen, "South Bend, Indiana," *SV*, January 1, 1935, 5.
67. Adolph Petersen, *SBT*, September 17, 1927, 7; December 28, 1929, 5; J. H. Bostrom, *SBT*, January 12, 1929, 4; December 29, 1928, 4; H. Johnson, *SBT*, February 23, 1929, 4; P. C. Nelson, *SBT*, Jun. 14, 1929, 33; Frank W. Jewell, *SBT*, September 29, 1930, 5; B. M. Johnson, *SBT*, January 2, 1930, 8; December 28, 1929, 5; B. Davidson, *SBT*, December 6, 1930, 12; Ada Peterson/ Uldin, *SBT*, August 25, 1928, 4; November 30, 1938, 24; "South Bend, Ind.," *PE*, January 27, 1934, 12; Hilda Bresch, *SBT*, September 14, 1929, 3; Jul. 6, 1931, 6; Jul. 11, 1931, 5; July 24, 1931, 26; November 10, 1933, 15; August 29, 1934, 5; November 24, 1935, 32; Mae E. Frey, *SBT*, March 24, 1934, 10; Ruth Johnson, *SBT*, January 2, 1930, 8; May 10, 1930, 5; Mina Seaholm, *SBT*, November 14, 1934, 27; Peter Jepsen, September 10, 1936, 5; August 30, 1936, 7; Carl Swanson; *SBT*, November 20, 1932, 24; Niels Thompson, *SBT*, July 5, 1933, 17; Rev. A. G. Ericson, *SBT*, April 24, 1934, 11; E. Bartlett Peterson, *SBT*, June 18, 1933, 6; Anna C. Berg, *PE*, July 2, 1938, 10. For P. C. Nelson, see Sumrall, *Pioneers of Faith*, 103–9.

E. Bartlett Peterson	1933
Niels Thompson	1933
A. G. Ericson	1934
Mae E. Frey	1934
Mina Seaholm	1934
Peter Jepsen	1936
Anna C. Berg	1938

On multiple occasions, Petersen led minister fellowship meetings, church conferences, and the Annual AG Convention of Indiana.[68] While in South Bend, he served multiple terms as general presbyter of the AG Central District which included Indiana, Michigan, and Ohio.[69]

Early church leaders of SBGT gave definition to the Pentecostal faith and church life. They laid the groundwork for what became the largest Assembly of God congregation in Indiana, and the second largest in the country. Many of the children and grandchildren of the pioneering families went on to become ordained pastors, evangelists, and missionaries.

SBGT's Pentecostal Faith Formation

The story of SBGT includes the formation of the Swedish Baptist Church, its dissolution, and (re)formation of the South Bend Gospel Tabernacle. The story also includes the spiritual formation of congregational members. Many of the beliefs, values, and practices integral to Scandinavian pietism, revivalism, and the holiness movement shaped the nature and practices of SBGT. However, its Pentecostal theology and practices yielded a distinctly Pentecostal spirituality and Pentecostal faith formation.

Several intersecting values permeated the Pentecostal faith, culture, and practices at SBGT. The priority placed on a personal encounter with the Holy Spirit stood in stark contrast to the formalism and nominalism of state churches in the Scandinavia motherlands, remembered by many of the immigrants. In America, they abandoned what they perceived as a superficial or abstract spirituality of the state churches

---

68. *PE*, May 27, 1933, 14; December 12, 1931, 14; *SBT*, October 9, 1936, 9.

69. *SBT*, May 7, 1934, 18. Though most of the SBGT pastors that followed Petersen were not of Scandinavian descent, the Scandinavian influence continued through Petersen's legacy and many of the life-long Scandinavian lay leaders. Pastor Petersen returned to SBGT in retirement and resided in South Bend until his death, June 26, 1949.

(and their American counterparts) for the supernatural and embodied spirituality of Pentecostalism.

Revivals
Salvation, Healing, Miracles, Spirit-Baptism

The importance of spiritual encounters took many forms at SBGT but nothing ranked higher than "getting saved" and "staying saved," and revival meetings were the primary means. Revival meetings and evangelistic crusades were often held in tents in a public lot in order to gain the attention of, and be accessible to, those outside the church and outside the Christian faith. This practice of holding revival meetings, already mentioned, continued for decades at SBGT.

Between 1949 and 1978, two Scandinavian-American evangelists, Sweden-born Einar Waermo (1901–1983) and AG minister Clifton Erickson (1915–1998), son of Norwegian immigrants, conducted multiple revival crusades at SBGT. One member of the church recalled, "Clifton Erickson came to town with a revival ... and his associate helped me to accept my salvation."[70] Another person remembered, "What attracted mom and dad's attention was what the neighbors were calling 'the hillbilly circus' that was coming to town ... They didn't have any idea what it was, and decided to go. So, the first night they went ... they gave their hearts to the Lord."[71]

In addition to gospel preaching with a view toward salvation of the soul, Clifton Erickson's revival meetings "concentrated on healing and prayer," especially prayer to heal the physically sick.[72] It was said that Erickson "probably had the greatest impact on the attendance at Calvary Temple, remembered for healing services with numerous testimonies of miracles by those who attended."[73]

---

70. Interview DM620009.
71. Interview DM620038.
72. Interview DM620017.
73. Murray, interview.

South Bend Gospel Tabernacle, 1949, Collection of Beverly Johnson-Miller

Belief in divine healing at SBGT did not exclude human medical care, but the pursuit and expectation of healing through the laying on of hands and prayer was the normative mindset and practice. Numbers of people shared testimonies of healing. One person said, "I can remember seeing legs . . . shortened legs grow out, and [a] goiter . . . it disappeared."[74] Another testified, "I had rheumatic fever and had been in bed for months. On the last night of the meetings, I was in the line, and the Lord healed me completely that night."[75] *Another person* said, "Clifton Erickson once prayed for a woman at a healing service and the power was so great [that] it knocked her down on the ground."[76]

In SBGT, of second importance to personal salvation was a person's baptism in the Holy Spirit, followed by the evidence of speaking in tongues. The congregation's emphasis on this involved an explicit expectation, persistence, urgency, and ample opportunity to seek it. Baptism in the Holy Spirit empowered "the saved to stay saved," to grow in holiness, and to win as many souls to Christ as possible before the "imminent rapture" that would precede Jesus' Second Coming. One member of the church recalled, "At the end of all the services, people would go and pray. You have a prayer room, even at a tent revival . . . I was probably 14 . . . I was slain in the Spirit, and evidently, I lay there for 20–30 minutes, speaking in tongues. It was kind of like all of a sudden,

---

74. Interview DM620016.
75. Interview DM620038.
76. Interview DM620015.

I came to or woke up, and my folks and a couple of other people were sitting around me, and everyone else was gone."[77]

Of course, Pentecostal baptism could happen at home, as well as during a revival meeting or at the end of Sunday worship service. Another member of SBGT recalled: "I began speaking in tongues, and it was just like a big well of spring water springing up through me, and out of my mouth through the top of my head. I got out of my bed . . . and knelt down by our little window . . . it was just bubbling out for two hours."[78]

Similar testimonies of Spirit-baptism were told throughout the history of SBGT. Even as early as 1910, Gunnar Vingren had reported, "On the first week, Jesus baptized ten people with his Holy Spirit and with fire," and in 1934, Adolph Petersen reported," We have just closed a 5 weeks' revival meeting . . . A number were saved, 16 were baptized with the Holy Spirit, and the entire assembly was refreshed. The fire is still falling and others are getting the Baptism."[79]

In the mid 1960s, through leadership in the Full Gospel Businessmen's Fellowship, SBGT lay leader Ray Bullard, began holding weekly prayer meetings in his home basement. Interestingly, Notre Dame students and several Roman Catholic priests attended these meetings and experienced the baptism of the Holy Spirit.[80] This was instrumental in the birth of the Catholic Charismatic Renewal at the University of Notre Dame.

Worship Practices
Music, Prayer, Testimonies, Altar Calls

Expectations of supernatural phenomena applied to worship practices that included "heavenly" music, passionate preaching, intercessory prayer, testimonies, and altar calls. The spiritual significance of these practices that were carried forward from the Scandinavian free-church movement, escalated with the exercise of spiritual gifts, and normalized expectations of the miraculous.

---

77. Interview DM620026.
78. Interview DM620010.
79. Vingren, "Gunnar Vingren: The Pioneer's Diary," 172; *PE*, January 27, 1934, 12.
80. Ciciliot, "Origins of the Catholic Charismatic Renewal in the United States," 150.

Music had many expressions such as congregational singing of hymns and gospel tunes, children's Sunday School songs, choirs, singing evangelists, stringed quartets, and solos. Through the act of singing, theological expressions of lyrics formed and transformed the worshipers.[81] One member of SBGT said, "You know, singing back then, they just sang basically hymns and some choruses . . . just lifting their voices in praise of the Lord. . . . As a kid . . . it just seemed to really stick in my heart that God was . . . in those services."[82]

In the early history of SBGT, those who had been part of the Swedish Baptist Church had sung hymns and songs from *Nya Psalmisten* (New Psalmody) published by the Swedish Baptist General Conference.[83] Swedish Baptists possessed a passion for enthusiastic singing.[84] SBGT maintained ties with its Scandinavian Pentecostal heritage of music. Lester Sumrall, who began as pastor of SBGT in 1947, recalled, "At one time, [Lewi] Pethrus sent fifty Swedish preachers to my church in South Bend. They called the group 'the Swedish Men's Choir.' Our people kept these men in their homes and fell in love with them, although most of them could not speak English."[85]

At SBGT, congregational singing not merely prepared seekers to hear messages of the preachers but the lyrics instructed and reinforced the Pentecostal message. One member of SBGT recalled, "I just loved being a part of the music, and that's when my heart would swell . . . the music ministered to me greatly during that time . . . made me feel the connection more than any other time 'cause . . . I'm not a big prayer [person] . . . music is where my spiritual connection comes better than anything."[86] Another said, "I just remember the music . . . the organ and the orchestra and the quartets, and the music . . . prepared the heart for the Word. Music soothes the soul, and I have a saying that 'music is the best stress reliever on this side of heaven.'"[87]

Adolph Petersen, as well as the SBGT pastors who followed him, were gifted preachers.[88] Their preaching styles varied, yet all held in

---

81. Ward, *Introducing Practical Theology*, 15.
82. Interview DM620046.
83. See *Nya Psalmisten: Sånger för Allmän och Enskild Uppbyggelse.*
84. Olson, "Neither Jew nor Greek," 37.
85. Sumrall, *Pioneers of Faith*, 116.
86. Interview DM620009.
87. Interview DM620045.
88. Additional pastors of SBGT were: Thomas F. Zimmerman, C.C. Burnett, Glen

common a commitment to Scripture as the divinely inspired and inerrant authority for life and faith. They recognized the essential need of the Holy Spirit's presence, anointing, illumination, and empowerment. Someone described Adolph Petersen as "unctioned with the Holy Spirit," and said that he "possesses that quality peculiar to a successful ministry."[89] The goal of preaching by ministers of the SBGT was spiritual transformation of the hearers.

In general, preaching was given often to the emotional engagement of the listeners through storytelling and testimony, rather than in-depth critical or scholarly engagement with Scriptures. The most-dramatic and often fear-driven or hell-fire preaching came from visiting evangelists.[90] A member of SBGT said, "I can remember that . . . whenever [guest] ministers . . . would come . . . there was a lot of hell fire and brimstone, you know, and just scared the bejeebers out of 'ya, you know . . . you were being scared into something, instead of drawn in to it."[91]

The prophetic significance of world events, the urgency of salvation before the end times of human history, the baptism of the Holy Spirit, supernatural healing and miracles, the call to holy living, and the need to share the gospel, were common sermon subjects. One member recalled, "Preaching [focused on] messages related to major world situations such as WWII . . . with [a] major emphasis and urgency regarding the Second Coming of Christ . . . ."[92] Another person commented: "The thing . . . I remember is the preaching, and the people just really responding to the Lord, and then the number of hours that we spent praying at the altar after the preaching of the message . . . and people being baptized in the Holy Spirit; in some cases, even people being delivered of some demons."[93]

Hurst, Lester Sumrall, Nelson Hinman, Bob McAlistar, Morris Cerullo, Roy Wead, and Jack West.

89. *The Selma Enterprise* (California), September 11, 1925, 3.

90. Lester Sumrall had a reputation for generating fear in many congregants. Those drawn to the fear-focused approach were usually disappointed in the preaching of Nelson Hinman, Roy Wead, and others with a more sensitive and positive presence and message. Pastors such as Roy Wead supplemented their calm, steady style with hell-fire evangelists, such as the Bruce Thumb Sunshine party and associate ministers such as Carl Strader.

91. Interview DM620022.

92. Interview DM620046.

93. Interview DB00007.

Along with preaching, prayer was deemed essential for Christian growth, holy living, and the advancement of God's work in the world. The church strongly encouraged and provided various forms and opportunities for prayer—women's prayer meeting, men's prayer meeting, revival service prayer, daily prayer, and intercessory prayer.

The prayer room at SBGT was to many people a meaningful place. One member recalled: "We would always flock to the prayer room to really intercede for missionaries and people, and people's needs . . . and those were such rich times . . . of the deacons, Sunday School teachers, and leaders coming and praying for us."[94] Another echoed the importance of the prayer room, saying: "Every Sunday night we . . . spent time in the prayer room . . . a lot of people would get filled with the Spirit . . . or get healed or whatever 'cause . . . people used to go around and pray for people."[95]

Personal testimonies took many forms as acts of worship, as well as witness to those outside Christian faith. Mid-week services generally provided congregants, including children, ample opportunity to share with others about the concrete ways in which God was present, personal, and powerfully at work in their lives. Testimonies were often incorporated into Sunday services, revival meetings, youth services, and Sunday School. The weekly AG periodical, *The Pentecostal Evangel*, published testimonies of many kinds and from many places, at home and abroad. For example, in 1947, Lester Sumrall told the story of Walter Gundt, a sailor who was invited to church but refused. Sumrall shared Gundt's story, saying,

> The Lord began to show Walt His [God's] goodness. He laid it on the heart of Mrs. Engstrom, a Christian lady in South Bend whose son was a good friend of Walt's, to take him into her home. She longed to lead him to Christ. Walt did not respect her motive at the time, but today he believes that if the Engstroms had not taken him into the happy atmosphere of their home he probably would have had a nervous breakdown, and might have ended [in] a suicide. For some time he persisted in his careless ways, wasting his money in taverns and hell holes, but the Engstroms would not turn him out into the street. They

---

94. Interview DM620038.
95. Interview DM620017.

were praying for him, and believed eventually he would come to Christ."[96]

Testimonies like that of Walt Gundt, who came to faith, revealed God's activity in everyday people, cultivating encouragement, hope, and perseverance.

Altar calls followed passionate sermons that were filled with dramatic stories of spiritual failures and successes. Creating a space for personal examination via altar calls served as a means of internalizing the congregation's beliefs, values, expectations, and boundaries, as well as a means of bringing all aspects of one's life into conformity with the church's prescribed way of faith and Christian life. One member recalled, "We were all equal at that altar, and as youth—as we got older—that altar bound us together. We prayed for each other; we cried with each other; we knew what our problems were in our personal lives, and we prayed about 'em at the altar."[97]

Participation in Congregational Life
Sunday School, Service, and Mission

Church attendance ranked supreme among the many standards and expectations that defined Christian living, and anything that interfered, other than employment or illness, was inexcusable. Church was in session at least three times a week, all year long, not including involvement in prayer meetings, teaching meetings, youth meetings, choir or orchestra practice, street witnessing, men's and women's ministry meetings, and fellowship meetings. One person commented, "We lived and breathed . . . church every day . . . on Monday nights . . . I led a nursing home ministry . . . I don't remember Tuesday. Wednesday, of course, was youth, and Thursday . . . Bible study, and then we had the morning Bible studies and prayer meetings before school . . . [in] high school . . . ."[98]

Frequent camp meetings, healing campaigns, and revival services took place several times a year and lasted for at least one to three weeks, with six or more services each week. Summer camp meetings often involved two to three services each day. The consuming nature of church

---

96. *PE*, July 5, 1947, 15.
97. Interview DM620035.
98. Interview DM620035.

participation cultivated deep belonging, personal care, and life-long relationships. One member of SBGT said, "I can remember, as a young kid, that the church was everything, and that was our country club, you know. I mean, that was our social life; that was—you know, because in the Scripture somewhere it says, 'Be separate from the world.'"[99]

Sunday school played an important role in forming a distinctly Pentecostal spirituality and identity. Of course, the institution of Sunday school spread decades earlier among the free-church congregations of Sweden, as well as in England and America. Swedish Baptist pastor Theodor Truvé edited the first Sunday School paper titled *Bikupan* (Beehive) and another called *Sondagsskolläraren* (The Sunday School Teacher).[100] In America, the Swedish Baptists and other immigrant churches adopted the latest methods of Sunday school—age-graded classes, institutes, rallies, and conventions—and promoted Sunday school with a passion.[101]

Henry Nelson served for several years as the Swedish Baptist Conference's Sunday school missionary, and C. M. Uldin, brother of O. A. Uldin, taught a session of the Swedish Baptist Conference on the topic, "The Sunday School Teacher and the Home."[102] The Swedish Baptist's enthusiasm for hosting Sunday school conventions continued and expanded at SBGT.[103]

At SBGT, the Sunday school was a major means of evangelism, Bible instruction, and church growth. One member remarked, "Well, the thing that really impressed me was, you know, [the teachers] were just a few years older than I was. I was 12, and they were probably 18 . . . the interesting thing was their passion for the church and for the Lord. I mean, this was all serious business to them, and, in every class, they prayed such beautiful prayers for us, and with us, and almost every Sunday, they would ask, 'Have you received Christ?' . . . [as a non-churched bus kid] I wasn't really quite sure, but about the third or fourth Sunday, after hearing the lessons and the teachings, I began to understand what it meant to

---

99. Interview DM620021.

100. Stephenson, *Religious Aspects of Swedish Immigration*, 87–88.

101. Stephenson, *Religious Aspects of Swedish Immigration*, 87; Ericson, *Harvest on the Prairies*, 108.

102. "Rev Charles Palm Conducts Services at the Swedish Baptist Church," *SBT*, May 2, 1902, 1.

103. "Swedish Baptist Sunday School Convention, *SBT*, November 12, 1904, 1; Henry Nelson, "Of Great Interest Was the Swedish Conference." *SBT*, June 23, 1894, 4.

be saved and to receive Christ into our hearts, and so it was in the Sunday School class... that I gave my heart to the Lord..."[104]

Everyone, from all ages, "the churched" and "the non-churched," attended Sunday School. The congregation worked vigorously to maximize weekly attendance. If needed, teachers arranged for children who were bussed from poor neighborhoods to have "Sunday clothes." Bus routes were added over the years to ensure that everyone had transportation to the church. In the 1959 annual church report, Sunday School director Ed Engstrom, reported: "The Sunday School is a very important outreach ... [and] a teaching arm of the church ... During the past year several new attendance records were set. We entered into the 1,700s for the first time and set a new high of 1,727 ..."[105] By 1959, SBGT had more than 150 Sunday School teachers and workers.

Children's classes included opening exercises with singing and prayer requests, as well as welcoming first-time visitors. Birthdays were celebrated with treats from the "treasure chest." Bible instruction with memory verses was part of the activity. Sunday school classes focused on the study of Scripture along with frequent opportunities and invitations for personal salvation in Christ. Teachers tracked attendance, sent post cards for every absence, and visited the homes of children whose parents did not attend. Sunday school nurtured belonging, personal faith, and Bible literacy.

Everyone had a role and responsibility when it came to ministries in the church, regardless of age, education, male, or female. While not everyone's particular talents fit the typical church ministry roles, church members took it upon themselves to help people find places to contribute, and places of personal significance within the life of the church. One member said, "We are supposed to be—every one of us—a minister. [All of us] are gifted in the Spirit of God in one way or another, and it is—the most important thing in life is—like I said, to pass it on ... help others, spiritually, physically, mentally, any way you can."[106]

The responsibility for ministry extended even to the young. In the Pentecostal stream, when it came to spiritual blessings and responsibilities, service to God was not partial to age. Because Pentecostals believed that God poured out the Holy Spirit on the young as well as the old, the

104. Interview DM620047.
105. "Calvary Temple-South Bend Gospel Tabernacle, Inc., South Bend, Indiana, Annual Business Meeting, September 21, 1959," 5.
106. Interview DM620006.

young were rallied together, encouraged, and given opportunities for Christian service.

Children as young as eleven or twelve years old assisted with younger children in Sunday School and summer Vacation Bible School. It was common for high school age youth to teach Sunday School classes. Children and youth helped peers in various ways such as Scripture memorization. Youth were active in the leadership of their own Sunday School classes and the youth group, named Christ's Ambassadors (CA), elected their own officers and led worship for the meetings.

Moreover, youth were challenged and mobilized to recruit other youth to meetings. Special youth services were designed to appeal to those outside the church. Youth canvassed neighborhoods distributing invitation fliers for the special youth services that were commonly tied to all-church revival meetings. This activity spilled over into evangelism as one member explained, "We were motivated to go out . . . on the street and pass out tracts."[107] This happened in South Bend, but trips were also made to Gary, Indiana, to engage in evangelism with other CA youth. One person recalled that the youth "would do street evangelism, street meetings, and play their instruments and things like that. Elsie Anderson used to tell such wonderful stories of how they enjoyed going to Gary . . . That was just a marvelous part of their lives . . . that really helped to shape the young people into the fellowship [with other] Pentecostal young people."[108]

Conclusion

The story of SBGT provides a microcosmic view of the Scandinavian immigrant role in birthing, shaping, and spreading of Pentecostal spirituality. Leaving behind the nominal religion of the homeland kindled a passion and precedence for phenomenal faith and spiritual experience desired in the American promised-land. Though participation in Pentecostalism triggered conflict within some Scandinavian-American congregations, it also made space for continuity and creativity; merging spiritual values and practices of the past with the prophetic voice and vision giving rise to the Pentecostal movement.

---

107. Interview DM620032.
108. Interview DB00005.

An examination of the history of SBGT sheds light on the shape and scope of Scandinavian influence in American Pentecostalism, as well as the nature of distinctly Pentecostal spirituality, formation, and faith-transformation. A look at the history reveals how a repulsion toward the spiritual oppression of the homeland state-church and the embrace of Pietistic and holiness traditions set the stage and provided theological groundings for the visionary leadership roles and enthusiastic response of Scandinavian immigrants which defined the burgeoning heart-felt, revivalist, phenomena-centered spirituality of SBGT and the Pentecostal movement at large.

The driving passion of SBGT for evangelism and church growth took the form of life-encompassing, sometimes fear-inducing, emotional revival practices; gifted, gender-inclusive leadership; and, lay-led, outreach-oriented Sunday School programs. The all-consuming church involvement contributed to bonding of the faith community and caregiving among the members. The belief and practice of everyone embracing their ministry responsibilities within the church played a major role in the multifaceted web of belonging, and the experience of belonging to one another stemmed from the shared meta-understanding of belonging to God.

Bibliography

Primary Sources

Newspapers Used

The Brainerd Daily Dispatch, Brainerd, MN, 1901–
Bridegroom's Messenger, Atlanta, GA, 1907–1970
Elkhart Weekly Review, Elkhart, IN, 1879–1897
The Herald-Palladium, Benton Harbor, MI, 1859–
The Herald-Press, Saint Joseph, MI, 1901–1975
Latter Rain Evangel, Chicago, 1908–1939
The Minden Courier, Minden, NB, 1893–
Nya Wecko-Posten (NWP), Chicago, 1884–1918
The Pentecostal Evangel (PE), Plainfield, IN, Springfield, MO, 1913–2014
Pentecostal Testimony (PT), Chicago, 1909–1912
Sanningens Vittne (SV), Minneapolis, 1911–1939
The Sauk Centre Herald, Sauk Centre, MN, 1886–
The Selma Enterprise, Selma, CA, 1888–
South Bend News-Times, South Bend, IN, 1913–1938
The South Bend Tribune (SBT), South Bend, IN, 1872–

Sterling Daily Gazette, Sterling, IL, 1927–1951
The Weekly Republican, Plymouth, IN, 1911–1922
Word and Witness, Malvern, AR, 1912–1915

OTHER PRIMARY SOURCES

Årsbok för Svenska Baptistförsamlingarna inom Amerika, *1910–1911*. Chicago: Swedish Baptist General Conference, 1911.
Calvary Temple-South Bend Gospel Tabernacle, Inc., South Bend, Indiana, Annual Business Meeting, September 21, 1959.
Cederoth, Erik and Gust Jahnson, History of the Swedish Baptist Congregation, South Bend, Indiana, 1897. Bethel University Library, St. Paul, MN; History Center; Archives.
Murray, Paul. Interview by Beverley Johnson-Miller, South Bend, Indiana; January 14, 2017.
Nya Psalmisten: Sånger för Allmän och Enskild Uppbyggelse. Chicago: Swedish Baptist General Conference, 1903.
Svenska Baptisternas Årsbok, Galesburg, Ill., 1912. Chicago: J. V. Martenson, 1913.
Svenska Baptisternas Årsbok,, 1913–1914. Chicago: J. V. Martenson, 1914.
Uldin, Howard. "Calvary Temple History." Unpublished.
Vingren, Gunnar. "Diary, 1912 Agenda." Gunnar Vingren Memorial Archives, CPAD, Rio de Janeiro, Brazil.

Secondary Sources

Blumhofer, Edith L. "Urban Pentecostalism: Chicago, 1906–1912." In *Turning Points in the History of American Evangelicalism*, edited by Heath W. Carter and Laura Rominger Porter, 154–79. Grand Rapids: Eerdmans, 2017.
Ciciliot, Valentina. "The Origins of the Catholic Charismatic Renewal in the United States: The Experience at the University of Notre Dame and South Bend (Indiana), 1967–1975" In *Transatlantic Charismatic Renewal, c. 1950–2000*, edited by Andrew Atherstone et al., 144–64. Leiden and Boston: Brill, 2021.
Contat, Odessa, et al. *History of First Assembly of God Mishawaka*, July 1980.
Ericson, Carl G. *Harvest on the Prairies: Centennial History of the Baptist Conference of Illinois, 1856–1956*. Chicago: Baptist Conference Press for Baptist Conference of Illinois, 1956.
Gohr, Glenn. "A Harvest in Minnesota: The Story of A/G Pioneer Frank J. Lindquist: Evangelist, Church Planter, Pastor, Bible College President, and Friend." *Assemblies of God Heritage* n.d. (1990) 10–13.
Ljungmark, Lars. *The Swedish Exodus*. Translated by Kermit B. Westerberg. Carbondale, IL: Southern Illinois University Press, 1979.
Olson, Adolf. *A Centenary History as Related to the Baptist Conference of America, 1852–1952*. Chicago: Baptist Conference Press, 1952.
Olson Gustafson, Anita. *Swedish Chicago: The Shaping of an Immigrant Community, 1880–1920*. Dekalb, IL: NIU Press, 2018.

Olson, Virgil A. "Neither Jew nor Greek: A Study of an Ethnic Baptist Group, the Swedish Baptists, 1850–1950." *Baptist History and Heritage* 25 (1990) 33–43.

Schön, Anders, et al., eds. *History of the Swedes of Illinois*. Chicago: Engberg-Holmberg, 1908.

Stephen Miceli, "Industrialization and Immigration: Labor at the River's Bend." PhD diss., University of Toledo, 2009. http://rave.ohiolink.edu/etdc/view?acc_num=toledo1241383946.

Stephenson, George M. *The Religious Aspects of Swedish Immigration*. New York: Arno Press, 1969.

Sumrall, Lester. *Pioneers of Faith*. South Bend, IN: LeSea, 2018.

Ward, Pete. *Introducing Practical Theology: Mission, Ministry, and the Life of the Church*. Grand Rapids: Baker Academic, 2017.

Vingren, Ivar. "Gunnar Vingren: The Pioneer's Diary." In *Latin American Religions: Histories and Documents in Context*, edited by Anna Lisa Peterson and Manuel A. Vásquez, 170–76. New York: New York University Press, 2008.

Chapter Eleven

From Scandinavian-American to Trans-Atlantic Relations of Neo-Pentecostals in Sweden and the United States, 1965–2014

Torbjörn Aronson

Neo-Pentecostalism in Sweden began from Scandinavian-American relations in the late 1960s and the early 1970s, and was then extensively shaped by trans-Atlantic relations in the 1980s and 1990s. This chapter discusses and analyzes three major Neo-Pentecostal developments in Sweden from the perspective of the timeline of this book, that is Scandinavia and America, 1880s to 1930, Scandinavian-American, 1930 to 1970, and trans-Atlantic American and Scandinavian relations, 1970 to 2020.

The late 1960s and the early 1970s was a period of transition from the Scandinavian-American to the trans-Atlantic relations, and during the following decades the latter is all but dominating. The description "Neo-Pentecostalism" or "Neo-Pentecostal" is here used as an umbrella concept, referring both to the Charismatic renewal from the 1960s until present, the Jesus People movement of the 1970s, and different later

Neo-Charismatic churches and movements. These three are developed in the main sections of this chapter:

- Full Gospel Business Men's Fellowship International's role in the beginning of the Charismatic Renewal and the Jesus People movement in Sweden, 1965–1974 and its long-term effects,
- Ulf Ekman and *Livets Ord* (Word of Life) and their role in the disseminating of American Neo-Pentecostalism in Sweden, 1983–2014,
- John Wimber's influence in Sweden and the birth of Vineyard Nordic, 1982–1998.

The Charismatic Renewal and the Jesus People movement arrived and began to flourish in Sweden through the Scandinavian-American links provided by the Full Gospel Business Men (FGBM). One of the converts from FGBMs evangelistic outreaches through the American Jesus People was Ulf Ekman (1950–). He became the most important Neo-Pentecostal leader in Sweden from the middle of the 1980s until he became a Roman Catholic in 2014. John Wimber (1934–1997), leader of the Association of Vineyard Churches in America, became a major influence in the Charismatic renewal in the Church of Sweden and also made possible a Vineyard movement in the Nordic countries.

Most of the historic overview below is based on monographs, articles, and dissertations published in Swedish, and important primary sources are listed in these books and articles. The section dealing with John Wimber is less so, because of the lack of scholarly writings about his visits and influence in Sweden. Personal recollections and newspaper articles have served as the material for that section.

FGBM and the Early Charismatic Renewal and the Jesus People Movement in Sweden

Below, we will discuss and analyze the start of FGBM in Sweden, FGBM's Airlifts to Gothenburg/Stockholm, 1965–70, FGBM's sponsoring of American Jesus People to Sweden, 1969–74, and the longstanding effects of FGBM's initiatives within the context of the Scandinavian-American and trans-Atlantic Pentecostal relations.

FGBM was founded in 1951 by sponsors of the Oral Roberts Evangelistic Association (OREA). Oral Roberts (1918–2009) had at that time become one of the most well-known healing evangelists in American Pentecostalism. His crusades were financially supported by business people with a background in classical Pentecostal denominations and some of them coalesced in this new evangelistic initiative that was FGBM. Demos Shakarian (1913–93), an Armenian-American businessman, became FGBM's first president and Oral Roberts and other American healing evangelists, supported the early activities of the organization. In 1953, *The Voice*, the monthly journal of the FGBM, was launched and in the same year the first national conference of the organization was arranged in Los Angeles. During the following decades, FGBM grew strongly and had more than three hundred local chapters in the middle of the 1960s and more than 250,000 members by the beginning of the 1970s. FGBM was a laymen's organization and independent of the classical Pentecostal denominations in America. FGBM organized informal services and prayer gatherings at workplaces and restaurants and often invited people from the workplaces of their members to attend. The result was a kind of grass root ecumenism where testimonies about born again-experiences, healing, and baptisms in the Spirit were disseminated, which in turn contributed to the early Charismatic renewal in mainline churches in the United States.[1]

The national conferences of FGBM often became a platform for healing evangelists and ministers related to the Latter Rain Movement. Their spirituality was spread through FGBM and would come to characterize much of the major conferences of the organization, which meant a focus on evangelism, healing, baptism in the Spirit, and gifts of the Spirit such as tongues and prophecy.

FGBM came to Sweden through a Swedish couple with an international network, Robert and Siv Pellén. He was an entrepreneur and she was an opera singer and both of them had lived in Central Europe for several years in the 1950s. They met FGBM at a conference in Switzerland in 1964 and experienced a call to launch the organization in their homeland. In 1964, they met with Lorraine Wise (1913–2016), who was one of the current leaders of FGBM, while attending the World Pentecostal Conference in Helsinki. Wise introduced the Pellén couple to Demos Shakarian. Shakarian supported their interest in launching FGBM in Sweden after having consulted Lewi Pethrus (1884–1974).

---

1. Harrell, *All Things Are Possible*, 146–49, 225; *The Voice* 1:1 and 1:2 (1953). *The Voice* 8:6–7 (1960).

Lewi Pethrus, former pastor of the Filadelfia Church in Stockholm (1911–58), was at that time residing in the U.S. and met with Shakarian. Both of them encouraged the Pellén couple to launch FGBM in Sweden. This took place in 1965. In that year, FGBM organized its first major conference in Europe, held in London. The conference was marketed in Sweden through the efforts of the Pellén couple. More than 15,000 people attended the conference which had the following main speakers: Oral Roberts, Derek Prince (1915–2003), Nicky Cruz (1938–), Harald Bredesen (1918–2006), Dennis Bennett (1917–91), David du Plessis (1905–87), John Sherrill (1923–2017), and Michael Harper (1931–2010). The conference represented through their main speakers a showcase of the early Charismatic renewal that had begun in the U.S. and Britain. All of the main speakers would in the following decade become staple names in Charismatic renewal conferences in different parts of the world.

Already at this time, FGBM had established contact with David Wilkerson (1931–2011) and Teen Challenge and their work among young drug addicts and gangs in New York. Wilkerson began his work in New York in 1958. In the London conference, the connection to Teen Challenge was represented by Nicky Cruz and an evangelistic outreach was organized in districts in London similar to those in New York where Teen Challenge worked. This evangelistic outreach led to spontaneous conversions among young drug addicts and to the founding of a rehabilitation center in London, sponsored by FGBM. All of the elements of the conference in London in 1965 were present when FGBM was launched in Sweden and were to characterize FGBM's activities in Sweden during the following decade. This meant especially conferences that promoted Charismatic renewal in mainline Protestant churches and evangelism among young drug addicts. The latter effort led to a close cooperation between FGBM and the American Jesus People movement.[2]

FGBM organized conference teams of American businessmen from 1965–1974, and evangelistic teams from the Jesus People movement to Sweden from 1969–1974. Several of these teams had a connection to the Scandinavian-American Pentecostal churches in Chicago and/or Oregon. The conferences of FGBM in Stockholm 1966, 1968, 1969 and 1970 pioneered the Charismatic renewal and the Jesus People movement in Sweden and received a wide public coverage by the churches and Christian and secular media, national television included. They helped give birth to

---

2. See Aronson, "När svenskamerikanska affärsmän sponsrade kristna hippies." See also *Voice of Healing* 8:7 (August 1955), 6, 18–19; *The Voice* 12:12 (December 1964) 18.

these types of movements in Sweden. These movements then continued within the national and international contexts of Pentecostalism, developing contacts and networks of their own.

The FGBM conferences, so-called Air Lifts, in Stockholm were huge undertakings. The FGBM conference in Stockholm 1966 represented the major launching of the organization in Sweden. More than 100 American businessmen were flown to Stockholm and during one week preached in the major churches of the Swedish capital and participated in small and large public events, like prayer breakfasts and lunches. The conference was publicly supported by Lewi Pethrus and many of the major churches of the city opened their doors. The result was a small beginning of Charismatic renewal in Stockholm where people from mainline churches experienced baptism in the Spirit and healing. There was also public discussion around the growing problem with young people addicted to drugs.[3]

Aside from Robert and Siv Pellén and Lewi Pethrus, several of the major personalities and networks behind FGBM's mission to Sweden from 1965 to the mid-1970s were connected to the Scandinavian-American Pentecostal churches in Chicago, that is Philadelphia Church and Faith Tabernacle, or similar churches on the American West Coast and especially in Oregon and Washington (Seattle and Portland). The context of FGBM's mission to Sweden, and the spreading of American Charismatic renewal and the Jesus People movement to Sweden, was then both the more general trans-Atlantic Pentecostal contacts and the Scandinavian-American Pentecostal network centered on Chicago and the American West Coast.

The Scandinavian-American connection was very much represented by one of the originators and main speakers of the first FGBM conference in Sweden in 1965 (Gothenburg) and the FGBM conferences in Stockholm in 1966, 1968, 1969, and 1970, Henry F. Carlson. Henry F. Carlson was president of FGBM in Chicago and was a member of the national leadership of FGBM. He had been part of the Latter Rain Movement in the 1950s and was an elder of Faith Tabernacle, one of the Swedish-American Pentecostal churches of Chicago.[4] Faith Tabernacle had been founded in 1962 by former members of the major Swedish-American Pentecostal church of the city, namely, Philadelphia Church. Joseph

---

3. Aronson, "När svenskamerikanska affärsmän sponsrade kristna hippies," 178–79.
4. *The Voice* 4:6 (1956); 11:11 (November 1963) 5; 30:1 (January 1982) 12.

Mattson-Bozé (1905-89), a well-known Swedish Pentecostal evangelist who immigrated to America in the 1930s, had pastored Philadelphia Church (1933-39 and 1941-58) and was at the same time part of the loose network of the American healing evangelists and the Latter Rain Movement. Mattson-Bozé was a longtime close friend of Lewi Pethrus and important link between the Scandinavian-American Pentecostals and *Pingströrelsen* (Pentecostal Movement) in Sweden. Faith Tabernacle and Philadelphia Church cultivated contacts with preachers associated both with the Latter Rain Movement and with *Pingströrelsen* in Sweden. It was no surprise then, that FGBM in Chicago got a backing and stronghold in these two Swedish-American churches, which then became a launching pad for FGBM to Sweden and Scandinavia.[5]

Together with the Pellén couple and Lewi Pethrus, Henry F. Carlson was the driving force behind the conferences in Stockholm and FGBM's sponsoring of teams from the American Jesus People to Sweden. Several of the main speakers of the conferences and leaders of the evangelistic teams were recruited by Carlson and related to the Swedish-American churches in Chicago or the American West Coast. The first conference was held in Gothenburg in late 1965 during a weekend and had a smaller format in comparison with those that would follow.[6] Main speakers were Henry F. Carlson, Clifton Erickson, and Harald Bredesen. Clifton Erickson (1915-98) was born to a Norwegian family in Chelan, Washington, and was converted at the age of eighteen. In 1945, Erickson became licensed with the Assemblies of God and in 1948 an ordained minister. He was one of the speakers at the first Voice of Healing Convention in Dallas in 1949 and was prayed for by Oral Roberts. After this, Erickson's ministry became fully focused on healing and tent evangelism. Erickson's ministry became international in the 1950s, ministering in Chile in 1952 and in 1954 in the Philippines with Lester Sumrall.

In 1962, Erickson and Sumrall together began the *World Harvest Magazine*.[7] Harald Bredesen (1918-2006) was born in Rugby, North Dakota, to a Norwegian family. His father was the pastor of a local Lutheran Church. Bredesen attended Luther College in Decorah, Iowa, and was ordained into the ministry in 1945. In 1946, he went to a Pentecostal camp meeting where he received the baptism of the Holy Spirit and

5. See Malmström, "Han arbetar efter amerikanska metoder," 81-137.
6. Aronson, "När svenskamerikanska affärsmän sponsrade kristna hippies," 177-80.
7. *Voice of Healing*, August 1955, 2, 8. See Shemeth, "Clifton O. Erickson," in *New International Dictionary of Pentecostal and Charismatic Movements*.

was one of the first ordained ministers from mainline denominations to experience this and keep his ordination and credentials. In 1959, Bredesen became pastor of First Reformed Church of Mount Vernon, New York. Together with his co-pastor, the future Christian broadcaster and Presidential candidate, Pat Robertson (1930–), he made the church an early center for Charismatic renewal. To conclude, all three of the main speakers of FGBM's first conference in Sweden had a Scandinavian-American background and they belonged to the network of healing evangelists and early Charismatic renewal in America.[8]

The main speakers of the first major conferences in Stockholm in 1966, 1968, 1969 and 1970 and were Demos Shakarian, Henry F. Carlson, Wendell Wallace (1923–2009), Harald Bredesen, and Nicky Cruz. Wendell Wallace was an African-American pastor and civil rights activist from Portland, Oregon. He pastored Maranatha Evangelistic Center in Portland, which was a groundbreaking church in being multi-racial and became a center for the Jesus People movement in the late 1960s. Many young hippies were converted there and became members of the church and Christian hippie communes were founded in connection with the church.[9] Wallace's involvement with FGBM strengthened the efforts of the organization to reach out to drug addicts and ministries devoted to their situation and finally, to the Jesus People movement. Already in the first Air Lift to Stockholm in 1966, there was a concerted effort to reach out to young people addicted to drugs. Arthur F. Johnson (1934–) from Seattle was part of this effort, having worked with a similar type of evangelistic outreach in the Seattle area. Johnson came to Sweden with FGBM's team and decided to stay in Gothenburg, Sweden, as a missionary to young Swedes. From 1969 to the mid-1970s, he helped to accommodate American Jesus People coming to Sweden to evangelize.[10] Through the evangelism partly organized by Johnson, the earlier mentioned Ulf Ekman was converted in Gothenburg 1970.[11] The first group from the Jesus People movement in California came to Sweden with FGBM's AirLift to Stockholm in 1969.

8. *The Voice* 8:6–7 (1960); Myrin, *Sänd till världsledarna*, 12–27.

9. *Christianity Today* 13:22 (August 1, 1969).

10. Aronson, "När svenskamerikanska affärsmän sponsrade kristna hippies," 181, 185–186.

11. Aronson, "När svenskamerikanska affärsmän sponsrade kristna hippies," 185–86.

The group was led by Devore Walterman (1919–2004) and was not labeled "Jesus People" but was advertised as "three converted drug addicts from San Francisco." They participated in services and evangelistic outreach in Stockholm. Walterman came originally from Texas and had served as pastor in different Pentecostal churches in Chicago and became involved with Philadelphia Church and Faith Tabernacle in the 1960s. During his time at Faith Tabernacle, he started a rehabilitation center for drug addicts.[12] In 1967, he founded National Council for Prevention of Drug Abuse and shortly after that, the first local center for Teen Challenge in the Chicago area. He moved from Chicago to northern California a year later to become director for Teen Challenge in San Francisco, where he came into contact with the early Jesus People revival.[13]

Walterman's contacts with the Swedish-American churches in Chicago and FGBM's support of evangelistic outreach to young drug addicts was the background of his participation in the AirLift to Stockholm in 1969. Walterman's visit and instructions helped Swedish Baptist and Pentecostal churches in Stockholm to begin a similar work as he was doing in San Francisco. Claes-Göran Bergstrand (1940–) was an evangelist in *Svenska Baptistsamfundet* (the Baptist denomination in Sweden) and experienced the baptism in the Spirit during the FGBM conference in Stockholm in 1969. With the support of Walterman, Bergstrand began an evangelistic outreach to young people in Stockholm and later evolved to become the major leader of the Charismatic renewal among Swedish Baptists in the 1970s.[14] Coming with FGBM's AirLift to Stockholm in 1969 was also Bill Lowery, who would become one FGBM's most important links to the Jesus People movement in the early 1970s. Lowery would lead several Jesus People groups to Sweden 1970–1975, sponsored by FGBM. Already in 1968, he had launched a small evangelistic ministry, *Christ Is The Answer* (CITA), which later would organize large evangelistic teams going to Scandinavia and other parts of Europe.[15]

In October 1970, Lowery came to Sweden for the second time and brought with him a group of American Jesus People. They took part in conferences organized by FGBM in Gothenburg and other parts of the country. After the end of the conference in Gothenburg, Lowery travelled on to Central Europe while parts of his group remained in the city and

12. *Michigan State News* 2:8 (August 5, 1966) 8.
13. Watson, *Directory of Narcotic Addiction Treatment Agencies*, 30.
14. Bergstrand, *Den karismatiska väckelsen*, 27.
15. Eskridge, *God's Forever Family*, 150, 153–55.

continued their evangelism. Among them were Jim Macinnes and Bill Bullard, who both came from the Chicago area. The evangelistic outreach of Macinnes and Bullard on the streets and in schools in Gothenburg was successful and a youth revival broke out, leading to the establishment of *Jesushuset,* the first "Jesus House" or Jesus People community in Sweden. It was organized in a former elementary school building and was initially supported by Arthur F. Johnson and by *Björngårdsvillan,* the ecumenical youth center of Gothenburg.[16] "Jesushuset" in Gothenburg quickly received wide and national publicity and became a model and an example for many other similar initiatives in different parts of Sweden.

The leaders of *Jesushuset* were invited to churches and conferences in Sweden and Norway and became major figures in evangelistic outreach. In 1971, *Sanningen* (The Truth), the first Christian counterculture newspaper in the country was launched by *Jesushuset.* In 1972, the members of *Jesushuset,* bought an old farm, *Jutatorpet,* about 150 km west of Gothenburg. *Jutatorpet* gradually became a national center for Charismatic renewal during the 1970s, with conferences, a publishing house, Bible school, and a base for different American Jesus People groups visiting Sweden. The conferences of *Jutatorpet* sometimes had up to 2,000 people attending, with speakers like Joseph Mattson-Bozé, Cookie Rodriguez, and David du Plessis. The visit of Joseph Mattsson-Bozé underlines the continued contacts between *Jutatorpet,* FGBM, and Scandinavian-American Pentecostals.[17] At approximately the same time, Faith Tabernacle in Chicago, for a shorter period (1973–74) housed the newly founded community *Jesus People USA.* Jesus People USA would develop into the longest surviving Jesus People community, with its permanent base in a ten-story building on 920, W. Wilson Abbey, in the heart of Uptown Chicago.[18]

Jutatorpet and FGBM were both non-denominational and parachurch organizations. In the later part of the 1970s, this began to arouse controversy in Sweden. New ecumenical charismatic communities were founded, new parachurch organizations for evangelistic and missional purposes started, and the older Swedish free churches became alarmed and felt threatened, worrying about losing young members to these

16. Aronson, "När svenskamerikanska affärsmän sponsrade kristna hippies," 187–89.

17. Aronson, "När svenskamerikanska affärsmän sponsrade kristna hippies," 188–91.

18. Eskridge, *God's Forever Family,* 151–53.

organizations. At the same time, controversies evolved around the so-called shepherdship teaching of Christian Growth Ministries in Fort Lauerdale (Derek Prince, Bob Mumford, Charles Simpson, Ern Baxter, and Don Basham). As a result, *Pingströrelsen* took an increasingly negative stand to all parachurch organizations and the teams and conferences of *Jutatorpet* were more or less boycotted. The Methodist Episcopal Church in Scandinavia took a different stand. Ole Borgen, the bishop of the church, opened the doors and the teams of *Jutatorpet* made a major contribution to revival and renewal in the Methodist churches of Norway and Sweden at this time. In the late 1970s, *Jutatorpet*, was dissolved and its members moved on to found new charismatic churches during the 1980s or became involved in the ministries of *Livets Ord* (Word of Life) in Uppsala (see below).[19]

Henry F. Carlson befriended and invited through FGBM an additional Jesus People group from Milwaukee and Chicago to Europe and the Nordic countries in 1972. This group was led by Jim Palosaari (1939–2011), who had a Finnish ancestry and who had been converted through the Jesus People Army (JPA) in Seattle in 1969. Palosaari was an entrepreneur and rock musician and founded a large Jesus People community in Milwaukee in 1971. Out of this community eventually *Jesus People USA* was founded when the Milwaukee community broke up in 1972. Another part of the Milwaukee community joined Bill Lowery's evangelistic ministry called *Christ Is The Answer* (CITA). Palosaari, together with the Christian rock group *The Sheep*, traveled with FGBM to Copenhagen for a conference and an evangelistic outreach during Easter 1972. Publicized through national television and newspapers, it made a huge impression on the Danish public, when the upper middleclass Scandinavian-American businessmen of FGBM and long haired American Christian hippies joined in a Pentecostal conference.[20] Palosaari and his team continued to Sweden and Finland and took part in great public events in both countries.

In Finland, Palosaari was invited to preach in the *Temppeliaukio Church*, in Helsinki. This Modernist type of church building was designed by architects and brothers Timo and Tuomo Suomalainen and opened in 1969. Built directly into solid rock, this church of the Evangelical

---

19. Aronson, "När svenskamerikanska affärsmän sponsrade kristna hippies," 188–89, 196–202.

20. Aronson, "När svenskamerikanska affärsmän sponsrade kristna hippies," 193–96.

Lutheran Church of Finland, is also known as *The Church of the Rock*. This got a particular meaning when *The Sheep* was offered to record its first album, *Karitsat Jeesus-rock*, in the same building! After this, Palosaari and his team were invited to England, where they eventually settled and where Palosaari would initiate a number of evangelistic initiatives involving popular music, for example the *Greenbelt Festival*.[21]

To sum up, FGBM's conferences and evangelistic outreaches in Sweden 1965–74 had a longstanding impact through initiating Charismatic renewal and a new era of evangelism in Scandinavian Protestant churches. It also led to conversions of a number of people who would pioneer new parachurch initiatives and organizations and new charismatic churches in Sweden in the 1970s and the 1980s. It also helped to give birth to new Christian popular music both in the Nordic countries and England. Most of FGBM's conferences and evangelistic outreaches during these years grew out of the Scandinavian-American Pentecostal network of FGBM and churches in Chicago and the American West Coast. This Scandinavian-American network was embedded within more general Transatlantic relations between Pentecostals in the United States and Scandinavia and was undergirded by a broad U.S.-friendly orientation in the Scandinavian countries after the end of the Second World War.[22]

Ulf Ekman, Livets Ord, and American Neo-Pentecostals, 1983–2014

Ulf Ekman was born in a working-class family in Gothenburg, Sweden in 1950 and grew up without any deeper contact with churches and the Christian faith, except for being baptized and confirmed in the Church of Sweden. In 1970 he was converted, shortly after a close friend of his, the later Lutheran reverend and Karl Barth-scholar, Axel W. Karlsson (1948–), had become a Pentecostal. Both of them were strongly influenced by American Jesus People who had come to Gothenburg through the conferences and evangelistic outreach of FGBM. Fall semester 1970, Ekman began academic studies at Uppsala University, graduating in 1978 with two BA-degrees, majoring in History and Theology. While studying, he was

---

21. Aronson, "När svenskamerikanska affärsmän sponsrade kristna hippies," 193–96; Eskridge, *God's Forever Family*, 202–5.

22. Aronson, "När svenskamerikanska affärsmän sponsrade kristna hippies," 171–73.

active in the Navigators, an American evangelical organization specialized in evangelism and Bible studies among university students.

Ekman was influenced by American-Dutch Reformed theology and also took part in Lutheran High-Church congregational life in Uppsala. Contacts with the Swedish Charismatic renewal began to grow after having married Birgitta Nilsson (1948–), daughter of Sten Nilsson (1915–2009), a Methodist minister and former missionary to India. Sten Nilsson was a co-worker of E. Stanley Jones (1884–1973) and leader of the European branch of the Ashram-movement and a frequent traveler to different types of Charismatic renewal conferences in the U.S. during the 1960s. In Sweden, his leadership of the Ashram-movement made it a platform for Charismatic renewal and Faith teaching during the 1970s. Sten Nilsson embraced the Faith teaching and introduced Ulf Ekman to different American Word of Faith ministries, especially Kenneth Copeland (1936–), Kenneth E. Hagin (1917–2003), and also Lester Sumrall (1913–96). After having completed his theological studies at Uppsala university, Ulf Ekman was ordained a Lutheran minister in the Church of Sweden in 1979. He worked as a university chaplain in Uppsala until 1981.[23] As a whole, Ulf Ekman's early formation, aside from his conversion, took place within a more general trans-Atlantic Evangelical and Pentecostal context. This would also characterize much of his ministry in Sweden during the following decades. But there was one Scandinavian-American contact during these early years of ministry, Harald Bredesen, while both of them at this stage belonged within the circles of Lutheran Charismatic renewal. Ekman was the interpreter for Bredesen during a preaching tour in Sweden in 1980.[24]

Ulf Ekman visited Rhema Bible Training Center, Tulsa, Oklahoma for the first time in 1980 and studied there 1981–82.[25] In 1983, Ulf Ekman and Sten Nilsson together founded *Livets Ord Bibelcenter* (Word of Life Bible Center), and *Församlingen Livets Ord* (Word of Life Church), a non-denominational charismatic Bible school, and a local church in Uppsala. The different branches of ministry were held together in *Stiftelsen Livets Ord* (Word of Life Foundation), which was the major legal entity. The Bible school was partly modeled on RBTC, focusing on Faith teaching combined with mainstream Evangelical and Pentecostal

---

23. See Torbjörn Aronson, "Ekman, Ulf" in *Brill's Encyclopedia of Global Pentecostalism*; Ekman, *Memoarer. Del 1*; Nilsson, *Ledd av Guds hand*.

24. Ekman, *Memoarer. Del 1*, 274–78.

25. Ekman, *Memoarer. Del 1*, 253–95.

theology. During its first six years, *Livets Ord Bibelcenter* was regularly visited by Bible teachers affiliated with RBTC in Tulsa or the Word of Faith-movement in the U. S., for example, Sandy Brown, Mark Brazee, Patsy Behrman (later Cameneti), Jim Kaseman, Sam Whaley, Kenneth Copeland, Jerry Savelle, and Bobbie Jean Merck.[26]

Församlingen Livets Ord grew to a megachurch during the 1990s, having 3,300 members in 2009. The enrollment in *Livets Ord Bibelcenter* soared to around 1,000 students per year in the first part of the 1990s, reaching a total of about 10,000 students in 2009. Several associations of Neo-Pentecostal churches in the former Soviet Union developed out of the missionary efforts of the church and its network of churches, organizations, and individuals in Scandinavia. The mission of *Livets Ord* in the former Soviet Union began in 1989 and the theology of Ulf Ekman became a shaping force in determining theology, practice, and social ethics of the Russian and Ukrainian churches that were founded and supported. Between 1989 and 1996 about 1,000 new local churches were planted and/or supported by *Livets Ord* and its network through conferences, missionaries, short-term volunteers, and Bible schools in different parts of the former Soviet Union.[27]

Ulf Ekman became a public figure of major importance in Sweden after having assailed the Swedish brand of socialism in 1985, the Swedish abortion law in the early 1990s, and founded one of the largest private Christian schools of the country in 1985. He also encouraged a stronger Christian involvement in Swedish politics, which in the long run has resulted in several members of the Swedish parliament and the present Swedish government (2022–) having their spiritual background and formation in the elementary school, Bible school, church, or *Livets Ord* movement.[28]

The close relationship between *Livets Ord* and Rhema (Tulsa) came to an abrupt ending in the late 1980s because of a schism within the network of Rhema (Tulsa) around the ministry of Sam and Jane Whaley. Sam Whaley had been part of the staff at RBTC in the early 1980s, but had left

---

26. Aronson, *Guds eld över Sverige*, 248–58; Ekman, *Memoarer. Del 2*, 33–124.

27. Aronson, *Guds eld över Sverige*, 259–327; Aronson, "Ryssland och några tidigare Sovjetrepubliker," 170–74.

28. Aronson, *Guds eld över Sverige*, 251–54, 265–72, 284–85, 295–97. Ekman, *Memoarer. Del 2*, 233–305. See Ekman, *Gud, staten och individen*; *Expressen*, September 18, 2013, *Aftonbladet*, March 16, 2015; *Dagens Nyheter*, September 19, 1998; *Aftonbladet*, January 13, 2013.

it and together with his wife operated a church of their own in Spindale, North Carolina.[29] Their practices concerning deliverance and loud prayer were not accepted by Kenneth Hagin and RBTC and they broke off their relations with the Whaley couple. In spite of this, Ulf Ekman continued his cooperation with the Whaleys, which eventually led to a strained relationship between Ekman and RBTC and an end to further cooperation between them. Ekman soon came to the same conclusion as Hagin and RBTC concerning Whaley's form of prayer and deliverance practices and terminated his contact with them in 1990. In 2001, Ulf Ekman visited Tulsa and met with Kenneth E. Hagin Jr. and reconciled with RBTC. Although this happened, it did not lead to any preachers from Rhema ministering at *Livets Ord Bibelcenter* in Uppsala again.[30]

By 1990, Ulf Ekman had already acquired an international renown of his own and independent extensive contacts with many of the major preachers and personalities of Anglo-American Pentecostalism. During the following decades the annual summer conference of his ministries in Uppsala, *Europakonferensen* (The Europe Conference), became a showcase of this. Among those ministering at the conference during these years were, for example, Benny Hinn, T. L. Osborn, R. W. Schambach, Richard Roberts, Bob Weiner, John Avanzini, Morris Cerullo, Rod Parsley, and Colin Urquhart.[31]

Important personal mentors for Ulf Ekman during the initial years of *Livets Ord* were, aside from Sten Nilsson, Lester Sumrall (1913–96) and Bror Spetz (1926–2007). Spetz was pastor of *Södermalmskyrkan* (now WAO Church), which was and is a major Pentecostal church in Stockholm. It became an early platform for the dissemination of the Faith teaching through Ulf Ekman. Lester Sumrall visited *Livets Ord* regularly between 1985 and 1996 and influenced Ekman in the area of mission and support of the State of Israel. Sumrall was one of the main speakers at the summer conferences of *Livets Ord* during these years.[32] Sumrall's support and mentoring of Ekman made headlines in *Pingströrelsen's* newspaper *Dagen* and probably strengthened Ekman's credentials with *Pingströrelsen*. Like Kenneth E. Hagin, Lester Sumrall had his Pentecostal background in the Assemblies of God, but associated himself with the healing evangelists during the 1950s and launched

29. *Albuquerque Journal*, February 26, 2017.
30. Ekman, *Memoarer. Del 2*. 100–109; *Dagen*, April 3, 2001.
31. Aronson, *Guds eld över Sverige*, 260–61.
32. Ekman, *Memoarer. Del 2*, 13–32, 106, 120–22.

an independent Pentecostal church in South Bend in the early 1960s. Sumrall had extensive Scandinavian-American contacts and had published several books in Swedish with the publishing house of Filadelfia church in Stockholm.[33] One of the books was a biography of the Swedish-American general superintendent of Assemblies of God 1949–52, Wesley Steelberg (1902–52).[34]

Pingströrelsen was initially skeptical of *Livets Ord* and became very critical in 1986, when several of its leading pastors questioned the theology of *Livets Ord* and Ulf Ekman because of the use of booklets by E.W. Kenyon in its Bible school. In some of these booklets there were references to Kenyon's teaching about the death of Christ, where Kenyon claimed that Christ had suffered in hell after the death on the cross, the so-called JDS-doctrine (Jesus Died Spiritually). This doctrine now was considered heretical by *Pingströrelsen*, who referred to this doctrine as a reason for breaking all forms of public relations with *Livets Ord*. Although Sten Nilsson espoused this doctrine, Ulf Ekman never did this either in speaking or printing. For this, and other reasons, during the second half of the 1990s the relations between *Livets Ord* and *Pingströrelsen* was gradually normalized. Lester Sumrall's involvement with Ulf Ekman and Livets Ord may have played a role in this. In 2006, Ulf Ekman finally got the opportunity to preach at Filadelfia Church in Stockholm.[35]

In 1994 Ekman founded the Livets Ord University (LOU), which became a fully accredited affiliation of the Oral Roberts University in 1997. Richard Roberts (1948–) visited *Livets Ord* in 1994 and from 1996 to 2014, teachers from Oral Roberts University regularly went to Uppsala to teach courses and examine students. Ulf Ekman was in 1996 elected as a member of the board of regents of ORU. Through LOU, theological education was supplied for pastors in the new churches in Scandinavia, Central Europe, and former Soviet Union.[36]

Between 2004 and 2014, Ulf Ekman developed increasingly close contacts with the Catholic Charismatic renewal and the Roman

---

33. Aronson, *Maranata! Väckelse och samhällsförändring 1960 tal till 1990 tal*, 124–25; *Voice of Healing*, August 1955, 2, 8. See Strang, "Sumrall, Lester Frank," in *The New International Dictionary of Pentecostal and Charismatic Movements*.

34. Sumrall, *Svenskättlingen som blev pingstledare i USA*. The other books were Sumrall, *Med en moders kärlek* and *Handbok för människofiskare*.

35. Aronson, "Ekman, Ulf."

36. Aronson, *Guds eld över Sverige*, 312–13; Ekman, *Memoarer. Del 2*, 263–85. Cf. Aronson, "Ryssland och några tidigare Sovjetrepubliker," 170–174; *Dagen*, February 11, 2007; *Världen idag* (*VI*), January 21, 2010; *VI*, February 11, 2014.

Catholic Church in general, leading to his conversion to this church in 2014. He left the role as senior pastor of *Församlingen Livets Ord* in 2013 and the ministry board in 2014. After conversion and retirement, Ulf Ekman has continued his ministry as an author and speaker but at a considerably slower pace, while being a Catholic layman.[37] As a result of its emphasis on missions, *Livets Ord*'s international network comprised about 1,500 churches in the former Soviet Union, East and Central Europe, Central Asia, and Scandinavia around 2010. Ekman's conversion to Catholicism threw his church and its national and international networks into turmoil and confusion. After a period of reconstruction, Word of Life International consists at present of about 800 local churches in Europe and former Soviet Union.[38]

To conclude, Ulf Ekman and *Livets Ord* became major actors in the religious and political landscape of Sweden from the middle of the 1980s to the middle of the 2010s. At the same time, *Livets Ord* became a platform for disseminating different aspects of American Neo-Pentecostalism in Sweden. Many of the initiatives of Ulf Ekman and *Livets Ord* were inspired or anchored in close cooperation with different American ministries, preachers, churches, and other institutions. This cooperation had mainly a trans-Atlantic character, although Scandinavian-American contacts occasionally would surface.

John Wimber and Sweden: Visits and Repercussions, 1982–1997

John Wimber was converted in 1963 and ordained as a Quaker minister after theological studies at Azusa Pacific College in California. His success as a church leader paved the way for an appointment to founding director of the Department of Church Growth at the Charles E. Fuller Institute of Evangelism and Church Growth 1974–1978. This institute was founded by the Fuller Theological Seminary and the Fuller Evangelistic Association. During this period, Wimber left the Quakers after having been asked not to emphasize the gifts of the Spirit in teaching and

---

37. Ekman and Ekman, *Den stora upptäckten*. His theological development leading to the conversion is well documented in Ekman, *Andliga Rötter* and Ekman, *Urgamla stigar*.

38. Aronson, "Swedish Mission and the Growth of Neo-Pentecostal Churches in Russia"; Aronson, "Neopentekostal mission," 94–96; Aronson, "Ryssland och några tidigare Sovjetrepubliker," 170–74.

practice. Instead, he began forming a house church, which eventually would become the Vineyard Christian Fellowship (VCF) of Anaheim in 1982. Wimber's house church was initially a member of Calvary Chapel, but left due to differences in theology and practice concerning the gifts of the Spirit. Wimber's church joined instead the Vineyard movement that had been founded by Norwegian-American Kenn Gulliksen (1945–) in the middle of the 1970s in the Los Angeles area. Gulliksen had started a network of Bible study groups in Beverly Hills in 1975, and these grew into churches. In 1982, eight churches founded the Association of Vineyard Churches and Gulliksen turned over the churches under his oversight to Wimber. Already, this same year, that is in 1982, the first team from Vineyard visited Sweden. This was in fact an initiative of a Swedish-American couple, Brent (1945–93) and Happy Rue, that had an active role in the Vineyard movement in its early stages. Brent Rue had a Catholic upbringing but come to a personal faith in Christ in 1973. Happy Rue was born Gladys Winblad and came from a Swedish-American family that had emigrated to the US when she was a small child. In 1975, they joined one of the churches Kenn Gulliksen had started and the same year they also did their first mission trip to Sweden. In 1977, Gulliksen asked Brent and Happy Rue to pastor a Vineyard church in Lancaster, California, which they did. Happy Rue felt a calling to bring Vineyard to her home country and this was accomplished for the first time in 1982, after a prophecy by Lonnic Frisbee (1949–93) that same year. She became part of a Vineyard team that visited several churches belonging to Svenska Baptistsamfundet (The Swedish Baptist Denomination), which had been touched by the Charismatic renewal. It was also from the Swedish Baptists that several of the later leaders of the Swedish branch of the Vineyard movement would come. The Vineyard team visiting Sweden in 1982 also helped prepare the way for John Wimber's first tour to Sweden in 1983.[39]

At that time, the name of John Wimber was becoming known among people in Europe that had been awakened by the Charismatic renewal. Wimber now was invited to speak at international charismatic conferences with a focus on what he called "Power Evangelism" and healing through the power of the Holy Spirit. John Wimber's first visit to Sweden in late Summer 1983 was organized by Baptist and Pentecostal churches in Gothenburg and Stockholm. In Gothenburg, the oldest

---

39. Freij, *Vinrankan*, 6–13.

Baptist church of the city, *Tabernaklet* (The Tabernacle), opened its door for a three-day seminar on healing, and in Stockholm, *Filadelfia church* housed major teaching sessions on the same subject by Wimber. The teaching sessions in Gothenburg were of seminal importance for the formation of an organized Charismatic renewal movement within Church of Sweden. A number of Lutheran ministers with close ties to the bishop of Gothenburg, Bertil Gärtner, participated and later in the Fall of 1983, *Referensgruppen för Andlig Förnyelse i Svenska kyrkan* (Reference group for spiritual renewal in the Church of Sweden) was founded. In 1989, the organization changed its name to *Oasrörelsen* (The Oasis Movement), and is to this day the major organization for Lutheran Charismatic renewal in the country.[40] Wimber's teaching on healing and the gifts of the Spirit became a strong influence on the practices of the movement, especially after Wimber's second and third visits to Sweden in 1988 and 1990 (see below).

Wimber's teaching session in Filadelfia Church also had a long-term impact on *Pingströrelsen*. In 1986 and 1987, two of Wimber's major books, *Power Evangelism* (1986) and *Power Healing* (1987) were translated to Swedish and published by the book club of *Pingströrelsen*, *Den kristna bokringen* (The Christian Book Circle), and provided basic teaching for a renewal of the gifts of the Spirit.[41]

In 1986, John Wimber was one of the main speakers at a Charismatic renewal conference in Birmingham, *Acts' 86*, where a Swedish group led by Bertil Gärtner participated. Gärtner approached Wimber directly and asked him to consider an invitation to Sweden in order to boost the Charismatic renewal, which, according to his estimate had stagnated. Gärtner had the backing of other churches and organization and Wimber responded positively to the request. This led to a leaders' conference in Gothenburg in May 1988 with *Evangelism in the Power of the Holy Spirit* as its theme. The conference was organized by the Lutheran renewal organizations in Sweden, Norway, Denmark, and Finland but had also a backing from charismatics in the Swedish Baptist Denomination. Bertil Gärtner was the official host of the conference, which made it a major ecclesial event. This aroused criticism from groups of liberal ministers in the Church of Sweden, who were confronted by Wimber, challenging them to accept the authority of Scripture and at the same time to do

40. Freij, *Vinrankan*, 13–23.
41. Wimber, *Övernaturligt: Om under och tecken i evangelisationen*; Wimber, *Helandets kraft*.

away with a cessationist theology. Around 2,000 leaders from the Nordic countries participated and among them also Hans Sundberg, who would be the pastor of the first Vineyard church in Sweden in 1992. Hans Sundberg was a pastor in *Svenska Baptistsamfundet* and had recently received a doctoral degree in systematic theology (1986) at Uppsala University. Along with Wimber, several other leaders of the Vineyard movement ministered: Brent Rue, Richard Foster, Dennis Pedersen, Bob McGee, and Ken Blue.[42] More or less directly after the ending of the leaders' conference in 1988, the preparations for a major popular and ecumenical conference in Gothenburg began. It was arranged for July 4–8, 1990, and became a peak and final breakthrough for Wimber's personal mission to the Nordic countries. *Norden för Kristus* (The Nordic Countries for Christ) was the theme of the conference and behind the conference stood a multinational ecumenical committee headed by bishop Bertil Gärtner. The purpose of the conference was to comfort, heal, equip, and empower the people of God. More than 7,000 people came to the conference, which was housed in the sports arena *Scandinavium*. Several bishops of the Church of Sweden participated in the conference. John Wimber was the main speaker but had also brought with him the prophet Paul Cain. Cain's prophetic word to Hans and Lotta Sundberg, the future leader couple of Vineyard Nordic, was a major source of inspiration for the start of the first Vineyard church in Sweden in 1993.[43]

Two additional large leaders' conferences were organized, in 1990 in Stockholm (with Brent Rue and Rick Joyner as main speakers), and in 1991 also in Stockholm with Wimber and Paul Cain (*Stockholm 91*). The conferences helped directly to prepare the way for the launching of a movement of Vineyard churches in Sweden, although the conferences had an explicit ecumenical profile. A new church plant was organized in Stockholm in 1992 under the leadership of Hans Sundberg, Hans Johansson, and Ted Jeans. Hans Johansson was a pastor in *Örebromissionen* (The Örebro Mission) a smaller Swedish holiness Baptist denomination. Ted Jeans was an American pastor married to a Swedish wife, Siv, who also became part of the team of leaders of the new church plant.[44] In 1993,

---

42. Freij, *Vinrankan*, 26–34; Sundberg, "Konferenser som plöjde mark i svensk kristenhet."

43. Freij, *Vinrankan*, 35–46; Sundberg, "Konferenser som plöjde mark i svensk kristenhet."

44. Freij, *Vinrankan*, 47–51, 57–69; Hans Sundberg, "Vineyard-profeter: Sveriges kristna är andliga vikingar," *VI*, July 22, 2020; Hans Sundberg, "Stockholm Vineyard

John Wimber informed Hans Sundberg that the new church plant was received as a member of the Association of Vineyard Churches. This was the beginning of the Vineyard movement in Sweden and Vineyard Nordic.[45]

This is not the place to write the full history of Vineyard in Sweden or Vineyard Nordic. In 2023, Vineyard celebrated its thirtieth anniversary in Sweden. Stockholm Vineyard, that became the new name of the first church plant in 1993, experienced a major revival in 1994–97. The revival was linked to the Toronto Blessing and brought its expressions to Sweden, with thousands of people taking part in renewal services at Stockholm Vineyard these years. The revival went on in different forms for a couple of years and led to renewal in different churches, the start of several new Vineyard churches in Sweden and other Nordic countries, and missionaries being sent out to Siberia and other parts of the world. In 1998, Vineyard Nordic was founded, which today consists of thirty churches in the Nordic countries. Vineyard did not become a big movement in Sweden or in the other Nordic countries but its influence has been considerable, through its forms of worship, its songs, its summer camp, and as a permanent platform for John Wimber's theology.[46]

In the perspective of this article, the role of John Wimber and the Vineyard movement in Sweden is primarily a result of trans-Atlantic relations. But important Scandinavian-American relations have continued to exist and play a role within the broader Pentecostal pattern of trans-Atlantic relations. Kenn Gulliksen and Brent and Happy Rue had a Scandinavian-American background and played pivotal roles in establishing the Vineyard movement in the United States and Sweden.

Conclusion

The Charismatic Renewal and the Jesus People movement arrived and began to flourish in Sweden through the Scandinavian-American links provided by FGBM. One of the converts from FGBMs evangelistic outreaches through the American Jesus People was Ulf Ekman. He became the most important Neo-Pentecostal leader in Sweden from

---

etableras och får egen lokal," *VI*, July 29, 2020.

45. Hans Sundberg, "Stockholm Vineyard startar," *VI*, July 28, 2020.

46. Hans Sundberg, "Torontovälsignelsen," *VI*, August 4, 2020; August 5, 2020. Cf. Hans Sundberg, "Andlig förnyelse spred sig från Sverige till andra länder," *VI*, August 11, 2020; Hans Sundberg, "Förnyelse och väckelse skapar både glädje och motstånd," *VI*, August 19, 2020.

the middle of the 1980s until he became a Catholic in 2014. From the mid 1980s to 2014, Ulf Ekman and *Livets Ord* in Uppsala were very much at the center of Neo-Pentecostalism in Sweden through the Bible school, conferences, college, Christian school, network of churches, missions work, etc. Ulf Ekman became part of a trans-Atlantic network through Kenneth E. Hagin and Rhema Bible Training Center in Tulsa, Oklahoma in 1981–82, but this was early on replaced by other contacts, especially by Lester Sumrall and his church and ministries located in South Bend, Indiana, and by Richard Roberts and Oral Roberts University, Tulsa, Oklahoma. Among these, only Lester Sumrall had an earlier relationship to Classical Pentecostalism in Sweden, which included Scandinavian-American Pentecostals in the United States. John Wimber came to Sweden mainly as a result of the growing trans-Atlantic relations between Classic Pentecostals and Neo-Pentecostals in Sweden and the U.S. but there were also individual examples of Scandinavian-American contacts playing a major role. Wimber's visits to Sweden in 1983, 1988, 1990 and 1991 paved the way for Vineyard Nordic and contributed profoundly to a renewal of spiritual gifts in Classical Pentecostal churches, among Swedish Baptists and in the Charismatic renewal movement in the Church of Sweden.

Bibliography

Primary Sources

NEWSPAPERS

Aftonbladet, Stockholm, Sweden, 1830–
Albuquerque Journal, Albuquerque, NM, 1880–
Christianity Today, Carol Stream, IL, 1956–
Dagen, Stockholm, Sweden, 1945–
Dagens Nyheter, Stockholm, Sweden, 1864–
Expressen, Sweden, Stockholm, 1944–
Michigan State News, East Lansing, MI, 1962–
The Voice (*Full Gospel Men's Voice*), Los Angeles, 1952–
The Voice of Healing, Shreveport, LA, 1948–1955
Världen idag (*VI*), Jönköping, Sweden, 2001–

Secondary Sources

Aronson, Torbjörn. "Ekman, Ulf." In *Brill's Encyclopedia of Global Pentecostalism.* edited by Michael Wilkinson. Leiden: Brill, 2021.

———. *Guds eld över Sverige: Svensk väckelsehistoria efter 1945.* Uppsala: Livets Ords Förlag, 2005.

———. *Maranata! Väckelse och samhällsförändring 1960 tal till 1990 tal.* Uppsala: EFS Budbäraren, 2021.

———. "När svenskamerikanska affärsmän sponsrade kristna hippies. Full Gospel Business Men och det amerikanska Jesusfolkets resor till Sverige 1969–1974." In *Varför reste Lewi Pethrus just till Chicago? Relationer mellan Sverige och USA inom ramen för pentekostalismen,* edited by Jan-Åke Alvarsson, 165–212165–212. Skellefteå, Sweden: Artos, 2019.

———. "Neopentekostal mission." In *Svensk mission och kyrkorna som växte fram,* edited by Klas Lundström et al., 94–96. Skellefteå, Sweden: Artos, 2021.

———. "Swedish Mission and the Growth of Neo-Pentecostal Churches in Russia." *Religion in Eastern Europe* 41 (2011) 33–40.

Bergstrand, Claes-Göran. *Den karismatiska väckelsen: Vad hände?* Handen, Sweden: XpMedia, 2018.

Ekman, Ulf. *Andliga Rötter.* Uppsala: Livets Ords Förlag, 2011.

———. *Gud, staten och individen.* Uppsala: Livets Ords förlag, 1987.

———. *Memoarer. Del 1. De första stegen 1950–1983.* Uppsala: Livets Ords Förlag, 2011.

———. *Memoarer. Del 2. I medvind och motvind 1983–1994.* Uppsala: Livets Ords Förlag, 2013.

———. *Urgamla stigar.* Uppsala: Keryx Förlag, 2014.

Ekman, Ulf, and Birgitta Ekman. *Den stora upptäckten. Vår väg till Katolska kyrkan.* Ängelholm: Catholica, 2015.

Eskridge, Larry. *God's Forever Family. The Jesus People Movement in America.* Oxford: Oxford University Press, 2013.

Freij, Torbjörn. *Vinrankan. Vineyards 30 (40) år i Sverige.* Sollentuna: Eagle Perspective, 2022.

Harrell, D. E. *All Things Are Possible. The Healing and Charismatic Revivals in Modern America.* Bloomington: Indiana University Press, 1979.

Lundström, Klas, et al., eds. *Svensk mission och kyrkorna som växte fram.* Skellefteå, Sweden: Artos, 2021.

Malmström, Nils. "Han arbetar efter amerikanska metoder: Joseph Mattsson-Boze, ett liv i skärningspunkten mellan amerikansk och svensk pingströrelse." In *Varför reste Lewi Pethrus just till Chicago? Relationer mellan Sverige och USA inom ramen för pentekostalismen,* edited by Jan-Åke Alvarsson, 81–137. Skellefteå: Artos, 2019.

Myrin, Ingmar. *Sänd till världsledarna.* Örebro: Evangeliipress, 1983.

Nilsson, Sten. *Ledd av Guds hand. Memoarer.* Uppsala: Livets Ords Förlag, 1986.

Shemeth, Scott. "Erickson, Clifton O." In *The New International Dictionary of Pentecostal and Charismatic Movements,* edited by Stanley M. Burgess and Eduard M. van der Maas. Grand Rapids: Zondervan, 2002. https://healingandrevival.com/BioCOErickson.htm.

Strang, Steven. "Sumrall, Lester Frank." In *The New International Dictionary of Pentecostal and Charismatic Movements,* edited by Stanley M. Burgess and Eduard

M. van der Maas. Grand Rapids: Zondervan, 2002. https://healingandrevival.com/BioCOErickson.htm.

Sumrall, Lester. *Svenskättlingen som blev pingstledare i USA. En bok om W. R. Steelberg.* Stockholm: Normans Förlag, 1959.

Watson, Deena. *Directory of Narcotic Addiction Treatment Agencies in the United States.* Fort Worth: Texas Christian University, 1970.

Wimber, John. *Helandets kraft.* Stockholm: Den Kristna Bokringen, 1987.

———. *Övernaturligt—om under och tecken i evangelisationen.* Stockholm: Den Kristna Bokringen, 1986.

Afterword

David Bundy

AMERICAN HISTORY AND AMERICAN Pentecostal history have often been viewed as English language projects. Books devoted to the development of Pentecostal Christianity in the world have too frequently been without mention of the Nordic, or other non-USA contributions. This has added to the worldwide perception that Pentecostalism is an American invention that sold well in the marketplace of religion.

Contributions of this Volume

This volume, reflecting the work of an international team of scholars, addresses one aspect of Pentecostal identity, focusing on Scandinavian presence in, and contributions to, the formation of Pentecostalism in North America. In doing this they have used and made available documentation of Scandinavian-American Pentecostalism that has seldom been used including archival collections and rare periodicals. Individuals known only in lists of names have been rescued from oblivion using genealogical data and newspaper files in diverse languages.

In doing so, these scholars have again demonstrated the inadequacy of the previous narratives of Pentecostal origins and developments in the USA. The binary USA race-oriented Black and/or Anglo-White theories of Pentecostal origins are no longer tenable. Voices have spoken contesting the dominant Anglophone theories, highlighting Russian, Ukrainian,

Bulgarian, and diverse Hispanic contributions, but these have not yet made much of a difference in the meta narrative.[1]

Despite the slow evolution of the historiography, this volume adds support to the contentions of earlier scholars who have worked on the non-English materials: any conception of Pentecostal foundational identity in the USA, Canada, and beyond, must reflect the diversity of the sources, participants, and influences. Simplicity in Pentecostal historiography is not a virtue.

The development of significant collections of European (and Asian and African) language publications and oral histories in the USA and around the world documenting Pentecostalism, allows for a more accurate and complex narrative of Pentecostalism. As the narrative is developed, it will also be important to think about what was lost to American Pentecostalism as political pressures and pragmatic considerations led to the suppression of non-English European languages during and after World War II. This volume has implications for other ethnic traditions as well. Besides Scandinavian-Americans, other groups need to reclaim their histories in American and worldwide Pentecostal history.

These histories cannot be understood without including the people and their texts who swelled (and swell) the ranks of rolling waves of immigration and reverse migration. A "New Frontier" for USA (and Canadian) Pentecostal studies remains the identification, collection, and interpretation of sources related to non-Anglophone contributions. It discredits the narrative of an Anglophone-origins narrative into which persons of other linguistic and religious traditions were sucked in. The Flower Pentecostal Heritage Center in Springfield, Missouri, under the leadership of Darrin Rodgers, has worked assiduously and creatively to document diverse aspects of Pentecostalism, and has supported extensively this book project.

In addition to the related areas of World Pentecostal historiography and documentation, this project is a contribution to at least three other areas of research: (1) migration; (2) transatlantic religion and

---

1. Dony K. Donev, *The Life and Ministry of Rev. Ivan Voronaev: Now with a Special Addition of the (Un)Forgotten Story of the Voronaev Children* (n.p.: Spasen, 2011); Gastón Espinosa, "'El Azteca:' Francisco Olazábal and Latino Pentecostal Charisma, Power, and Healing in the Borderlands," *Journal of the American Academy of Religion* 67 (1999) 597–616; and, idem, *William J. Seymour and Origins of Global Pentecostalism* (Durham, NC: Duke University Press, 2014); Daniel Ramirez, *Migrating Faith: Pentecostalism in the United States and Mexico in the Twentieth Century* (Chapel Hill, NC: University of North Carolina Press, 2015).

Scandinavian diaspora studies; and, (3) religion in the USA during the Progressive Era.

Migration Studies

The Scandinavian data on immigration patterns to the USA and the return migration back to Scandinavia are particularly well documented for the late nineteenth and early twentieth centuries.[2] While representation of religious affiliations of the migrants based on religious emigration interviews with Scandinavian clergy may be misleading given the different understandings of ecclesiology and religious networks on all sides of the discussions, the data provides a beginning basis for research. The work of Jon Gjerde suggested that a primary goal of immigrants to America was to recreate their village and agriculturally based lives, although seeking to amend the contextual social structures, in the Midwest and Canada.[3] Charles W. Estus, Sr. and John F. McClymer discussed the economic migration to New England and the Americanization pressures applied by Scandinavian-American political and business leaders on immigrants, as well as their support for diverse respectable churches.[4] Bergland and Lahram documented the evolving roles of Norwegian women, with minimal attention to religion and with no attention to Pietist, Radical Holiness Scandinavian networks or organizations.[5] The studies in this volume suggest that the work of the earlier scholars on migration may require rethinking with regard to religious participation of immigrants and their evolving participation, sometimes in multiple networks.[6]

2. Hans Norman and Harald Runblom, *Transatlantic Connections: Nordic Migration to the New World after 1800* (Minneapolis: University of Minnesota Press, 1976).

3. Jon Gjerde, *From Peasants to Farmers: The Migration from Balestrand, Norway to the Upper Middle West* (Cambridge: Cambridge University Press, 1985).

4. Charles W. Estus, Sr. and John F. McClymer, *Gå till Amerika: The Swedish Creation of an Ethnic Identity in Worcester, Massachusetts* (Worcester, MA: Worcester Historical Museum, 1994).

5. Betty A. Bergland and Lori Ann Lahram, *Norwegian American Women: Migration, Communities, and Identities* (St. Paul, MN: Minnesota Historical Society, 2011). Compare: J. Augestad, "Eit norsk-amerikansk skuleprosjekt i haugiansk vekkingstradisjon," in *Åndelige strømninger mellom Norge og Amerika i emigrantperioden: Foredrag fra seminar 3. juli 2004 ved Vestnorsk utvandringssenter, Sletta, Radøy*, edited by Jenny Marie Helland and Rolf Svellingen (Bergen: NLA-forlag, 2005), 80–95.

6. See, for example also D. Nygård, "Religionsfrihet og emigrasjon: idehistorisk og religionspolitisk perspektiv på emigrasjonen," in *Åndelige strømninger mellom Norge og Amerika i emigrantperioden*, 51–62.

It is important that Pentecostals were not the first immigrants or reverse immigrants: Mormons, Methodists, Baptists, and other Free Church believers migrated, frustrating mission executives who could not understand why their denominations were not growing in the Nordic countries despite foreign financial support.[7] Large numbers of Scandinavian state church members, who in North America self-identified primarily as Lutherans, also made the transatlantic voyage.[8]

The reverse migration was significant: Nugent's analysis suggests that the average annual rate of return of former emigrants to Scandinavia (1896–1914) was 19.0%.[9] Well known Scandinavians who were part of Pietist and/or Radical Holiness and/or Pentecostal Networks became reverse immigrants to Scandinavia. Examples include John Ongman (Baptist, Radical Holiness, Baptist-Pentecostal), Albert Lunde (Salvation Army, influenced by D. L. Moody and G. Campbell Morgan), and Sigbjørn Olsen Modalsli, who after a trip from Norway to the USA, about which little is known, partnered with reverse migrant Albert Lunde, and Ludvig Hope, who would later become a reverse migrant, in ministry in Norway.[10] Andrew Johnson-Ek, Azusa Street Mission participant and missionary to Scandinavia, China, and Austria, may never have returned to the USA after 1906.[11] All these individuals became important religious

---

7. William Mulder, *Homeward to Zion: The Mormon Migration from Scandinavia* (Minneapolis: University of Minnesota Press, 2000); Arlow W. Andersen, *The Salt of the Earth: History of Norwegian-Danish Methodism in America* (Nashville: Parthenon Press for the Norwegian-Danish Methodist Historical Society, 1962).

8. See for example: Dag Blanck, *The Creation of an Ethnic Identity: Being Swedish American in the Augustana Synod, 1860-1917* (Carbondale: Southern Illinois Press, 2006); V. D. Anderson, "The Lutheran Church among Norwegian-American Immigrants and Their Descendants: A Religious Heritage Transplanted from Norway," in *Åndelige strømninger mellom Norge og Amerika i emigrantperioden*, 9–20.

9. Walter Nugent, *Crossings: The Great Transatlantic Migrations, 1870-1914* (Bloomington, IN: Indiana University Press, 1992), 55-62.

10. John Magnusson, *John Ongman, en levnadsteckning* (Örebro: Örebro Missionsförening Förlag, 1932); M. Lunde, *Albert Lunde: Minner fra hans liv* (Oslo: Aschehoug, 1939); A. Prøis, *Vekkelsens budbringere gjennom hundre år* (Oslo: Lunde, 1995); Ingulf Diesen, "Om Albert Lunde: ein "heimatkomen" emigrant med nedslag i Norsk vekkelsestradisjon," in *Åndelige strømninger mellom Norge og Amerika i emigrantperioden*; Sigbjørn Olsen Modalsli, *Fra vækkelse i Norge: Taler af S. O. Modalsli* (Kristiania: Johannes Bjørnstads Forlag, n.d.), 9–14; and, O. J. Jensen, "Ludvig Hope som formidler av amerikanske impulser i den norske lekmannsbevegelse," in *Åndelige strømninger mellom Norge og Amerika i emigrantperioden*, 71–75.

11. David Bundy, *Visions of Apostolic Mission: Scandinavian Pentecostal Mission to 1935* (Uppsala: Uppsala Universitet, 2009), 128, 174, 181–86, 247–54, 404–13; Jan-Åke Alvarsson, *Om Pingströrelsen ... Essäer, översikter och analyser* (Skellefteå: Artos, 2014).

leaders in Scandinavia. Famously the already influential Lewi Pethrus (Baptist, influences of Salvation Army, Radical Holiness, Pentecostal, immigrant-reverse immigrant) moved to and from the USA.[12] The intense communication between Scandinavia and North America during the period of most intense migration, 1870-1914, and its significance for Scandinavian and North American cultures remains a desideratum for research.[13] The studies in this volume suggest that significant numbers of Scandinavians found religious affinity within the Pietist, Radical Holiness, and Pentecostal networks as well as among other heirs of Pietism.

In addition to the reverse migration, there was what one might call "pass-through" migration. "Pass-through" migration was characteristic of many of the missionaries studied in this volume, and of a yet unknown number of Pentecostal missionaries around the world. Rakel Ystebø Alegre and I have studied Berger N. Johnsen who came to the USA as a worker-immigrant, became Pentecostal, stayed briefly in a school/commune in Alliance, Ohio, and went to Argentina as a missionary. He appears never to have become a USA citizen, although he visited New York on his return trips to Norway to raise funds, which he also did by communicating with diverse networks and their periodicals in the USA and Norway.[14]

Transatlantic Religion

The studies in the volume also make important contributions to trans-Atlantic religion. Most trans-Atlantic research on religion, especially related to revivalistic traditions, has focused on the USA and UK. This work makes clear that that future analysis must include the Scandinavian

---

12. Jan-Åke Alvarsson, ed. *Varför Reste Lewi Pethrus Just Till Chicago?: Relationer mellan Sverige och USA inom ramen för Pentekostalismen* (Skellefteå: Artos & Norma, 2019).

13. See for example: O. Nilsen, "Hvorledes åndelige impulser fra Amerika har påvirket kristenlivet i Norge," in *Åndelige strømninger mellom Norge og Amerika i emigrantperioden*, 63–70.

14. Bundy, *Visions of Apostolic Mission*, 98, 237, 239–40, 345–50, 444; Rakel Agathe Ystebø, "La Misión Pentecostal en Embarcación: Conversiones y cambios socio-culturales entre los indígenas afectados por la misión de Berger Johnsen (1916-1945)," (Thesis, Estudios Latinoamericano, Facultad de Humanidades, Universidad Nacional de San Martín, Buenos Aires, 2010). David Bundy, "Berger N. Johnson: Un Pietista Luterano y las redes del movimiento radical de santidad y misión en Argentina," *Hechos* 5 (June 2023) 49–77.

North-American routes of influence as well. As in the USA-UK exchange, the impact of cultural influences was bi-directional.

Progressive Era and New Era Religion

Immigration to the USA and Canada expanded radically during the Progressive Era (c. 1896–1919) and began to slow during the New Era (1919–1929). Radical Holiness and Pentecostal networks grew rapidly during these periods, although not as rapidly as in the "Americanized" post-World War II era. While the work cited above by Gjerde, Norman and Runblom, Estus and McClymer, as well as Bergland and Lahram suggest economic and cultural components were paramount, the essays of this volume suggest that religion must be considered more fully as a component of the development of Scandinavian culture and influence in the North American contexts. The studies presented here may be considered by some to be quirks, almost anecdotal, rather than trends, but there is sufficient evidence presented to suggest that a more quantitative study of religious participation in Scandinavian Pietist, Radical Holiness, and Pentecostal communities may be worth undertaking.

Future Avenues of Research

Any ground-breaking scholarly undertaking cannot address all significant issues and questions raised in the initial examination of previously neglected communities. There is only space here to list a series of such items that may be worth exploring which have arisen in the mind of this writer through interaction with this book.

- Finland, Denmark, and Iceland were smaller contributors to the Nordic diaspora. The impact on North American and World Pentecostalism of these smaller Pentecostal churches remains important for future study, both as to why they remained less important in their original and diaspora contexts, albeit with important regional influences in the world. It would be valuable to examine the diachronic shifts of influence and the implications of them on the development of World Christianity.

- Attention should be given to quantitative and cultural mapping religious participation of emigrants from Scandinavia, with attention to Pietist streams in the Scandinavian state churches, Pietistic free churches of Scandinavian origin, Baptist, Methodist, Methodist Holiness, Radical Holiness, and LDS denominations and networks to see if there are correlations with religious participation of immigrants from these traditions across the broader landscape of North American Christianity before 1906. It will be quite illuminating in regards to Pentecostal origins to map the religious background of as many converts to Pentecostalism as can be reliably documented.

- The current work could not include all nodes of Scandinavian Radical Holiness and Pentecostal networks in the USA. In this and earlier research, the important centers of Scandinavian revivalist networks have been noted in the New York City area, Chicago, Indianapolis, Fort Wayne, Indiana, Alliance, Ohio, Spokane, and Seattle. There are others throughout the USA and Canada, as well as smaller Scandinavian immigrant communities in Brazil, Argentina, and Chile.

- Possible correlations of regional identities of persons and their post-immigration goals, expectations, and religious participation in North America needs examination. Is the research of Jon Gjerde on emigrants from Balestrand, Norway, mentioned above, replicable? Related to this would be an examination of the social class and educational levels of immigrants who became adherents of revivalist networks in Scandinavia and/or in North America.

- A thorough study of Scandinavian-American missions is a desideratum. Important to this study would be patterns of mission funding and the question of how Scandinavian immigrants in the USA understood their relationships with their original and new countries. There is some evidence that many Scandinavian-Americans did not quickly differentiate their two identities and may have resisted doing so. This double identity is suggested in the fund-raising efforts by missionaries in multiple countries.

This volume makes many contributions, in its historiographical agenda and sources identified, as well as in the implicit questions for future research. Its focus on the Scandinavian-American sources and historiographical questions will serve as a model for similar efforts. This work "changes the game" for Pentecostal studies in North America and in other areas where Pentecostal evangelists and missionaries of Scandinavian and Scandinavian-American identity have been active. The editors and authors are to be congratulated for an original and provocative contribution to scholarship.

Appendix
Successor Associations in America Today

THE MOVEMENT OF SCANDINAVIAN-AMERICAN Pentecostals, beginning with the Azusa Street revival in Los Angeles in 1906, as the rallying point of the Pentecostal movement, expanded to other regions of the United States and Canada. In 1914, the General Council of the Assemblies of God (AG) of Springfield, Missouri, was established. A few Scandinavian immigrant preachers and missionaries joined this ministerial association. In 1918, a separate group of Scandinavian immigrants formed the Scandinavian Assemblies of God (SAG), and in 1922, another group, comprised mostly of Scandinavian immigrants, formed the Independent Assemblies of God (IAG).[1] During these early years, some of the newly-formed congregations, for example, supported the missionary work of Gunnar Vingren and Daniel Berg who founded the Assembleias de Deus (Assemblies of God) of Brazil.

The Scandinavian Assemblies of God (SAG) and Independent Assemblies of God (IAG) merged in 1935 to become the Independent Assemblies of God (IAG non-incorporated). However, during the second half of the twentieth century, the IAG split into three associations of ministers and churches that continue today. Therefore, these three bodies, along with Scandinavian-founded congregations of the Assemblies of God (AG), have roots in Scandinavian-American Pentecostalism. The complex history of these associations (with similar names) is illustrated in the following diagram. The four associations which continue today are highlighted in bold.

---

1. Ron Rhodes, *The Complete Guide to Christian Denominations: Understanding the History, Beliefs, and Differences* (Eugene, OR: Harvest House, 2015), 357.

APPENDIX—SUCCESSOR ASSOCIATIONS IN AMERICA TODAY

Diagram
Associations of Scandinavian-American Pentecostals

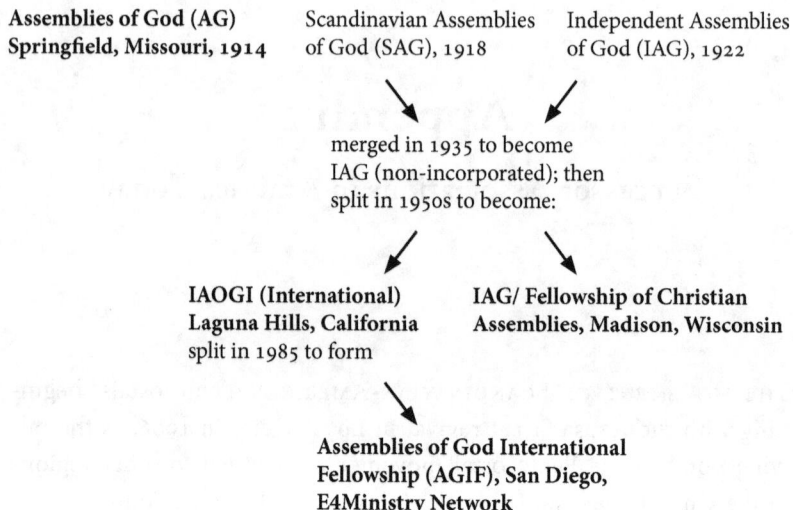

A brief description of these four bodies is provided.

Scandinavian-American Congregations of the Assemblies of God (AG) Springfield, Missouri

In 1914, when the Assemblies of God (AG), Springfield, Missouri, formed as an association of ministers, a small number of Scandinavian-American Pentecostals joined this American, English-language fellowship. Subsequently, numbers of congregations of Scandinavian immigrants joined the AG denomination, as shown in Chapter Five. These Scandinavian-American congregations were located primarily in cities, towns, and rural areas of the Midwest, Upper Midwest, and Pacific Northwest where Scandinavian immigrants settled.

Independent Assemblies of God International (IAOGI) Laguna Hills, California

The IAG (non-incorporated) which came about from a merger of the SAG and IAG, described above, divided in 1951 into two groups, each with similar names. This split happened when the IAG was disrupted by a revival movement promoted by A. W. Rasmussen (1905-1996) and Joseph Mattsson-Boze (1905-1989). They taught that the "New Order of the Latter Rain" was the instituting of spiritual gifts through the office of prophets and apostles and given authority from God to direct congregations.[2] Debates over this began in 1947 and by 1951, the pro-New Order of the Latter Rain group formed a separate association.

This pro-New Order of the Latter Rain group was the smaller of these two groups, and modified its name to the Independent Assemblies of God International (IAOGI). This association located its headquarters in San Diego, California. It legally incorporated in 1964, and later relocated its headquarters to Laguna Hills, California.[3] IAOGI began under the leadership of A. W. Rasmussen who was succeeded by his son, Philip A. Rasmussen. The IAOGI's periodical, *Herald of Faith*, began publication under Joseph Mattsson-Boze in Chicago in 1951. This was the organ of the New Order of the Latter Rain movement. In 1959, the IAOGI formed a Canadian branch with Stanley M. Hammond as the general secretary. Canadian headquarters were established in Smiths Falls, Ontario. The periodical *Herald of Faith* continued until 1971.

Joseph Mattsson-Boze also founded the mission arm of the IAOGI that was named Herald of Faith Mission. This mission society was founded to train national pastors, as well as to strengthen their churches. The initial work began in Kenya but soon branched to other African nations, as well as to Guatemala, India, Mexico, Philippines, and Romania.[4]

Fellowship of Christian Assemblies (FCA)
Madison, Wisconsin

In 1951, when the IAG (non-incorporated) divided, as mentioned above, the larger of the two groups sought stricter theological standards for its ministers, mostly due to the controversy over the New Order of the Latter Rain, which it opposed.[5] In 1973, the larger group

---

2. Granquist, "Smaller Religious Groups in the Swedish-American Community," 225.
3. R. G. Robins, *Pentecostalism in America* (Santa Barbara, CA: Praeger, 2010), 80.
4. Paul McPhail, "Revival and Independence," *Faith Today* 29 (Nov/Dec 2011) 41.
5. Warren Heckman, *The History of the Fellowship of Christian Assemblies* (HFCA) (Beaverton, OR: Good Book, 2011), 87.

took the name Fellowship of Christian Assemblies (FCA).[6] With the loss of its periodical to the IAOGI as a result of the split in 1951, this larger body launched a new periodical titled *Herald of Pentecost*. It was begun by E. C. Erickson and Henry Jauhiainen in Duluth, Minnesota, and was edited by Ted Lanes in Rockford, Illinois.[7]

In 1963, this fellowship began a periodical titled *Conviction*, published by Fellowship Press.[8] The Fellowship of Christian Assemblies (FCA) established its headquarters in Madison, Wisconsin.[9] In 1989, its periodical was renamed *Fellowship Today*.[10]

Assemblies of God International Fellowship (AGIF) or E4Ministry Network, San Diego, California

In 1985, the Independent Assemblies of God International (IAOGI) led by A. W. Rasmussen, mentioned above, divided into two groups. The new group that emerged took the name Assemblies of God International Fellowship (AGIF), known today as E4Ministry. The AGIF was led by Ted Lanes, beginning in 1986. This fellowship established headquarters in San Diego, California.[11]

Decades earlier, in 1964, when Ted Lanes relocated to San Diego to start a printing and publishing business, he became reacquainted with A. W. Rasmussen. The two men knew each other since the 1940s when they worked together on the pastoral staff of the Philadelphia Church in Chicago.[12] Later, in San Diego, as A. W. Rasmussen was nearing retirement, he decided to name Ted Lanes as his successor to oversee the International Assembles of God International (IAOGI). When this did not materialize, the majority of ministers formed a new association, the Assemblies of God International Fellowship (AGIF). Lanes was elected as president and Winston Mattsson-Boze, son of Joseph Mattsson-Boze, became vice president. In 2019, the Assemblies of God International Fellowship (AGIF) changed its name to E4Ministry Network.

6. Rhodes, *Complete Guide to Christian Denominations*, 354–55.
7. Heckman, *HFCA*, 88.
8. Heckman, *HFCA*, 88.
9. Heckman, *HFCA*, 16, 94.
10. Heckman, *HFCA*, 16.
11. J. Gordon Melton, *Encyclopedia of American Religions* (Detroit: Gale Research, 1996), 414.
12. "Honor to Whom Honor," *Fellowship: Assemblies of God International Fellowship* (Winter 2004) 2.

Contributors

RAKEL YSTEBØ ALEGRE, PhD Regent University, is Associate Professor of Church History at Norwegian School of Leadership and Theology, Oslo, Norway, and Dean of the School of Social Sciences at la Universidad Evangélica in Buenos Aires, Argentina.

JAN-ÅKE ALVARSSON, PhD Uppsala University, is Professor Emeritus of the Department of Cultural Anthropology and Ethnology at Uppsala University, Honorary Associate Docent at Åbo Akademi, Finland, and former Director of the Institute for Pentecostal Studies, Uppsala.

ISAEL DE ARAUJO is Historian, and Director of Evangelical College of the Assemblies of God, Rio de Janeiro, Brazil, and Founder of the Vingren Memorial Center and Archives Center at the Casa Publicadora Assembleias de Deus in Bangu, Rio de Janeiro.

TORBJÖRN ARONSON, PhD Lund University, ThD Uppsala University, Sweden, is Rector and Professor of Church History at Scandinavian School of Theology, Uppsala, Sweden, and Professor-at-large at Southeastern University, Lakeland, Florida.

DAVID BUNDY, PhD Uppsala University, is Associate Director of the Manchester Wesley Research Centre in Manchester, England, scholar of Holiness and Pentecostal Movements, and contributor to the *International Dictionary of Pentecostal and Charismatic Movements*.

TOMMY DAVIDSSON, PhD University of Birmingham, is Associate Professor of Historical and Pentecostal Theology at the Norwegian School of Leadership and Theology, in Oslo, Norway. He has authored the book *Lewi Pethrus' Ecclesiological Thought 1911–1974*.

CONTRIBUTORS

DAVID M. GUSTAFSON, PhD Linköping University, DMin Fuller Theological Seminary, is Professor and Chair of Mission and Evangelism at Trinity Evangelical Divinity School, Deerfield, Illinois, and Affiliate Docent at Johannelund School of Theology in Uppsala, Sweden.

BEVERLY JOHNSON-MILLER, PhD Claremont School of Theology, served in the Beeson School of Practical Theology at Asbury Theological Seminary, Kentucky, with emphases in the history of Christian Education, practical theology, and congregational formation.

RUTH MA is a PhD student in Intercultural Studies at Trinity Evangelical Divinity School in Deerfield, Illinois. Her research has focused on missiology including mission history and teaching cross-culturally.

CECIL M. ROBECK JR, PhD Fuller Theological Seminary, is Senior Professor of Church History and Ecumenics at Fuller Theological Seminary in Pasadena, California. His historical research centers on the Azusa Street Mission and Revival and its pastor, William Seymour.

DARRIN J. RODGERS, MA Assemblies of God Theological Seminary; JD University of North Dakota School of Law, is Director of the Flower Pentecostal Heritage Center in Springfield, Missouri. He is the author of *Northern Harvest*, a history of Pentecostalism in North Dakota.

KRISTINA UNDHEIM, MA Norwegian School of Theology, MATS Assemblies of God Theological Seminary, is an Assistant Professor at the University of South-Eastern Norway. Her research relates to Pentecostal theology.

JOEL W. WRIGHT, MDiv, Trinity Evangelical Divinity School, serves with the Brazilian Diaspora/ Global Diaspora Ministries of Converge Worldwide, Illinois. He taught at the Baptist Theological Seminary of São Paulo, Brazil, from 1991 to 2007.

Name Index

(Å and Ä are treated as A,
and Ö is treated as O)

Ahlberg, Arthur, 125
Ahlberg, Sara, 226
Albuquerque, Celina, 219–20
Albuquerque, Henrique, 220
Aldeen, C. A., 81
Alvarsson, Jan-Åke, xxix, xxx, 4, 193
Andersen, August A., 159
Anderson, C. A., 164
Anderson, Carrie P., 120–21, 157
Anderson, Elsie, 279, 291
Anderson, Ida, 4, 15–19, 24
Anderson, John J., 95
Anderson, Mrs. C. M., 275
Anderson, Nels, 41, 155–56
Andreasen, Paul J., 121
Apostolic Faith Mission, Los Angeles, see Azusa Street Mission
Argue, A. H. xxvn9, 38, 74, 158–59
Armstrong, Edward, 148
Arnesen, A. E., 106
Arneson, Laura Elizabeth, xv
Arneson, Oscar C., 129
Aronsson, Peter, 8
Asberry, Ruth and Richard, 58
Ashcroft, John J., 164
Assembleias de Deus, Brazil, 208, 211n13, 225, 232, 235, 327
Assemblies of God (AG), Springfield, Missouri, xix, xxx, 21, 55, 82, 118–46, 147, 150, 176, 189, 204, 259, 267, 279, 327–28

Assemblies of God International Fellowship (AGIF), see E4 Ministry Network
Avanzini, John, 308
Azusa Street Mission, xvi–xix, xxv, xxvii–xxxii, xxxiii–xxxiv, 1, 2, 4, 10, 24, 28, 29n8, 34–38, 44, 55–56, 59–64, 66, 69, 91–93, 95–97, 113, 119–20, 128, 133, 136, 154–55, 173, 181–82, 198–99, 241, 245–49, 250n51, 267, 269, 322, 327

Bakke, Alf, 17
Bakken (Balken), Jakob O., 20, 24
Baptists, xvi, xxiii–xxv, xxix, 5, 27–52, 57, 63, 66–68, 80–81, 130, 186, 212–13, 215, 219, 272, 285, 289, 302, 311, 315, 322, also see Swedish Baptist Theological Seminary
Barratt, Laura, 91, 105, 107, 111
Barratt, Mary Ball, 109
Barratt, Thomas Ball, xvii, xxvi, xxix–xxx, 14, 24, 49n112, 61, 64, 69–70, 73–75, 87–109, 111–15, 134, 137, 159n41, 169, 179, 182, 185–86, 188–89, 193, 195–96, 198, 200-1, 204
Bartleman, Frank, xviii, 67n50, 104
Basham, Don, 304

NAME INDEX

Bau Yien-Ching, 254–55, 263
Baxter, Ern, 304
Bays, Daniel H., 250
Beck, Edwin A., 128
Beckdahl, Agnes N. Thelle, 76, 97–98, 121
Beckdahl, Christian, 121
Bell, E. N., 38, 55–56, 158, 200
Bendiksen, Edwin and Jennie 121
Bennett, Dennis, 298
Berg, Anna Hanson, 129, 281
Berg, Arthur F., 127–28
Berg, Daniel G., xxxi, 47–48, 184, 208–10, 212–13, 217–29, 231–35, 249, 272–73, 327
Berg, Sara Ahlberg, 226–29, 233
Bergstrand, Claes-Göran, 302
Bergström, Wilhelm, 17
Berntsen, Bernt, xxxi, xxxiii, 64–65, 99, 107n108, 120–24, 241–50, 259–60
Berntsen, Magna, 99, 120, 121, 124, 242, 243, 246, 249, 259n92
Bjork, C. A., 6
Bjorkman, Carl, xvii
Bjorkman, Mary, xxxiii, 62, 248–49
Bloch-Hoell, Nils, xviii
Blumhofer, Edith L. W., 3, 269
Booth, William and Catherine, 181
Borgen, Ole, 304
Bostrom, J. H., 278, 280
Bosworth, F. F., 82, 270–71
Boyles, William H., 119
Branham, William, 141, 174–75
Brazee, Mark, 307
Bredesen, Harald, 159, 298, 300–301
Bresch, Hilda, 280
Briem, Efraim, xviii
Brown, Robert and Marie Burgess, 104, 112
Brown, Sandy, 307
Brumback, Carl, 3
Bullard, Bill, 303
Bullard, Ray, 284
Burt, William, 90
Buss, Albert E., 270
Butsch, J. A., 8–9

Cameneti, Patsy Behrman, 307
Campbell, Jeanie, 270
Carlson, Charles O., 120
Carlson, David M., 128
Carlson, G. Raymond, 127
Carlson, Henry F., 299–301, 304
Carlson, Joel and Signe, 226, 233
Carlson, Martin, 42–43, 45, 272, 275
Carlyss, S. Paul, 160
Carvalho, José Batista de, 218–19
Cerullo, Morris, 308
Charismatic Movement (renewal), xxxii, 309, 311–12, 314–15
Christ's Ambassadors, 291
Christensen, Theodor "Tom" G., 75, 97, 112, 150, 169, 228
Christiansen (Kristensen), Rasmus, 18–20, 24
Christophersen, C., 95
Clafford, Thorsten, 38
Colletti, Joseph, 189
Conlee, Joseph R., 66
Conventicle Law, 6, 9
Cook, Glen A., 199
Copeland, Kenneth, 306–7
Copley, A. S., 183
Costa, Emília, 229
Costa, José Plácido da, 218–19, 222
Craig, Robert J., 114
Cruz, Nicky, 298

Dahl, Arne, 108–12, 154, 169
Dahl, Berthine H., 63
Dahl, Levone Katherine, 125
Dahlman, P. A., 41, 49, 155
Dahlstein, Gideon A., 121
Davis, August, 4, 11–16, 18, 20, 24, 36, 70, 268
Dayton, Donald, 181
Diltz, Carrie, 271
Dixon, A. C., 106
Dowie, John Alexander, 29, 136, 182, 270
du Plessis, David, 298, 303
Durham, Bessie Mae, 43
Durham, William H., xxv, xxvi, xxix, xxx, xxxiii, 23, 34–45, 48, 51, 55–57, 61–62, 67–74, 154–59,

334

182–87, 199, 204–5, 215–18, 225, 241, 246–50, 269–70, 272, 274, 276

E4 Ministry Network, 328, 330
Edgren, J. August, 163
Edwards, Gust A., 149
Ekberg, Einar, 173
Ekman, Ulf, 296, 301, 305–10, 314–15
Engquist, Almeda, M., 165–66
Engquist, Charles, 165–66
Engstrøm, Dagmar Gregersen, 76, 97–98
Engstrom, Ed, 290
Engstrøm, Henrik, 98
Erickson, Clifton, 282–83, 300
Erickson, E. C. (Elmer Claude), 72, 82, 121, 124, 138, 148, 150–1, 154, 166–68, 173–74, 330
Erickson, Emma Brun, 121
Erickson, R. L. (Rasmus Lee), 119–20
Ericson, A. G., 281
Ericson, C. George, 29, 50
Evangelical Covenant Church of America, xvi, 5, 12, 170, 187–88
Evangelical Free Church of America, xiii, xvi, xxiv, xxxiv, 1, 4–5, 11, 15, 18, 20, 23, 27, 36, 66n48, 69–70, 75–76, 92, 97, 160, 162, 173, 187 See also Scandinavian Mission Society U.S.A.
Ewart, Frank J., 199, 203

Farrow, Lucy, 59
Fellowship of Christian Assemblies (FCA), 141, 328–30
Filho, Isidoro, 222
Fink, G. F., 67, 100–101
Finney, Charles G., 91, 181
Fjermedal, Olav, 104, 200–201
Flower Pentecostal Heritage Center, Springfield, Missouri, xiii, xxxiv, 122, 320
Flower, J. Roswell, 139–40, 200
Fockler, C. B., 270–71
Forseth, Ole, 74, 174
Fraim, Efraim, 113, 161
Francescon, Luigi (Louis), 38, 209

Franklin, A. P., 229
Franson, Fredrik, xxvi, 6, 11, 20n90
Fredrickson, Gust, 275
Free-Free, see Scandinavian Mission Society U.S.A.
Frey, Mae E., 281
Frizen, John, 41, 155
Frizen, Oscar, 41, 155
Frodsham, Stanley H., 2–3, 113
Full Gospel Business Men's Fellowship International (FGBM), 284, 296–304, 314

Gabrielsen, T., 108
Galvão, Josina, 221
Garr, A. G., 82, 119, 240
Gentry, William D., 57–58
Gjerde, Jan, 321, 324–25
Gordh, Arvid, 38
Gordon, A. J., xxiv, 29, 181
Graves, F. A., 28–29, 149
Great Commission, 5
Greisen, Victor G., 128
Griffin, Thomas and Emily, 158
Grönlund, H., 192
Gross, H. A., 139–40
Gulliksen, Kenn, 311, 314
Gundersen, Tønnes, 247
Gundt, Walter, 287–88
Gustafsen, Jens, 172
Gustafson, David M., 4
Gustavsen, Sverre, 108, 110, 113, 159
Gustavsson, Emil, 211

Hagen, Knut, 73
Hagen, Selh., 103
Hagin, Kenneth E., 306, 308, 315
Hagli, Bergine Engen, 172
Hagli, Martin J. N., 125, 159, 172
Hall, Nelly, 193
Hallden, Eric, 45
Halvorsen, Oscar, xxvi, 74–6, 94, 96–98, 169
Hammarberg, Agnes, 125
Hammond, Stanley M., 329
Hanger, Signe Alice, 125
Hansen, Abraham, 108
Hansen, Bendix, 65

NAME INDEX

Hansen, Emelia, 19–20
Hansen, Emma B. (Burns), 65, 248–49
Hansen, Folker, 19
Hansen, George (Jørgen), 37, 64, 164, 217, 241–45, 247, 249–51, 253–62
Hansen, Harold E., 120–21, 125, 256
Hansen, Helga, 242, 255, 260n95
Hansen, Jenny, 242, 255
Hansen, Lee, 5
Hansen, Margaret Tollefsen, 120–21
Hansen, Mikael, 75, 108, 112
Hansen, Minnie Florence, 261
Hansen, Samuel, 241–42, 255, 261–62
Hansen, Sophie, xxxi, 37, 64, 164, 217, 238–63
Hansen, Tønnes, 243
Hansen, Wesley Daniel, 125
Hanson, Carl M. "Daddy," 4, 21–24, 28–29, 35, 38, 44–46, 49, 51, 71, 82, 121, 126–28, 149–50, 152, 155, 158, 164, 171, 187, 249, 268
Hardin, Ben, 133
Harper, Michael, 298
Hauge, Hans Nielsen, 6
Haugland, Hazel Irene, 125
Hawtin, George, 174
Haywood, G. T., 200, 203
Heckman, Warren, 138
Hedeen, Carl, 33, 152–53, 161, 164, 173
Hedeen, John, 275
Hedeen, Olof, 30, 32–33, 38, 153
Hedlund, A. F., 168
Helland, Serena, 63
Helm, C. W., 48
Hempel, Kari Guttormsen, 5
Henricksen, Henry C., 19, 24
Herald of Faith Mission, 329
Hess, Roy and Lydia, 248–50, 255
Hinn, Benny, 308
Hjertstrom, J. W., xvi, xxiv–xxv, xxvi, xxix, 29–33, 39–42, 47, 50–51, 100, 159, 269, 271–72
Hollingsworth, Eric Carlsson, xvii, 62
Hollingsworth, Ida Magnusson, xvii, 62
Holm, Einar J., 170
Holmberg, David, 50
Holmer, Albin, 191

Holmes, Phoebe, 247
Holmgren, A. A. (Andrew August), xviii, xxxiii, 38, 45, 47–49, 65, 67–69, 73, 149–53, 165, 179–80, 184, 188–89, 193–94, 197, 201–3, 205, 223, 228, 233
Holmsten (Axberg), Hanna, xxxiii, 62, 248–49
Hope, Ludvig, 322
Horton, Webster I., 165
Hultgren, Petrus, 45, 73
Hunt, Percy, 174
Hydéhn, Magnus A., 164

Independent Assemblies of God (IAG), xix, xxii, xxx, xxxiv, 120, 137–42, 147–48, 151–54, 163–65, 168, 170, 173–77, 228, 233, 327–29
Independent Assemblies of God International (IAOGI), 328–30
Iversen, Maren, xxvi, xxxiii, 66–67

Jacobsen, Douglas, 180
Jacobson, Agnes "Annie," xvii, xxvi, xxxiii, 62
Jacobson, Jennie, xvii
Jaggers, O. L., 141
Jamieson, Hattie, 71
Jauhiainen, Henry, 330
Jeans, Ted, 313–14
Jensen, Bertine, 96, 99
Jensen, Clara, 125
Jepsen, Helen, 154, 166
Jepsen, Peter, 281
Jesus People Movement, 295–96, 298–305, 314
Jewell, F. W., 275, 280
Johanson, K. G., 106
Johansson, Anders, 231
Johansson, Hans, 313
Johansson, Svenning, 6
Johnsen, Berger N., 323
Johnsen, Ludwig, 75, 97
Johnson, Adolph, xxxiii, 62, 248
Johnson, Arthur F. (b. 1888), 6, 71–72, 82, 113, 121, 148–50, 153, 159–60, 166–67, 171, 174, 275

NAME INDEX

Johnson, Arthur F. (b. 1934), 301, 303
Johnson, Augusta, 17
Johnson, B. M. (Bengt Magnus), 29, 33, 38, 41–42, 45–47, 49, 51, 149, 155–57, 164, 171–2, 184, 189, 194, 215, 217, 223, 227–28, 249, 272, 280
Johnson, Beatrice "Beda" Farnlof, 71, 121, 159
Johnson, Eric E., 279
Johnson, Helen Louise, 125
Johnson, Herman G., 126-7
Johnson, Hjalmer M. and Olga, 126
Johnson, Linda Erickson, xxxiii, 62, 248
Johnson, Linnea Moberg, 279
Johnson, Mary, 4, 15–17, 19, 24
Johnson, Pauline, 157
Johnson (Creamer), Ruth A., 121
Johnson, Ruth, 280
Johnson, Sabina, 17
Johnson, Segrid A., 121
Johnson, Thea, 17
Johnson-Ek, Andrew G., xviii, xxvi, xxxiii, 34, 49n112, 60, 61, 182, 322
Johnsrud, Marie, 125

Karlsson, Axel W., 305
Kaseman, Jim, 307
Keener, Craig, 240
Kenyon, E. W., 309
Kerr, David W., 82, 200–203
Kihlstedt, C. J. A., 211
King, J. H., 104
Knudsen, Chrest and Amanda, 126
Knudsen, Nels 19
Knutson, K., 49
Koford, Olof K., 79
Konsmo, K. J., 172
Kringle, Nels, 21
Kristoffersen, L., 95–96, 100
Kvamme, John, 172
Kvamme, Martin and Martine, 63, 125, 172

Lagerstedt, Tytti, 103
Lanes, Theodore, 330

Langeland, Henrik S., 63–65, 98–99, 125
Larsen, Jacob, 108
Larson, Christina, 73
Latter Rain Movement, xix, xxx, 141, 148, 174, 177, 189, 297, 300, 329
Leatherman, Lucy, xvii, 34, 92–93, 246
Lee, Edward, 59
Lenander, Esther, 63
Levi, John, 57
Lidman, Sven, 190
Lima, Cicero de, 229, 231
Lindblad, Frank, 121, 125
Lindblad, Helmer, 112, 169
Lindblom, Harry, 162, 167
Linderholm, Emanuel, xviii
Lindquist, Frank L., 82, 113, 126, 129, 132–34, 136–37, 150, 277
Lindquist, Loth, 70–71, 100–102
Lindstrom, Emil J. G., 76–81, 120–21, 168, 173, 192
Livets Ord (Word of Life), 296, 304–10, 315
Lowery, Bill, 302, 304
Lund, Eric, 131
Lunde, Albert, 322
Lundgren, Ellen Carlson, xxxiii, 62, 248
Lundgren, Gustav S., xxxiii, 62, 248
Lundquist, David F., 172
Lutherans, xv, xvi, xvii, xxiii, 5–8, 21, 27, 33, 63–64, 66, 68, 91, 170, 210, 212, 270, 300, 305–6, 312, 322

Macalão, Paulo Leivas, 229
Macinnes, Jim, 303
Magnussen, Beda, 120
Malm, Peter, 78
Manley, William R., 58, 60
Martinson, N. A., 14, 185
Mason, Charles H., 119
Mathisen, Gustav, 89
Matos, José, 227
Mattson, Algot R., 125
Mattson-Boze, Joseph, 141, 154, 161–63, 169, 174–75, 300, 329, 330
McAlister, Robert E., 69–70, 74, 199–203
McGee, Bob, 313

NAME INDEX

McGee, Gary B., 3–4, 7
McIntosh, T. J., 240
McLean, Sigrid Bengtson, xvii
Melin, William, 16–17
Mellquist, C. Otto, 45, 48, 214
Mellquist, Hannah, 47–48, 214
Melo, Crispiniano de, 222
Menzie, James, 133, 277
Menzies, William, 3
Merck, Bobby Jean, 307
Merrin, J. W., 278
Methodists, xvii, xxiii–xxvi, 5, 12, 18–20, 27, 61, 66, 68, 70, 75, 88–92, 95, 102, 113, 181, 186, 218, 242–43, 247, 304, 306, 322, 325
Minnesota Historical Society, St. Paul, xxxiv
Modalsli, Sigbjørn Olsen, 322
Moen, Ida C., 17
Moline, John, 17
Montgomery, Carrie Judd, 81, 114, 260n98
Moody Bible Institute, 74, 170
Moody, Dwight L., xxiv, 11, 29, 181, 322
Morin, Antonio Ríos, 119
Morken, Anders O., 1, 20–21, 24
Moseid, C. Albert and Ella, 121, 228
Moseid, John, 149, 228
Mumford, Bob, 304

Nankivell Evangelist Party, 278
Nazaré, Maria de Jesus, 219
Nelson (Nilson), Henry, 32–33, 38–39, 45, 216, 218, 223, 268, 271–72, 289
Nelson University, Waxahachie, Texas, 129
Nelson, Albert A., 17
Nelson, Eric, 218
Nelson, Nels Julius, 226, 231
Nelson, Olga, 22–23
Nelson, Otto and Adina (Lydia), 223, 226
Nelson, P. C. (Peter Christopher), 129–32, 280
Ness, Henry H., 8, 14–15, 18, 20, 22, 24, 82, 113, 127, 129, 134–35

Newman, H. A. (Herman August), 79–80, 168, 193, 196–98
Nielsen (Nilsen), N. G. (Niels Gabriel), 76, 97, 106, 121, 126, 196
Nilsen, Bernhard, 75
Nilsson, Birgitta, 306
Nilsson, Ernst L., 171
Nilsson, Sten, 306
Nobre, Raimundo, 219
Nordin, Carl. O., 74
Nordling, David, 114, 164
Nordquelle, Erik Andersen, 94, 107
Norli, Ingeborg, 121
Norlin, Victor, 113, 161
North Avenue (Full Gospel) Mission, Chicago, xxv, xxix, 23, 34–37, 41–44, 55, 57, 61–62, 64, 71, 110, 154, 155, 158, 164, 183–84, 187, 213, 215, 217, 241, 245–47, 249–50, 269, 272, 276
North Central University, Minneapolis, 129, 132
Northwest University, Kirkland, Washington, 129, 134
Nylander, Carolina, 121, 125
Nyström, Lina, 223
Nyström, Samuel, 223, 225, 227, 231, 233

Ödman, Adolf, 78–81, 106, 168, 191–98, 201, 204
Ohrnell, Arvid, 125, 152, 160–61, 171
Olofsdotter, Karin, 7
Olsen, Adolph, 275
Olsen, Oscar, 122
Olson, Louis, 17
Olson, Roger E., 4–5
Ongman, John, xxvi, 322
Oral Roberts University, 309, 315
Osborn, T. L., 308
Osterberg, Arthur, xvii, 36, 56, 82, 128, 173
Osterberg, Cenna and Louis, viii, xxxiii, 34, 36, 56–58, 60–62

Palestine Missionary Band, 34–35, 182
Palmberg, Karl, 6
Palosaari, Jim, 304–5

NAME INDEX

Parham, Charles F., 4, 29n8, 35n38, 38n55, 136, 198n107, 199
Parsley, Rod, 308
Patterson, S. H., 113
Paulsen, Jacob, 102
Paulsen, Paul, 102
Pearson, Edna O., 125
Pellén, Robert and Siv, 297–300
Pendleton, William, 66
Pentecostal Assemblies of the World, 260
Petersen, Adolph, 158, 268, 276, 279, 280, 284–86
Peterson Uldin, Ada Terés, 277–78, 280
Peterson, Dagny Marie, 125
Peterson, E. Bartlett, 281
Peterson, Rangor S., 82
Pethrus, Lewi, xxvi, xxx, 41n66, 69, 80n114, 105, 107, 137, 151–53, 157, 160–62, 166–68, 171–72, 174–75, 179, 186, 188–90, 193–98, 200–201, 212–13, 223, 226, 230–31, 234, 285, 297–300, 323
Pethrus, Oliver, 162
Pettersen, Jens, 159
Piano, Absalão, 222
Pietist Movement, xvi, xxiii–xxiv, xxviii–xxix, xxxi, 2, 4–7, 11, 20, 23, 29, 56, 68, 83, 180–82, 199, 281, 292, 321–24
Piper, William H., 38, 46
Pohl, August, 6
Pöysti, Nicolai J., 169
Price, F. O., 158
Prince, Derek, 298, 304
Princell, John Gustav, 6, 187

Rasmussen, Andrew W., 162-3, 169–70, 172–75, 329–30
Rasmussen, Anna C., 122
Rasmussen, James E., 82, 122, 125
Rasmussen, Philip A., 329
Rasmussen, Rasmus S., 82, 122
Reed, David, 185, 199
Rhema Bible Training Center, 306–8, 315
Richmann, Christopher, 183, 204–5
Ring, Frederick, 90

Ring, Harry, 109, 163, 167, 169–70
Robeck, Axel Edwin, xv
Roberts, Evan, 181
Roberts, Oral, 296–98 300
Roberts, Richard, 309, 315
Robertson, Emelia Hansen, 19
Robertson, Pat, 301
Robertson, Rasmus, 19, 20n90
Rodgers, Darrin J., 1, 3-4, 6
Rodrigues, Manoel Maria, 219
Rodriguez, Cookie, 303
Roman Catholic Church, 267, 284, 296
Ronnberg, Alma, 62
Rønnestad, Kari S., 125
Rosenius, Carl O., xxiv, 6, 11, 29
Rue, Brent and Happy (Gladys Winblad), 311, 314
Russum, Hendrick N., 22
Ruud, Hjalmar, 159

Salvation Army, 22, 75, 92, 100, 170, 276, 279n63, 322–23
Samuelson, Emil, 82
Sanders, Anna Jensen, 74
Sandford, Frank, 136
Sandgren, F. A. (Ferdinand Alexander), 29, 35, 37–38, 43–46, 48–49, 55, 56n1, 76–78, 91, 155, 164–65, 215, 216n32, 249–50, 268, 272–74
Savelle, Jerry, 307
Scandinavian Mission of Los Angeles, xvi, xxix, 59, 61–62, 64, 173, 247
Scandinavian Mission Society U.S.A., 4, 11, 14–18, 19, 24, 187
Schaff, Philip, 8
Schambach, R. W., 308
Seaholm, Mina, 281
Second Coming of Christ, 21, 182, 202n129, 283, 286
Seehuus, Carl Magnus, 94, 186
Segerquist, Arthur Helmer, 125
Segersven, Ida E. 73
Seiss, Joseph A., 253
Semple, Robert, 156, 217, 247
Semple-McPherson, Aimee, 38, 113, 156, 158, 217, 247
Seymour, Isaac "Chicago," 57

339

NAME INDEX

Seymour, Jenny Evans Moore, 59
Seymour, William J., xvii, 2, 8, 34, 36, 38n55, 58–59, 62, 64, 83, 198n107, 199,
Shakarian, Demos, 297–8, 301
Sherrill, John, 298
Shulene, Jonas Magnus, 71
signs and wonders, xxv, xxviii, 3, 15, 52, 79, 244–45, 254, 258–59, 282, 286
Silva, João Trigueiro da, 224
Simonsen, N. E., 90
Simpson, A. B., xxiv, 76, 91–92, 97, 182
Simpson, Alma Ekvall, 158
Simpson, Charles, 304
Simpson, W. W., 158
Sjölander, Christina, 17
Sjoli, Juehl, 155
Sjoli, Lotten Tenman, 157n41
Skipple, Martha, 102
Skoog, Harold Maynard, 125
Small, Franklin, 203
Smidt, Gerhard Olsen, 67, 100–102
Smyth, John, 186
Snartemo, Ole, 172
Sobrinho, Almeida, 224, 227
Söderholm, G. E., xviii
Sorensen, Annina, 122
Sorensen, Niels C., 120
South Africa Missionary Band, 19–20
South Zhili Mission, 121, 243
Southwestern Bible Institute (Southwestern Assemblies of God University), see Nelson University
Spener, Philip Jakob, 5
Spetz, Bror, 308
Spurgeon, Charles Haddon, xxiv, 29, 181
Starkenberg, Alma, 62
Steelberg, Wesley, 309
Stokkan, John Arn and Carrie Romenstad, 126
Stolsen, Karl G., 171–72
Stone, A. L., 13
Stone, E. S., 69–70

Strand, Algot, 68
Strand, Josef N., xxix, xxxiii, 62
Strong, Augustus, 129
Sulger, Aage L., xvii, xxxiii
Sumrall, Lester, 285, 287, 300, 306, 308–9, 315
Sundberg, Hans, 313–14
Swanson, Carl, 280
Swanson, Edwin, 125
Swanson, Samuel, 125
Swartz, Gordon P., 163, 243n20
Swartz, Petrus, 29, 32–33, 38–39, 45–46, 51, 159, 163, 228, 272
Swedish Baptist Theological Seminary, Chicago, 30, 33, 42, 46–47, 80, 153, 211, 275

Tangen, Karl Inge, 186
Tangen, Robert Ball, 126
Teen Challenge, 298, 302
Thomas, Ellsworth S., 119
Thompson, John, 11, 14–15, 17, 20, 24, 36, 121
Thompson, Niels, 281
Thompson, Peter B., 15, 82
Thompson, Thomas, 76, 102
Thomsen, Niels P. and Ellen K., 122
Thunborg, Mårten Larsson, 7
Timrud, Ketil and Gertrude, 122
Tonnesen, Tobias E., 63–64
Torrey, R. A., xxiv, 75, 181
Truvé, Theodor, 31, 289

Udd, Magnus Emanuel, 126
Udd, Ragnar E., 126
Uldin, Carl Magnus, 271
Uldin, Esther, 273–4, 276
Uldin, G. A. (Gedion Adolph), 268, 276–77
Uldin, Olof Adolf, 48, 215–7, 224, 268, 271, 273–74, 276, 279–80, 289
Ulness, Sivert V., xxvi
University of Notre Dame, 284
Urquhart, Colin, 308
Urshan, Andrew D., 38, 45

NAME INDEX

Villadsen, Christine, 19
Vineyard Christian Fellowship, Anaheim, California, 311
Vingren, Carl A., 38, 46
Vingren, Frida Strandberg, 224, 231
Vingren, Gunnar, xxxi, 46–49, 149–50, 184, 194, 197, 208–35, 249, 268, 272–74, 284, 327

Wacker, Grant, 240
Waermo, Einar, 162, 173, 282
Wahl, Gilbert, 21
Wahl, John, 21
Walblom, Carl, 126
Waldenström, P. P., 6, 11–12
Walker, Watt, 119
Wallace, Wendell, 301
Walle, Barratt, 96
Walterman, Devore, 302
Wanghow Chang, 252–53, 263
Watland, L. L., 65
Weiner, Bob, 308

Wellard, Thomas W., 277–78
Westman, John A., 157
Whaley, Sam and Jane, 307–8
White, Alma, xvii
Wigglesworth, Smith, 164
Wikstrom, G. Algot, 165, 113, 152
Wilkerson, David, 298
Wilkinson, W. M., 8–9
Williams, Maud, 93
Wimber, John, 296, 310–15
Wingard, Adolph C., 126
Wise, Lorraine, 297
Woodberry, John, 253
Woodberry, Katherine C., 252–53, 263
Woodworth-Etter, Maria B., 81
World's Faith Missionary Association, 36

Ystrom (Ystrøm), Joseph, 159

Zettersten, Paul, 173

www.ingramcontent.com/pod-product-compliance
Lightning Source LLC
Chambersburg PA
CBHW071147300426
44113CB00009B/1115